DISCONCERTING ISSUE

SYMBOLIC ANTHROPOLOGY

Series Edited by
David W. Crabb

DISCONCERTING
ISSUE

Meaning and Struggle in a
Resettled Pacific Community

Martin G. Silverman

With a Foreword by
David M. Schneider

The University of Chicago Press
Chicago and London

International Standard Book Number: 0–226–75750–1
Library of Congress Catalog Card Number: 70–133490
The University of Chicago Press, Chicago 60637
The University of Chicago Press, Ltd., London
© 1971 by The University of Chicago

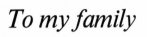

To my family

CONTENTS

List of Illustrations ix
Series Editor's Preface xi
Foreword xiii
Acknowledgments xv
Abbreviations 2

INTRODUCTION 3

PART I   BLOOD, LAND, AND TRADITIONAL BANABAN CULTURE   21
   1 Traditional Social Organization (H. C. Maude and
     H. E. Maude)   23
   2 The Traditional System Revisited   48

PART II   THE TRANSFORMATION OF OCEAN ISLAND   83
   3 Christianity, Phosphate, and Colonial Beginnings   85
   4 Opposition and Political Consciousness   106
   5 Codification and the War   139
   6 The Transformation of Banaban Culture   149

PART III   TESTING OUT ON RAMBI ISLAND   157
   7 Arrival, and the Integral Model Explored   159
   8 Two Crucial Decisions   166
   9 The Integral Model Examined: The Banaban Community Store   173
  10 Banaban Identity and Community Action   180
  11 People, Lands, and Localities on Rambi   210

PART IV   KINSHIP, DESCENT, AND AFFINITY   229
  12 Kinship and Vocabulary   231
  13 Kinship and Ritual I: Consanguinity and Affinity   262
  14 Kinship and Ritual II: The Descent System   303

viii   *Contents*

CONCLUSION: THE QUEST FOR A CIVIL RELIGION   329
Epilogue   333
Appendixes   335
References   347
Index   355

ILLUSTRATIONS

Figures

1 Sex and Succession   32
2 Adoption and Succession   33
3 Sitting Places   36
4 Some Ritual Circuits   50
5 Links in a Gift at Death   274
6 A Controversial Marriage   286
7 Kinship, Descent, and Affinity   306
8 Utu Representation   308
9 Units in Marriage Gifts   311
10 A Descent Unit Dispute   314

Map

Ocean Island (Banaba)   335

Tables

1 Population of the Resettlement Group   162
2 Componential Analysis   239

SERIES EDITOR'S PREFACE

This book makes a significant contribution to the definition of the interfaces of symbolic anthropology with other disciplines in the social sciences, for Dr. Silverman has here skillfully combined the presentation of ethnographic data gathered on a Pacific island with the larger concerns of the science of human interaction. He has accomplished this on a variety of levels simultaneously, and he has also used the inherent properties of symbolic systems to provide a multiplicity of scale.

In the spirit of Dr. Silverman's plays on words (as opposed to the dramaturgical analysis of plays themselves which was presented by the first author in this series, Dr. Peacock), one is tempted to point out that a large part of his analysis is devoted to the *properties* of *property*. He thereby provides a convincing realization of the local symbolic system *on the ground*, as it were. Additionally, students of sociocultural change and of modernization can find realizations of social *movement* which elegantly exemplify both senses of the word at the same time.

The gestation period for such a many-faceted work is necessarily a long one, and it is instructive to note that this book is the product of many visits to the field (including two for really extended periods), several years of presenting aspects of the material in the classroom, a novel use of the computer, and a series of meetings with fellow scholars culminating in an international conference for which substantial portions of the final version of the book were written. All of this was in addition to, among other things, extensive correspondence with others who had first-hand knowledge of the problems involved, and personal investigations in various archives. Fortunately, the issue of this labor is now given unto us.

DAVID W. CRABB

FOREWORD

The title of this book carries a load of information about it.

This book is about the Banabans, the people of Ocean Island in the Gilbert and Ellice Islands Colony, whose island was put into ships and carried away to be made into fertilizer. Ocean Island would not be habitable after the projected exhaustion of its mineral resources, and the indigenous community was relocated on Rambi in the Fiji Islands, many miles from their Ocean Island home. The book describes the traditional social order of the Banabans and then recounts in detail their history from the traditional period through Christianization, colonization, and the commercial exploitation of the phosphate on Ocean Island, to their present situation on Rambi. It analyzes the changes which have taken place, as well as the newly emerging social order on Rambi.

"Issue" refers both to kinship and politics: in particular, the descent system, the dispute over phosphate rights, and the problem of how the community is to organize itself on a new island, and the relationship between these issues. "Disconcerting" applies to these related issues: they disconcert the community in the sense that they divide it, they disconcert individuals in the sense that the individuals are in a state of confusion about these issues, and they disconcert the anthropologist in that the conditions of rapid change, confusion, and ambiguity present analytic problems which are difficult to deal with.

But which of the disconcerting issues in this book is the most important? Is it the superb treatment of the interrelationship between culture and social system over time, as history, using a sophisticated conception of culture and symbol? Is it the demonstration that kinship as a distinct, analytic isolate is no longer a viable entity? Is it the brilliant demonstration of the emergence of a communal identity from the events of the past, or is it rather the demonstration of how to analyze and understand an emerging social order, one important part of which is a communal identity? Perhaps it is really the useful notion of "testing out" which is introduced and developed in the analysis of the actor's problem of translating sets of concepts and symbols into actable, workable norms for conduct. Or is it really the major problem of the relationship between culture and behavior, thought and action, and the remarkable demonstration of the important place which the value system occupies, articulating the symbols of culture with the patterns for and of behavior?

The title of this book carries a load of information about it. But it does not say one important thing: it does not tell how what appear at first sight as a series of utterly disconcerting issues soon become woven into an understandable whole in Dr. Silverman's skillful hands.

It is indeed a privilege and a pleasure to contribute the foreword to this very fine book. I could wish for only one more thing; I wish that I had written it.

DAVID M. SCHNEIDER

ACKNOWLEDGMENTS

To construct a coherent account of the cultural experience of the Banaban people on Ocean Island in the Gilbert and Ellice Islands Colony, and on Rambi Island in Fiji, to which they moved, has been almost an *idée fixe* with me for eight years. Until the writing was well underway, I combed practically everything in anthropology and related fields which I read or heard about for its relevance to the Banaban situation, with the hope that breadth would not degenerate into theoretical promiscuity.

My debts to authors and colleagues are thus truly enormous. Many have unwittingly contributed to this book.

My greatest debt is to the people of Rambi Island, who in a time of great turmoil allowed me to share in their joy and their suffering. The Banabans have a great deal to offer the anthropologist. What this anthropologist has to offer the Banabans, beyond deep gratitude, is as meaningful an interpretation as he can now render of certain aspects of their past and their present.

I owe special gratitude to the officers and employees of the Rambi Island Council, the Banaban Funds Trust Board, and the Banaban Co-operative Association; to my Banaban assistants, Iotua Itiennang, Kauongo Bio, and Kaintong Tenangiro; and to the people of the many families, villages, and churches whose hospitality is unmatched.

Two scholars have haunted my investigations almost since their inception. H. E. Maude of the Department of Pacific History, the Australian National University, Canberra, first put me in touch with the Banaban situation and gave of all the help I was intelligent enough to ask for. Almost all the documentary and published historical sources were uncovered by him. He has been an historical prod in my intellectual ribs throughout, and if this book goes even a small way toward meeting his rigorous and humane standards, I will be very pleased indeed. Thanks also to Mrs. Maude.

David M. Schneider of the Department of Anthropology, University of Chicago, entered the scene when he helped me to realize what to do with the spotty data I had brought back from a four months' visit to Rambi in

1961. A close intellectual collaboration has developed to the point where I no longer know which ideas are mine and which are his. On my return to Rambi I had the fantasy that he was hiding out in some corner of the island, instructing the people how to behave. Maybe he was.

Other teachers and students at the University of Chicago, during my education there and since, have been lively contributors to my thinking, and commentators on various writings. I must thank in particular Vern Carroll, Bernard S. Cohn, Fred Eggan, Lloyd A. Fallers, Paul Friedrich, Clifford Geertz, Nicholas S. Hopkins, and Nur Yalman—and elsewhere, Laura Thompson and George Grace. Conversations with two of my fellow students of societies in the Gilbertese culture area, Bernd Lambert and Henry Lundsgaarde, and comments from them never fail to have some consequence for my work. Recently I had an interesting if brief exchange with Jean-Paul Latouche on Gilbertese kinship.

Many figures in Fiji, both in the government and out, were extremely helpful and eased the difficulty of working in a politically very sensitive area. My chief continuing colleague there has been A. I. Diamond, Archivist of Fiji and the Western Pacific High Commission. P. D. Macdonald, Rupert Hughes, and Dr. Lindsay Verrier showed many kindnesses. The "European community" of Rambi Island at one time or another included Mr. and Mrs. A. F. Grant, Col. Paul B. Laxton, and Mr. and Mrs. W. D. B. Jobson and their children. I always had a generous welcome from them.

I owe much gratitude to the archivists and other personnel of organizations and agencies connected with my major documentary sources. These include A. I. Diamond, Central Archives of Fiji and the Western Pacific High Commission, Suva, Fiji; Rotan Tito, Kawate Maibintebure, Ioteba Karebanga, and Teem Takoto, Files of the Rambi Island Council, Rambi Island, Fiji; H. E. Maude, custodian of the Maude Papers, Grimble Papers, and Holland Papers, Canberra; Miss Mary Walker, Mrs. R. Ashenden, and Rev. Joan Jonas of the United Church Board for World Ministries, Boston and New York, for the Archives of the American Board of Commissioners for Foreign Missions, Houghton Library of Harvard University, Cambridge, Mass., and the Board's Boston office; Miss Irene M. Fletcher, Librarian and Archivist, and E. H. G. Blacklock, A.I.M.T.A., Administration Secretary, Congregational Council for World Mission, London, England, for the Archives of the London Missionary Society.

Various phases of fieldwork (conducted for a total of eighteen months, in 1961 and 1964–65), archival work, and writing were supported by the Social Science Research Council, the American Educational Foundation in Australia (Fulbright), the National Institutes of Health, the Coordinating Committee of Foreign and International Affairs and the University Committee on Research in the Humanities and Social Sciences of Princeton University, and the Wenner-Gren Foundation for Anthropological Research. I express my gratitude to them all.

To my colleagues in the Program in Anthropology of Princeton University at various times, David W. Crabb, A. Thomas Kirsch, Mark P. Leone, Alfonso Ortiz, Sherry Ortner Paul, and James L. Peacock, and to many students, my thanks are boundless. I must mention also Amélie Rorty of the Department of Philosophy, Douglass College, Rutgers University, an ex officio member of the Program. An *ambience* was established at the Princeton Program in which ideas were recklessly promulgated and exchanged. I must express particular appreciation to David W. Crabb for his editorial and linguistic advice, A. Thomas Kirsch for taking the trouble to teach me practically everything I know about cultural modernization (many of his ideas are in this book, too), and James L. Peacock III for introducing me to his own superb version of the dramatistic model of social analysis.

Mrs. Anne Benson, the Program Secretary, has been an unflagging ally in putting the manuscript together. Two student assistants, Carlos Dabezies and Larry Thompson, in an imaginative fashion relieved me of many details. Mr. Thompson, above and beyond the call of duty, drew all the diagrams except figure 4, which was drawn by Gustav Escher.

And finally gracias to Liz and Robin Fox, who, although they probably do not remember it, helped to dream up the title.

There is not much culture-by-culture comparison in this book. Some of that will emerge at another time. I do want to mention the feeling of déjà vu which emerged in reading certain books after my work was completed: Elizabeth Colson (1953) on the Makah—a book which I wish I had known about much earlier; Marshall Sahlins (1962) on Fijian kinship groups; Harold Scheffler (1965) on the Choiseulese; Ronald Frankenberg (1957) on Wales. David Schneider's *American kinship* (1968) was available to me in manuscript while I was working on my material. That manuscript and a few subsequent ones have been major theoretical inspirations of this book, although I have gone astray.

Great appreciation must be expressed to publishers, authors, or editors for permission to quote from the following sources: Arthur Grimble, From birth to death in the Gilbert Islands, *Journal of the Royal Anthropological Institute* 51 (1921): 25–54, by permission of the Royal Anthropological Institute of Great Britain and Ireland; Grimble, *We chose the islands* (New York: William Morrow; London: John Murray), © 1952 by Sir Arthur Grimble, by permission of both publishers; Grimble, *Return to the islands* (New York: William Morrow; London, John Murray, © 1954, 1957 by

Olivia Grimble, by permission of both publishers; H. C. Maude and H. E. Maude, The social organization of Banaba or Ocean Island, Central Pacific, *Journal of the Polynesian Society* 41 (1932): 262–301, by permission of the authors; Pacific Islands Monthly, *Pacific Islands Monthly* 36 (9):16, and 37 (8):19, © Pacific Publications Pty. Ltd., Sydney, Australia, by permission of the publishers; Talcott Parsons, *Societies: evolutionary and comparative perspectives,* © 1966 by Prentice-Hall, Englewood Cliffs, N.J., by permission of the publisher; Deryck Scarr, *Fragments of empire: A history of the Western Pacific High Commission 1877–1914* (Canberra: A.N.U. Press, 1967), by permission of the publisher and the author; David M. Schneider, *American kinship: a cultural account,* © 1968 by Prentice-Hall, Englewood Cliffs, N.J., by permission of the publisher; Schneider, Kinship, nationality and religion in American culture: Toward a definition of kinship, in Robert F. Spencer, ed., *Forms of symbolic action, Proceedings of the 1969 Annual Spring Meeting, American Ethnological Society* (Seattle: University of Washington Press, 1969), by permission of the publisher.

Certain sections of this book include material from the following previously published articles of mine, and I would like to express appreciation for permission from each of the publishers to use them as modified: Maximize your options: A study in values, symbols and social structure, in Robert F. Spencer, ed., *Forms of symbolic action, Proceedings of the 1969 Annual Spring Meeting, American Ethnological Society* (Seattle: University of Washington Press, 1969); Banaban adoption, in *Adoption in Eastern Oceania,* Vern Carroll, ed., © 1970 by the University of Hawaii Press, Honolulu; The historiographic implications of social and cultural change: some Banaban examples, *Journal of Pacific History* 2(1967): 137–47.

From two unpublished works, much has been directly lifted. I refer to my doctoral dissertation, "Symbols and solidarities on Rambi Island, Fiji," University of Chicago, 1966; and my paper, "Land as a medium of symbolic exchange: the Banaban case," Wenner-Gren Symposium no. 46, Kinship and locality, Burg Wartenstein, Austria, 23 August–1 September 1969. The paper was circulated among the conference participants, from whom I learned much. For availing me of the facilities of the Wenner-Gren Foundation, I conclude by expressing my appreciation to a gracious lady, Mrs. Lita Osmundsen.

DISCONCERTING ISSUE

Abbreviations

The following abbreviations are used for achival sources.

ABCFM   Papers of the American Board of Commissioners for Foreign Missions, Micronesia Mission, ABC 19.4, Houghton Library, Harvard University, Cambridge, Mass.

LMS   Papers of the London Missionary Society, Livingstone House, London.

RIC   Files of the Rambi Island Council, Rambi, Fiji.

WPHC   Central Archives of Fiji and the Western Pacific High Commission, Suva, Fiji.

Introduction

On the island of Rambi, in the colony of Fiji, stands one two-story building, which houses a number of small administrative offices. The office for the Rambi Island Council occupies half of the upper floor. It is often a lively office, and most visitors to that section stop before a counter between the door and the desks of the local officials. The population of the island is about two thousand, and most of the adults know one another. Those who come to the office on business share a broad range of experience with the relatives, friends, or acquaintances whom they see, and there is always much to talk about, commiserate about, joke about.

Copies of the *Fiji Times,* the colony's daily, and the *Pacific Islands Monthly,* the major regional magazine, are regularly received in the office, and the visitors who can read English or who enjoy seeing the pictures leaf through them on the counter. People who can read English do not scan the contents of these journals randomly. The items of greatest interest are about the people themselves; they are looking for themselves inside.

Island officials or typists may make copies of relevant articles for future reference. The articles are not only about the island of Rambi. They are also about Ocean Island and the Gilbert and Ellice Islands Colony, of which it is a part. The native name of the island is Banaba. Its indigenous inhabitants are known as Banabans. But its indigenous inhabitants are not on Ocean Island.[1] They are on Rambi and have been since 1945.[2] They are the people who read the articles.

This book is about one people and two islands: Ocean Island, the place from which most of the people (or their parents) came, and Rambi Island,

1. A Banaban representative is regularly on Ocean Island, however, and recently some Banabans have returned there to work.
2. Rambi is also spelled Rabi, Rabe, and Rambe. I use *Rambi* because the spelling best suggests the pronunciation to readers unfamiliar with Fijian orthography. For other Fijian names the Fijian orthography is used. For names and words in the Gilbertese language, the orthography now generally used in the Gilberts is adopted.

the place where they are now. The physical distance between the two places is about sixteen hundred miles. In some aspects of the people's lives, however, the conceptual distance between the two islands is minimal. What people know and feel about Ocean Island informs what people know and feel about Rambi Island. And what they know and feel about Rambi Island informs what they know and feel about Ocean Island: in contending with Rambi, people refer back to Ocean and thus shape the concept of Ocean itself. It is not only memory which shapes this concept. There are the articles in the journals, the reports of visitors, the statements of government officials, the inquiries of researchers. Ocean Island and Rambi Island, separated by over a thousand miles of sea but hovering in one another's shadow in people's minds, act as metaphors for each other. This is one of the major themes of *Disconcerting Issue:* the two-island theme.

Ocean Island has been the seat of an extensive phosphate mining enterprise since 1900. At that time there began an influx of foreign officials, laborers, and other employees who caused the Banabans to become a minority on their own island, which was transformed into a kind of company town. This transformation and the consequent resettlement of the Banabans on Rambi will be discussed in detail.

Since before the resettlement, there have been Banaban objections to the phosphate company's mode of operation. When the people moved to Rambi, they maintained land rights on Ocean Island, and mining continued there. Objections particularly to the ways in which phosphate profits are shared out have become a great source of friction between the Banabans and the British government and have culminated in a present state of confrontation politics. The Banabans recently sent a delegation to the United Nations asking for the independence of Ocean Island, as the only way through which what they consider present abuses can be corrected.[3] We are not dealing with a placid corner of the Pacific. The Banabans are a people who have had a massive grievance, which touches most aspects of their life. Their struggle is not only a "political" one in the narrow sense of the term. The Banabans are struggling to make sense out of their past and present, and to give direction to their future.

We will be primarily concerned with phosphate not as a concrete entity but as a symbol, as an embodiment of highly charged meanings, and as a partial transformation of a more central symbol in traditional Banaban culture: land. The notions about phosphate are intimately tied with the

---

3. Fiji became independent in October 1970, after the text of this book was written. Fiji's independence will no doubt change the context of the Banabans' political activity.

notions about land, and this fact informs the present social, political, and economic crisis of Banaban society. Land as a symbol is related to blood as a symbol in ways which will be explored in detail. Largely through the activities of the phosphate industry, the Banabans were drawn into a world system, and the people changed mightily. Yet, although transformed, land and blood have remained as two focal points in Banaban culture. This is another of our major themes, and indeed the central one: land and blood.

The expanding field of Pacific history is changing our view of the islands of Oceania. As research develops, the notion that before the arrival of Westerners the islands had isolated populations going their own unchanging ways is losing credibility. Things *happened* in the Pacific. The new Pacific history rightly concerns itself with the precolonial history of Pacific peoples.[4] Unfortunately, most of the verifiable history of Ocean Island before the arrival of representatives of the metropolitan powers is lost to us. There is much that can be reconstructed, however, from material emanating from the recent era, and we will be concerned with that.

The history of the Banabans is in part a history *about* history, and about culture. Circumstances over which the people had little or no control brought about a situation in which they were compelled to make explicit both to themselves and to outsiders what their custom was and what their history was. Outsiders made interpretations based on this information, their own preconceptions, and their own interests. The interpretations made by outsiders molded the people's own conceptions, which were then an input to subsequent interpretations by outsiders, and so forth in an unending series. This book is a moment in that process.

Records from earlier times, along with magazine and newspaper articles of today, are both historical documents and cultural documents—but documents which pertain to more than one culture. A variety of older documents and writings about the Banabans will be quoted at length in this book. A single document can have relevance in several ways. For example, it purports to record events of its time or events of an earlier time. And from the Banaban perspective, it may have been alive at the time because people knew of it then, or it may be alive in the present because people know of it now, or both. The Banabans stress historicity. Such documents are at least as relevant, and deserving of at least as much serious consideration, as legends, and at times their style is as revealing of the attitudes of actors in the Banaban drama as is their content.

4. The center of this work is the Department of Pacific History, Australian National University. See Maude 1968.

We are thus concerned with history in the common sense, but also with history as myth, and myth as history. We read from the past to the present and the present to the past, see-sawing from one to the other as do the people, and our purposes include the explication of how and why they do it. The people are in history, and history is in the people.

As for other times, so for other places and other peoples. Information from the outside which is salient to current Banaban problems of action also concerns Nauru, an independent, phosphate island to the west of Ocean Island, formerly under a different administration but mined by the same company. Banabans scan magazine articles about Nauru with great interest, and beliefs about what happened on Nauru have been a significant input to the Banaban scene for many years. As we will see, Nauru has taken on the nature of a model which the Banabans can follow. Not only do Nauru and the Nauruans exist as a place and as a people, they exist as part of Banaban culture in that they are symbols, as are the British and many other such categories. On the one hand, what Nauruans do and what the British do are objectively related to the Banaban situation. On the other hand, Nauruans and the British have been incorporated into Banaban culture in the sense that they are meaningful categories to the people, and with other categories, they define the people's world and inform their action. This raises another of our themes: the use of external models. The models are external in that they relate to people who are defined as being out-side the community's own boundary. The models are, however, internal in that they have been transformed to become part of the Banabans' own culture. Perhaps many modern societies in the Pacific have come to the point where definitions of the British, the Americans, the United Nations, and so on, have more relevance to a wider range of action than do treasured myths.

The dialectic of mutual interpretation (and misinterpretation), within the social context of which it is part, is a process which bears on all colonial societies. There is another dialectic (using the term broadly), which bears on all societies. Clifford Geertz outlines it in a discussion of "Modjukuto," an Indonesian town.

> Especially the years after the Revolution (that is, after 1950), when the whirl of innovation engulfed the entire scene, were marked by an increasing am-biguity of social behavior. And from this double observation comes the cen-tral theoretical argument, also double, of our study: namely, (1) that ordered social change involves the attainment by the members of the population con-cerned of novel conceptions of the sorts of individuals and the sorts of groups (and the nature of the relations among such individuals and groups) that comprise their immediate social world: and (2) that such an attainment of conceptual form depends in turn upon the emergence of institutions through

whose very operation the necessary categorizations and judgments can be developed and stabilized.[5]

One may gloss this as a dialectical view of the relations between conceptual form and institutional form. Thus emerges another theme of this book: the double dialectic of Banaban history. One part of the dialectic is that between the indigenous community and those superordinate to it, as we discussed above. The other part is that between conceptual form and institutional form. *Double dialectic* is a convenient slogan. The interrelationships, however, are far more complex, since the institutional forms, as we will see, were often creatures of outside forces, and the conceptual forms were themselves molded in relationship to outside forces.

The problem which Geertz is addressing is one of the core problems, not only of social science, but also of Western thought in general. It has often been glossed as the "idea-action problem" but in anthropology has been reconceptualized as the relationship between cultural (or symbolic) systems and social systems.[6] Earlier I mentioned that we will be concerned with phosphate, not as a physical object, but primarily as a cultural object, a symbol, a vehicle for a number of conceptions which are basic to the Banaban cultural system. What do we mean by "symbol" and "culture"?

A recent statement by David Schneider sets out the point of view adopted here.

> By symbol I mean something which stands for something else, or some things else, where there is no necessary or intrinsic relationship between the symbol and that which it symbolizes.
>
> A particular culture . . . consists of a system of units (or parts) which are defined in certain ways and which are differentiated according to certain criteria. These units define the world or the universe, the way the things in it relate to each other, and what these things should be and do.
>
> I have used the term "unit" as the widest, most general, all-purpose word possible in this context. A unit in a particular culture is simply anything that is culturally defined and distinguished as an entity. It may be a person, place, thing, feeling, state of affairs, sense of foreboding, fantasy, hallucination, hope, or idea. . . .
>
> It is important to make a simple distinction between the culturally defined and differentiated unit as a cultural object itself, and any other object elsewhere in the real world which it may (or may not) represent, stand for, or correspond to.
>
> A ghost and a dead man may be helpful examples. The ghost of a dead man and the dead man are two cultural constructs or cultural units. Both

5. Geertz 1965, p. 5. Geertz's points may be taken as constituting a definition of orderly social change (and, by implication, social order).

6. On this problem, see Geertz 1957; Kroeber and Parsons 1959; Parsons 1965, 1966; Schneider 1968; and on a related issue, Levy 1965.

exist in the real world as cultural constructs, culturally defined and differentiated entities. But a good deal of empirical testing has shown that at a quite different level of reality the ghost does not exist at all, though there may or may not be a dead man at a given time and place, and under given conditions. Yet at the level of their cultural definition there is no question about their existence, nor is either one any more or less real than the other.

In one sense, of course, both ghost and dead man are ideas. They are the creations of man's imagination or intellect, which sorts certain elements out and keeps others in, formulating from these elements a construct that can be communicated from one person to another, understood by both. Yet at that level of reality the question of whether one can actually go out and capture either a ghost or a dead man is quite irrelevant. . . .

Both "ghost" and "dead man" are words, of course, and it is certainly important to note that words "stand for" things. . . . But the question is not *what thing* they stand for in the outside, objective, real world, although with a word such as "dog," we can take that concrete animal, stand him on the ground, point to him, and say, "That is a dog." The question is rather *what different things* does such a word stand for. The word "dog" certainly is a cultural construct—in one of its meanings—and it is defined in certain ways as a cultural unit. Its referent in that context, then, is not the "objective" animal itself, but rather the set of cultural elements or units or ideas which constitute that cultural construct. . . .

Certainly culture is in one sense a regularity of human behavior, and as such it is quite objective and quite real. But this does not mean that any observable, definable, demonstrable regularity of human behavior is culture. Neither does it mean that culture can be directly inferred from any regular pattern of human behavior.

Among the different forms in which symbols can be cast, one consists of the definition and interrelation of persons in interaction. This is the set of rules which specify who should do what under what circumstances. . . . These are the standards, the guides, the norms for how action should proceed, for how people of different cultural definitions should behave.

But the cultural constructs, the cultural symbols, are *different* from any systematic, regular, verifiable pattern of actual, observed behavior. That is, the pattern of observed behavior is different from culture. This is not because culture is not behavior. Culture *is* actual, observable behavior, but of only one specially restricted kind. [Schneider 1968, pp. 1–5.]

Schneider's last point in particular needs underscoring, since some have misunderstood it. In talking about culture, about symbols, one is not entering an ethereal nonbehavioral realm. Cultural or symbolic systems are abstracted from aspects of live behavior and are no less real than technology.

People sometimes speak of culture as if it contrasted with behavior or with action. This is a subversive usage. Culture is abstracted from behavior, action or interaction; it is not opposed to them. This does not mean that an ideal construct of, for example, how government should function may not be different from how government actually functions. But it does mean that the ideal construct of how government should function is in no sense less real than the way in which government actually functions. Nor does it mean that the ideal construct exhausts the cultural aspects of "government." If people *suppose* that government functions in a nonideal way, or they *expect* government to behave in a nonideal way, this is an important fact and a *cultural* fact. In the cultural analysis of the "definition and interrelation of persons in interaction," to use Schneider's phrase, suppositions and expectations are as relevant as ideals (see Kroeber and Kluckhohn 1963; Oliver 1958).

The general aim of my research is to describe and explicate those aspects of Banaban culture which pertain to the definition and interrelation of persons in interaction, "the fabric of meaning in terms of which human beings interpret their experience and guide their action" (Geertz 1957, p. 33). In my earliest, largely untutored researches among the Banabans, history was in the foreground because I was diffusely interested in culture change. History receded into the background as I began to focus my interest on the bilateral descent and kinship systems as symbolic systems, because they presented certain theoretical problems of great interest in anthropology. History pushed into the foreground again as I became concerned with why the descent system, in particular, occupied the position which it did occupy within the cultural system. This was not really intentional. I began writing historical background sections to a revised version of my doctoral dissertation and found that the background was absorbing the foreground. The reason is, I think, very simple.

Cultural analysis is concerned very broadly with the problem of meaning. Banaban culture on Rambi Island does not present us with a system of calm categories neatly and unambiguously arrangeable. The problem of the definition and interrelation of cultural categories is a real problem to the people themselves. It is a painful problem to the people themselves. Symbols are being formed and reformed. People are actively fashioning, refashioning, and searching for the categories which might help to provide a comprehensible, livable life for them. They are concerned with building a society and constituting a culture. In order to describe this condition, and certainly to account for it, one must look to the past.

In parts 2 and 3 I present close analyses of a number of concrete events. There I am treading on dangerous ground. I am trained as an anthropologist, not as a historian. The historical sources are unevenly distributed, by their existence, their public availability, and my knowledge of them. Some sources I have unfortunately not yet had the opportunity to see. There is always the danger of assuming that the most critical events are the events reported in the sources. There is also the danger of knowing the way a situation turns out and structuring one's description so that the end points seem inevitable.

At times an almost microhistorical presentation is necessary because the time factors involved are extremely small. For example, the beginning of Christian conversion, the beginning of the phosphate enterprise, and the assumption of colonial control occurred within a period of fifteen years. Many important events were not initiated by the Banabans but were initiated by external forces or, rather (after a time), forces that had local establishments with which the Banabans participated and toward which Banaban culture and society were partially differentiating.

Thus, since it is with Banaban culture that I am primarily concerned, the major task is to assess (with little information available to me on individuals) how the Banabans marshalled their cultural and social resources to contend with the other factors in the largely expanded field of which they were part, and to assess the implications for future action of the ways in which those resources were marshalled.

The rapidity with which locally momentous events followed one another in the Banabans' experience relates directly to Geertz's "double" theoretical argument, on the attainment of novel conceptions and the emergence of institutions through which they "can be developed and stabilized." We do not know in any systematic fashion, alas, what are the limits in the capacity of members of a community to revise their behavior to cope in an ordered and satisfying fashion with such a rapidly changing milieu. One may reflect, however, that this capacity is not infinite, and one may contemplate the implications of a life in which today's conceptions have effectively put yesterday's experience into some kind of order, only to be challenged by tomorrow's reality.

The other half of our double dialectic also enters this picture. The Banabans have been faced with interpreting and, at the same time, being interpreted by different people (even different people in the same bureaucratic hierarchy), who arrived in uneven succession. This is no easy situation, to understate the case, in which to navigate.

It is hopeless to consider the Banaban situation at any time since at least 1885 from the point of view of an equilibrium state. And an anthropologist should not be restricted to equilibrium states. I therefore deal, not only with events, and consequences, but also with tendencies, or directions.

This book is a work in both anthropology and history. When historical data are lacking, I feel no constraint to avoid disciplined speculation (always labeled as such), both theoretically and comparatively based, to fill in the gaps.

As an anthropologist who uses the history of a particular people to construct a coherent account of that people, in order to clarify the theoretical concerns of anthropology, I do not use (or speculate about) all their history. I am primarily interested not in concrete individuals but in systems, and not in all systems but primarily in cultural systems. The set of criteria that I bring to bear to sort out relevant from irrelevant historical data is formed by the major themes I identify, and by a recognition of the central importance of one of the major concepts of social science: differentiation.

In a recent statement, Talcott Parsons discusses this concept.

A unit, sub-system, or category of units or sub-systems having a single, relatively well-defined place in the society divides into units or systems (usually two) which differ in *both* structure and functional significance for the wider system. To take a familiar example . . . , the kinship-organized household in predominantly peasant societies is *both* the unit of residence and the primary unit of agricultural production. In certain societies, however, most productive work is performed in specialized units, such as workshops, factories, or offices manned by people who are *also* members of family households. Thus two sets of roles and collectivities have become differentiated, and their functions separated. There must also be some differentiation at the levels of norms and some specification of common value patterns to the different situations. . . .

Differentiation processes also pose new problems of *integration* for the system. The operations of two (or more) categories of structural units must be coordinated where only one category existed before. Thus, in employment-occupational systems, the father of the household can no longer supervise production in his kinship role. Therefore, the producing organization must develop an authority system which is *not* embedded in kinship, and the producing and household collectivities must be coordinated within the broader system—e.g., through changes in the structure of the local community. [Parsons 1966, p. 22.]

Especially in sociology, the literature on differentiation is enormous. Differentiation is one of those concepts which can define the interface between social science and history. The social implications of differentiation, the kinds of problems in social structure that must be solved if the new form is to be more adaptive than the old form, or even if it is to survive, will not be discussed now directly. Rather I would like to focus attention very briefly on some of the cultural implications of differentiation, beginning with a discussion by Parsons.

Any given value system is characterized by a particular type of *pattern*, so that, when it is institutionalized, it establishes the desirability of a *general type of social system*. By what we have called specification, such a general valuation is "spelled out" in its implications for the various differentiated sub-systems and the various segmental units. Hence, the value orientation appropriate to a particular collectivity, role, or norm-complex is not the general pattern of the system, but an adjusted, specialized "application" of it.

A system or sub-system undergoing a process of differentiation, however, encounters a functional problem which is the opposite of specification: the establishment of a version of the value pattern appropriate to the new *type* of system which is emerging. Since this type is generally more complex than its predecessor, its value pattern must be couched at a higher level of *generality* in order to legitimize the wider variety of goals and functions of its sub-units. The process of generalization, however, often encounters severe resistance because commitment to the value pattern is often experienced by various groups as commitment to its particular content at the previous, lower level of generality. Such resistance may be called "fundamentalism." To the fundamentalist, the demand for greater generality in evaluative standards appears to be a demand to abandon the "real" commitments. Very severe conflicts often crystallize about such issues. [Parsons 1966, p. 23.]

Differentiation thus involves changes, not only in the lineaments of social structure, but also in values.[7] "Solutions" to the problems of integration and generality are in part cultural solutions. Parsons seems to be writing from the perspective of differentiation which is internally based rather than externally oriented, as it may be in colonial systems. In both cases, however, some of the major implications are the same.

In order for integration and a higher level of generality to be achieved, it is important to remember, if perhaps obvious to point out, that real people must be doing real things. Such processes or achievements do not simply happen by the inevitable working out of some transcendent principle. One of the things that people will be concerning themselves with is the nature of the structures that have become differentiated—for example, religious and political structures which were once part of a relatively less differentiated matrix. They will try to systematize, or introduce a greater degree of logical coherence into, both the structure as a whole and the newly differentiated parts.

Although the subsystems are interdependent, as each becomes more autonomous it can assume some meaning by itself. A genuine innovative and creative upsurge may be experienced as people try to define the nature of each subsystem, and the nature of the system as a whole. New possibilities for action may be realized that were not realized, that could not be realized, before. This cultural elaboration might proceed so fast and in so many directions that social action in the direction of institutionalization becomes stymied, especially if there is no subunit with the legitimate authority to sort out the elaborations. This feature has particular salience for colonized societies, in which the institutionalization and specification of new values and concepts may be blocked as well.

---

7. I have elsewhere argued for the possible desirability of separating value systems from cultural systems; see Silverman 1969a. But I will not recast the analysis in those terms here, since some excruciating theoretical excursions and transformations would have to be made.

Where the elaborations in the cultural sphere are not institutionalized socially, or where the level of generality is great (thus requiring a chain of specifications to reach the level of concrete action), we may speak of a greater degree of analytic differentiation *between* the cultural and social systems. Specific cultural forms are less tied to specific social forms. Literacy has been invoked as one factor in such a differentiation: there are books and records which transcend particular social structures and social circumstances.

In colonial societies the differentiation of cultural and social systems often takes the following form: Speaking only of social structure, the difference between the ideal nature of the social world and the actual nature of the social world becomes a difference in kind rather than in degree. The ideal order and the actual order are in radical disjunction. If, however, we admit not only ideals but expectations as cultural phenomena, and if there is also a disjunction between the ideal order (what should be) and the suppositional order (what people believe actually is), then there has also been a differentiation within the cultural system. Whether one looks at the differentiation as intracultural, or cultural-social, or even intrasocial, the consequence is the same: a tension, and a leverage for change.[8]

How does one look at these developments from the point of view of the individual? With the problems of order to be solved (problems which are radical in a situation of rapid change), with the possibilities for creativity and elaboration increased, with differentiation between cultural and social spheres, objectification and the growing systematization of the culture which we have remarked become correlates at the individual level. This means that the individual stands further back, as it were, from the concrete circumstances in which he finds himself. He can contemplate his own cultural and social systems as objects, which thus can be creatively manipulated and changed. He can contrast the situation as it is now with the situation as it was then, in a relatively less differentiated context. The more options he is aware of, even if he rejects them all, the less engulfed he is in the system of which he is part.

Another factor which leads to systematization and objectification, I suggest, is the appearance of a genuine cultural contrast category on the local scene. Horton (1967*a*, 1967*b*) has quite correctly drawn our attention to this important moment, or set of moments, in the history of any people. Such a moment occurs when people are aware that another cultural system, based on quite different basic premises, could work in their own situation.

8. The points here are a reduction of concepts found in Bellah 1964, 1965; Eisenstadt 1964; Parsons 1966; and many conversations with A. Thomas Kirsch.

One may speculate that given this condition, people articulate their own system, systematize it further, and objectify it, and thus increase the differentiation between cultural and social systems.

Does this conceptual apparatus really have anything to do with the Banaban people?

At the beginning of this Introduction, I mentioned that when the Banabans look at certain magazines, they look for themselves inside. This is a special case of a more inclusive phenomenon: they are looking for themselves in general. They are trying to clarify who they are, how they got where they are, what they are doing and what they should do, where they are going and where they should go.

The Banaban dilemma is a product of both rather unusual historical circumstances and the more widespread phenomenon of a relatively undifferentiated society and culture becoming relatively more highly differentiated within a colonial structure.

In part 3, I label the major process occurring on Rambi Island, the creative disorder through which the dilemma is concretely being realized, as one of "testing out." "Reality-testing" or even "experimenting" might do. In this process, conceptions drawn from the past and present, at times differently elaborated by different individuals, are played out to construct and construe differentiating social forms. The testing is in part a means to clarify what those conceptions are, and there is, as Geertz insists, a feedback process. In the colonial framework on Ocean Island, many values and ideas about social life were developed within the setting of increased systematization and objectification, which could not be actualized. The disjunction between cultural and social systems occurred. The resettlement situation provides a field within which actualization of the values has become more feasible and more urgent. But the implications of actualizing these values and ideas were not thought out, and conflicts and confusions have arisen as they have become manifest. Testing out means that through social action individuals and groups are testing out these ideas against other ideas (or one differentiated bit against another differentiated bit), against themselves and against reality, not always sure of what the results will be. Through testing out, tangible form (institutions) is given to the conceptions which have developed, and those tangible forms then begin to reshape the conceptions themselves.

As a people in such circumstances encounter the conditions of the social world, conceptions which they have developed suggest rather vague *ranges of variation* of mandatory, acceptable, and prohibited behavior (or at least ranges to which people are not strongly committed). Testing out refines the boundaries of those ranges of variation, and the redefined ranges themselves interrelate with the concepts.

Kinship and descent, politics, economics, and religion are implicated in the testing-out process. Through this process Banaban culture evolves, and individuals try to give sense to and make sense from their experience. Their experience is neither personally nor historically static. It is calamitous; and the experience of their parents and grandparents, transformed, is alive within them. Again, they are in history and history is in them.

A particularly poignant problem for the Banabans, as for any people, is the role to be played by very meaningful institutions which have in some sense been "pushed to the wall" in the differentiation process. What happens to these institutions as their social environment becomes more complex? How are they redefined, as they must be? In the Banaban case, the institution which invites analysis from this perspective is the bilateral descent system. I will discuss this at length.

In the first discussion of the descent system, I will begin building evidence for a hypothesis about the Banaban value structure, about the principles which structure the relationship of actors to cultural objects. I underscore that this is a hypothesis, because it was formulated mainly from field data after I left the field, and I did not test it on genuinely new data. I term the value of highest generality in the hierarchy of values that of "Maximize your options," or "Keep your options open" (see Silverman 1969a). It seems to me that when this value (which is about commitment itself) is at the highest level in a hierarchy of values, its institutionalization should produce a definite configuration. Stating it will be stating something of an "ideal type," since implicitly we are making comparisons with other systems, and the dimensions of contrast are relative, not absolute. What are some of the characteristics of this type?

First, ends are multiple but the multiplicity is not institutionally ranked. Second, a "have your cake and eat it too" outlook dominates the manner in which alternatives are confronted; there is an attempt to get the best (or at least something) of all worlds. Third, there is a complex marked by the co-occurrence of fluidity of commitments, loosely defined expectations, conditional acceptance of decisions, and a magnified need for current information about individuals as a background for action. Fourth, there is a willingness to entertain propositions without feeling constrained to decide about their truth or falsity. Fifth, significant aspects of social integration are ego oriented rather than group oriented, so that social ties are widely disposed, and memberships tend to be overlapping rather than exclusive. And sixth, with maximizing options at the highest level, the community structure will be relatively undifferentiated, or the community will be a dependent one, or both.

The more direct relationship of this hypothesis to empirical data will be taken up again in parts 3 and 4; the kinds of data necessary for its explication are not as readily available for the period discussed in part 2.

In order for an anthropologist's statements to be convincing, the reader has a right to know how the anthropologist did what he did. At various points in this volume my style of research will emerge. I had contemplated presenting here a systematic account of my research, but having begun it, found that the task was too large and would in fact require another book. My material has remained unpublished too long, and I feel a responsibility to present it now. The delay of another year or two is simply too great.

I will merely say now that I did not engage in any form of exotic research activity. A combination of semidirected conversations, interviews, systematic observation and investigation of kinship and political events, household surveys, archival research, and a habit of keeping my eyes and ears open forms the basis of this study. My first interpreter-assistant gradually became an assistant, and most of my work was conducted in the Gilbertese language.

In addition to the technical gap, there is a comparative gap. The comparative problems to which this material is relevant are many: the study of social structures as systems of understanding, the nature of the colonial experience, the structures and functions of bilateral kinship and descent systems, the problem of resettlement, and the relation of anthropology and history. My presentation, however, is only erratically comparative. I intend to pursue the comparative aspects in future publications.

Before presenting a preview of the chapters, I recall to the reader's attention the general themes outlined above: the two-island theme, land and blood, external models (such as Nauru and the British), the double dialectic and the testing out process, the concept of differentiation as a meeting point between anthropology and history, and the value of maximizing options.

Chapter 1 is a reprinting of the most substantial contribution made to traditional Banaban ethnography: H. C. Maude and H. E. Maude's, "The Social Organization of Banaba or Ocean Island, Central Pacific," which appeared in the *Journal of the Polynesian Society* in 1932. The original article is reproduced unchanged except for stylistic modifications and the omission of photographs and three appendixes. Chapter 2 is a reanalysis of the traditional culture based on the Maudes' article conjoined with my own work, the notes of H. E. Maude and Sir Arthur Grimble, and travelers' accounts. In the reanalysis chapter, some issue is taken with a few of the points made in the Maudes' article, but that article still stands as a superb piece of work, and my interpretation of Banaban culture would have been impossible without it.

The social structural feature of central interest here is the system of linked, ranked bilateral descent units. The idea is mooted that in analyzing material pertinent to Banaban descent, the best procedure is to see "the system" in terms of the intersection of a number of more general systems. These systems include a kinship system (of which descent categories are one component), a locality system, a ritual circulation system, a precedence-complementarity system, and a "person" system. "The person" is being used in this context in a special sense, to refer to the person as a social category or unit in its own right, considered independent of other attributions—what the fact of being a person implies in the culture. Consideration of "the person" will recur in many chapters. The structural significance of the person is a point which in the culture today interrelates features of kinship (the "ego-oriented" aspects of the kinship system), religion (the notion of personal commitment), politics (the problems encountered in institutionalizing central authority), social integration in general, and values (for example, the option-maximizing complex).

The argument is made that in the traditional culture, the system of descent units functioned primarily as a ritual system, and in chapter 2 the basic symbolic point of this book is introduced: two symbolic complexes were the integrative complexes of the Banaban cultural system. One complex centered on common substance, blood, and the other complex centered on land, locality, and space. The interrelationship between these two complexes is discussed in terms of Schneider's (1968) distinction between *identity* and *code for conduct*.

Much of the rest of the book is a spelling out, in part speculative, of the fate of these two complexes as Banaban society partially differentiated and as the Banaban people moved to Rambi. The argument is made that land, in reference to blood, has operated in Banaban culture as a kind of medium of limited "symbolic exchange" between different domains. Different aspects of land as a symbol, and the set of conceptions embedded in it, are differentiated out into the different domains, or, from another perspective, one can move from one domain to another by considering land and adding some other factors. Through blood and land as symbols, different domains of social structure are ordered, as are the relationships between the individual and society; the past, present, and future; Ocean Island and Rambi Island; Christianity and the local idea of "custom"; and the Banabans and the world.

In chapter 3, I discuss three momentous events which occurred in a fifteen-year period (1885–1900): the arrival of a Protestant mission, the discovery of phosphate and the beginning of the phosphate industry, and the inclusion of Ocean Island within the Gilbert and Ellice Islands Protectorate. In this period Ocean Island became systematically related to the modern world. Our major concern is to discover how Banaban culture evolved in this new context, by trying to read from the data implications for the two central symbolic complexes.

At many points in the book a particular implication of Christianity will be stressed: the fact that Christianity presented a system of understanding and ethics which ideally transcended any particular people in any particular place. Traditional Banaban culture provided a system of understanding and ethics which focused on a particular people and a particular place: the Banabans and Ocean Island. This contrast grounded the Banaban cultural distinction between "Christianity" and "custom" which has had far-reaching consequences for many areas of the people's lives, from the nature of irony in "joking relationships" to the kinds of attitudes held toward the British government.

The Banaban concept of custom, I will argue, became a more highly articulated and generalized concept as Banaban culture developed in its now more complex setting. As that concept became more highly generalized, external models moved in to partially occupy the place that some traditional concepts had occupied within the cultural system. This "conceptual circulation effect," where as one set of concepts becomes more highly generalized, another set of concepts is either brought in from the outside or is redefined (perhaps downwards) from another domain (or level), is probably very common in situations of change and is probably necessary, although not sufficient, for a new stable order to emerge.

Chapters 4 through 6 present a description and suggested explanation of a growing opposition to external authority and the development of an ideology of autonomy. This development was represented in the political, religious, and economic domains, which were in the process of differentiating out of a relatively undifferentiated matrix. Events which bear on land and kinship are discussed in detail. The background of the resettlement move is also discussed, as is the dispersal of the community during the Second World War.

Part 3 presents the working of the testing out process discussed above. Chapter 7 contains a description of the arrival on Rambi and an outline of one attempted solution to the problem of community organization. This was an integral model, with three partially differentiated substructures: the Island Council as the political instrument of an integrated societal system, the Community Store as the economic instrument, and the London Missionary Society Church as the religious instrument. Chapter 8 is a chronological pause to consider a putatively final settlement with the phosphate company, and the decision to remain on Rambi. In chapter 9, I explore the failure of the integral model through a discussion of the rise and fall of the Community Store.

In chapter 10, I elaborate the complex of ideas surrounding Banaban communal identity and their implications for community action. In talking about Banaban communal identity, I present a construct of the Banaban value system and a discussion of its operation within the colonial framework. The argument is made that there is a basic "bind" in the value system (a bind which is probably widespread in societies without strongly legitimized central decision-making structures). The major concern is the implications of this developing value system for organization on Rambi. Chapter 11 contains an outline of some aspects of local organization and land distribution on Rambi.

Part 4 is about kinship and descent in the contemporary culture, intimately tied to blood and land. Chapter 12 is a detailed analysis of kinship terms and terms for kinsmen; I am concerned as much with "use" as with "structure" in the common senses. Terminological usage is one of the ways in which fundamental ideas about consanguinity and affinity are encoded. Chapter 13 explores the nature of consanguinity and affinity, taking off from some rituals. These rituals constitute another way in which fundamental ideas about consanguinity and affinity are encoded. As our observations on kinship accumulate, an interesting feature of the total kinship system emerges (though certainly one not distinctive to the Banaban kinship system alone). David Crabb has called this feature the "expansion-contraction model." Although the basic, defining symbols are constant, in action the vocabulary used to label kinsmen can expand and contract, the universe of concrete people recognized as kinsmen can expand and contract in time and in different contexts, the set of rituals which concern kinship can expand and contract with different individuals. The expansion-contraction model in this culture appears to gear well with the general option-maximizing orientation.

At the beginning of chapter 14, I formulate the relation between descent, consanguinity, and affinity, and speculatively apply that formulation to traditional Banaban culture. I discuss the structure and role of the descent system in the contemporary culture and society and make the point that the system serves a wide variety of functions for different individuals and groups. I also explore in detail how the system is related to other things, including political grievances and the question of organizing the resettled community.

In the Conclusion, I use Robert Bellah's notion of a "civil religion" to explore the nature of integration in Banaban culture, how the culture got where it is, and where it may be going.

PART I

Blood, Land, and
Traditional Banaban Culture

Traditional Social Organization
H. C. Maude and H. E. Maude

Banaba or, to give it its European name, Ocean Island, is an elevated coral peak about 3 miles long by 2.5 miles wide situated in latitude 0.53 south and longitude 169.35 east. The island is about 6 miles in circumference and is completely surrounded by a coral shelf, about 100 yards in width, from which it rises to a height, in the center, of 270 feet.

Except for the occasional visits of whalers and a few trading schooners, there was but little contact with Europeans before the discovery of phosphate in 1900,[1] though a number of deserters from whaling ships lived as beachcombers among the natives. As far back as the seventies, however, five black-birding ships visited the island and, finding the islanders in the throes of a severe drought and consequent famine, transported between one thousand and one thousand five hundred of them to Honolulu and Tahiti. This terrible famine, resulting in an enormous reduction in the population of the island through deaths and migration, had the effect of severely dislocating the social organization of the Banabans and caused many customs to decay even before the coming of the Europeans employed in the phosphate industry.

Christianity was brought to the island in 1885 by a native of Tabiteuea in the Gilbert group and the islanders were gradually converted, though even today a few professing pagans may still be found among the older generation. As the discovery of phosphate made the island of great value to the Empire, a protectorate was proclaimed over it by Great Britain in November 1900.

The islanders, as will be seen later, are identical with the inhabitants of the neighboring Gilbert group and are usually referred to as Micronesians, being an offshoot of the Malayo-Polynesian race. They speak the Gilbertese language, but with a distinct local accent and with the addition of a consider-

1. For a very interesting account of a landing on Banaba in 1851 see Webster n.d., pp. 39–50.

able number of words not used in the Gilbert Islands. From a count of old village and dwelling sites, it is calculated that the population of the island before the famine was in the neighborhood of 2,500, an estimate which is agreed to by the old men. By 1914 the population had sunk to little over 400, but since that year there has been a steady increase, the 1931 Census giving a total of 729.

In the following pages an attempt is made to describe certain of the more important aspects of the Banaban social organization. Several subjects, among them being the system of relationship, have been omitted, although they fall logically within the scope of this article, as they are being dealt with elsewhere. For almost the whole of the material on which the historical reconstruction is based, and for his valuable help and advice throughout our stay on Banaba, we are indebted to Mr. A. F. Grimble, C.M.G., whose unrivalled knowledge of the Gilbertese, gained during seventeen years of work among them, enables him to speak with unquestioned authority on all phases of their life.

HISTORICAL RECONSTRUCTION

According to local myth the original inhabitants of Banaba were Melanesian in type. They are described as being small-bodied, squat, crinkly-haired, large-eared, and black-skinned, and were skillful in sorcery. Their gods were the Spider (*Na Areau*) and the Turtle (*Tabakea*) and they were apparently associated with a fire-cult. They are reported to have been cannibals.

These autochthones appear to have been of the same race as the earliest inhabitants of the Gilbert group, for on nearly every island from Makin to Butaritari may be heard legends referring to the small, black, ugly folk who worshipped Na Areau and who were absorbed or killed off by the invaders. Christian records a similar tradition on Ponape, where the earlier inhabitants are described as being little dwarfish folk, dark-skinned and flat-nosed.[2]

The next invaders of Banaba were tall, fair-skinned people who, according to the evidence shortly to be published by Mr. Grimble [1933], came in a migrating swarm from Gilolo and its neighboring islands in the East Indies and overran the Gilbert group.[3] A portion of this host, whose ancestor was Auriaria, landed on Banaba and succeeded in overcoming the inhabitants,

2. Christian 1899, pp. 111, 112.
3. Cf. Grimble 1921a, pp. 53, 54, for a discussion of the identity of the Ancestral Lands.

"casting them into the sea," though they had a wholesome fear of their sorcery. In the words of a local myth, "they overturned Banaba, and imprisioned Tabakea the Turtle under the land, where he lies to this day."

However, it would appear from local tradition that not all of the black folk were killed, for a remnant appear to have been driven to the central plateau of the island, where they reappear later as the people of Tairua who fought with, and were beaten by, Na Kamta,[4] a chief of Tabwewa. Indeed there is evidence suggesting that they have, to some extent, kept their separate identity to this day and that they are none other than the people of Mangati—the fierce people—who form the division of Te Karieta or the Upland folk, one of the two sections into which the Tabwewa village district is divided. Until a few years ago the people of Mangati lived on the uplands above the present village of Tabwewa and in their territory may still be seen the cairns of rough stones which local tradition states to have been connected with the fire-worship of the autochthones.[5]

The invaders, who came without women of their own race, took their wives from among the earlier inhabitants and produced the hybrid Banaban type of today; however, the majority of them did not stay on Banaban long, but together with their relatives in the Gilberts they passed down the chain of atolls comprising the Gilbert and Ellice groups until they reached Samoa, where they formed part of the famous invasion of the Tonga-fiti folk. Another legend records how Samoa was first discovered by Banabans, who called it "Tamoa te Ingoa" or Samoa the Namesake, owing to its resemblance to the portion of Banaba lying below Tabwewa village, and known as Tamoa.[6]

The remnant left on Banaba settled down in their new surroundings and at length came to connect themselves so intimately with their new homes that in their creation-myth they made Banaba "the first of all lands, the navel of the universe and the home of the first ancestors."[7] However, intercourse was kept up with the Gilberts and especially with the island of Beru, and a member of the chief's family tracing his descent from Auriaria sailed

4. Na, Nam, Nan, or Nang is placed before names of males on Banaba and Nei before names of females.
5. Another myth runs as follows: "Nei Aro-Mangati and Nei Nou Mangati were known to be man-eaters. They lived at Banaba and tried to eat Auriaria (i.e., the invaders) when he visited there." This lends support to our identification of the people of Mangati with the earlier inhabitants. Many of the attributes of the autochthones, such as fierceness and skill in sorcery, are also considered by the Banabans to be characteristics of the present-day Mangati folk.
6. Grimble 1921a, p. 52.
7. Ibid., p. 52.

to Beru and married there a woman named Nei Angi-ni-maeao (Wind of the West) who, according to Banaban tradition was actually the descendant of a senior branch of the Auriaria family who had migrated to Samoa and had been driven back along the old track to the Gilberts, together with the rest of the Tonga-fiti host.

Whether this tradition is true or not, Nei Angi-ni-maeao came with her husband to Banaba, bringing with her a great many of her Beru relations led by Na Kouteba her brother, Na Mani-ni-mate, and Nei Te-borata. They apparently came at the invitation of the Banabans, who were few in number and anxious to increase the population of the island, but in any case the newcomers proceeded to partition the island in an arbitrary manner, and the older inhabitants, quite overawed, returned to their settlement on the flat seacoast land below Tabwewa.

This partition of Banaba made by Nei Angi-ni-maeao is of great importance, as the boundaries of the five village districts thus fixed stand unaltered to this day. An account of the partition, as obtained by Mr. Grimble from Nei Beteua, a direct descendant of Nei Angi-ni-maeao, is given in Appendix 2 [see pp. 336–39].

The result of the partition of Nei Angi-ni-maeao was to divide up Banaba as follows:

1. Na Kouteba and his followers took the north and east foreshores, forming the village district of Te Aonoanne.
2. Na Mani-ni-mate and his followers took the southeast foreshores, forming the village district of Uma.
3. Nei Te-borata and her followers took the south foreshores, forming the village district of Toakira.[8]
4. Nei Angi-ni-maeao and her followers took the southwest foreshores, forming the village district of Tabiang.
5. The former inhabitants retained the west and northwest foreshores, forming the village of Tabwewa.

The boundaries of each village district ran back from the measured foreshore toward the center of the island until they met the boundaries coming in from the opposite coast.[9]

Comparison of the genealogies of the village district chiefs shows that the migration from Beru to Banaba took place about eleven generations ago, and from that time until the coming of the Europeans the history of

8. The districts of Te Aonoanne and Toakira have been in recent years joined together by the government, forming the single village district of Buakonikai.
9. For the boundaries of the divisions see the map of Banaba given in Appendix 1.

the island has been uneventful.[10] The Beruans brought but few women with them and were thus compelled to marry the women of the *Bu-n Anti* (the breed of Spirits), as the descendants of Auriaria were called. Na Kouteba himself married one of the Tabwewans who, as will be seen later, retained many rights and privileges over the rest of the island. Continual intermarriage between the two divisions of Tabwewa and the people of the other four districts has long ago obliterated any differences which may once have existed in their physical characteristics. Intercourse too was kept up with the Gilbert group, though the island suffered from no subsequent invasion and, together with Makin and Butaritari in the Gilberts, escaped the domination of Tanentoa of Beru and the troubles caused by the wars of Kaitu and Uakeia, facts which add to the importance of the study of its system of social organization.

SOCIAL ORGANIZATION

In describing the social organization of the Banabans we have thought it advisable to proceed from the smaller units toward the larger, and the subject will be dealt with under the following four heads:
1. The Household
2. The Hamlet or *Kawa*
3. The Village District
4. The Overlordship of Tabwewa

The Household

As a general rule each family in a hamlet would occupy a separate sleeping house or *mwenga,* the Banaban family consisting of a man, his wife or wives, and their children. Besides a man's real children, he would often adopt someone else's child as *nati* (son or daughter). This child would live with his or her adoptive parent in exactly the same way as the natural issue of the family. We have dealt with the custom of adoption more fully elsewhere,[11] but since writing that article it has become apparent that adoption as a *tibu* (grandchild) is extremely rare on Banaba and is, in all probability, a recent importation from the Gilbert Islands. The family was

10. Cf. Grimble 1921a, p. 52. The statement that Banaba is inhabited by people who did not take part in the migration to Samoa is true only of the Tabwewa village district. The other districts were peopled by the immigrants from Beru and there is no reason to suppose that they were not descendants of the returned Tonga-fiti swarm. No doubt the newcomers adopted the creation myth of the original inhabitants, as has been the case elsewhere in the Pacific.
11. See Maude and Maude 1931.

patrilineal and usually patrilocal, though cases in which a man went to live in his wife's hamlet are not unknown. Although there was theoretically no limit to the number of wives a man could have, in actual practice it was unusual to have more than one.

A daughter would live with her parents until her marriage, which would normally take place soon after she reached puberty. A son would live in his parent's house until the time came for him to be initiated into manhood, which was soon after the appearance of his axillary and pectoral hairs. From this time onwards, until he became a *roro-buaka* (warrior) and could marry, he would spend a considerable portion of his time in the *uma-n roronga* (young men's house) or on the terraces of his village district, where the old men of his *utu* (kindred) would instruct him in the *kouti* magic and in his family traditions. He would, however, continue to regard his father's house as home until he married and set up a house of his own.[12] An elderly couple, after they had partitioned their lands, would usually live with each of their children in turn, who would look after them until their death.

The mwenga in its typical form was known as a *bata* and consisted of a rectangular roof of pandanus thatch supported well above the ground on four posts and containing a loft entered by a trapdoor. In this loft the family kept their valuables, more or less secure from the attacks of their enemies. Besides the bata, a family would also possess a small, open-sided, thatched shed forming a roof over the *umum* or cooking oven and a storeroom for miscellaneous objects which were not likely to be stolen. Most families would also have an *uma-n teinako,* a small house where the women of the family could be separated when menstruating.[13] The family would also own a canoe shed on one of the terraces belonging to its village group.

The Kawa *(Hamlet)*

The Banaban hamlet was a cluster of four or five, sometimes more, homesteads, situated somewhere on the land bearing the same name as the hamlet itself. The male inhabitants of each hamlet were all, theoretically at any rate, descended from a common ancestor and were considered to all belong to the same utu. However, although the members called each other brother, sister, etc., the kawa were not exogamous groups and, provided that they were not *te utu ae kan* (near kindred) and thus within the prohibited degrees, members of the same hamlet could marry each

12. Cf. Grimble 1921*a*, p. 32, for an account of one of the marriage customs in vogue on Banaba.
13. These "houses of separation" were also found on Hawaii. Handy 1927, p. 47.

other at will.[14] Each hamlet had a *unimane* (old man) who was the eldest descendant, in the male line, of the founder, and was consulted in all affairs affecting the hamlet as a whole. His also was the privilege of being spokesman for the group in ceremonial dealings with outsiders.

Our informants were clear on the point that formerly the inhabitants of a hamlet owned all the land around it, but through the marriage of the women of the kawa to outsiders much of the land has come, as the years have passed, to be owned by people who actually reside in other kawa and often in other village districts. For example, we doubt if more than half of the land block known as Aurakeia, and owned originally by the members of the kawa of Aurakeia, actually belongs to them today. The owners of the other half are, in all probability, scattered all over the island. This, of course, is counterbalanced by the fact that the people of Aurakeia own much land in other land blocks. If, however, a woman married and went to reside outside her kawa she would still consider herself a member of it and would be bound, if called upon, to assist the inhabitants in such matters as preparing food for a ceremonial feast. Her children, however, would definitely consider themselves as members of their father's hamlet.

In the ceremonies attendant upon births, marriages, and deaths, as well as in the important matter of ceremonial feasts, the hamlet acted as a unit. To give an example, should the hamlet of Aobike, as a whole, or any member of it, wish to give a feast in the *uma-n anti* [spirit house], word would be sent round and those related to Aobike would come from all over the island to bring food and assist generally; conversely should a feast be given by any other group in honor of a kawa member all his kawa relations would assist in eating it. Ceremonial presents given to a hamlet were divided up amongst its members.

Each hamlet had its own *boti* (sitting-place) in the uma-n anti and *maneaba* [meetinghouse] of its village district and the descendants of that hamlet had the right of sitting in their boti irrespective of where they were actually living at the time. In all the various ceremonies, feasts, and activities of the village district as a whole, such as the thatching of the uma-n anti or the welcoming of a stranger, each hamlet had its rights and privileges which were jealously guarded in the old days and are even valued to some extent by the present generation of mission trained youths. For example, in the ceremony mentioned above of *te kairua* (the welcoming of a

14. The utu (kindred group) was, on Banaba, the only regulator of marriage, the kawa having no such function. A Banaban was prohibited from marrying his direct ascendants, or the issue of his direct ascendants, up to and including his (or her) great-grandparents.

stranger), which was last performed on the High Chief of Tarawa Island in the Gilberts, one hamlet (or perhaps two or more jointly) would have the duty of calling the man to the maneaba, one would tie on his wreath of flowers, one would anoint him with oil, one would see to his food, one would keep him engaged in conversation, and so forth.

Here then, in the hamlet, we see a striking difference between the social organization of the Banabans and that of the neighboring Gilbertese. The hamlet is the central pivot of the Banaban social structure and a Banaban, when he tells one that he is *kai-n Eta-ni Banaba* or *kai-ni Mangati*,[15] has told one the most important single factor regulating his social life, for on it depends the locality of his home and his lands, the maneaba in which he will have a right to sit and the uma-n anti in which he will make his food offerings to the gods, the terrace where his son will learn the mysteries of magic, his position in the dance and in all ceremonies, and numberless other things.

In the Gilberts, on the other hand, the hamlet is comparatively unimportant, the supreme factor in social organization being the clan. Now a comparison between the Gilbertese clan and the Banaban kawa will show them to be two similar but distinct social groupings. Both are patrilineal and both determine the sitting place in the maneaba, but here the resemblance ends, as the kawa is essentially a geographical unit and the Gilbertese clan is certainly not, members of the same clan being found scattered over all the sixteen islands of the group. Again, the Gilbertese clan is an exogamous unit while no evidence has ever been obtained suggesting that the kawa is, or was at any time, exogamous.

The only reason which we have found to account for this difference between the Gilbertese and Banaban social structures is as follows. The old inhabitants of the Tabwewa village district, with the possible exception of the people of Mangati, were all descended from a comon ancestor, Auriaria, and were consequently all members of the same or allied clans; the later arrivals from Beru, again, are known to have been all, or nearly all, members of a clan claiming descent from Nei Tituaabine and having as their clan totem a stingray known as *te kerentari* or *te baimanu*. They also considered themselves to be, in some way, related to the Tabwewans. Consequently where all were members of one, or at the most two clans, the clan unit would rapidly cease to be of any importance whatever. When therefore Banaba was partitioned by Nei Angi-ni-maeao and her fellow voyagers, each family built their home on a suitable site within the boundaries of the land apportioned to them and their descendants would naturally tend to build their

15. *Kai-n* means inhabitant of. The *i* before Mangati is euphonic.

houses in the same place, thus forming the typical Banaban hamlet. In the maneba and the uma-n anti members of the same kawa would sit in the place where their ancestor had sat and act as a unit in ceremonies and functions of all kinds, and thus the hamlet would take much the same place in their social organization that, in the Gilberts, had been occupied by the clan.

The Village District

We have seen above how the five village districts of Tabwewa, Tabiang, Toakira, Te Aonoanne, and Uma came to be formed as a result of Nei Angi-ni-maeao's partition. Each district formed a very definite group under a chief and, with unimportant exceptions, owned in common:

1. A main maneaba in the interior;
2. Subsidiary maneabas, for kouti devotees, on the terraces;
3. An uma-n anti;
4. Terraces and kouti sites;

and, through the hamlets of which it was composed, owning:

1. Lands;
2. *Bangabanga* (water-caves.)

As a unit or through its hamlets the village district was organized for war, work, games, and feasting.

The village districts often, though not invariably, contained in addition an uma-n roronga. These were clubhouses for the unmarried men similar to the *bai* of the Carolines and elsewhere, but they had nothing like the same importance in the social structure, probably owing to the terraces usurping so many of their functions.

The village districts varied in size and in the number of their component hamlets, a list of which is given in Appendix 3 [see pp. 340–41]. According to the list, which as far as we could ascertain was complete, Tabwewa is seen to have eighteen kawa of which the Karia section had eight and the Karieta folk seven, three being mixed Karia and Karieta. Tabiang had twenty-three hamlets, Te Aonoanne thirteen, Toakira ten, and Uma twenty-three. A further basis of comparison, though inexact for the reasons mentioned above, is furnished by the number of lands owned by the inhabitants of each district, obtained by the Native Lands Commission which has recently sat on the island. This shows that 695 pieces of land are owned by people living in the Tabwewa village district, 291 by Tabiang, 650 by Uma, and 843 by the village of Buakonikai, formed by the recent fusion of Te Aonoanne and Toakira. We shall deal shortly with each of the main attributes of the village district, commencing with its head, the chief.

The Chief. The chief had definite but limited powers. For example, in any

major communal activity, such as the building of a maneaba or the prepara-
tion for a season's communal games, the chief's opinion would have considerable weight in deciding what was to be done and when to start, but the
people and not he would apportion the shares to be undertaken by each
hamlet or individual. When the question to be decided affected one village
group alone, such as the date for a feast or the punishment of a wrongdoer,
the chief of that village would call, and preside over, a meeting of the
inhabitants of the village group. The chief would outline the problem to the
people, after which a general discussion would take place, and any final
decison reached would be based on the opinion of the majority.

Should there be much sour toddy drinking or other trouble affecting the
island as a whole the chief of Tabwewa would call a meeting of all island
chiefs and landowners to decide on the steps which should be taken to stop
it. The village chief had the right of speaking first in the maneaba.

Succession to the chiefship passes to the eldest child, either male or female, but should the eldest child be a female, the nearest male descendant or
relative will perform the functions of the chiefship until the daughter has
a son who can do the work. The daughter will be called chiefess until her
death, when her son will take over the title as well as the duties of the office,
the Banabans considering that these duties are such that they cannot be
performed by a female. The genealogy in figure 1 will illustrate this point.
When Nei Tiara-n Uea was chiefess Na Bauro, the male grandchild of her
great grandfather's eldest brother, performed the work until her son Nan
Tabau came of age, when he took over the duties of office.

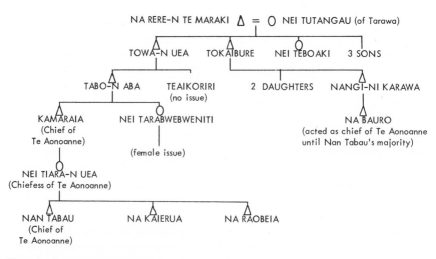

Fig. 1. Sex and Succession

An adopted child could become chief in exactly the same manner as an individual's natural issue, as is shown in the genealogy in figure 2. Here Na Raobeia, the youngest son of Nei Tiara-na Uea, was adopted as a nati by his great grandfather's grandson Te Aroua, the chief of Uma. On Te Aroua's death he succeeded to the chiefship and is the present holder of the office.

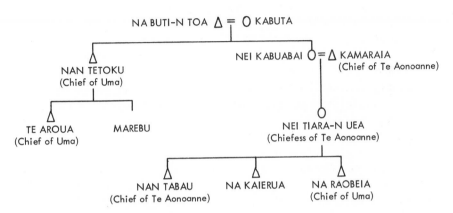

FIG. 2. ADOPTION AND SUCCESSION

Maneabas. The maneaba, or communal meetinghouse, was the focal center of the secular life of the village district. Here were held the meetings of the old men and the discussions on all matters affecting the village group as a unit and here the neighborhood would naturally gravitate at the end of the day's work, for games, dances, and gossip. While the edifice was regarded with some degree of veneration, being forbidden to noisy bands of children, it had nothing like the degree of sanctity which attached itself to the uma-n anti. A maneaba is best described as a high rectangular roof of pandanus thatch supported on large stone pillars, the shingle floor being covered with coconut-leaf mats, on which the people sit. To those accustomed to the large maneabas of the Gilbert Islands the smallness of the Banaban counterparts comes as a surprise, but they are adequate for the needs of the small village units.

Besides the main maneaba, which was built away from the seacoast, each village had its subsidiary maneabas situated on the terraces belonging to the group. These were used by people temporarily residing at the terraces for one or more of the purposes to be mentioned later. The following list comprises the main maneabas of the various village districts:

1. Tabwewa had formerly a maneaba which stood at Kaimatua (at the bottom of the present village and to the west of the railway). Later

this was demolished and the present maneaba called Tawanang was built. These maneabas were used by both Te Karia and Te Karieta.
2. The Uma maneaba was called Te Toka-ni Mane or Nariakaina.
3. The Te Aonoanne maneaba was called Takamoi. This was recently removed from its old site in the hamlet of Te Maeka-n Anti, by the Wireless Station, and placed in Buakonikai village.
4. The Toakira maneaba was called Te Toa. This no longer exists.
5. The Tabiang people, being few in number, had no proper maneaba, but used one or other of two large houses known as Te Nikora and Te Burabura. Recently, however, they have built a maneaba in the middle of their present village.

Uma-n anti. In structure the uma-n anti[16] were exactly the same as the maneabas but they held perhaps an even more important place in the life of the people, being used for magic and ceremonial purposes. They might be described as large communal eating houses in which everyone had their boti or sitting place. All ceremonial feasts took place inside the uma-n anti and here the food offerings were made to the various ancestral gods. These offerings were collected from the kawa and put together in one place outside the building. The following is a short account of a typical function in the uma-n anti. The firstfruits of the coconut, pandanus, and wild almond trees belonged, in Uma village, to the kawa directly descended from Na Mani-ni-mate. The firstfruits were collected by the members of these kawa and taken to the uma-n anti, where the hamlet of Te Tarine,[17] who were the head of the uma-n-anti, offered them to Nei Tituaabine, from whom the trees were held to have been originally obtained. While the coconut and pandanus cult was, in actual practice, confined to the section of Uma village descended from Na Mani-ni-mate, no one on the island could eat of the fruit of the wild almond tree until they heard that the season had been commenced by the firstfruits being offered to Nei Tituaabine.[18]

There were the following uma-n-anti on the island:
1. Tabwewa. (*a*) The Te Karia building called Bu-n tiritiri. Both sections used this until the separate Karieta one was built. (*b*) The Te Karieta building called Te Karawa ititi built by Na Ning, who was made a chief for his efforts. It was used, when first built, as an uma-n roronga for the young men of Te Karieta, but the people of Uma and Tabiang began bringing the stranded porpoises and other fish there[19] and so it became used as an uma-n anti.

16. *Uma* means house; *anti*, ancestral Gods, or literally, "the house of the ancestral Gods."
17. The name *Te Tarine* itself means the wild almond tree.
18. See Grimble 1921*b*, p. 83, for a discussion on the goddess Nei Tituaabine.
19. See below, p. 41.

2. Tabiang, called Tieraki-n te bong.
3. Uma, called Nei Karibaba. The timbers for this uma-n anti were brought by its builder, Na Mani-ni-mate, from Beru.
4. Toakira had two uma-n anti called Tabera-n nene and Tokia I-Matang.
5. Te Aonoanne apparently had no uma-n anti but used one or other of those belonging to Toakira.

Boti places in the maneabas and uma-n anti. As in the Gilbert Islands the interior of the maneabas were divided, either by the *oka* (roof-beams) or the *inaki* (rows of pandanus thatch), into boti or group sitting-places. But, whereas in the Gilberts a man's boti depends not on the locality of his dwelling-place and lands but on the sib of which he is a member, on Banaba the boti divisions were essentially hamlet divisions and an individual would sit in the boti of the kawa of which he or she was a member.

The uma-n anti were also divided into boti and, although the old men were not explicit on this point, it would appear that the sitting-places in the maneaba were more or less exactly duplicated in those of the corresponding uma-n anti. But while in the maneaba the people seldom sat in their correct boti except on ceremonial occasions, in the uma-n anti they invariably did, and as a consequence, with the early disappearance of the uma-n anti under mission influence, the position of the boti places, and even their names, were soon forgotten, and it was only with the greatest difficulty that we were able to reconstruct a fairly comprehensive list of the sitting-places in the old Tabwewa maneaba at Kaimatua and in Bu-n tiritiri, the Karia uma-n anti.

The boti in the old Tabwewa maneaba were as follows:

1. Kabwara
2. Te Bakoa
3. Karongoa
4. Bukiniwae
5. Nei Tebaobao
6. Baraua
7. Nukuao

In Bu-n tiritiri there were the following sitting-places:

1. Buariki
2. Tanneang
3. Te Koturu
4. Bukiniwae
5. Ria-n Matang
6. Te Inaki-ni mane
7. Te Rieta
8. Nukuao
9. Abero
10. Te Inaki-n te Maneaba

Very few of the sitting-places in the other maneabas and uma-n anti were remembered, and in only four cases were we able to establish the exact position of the boti in the building. These four positions are shown in figure 3, as it is possible that further research may reveal more.

Each of the boti places given in figure 3 belonged to a single kawa or to a group of neighboring kawa; for example Bukiniwae was the boti of Mangati, and Inaki-n te Maneaba belonged to the group of hamlets known as Te Maneaba. Many of them—Karongoa, te Bakoa, Buariki, Tanneang—bear the names of well-known Gilbertese clans and one—Bukiniwae—refers to privileges which the hamlet had in the functions centered round the building.[20] The meanings of the others are unknown.

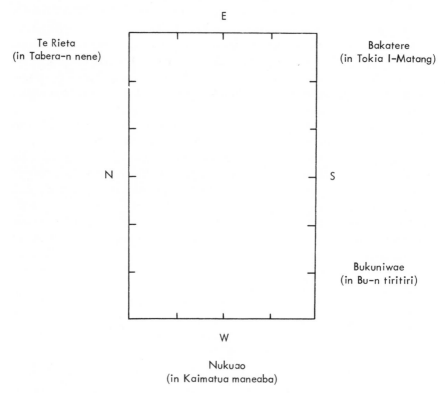

E

Te Rieta
(in Tabera-n nene)

Bakatere
(in Tokia I-Matang)

N

S

Bukuniwae
(in Bu-n tiritiri)

W

Nukuao
(in Kaimatua maneaba)

FIG. 3. SITTING PLACES

Within the maneaba or uma-n anti each important boti and therefore the principal kawa had their duties and their privileges. For example the main duties connected with the Tabiang uma-n anti, Tieraka-n te bong, were allocated as follows:

    1. The atu (head) was the kawa of Tabiang, which was Nei Angi-ni-maeao's own kawa. Its duties were to decide when all work connected

20. See below, p. 41.

with the uma-n anti was to be done and the date on which the various feasts were to be held.

2. The "dividers of the food" were the kawa group of Te Itiatia and Eta-ni Banaba.

3. The "cutters of the eaves" were Te Itiatia, and the fallen ends of thatch were collected and thrown away by Aba-uareke. Te Itiatia also had the duty of holding down the ridge capping during high winds.

4. The "thatchers of the roof" were Te Itiatia, Eta-ni Banaba, the kawa group of Nakieba and Aba-uareke.

5. The "plaiters of the floor mats" were Te Itiatia and Eta-ni Banaba. The speaking, distribution of food, etc., was in order of boti as in a Gilbertese maneaba.

The Terraces. As has been mentioned before each village group owned a series of terraces situated on the cliffs overlooking the seacoast of the district. The method of construction was first to build walls of uncemented stones along the edge of the coral bedrock to the required height and then to fill in the space behind with stones and earth. When the filling was brought flush with the tops of the walls, it was leveled and covered with a few inches of white coral shingle, thus resulting in a large, smooth, level platform.

The terraces varied in size, Ao-n te Tarine[21] being slightly above the normal. This terrace is kept in good repair by the old men of Buakonikai, in remembrance of their youth when they used to live there for several months at a time. The feature which marks it out from the other terraces is a line of seven stone monuments lying about ten feet back from the edge of the seawall. The center monument consists of two flat, tablelike slabs supported by a group of five smaller vertical stones. On either side of this table there are three groups of stones, each consisting of a large upright block in the center having its base surrounded by four flat slabs. The ruins of other tablelike structures can be seen lying further away from the seawall. Repeated questioning of the old men has elicited nothing further than that in their youth the monuments having central vertical slabs were used as seats and the tablelike stones for food offerings.

At the back of the terraces there used to stand a line of open-sided houses and on the more important ones a maneaba in addition. A complete list of the terraces on the island is given in Appendix 4 [see p. 342]. Some of these no longer exist, those belonging to Uma having been destroyed in the process of building a government cemetery and three belonging to Tabwewa being utilized for the old Pacific Phosphate Company's harbor works, but the

---

21. We are indebted to Mr. Grimble for allowing us to utilize his notes on the terrace of Ao-n Te Tarine, which he was the first to discover.

majority still remain in a state of fairly good preservation and, although usually situated on somewhat inaccessible cliffs, more than repay a visit of inspection. The authors have examined, at one time or another, every one of the seventeen terraces or terrace-sites and they have never failed to be impressed with the immensity of the task involved in the construction. Somewhat similar but far larger structures are found in the Carolines[22] as well as elsewhere in the Pacific, but nothing like them are found in the Gilberts, no doubt owing to the rarity of suitable stone.

Perched among the rocky pinnacles on the east coast and in the neighborhood of the terraces facing that direction are numerous platforms of rock and shingle, miniature counterparts of the terraces themselves but often so small as to be made of a single flat stone. These were the platforms where the men perched in the early morning to do the magic called kouti in order to insure their success and prowess. It is impossible to enter into any detail here as to the nature of kouti magic but it was essentially performed at sunrise, facing east, and consisted of a ritual washing with salt water from a special coconut shell followed by a massaging of the arms with smooth pebbles from the beach. The main consideration was that the rising sun must be faced, as from the sun came the essential principles of health and strength.

As the people of Tabwewa and the western coast were not able to see the rising sun from the normal kouti platforms they built large altarlike structures known as *teiabakana* from the top of which they could view the sun sooner than would be otherwise possible. These teiabakana, of which several exist in a good state of preservation, are rectangular in shape and about ten feet by six, the sides, which are vertical, being made of stone slabs and the interior filled and leveled as in a terrace. On the top of each is a stone slab lying on the shingle with an upright stone on its western side, thus forming an L. On this the kouti performer sat and rested his back, waiting for the rising sun to appear in the eastern sky.[23]

According to all our informants the terraces were primarily made not as a rendezvous for kouti devotees but usually for the catching and taming of the frigate-birds, which took up a large part of the leisure hours of the Banabans. Catching the frigate-bird was far more than a mere pastime with the Banabans, as an elaborate ritual was attached to it and to attain skill involved a lifetime of study and practice.[24] There were large *kai ni katiku* or platforms for the tame birds built on the terraces and here they were ten-

22. Cf. Christian 1899.
23. Cf. Grimble 1931, p. 205 n, where the similar but smaller structures of the Gilbert Islands, there called *buatarawa*, are described.
24. Webster n.d., pp. 39–50, frequently alludes to the importance which the Banabans attached to their frigate-birds.

dered and cared for daily by their owners. When twenty or more frigate-birds had been tamed they were set free and served to decoy other birds, which were brought down by the *ao ni kabane*, a bolas, formed by a stone, *te atau*, attached to the end of a string. The thrill in the game was in the skillful throwing of the ao ni kabane so that it fell over the bird's wings and body and brought it to the ground. There is an elaborate native terminology describing the various games and special movements to secure a bird, whether it be soaring, descending, wheeling, or flying level, the game mentioned above being known as *te kabaneitei*. It would, however, be wandering outside our subject to describe the sport further here.[25]

As it was absolutely forbidden for a woman to have any contact with a frigate-bird, a line of coconut string was stretched across the boundary of each terrace where birds were being kept, beyond which no female could pass. Hence, as it was also important in the proper performance of the kouti magic to be sure that one did not sleep on the same mat as a woman, or even go near one, the kouti platforms were built close to the terraces and the performers and learners used to live on the terraces for the nights previous to their ablutions.[26] A few men who were performing the kouti exceptionally seriously with a specific object in view, such as to become a champion fighter, might stay on the terraces for long periods until they felt themselves to be in a fit state, bodily and mentally, to return. In some of the more arduous types of the kouti magic, for those who were endeavoring to become champions at any pursuit involving intense physical strain, it was necessary to abstain from sexual intercourse for a year at a time, and such individuals would become more or less permanent inmates of the houses on the terraces.

Another purpose for which the terraces were used was in the training and education of the village youths. When the boy's time came for undergoing his haircutting ceremonies and trial by fire,[27] i.e., when his hair began to grow on his chest and under his arms, he would be sent to the terrace of his district to undergo instruction in the arts of life and the kouti magic from his grandfather or other elder relative. Here he would stay at intervals, with the other village youths of his age, until he passed into the ranks of the roro-buaka.

A second series of terraces, those on the west side of the island belonging

---

25. Cf. Woodford 1895, p. 347, for a description of the sport as practiced on Abemama in the Gilbert Islands; also Kennedy 1931, p. 294, where the weight for a similar bolas is also called *te atau*.

26. The reason why no woman should come near was for fear lest they might be menstruating, a menstruating woman having a lethal effect on magic. Cf. Handy 1927, p. 47.

27. See Grimble 1921a, pp. 40, 41, for an account of these ceremonies.

to the Tabwewa and Tabiang village districts, were built and used primarily as large platforms for the erection of the village *bareaka* (canoe sheds) and, in later years, for trading with the visiting schooners in search of palm oil.

Totemism. The evidence we were able to obtain concerning totemism suggests that the village districts founded by Nei Angi-ni-maeao and her fellow voyagers from Beru all had as their totem the kerentari or baimanu, a species of stingray. This fish was considered to be the *rabata* (body) of Nei Tituaabine, who was the *bakatibu* (ancestress) of the immigrants and their *anti* (ancestral goddess). To this day the villagers, should they meet a stingray when out fishing, will throw it morsels of anything in the way of food, tobacco, etc., that happens to be in their canoes, and formerly a portion of each meal was set aside as an offering to the totem-fish. It is said that if a member of the totem-group causes any harm to Nei Tituaabine as personified in the stingray he will inevitably suffer misfortune and nothing can be done to help him.

The group of clans in the Gilberts claiming descent from Nei Tituaabine and having as their totem one or other of the stingray family retain their veneration for their totem in a more marked form than any of the clan-groups. This is especially interesting since Christian in his book on the Caroline Islands states that Metalinim was destroyed by an invading host belonging to a clan known as Tip-en-uai (Tituaabine?), coming from a land in the south known as Panamai and having as their totem the stingray.[28] It would seem probable therefore that, as Christian himself suggests, the cyclopean buildings on Ponape were destroyed by an invasion from either the Gilbert Islands or even Banaba itself, which may possibly be the Panamai of Ponapean tradition. This would also account for the recorded similarity between Gilbertese and Ponapean root words.[29]

The totems of the Tabwewa community were two large stones standing in a *bangota* (sacred enclosure), close to the present village. These were the rabata of Tabuariki "the Thunder," and Bakatau, the two anti of the village.

The Overlordship of Tabwewa

As has been mentioned before, the Tabwewans retained many of their rights and privileges after the coming of the Beru settlers. These rights, excellently summed up by Nei Beteua in her account of the settlement of Beru given in Appendix 2 [see pp. 336–39], are as follows:

1. The right to board strange canoes or vessels—*wa-n n tieke;*
2. The right of taking the peace offering of food—*kana-n te amarake;*

28. Christian 1899, pp. 83–84, 108, 324.
29. Ibid., p. 85.

3. The right of anointing with oil—*kabira-n te ba;*
4. The right of garlanding the stranger—*mwae-n te kaue;*
5. The right to take the stranded turtle or porpoise—*kana-n te ika, te on ke te kua;*
6. The right to the stranded *urua* fish—*kana-n te ika te urua;*
7. The right to ordain the *ruoia*—*ruoi-n;*
8. The right to the governance of the land—*taeka-n ao-n te aba;*
9. The right to draw the measuring cord across the land—*katika-ni kora-n ao-n te aba*

The first four privileges fall into one group since they all refer to the treatment of strangers to the island. The chief of Tabwewa had the right of visiting all canoes or ships before anyone else, as well as to take possession of anything that arrived on the canoe or vessel. Should he think fit he could issue an edict that no one except himself could visit a particular canoe or ship, but once he had sent out word that it could be boarded anyone on the island could launch his own canoe and go out.[30] With this privilege went a corresponding duty, that of entertaining all canoe crews and other visitors. The crew would be brought to the Tabwewa maneaba and divided out among the various kawa, who would provide them with food, lodging, and entertainment until their departure. The owner of the canoe would invariably stay with the chief himself. The right of taking the peace offering of food, the right of anointing with oil, and the right of garlanding, all refer to the procedure of welcoming the visitors in the maneaba.

The right to take the porpoise, turtle, or *urua* fish when stranded on the foreshores of the island is the most jealously guarded privilege of the Tabwewans and around it has gathered a mass of interesting custom as to the duties of the various kawa and boti. If the fish was stranded on the foreshores of Te Aonoanne or Toakira it was brought by the people of those districts to the uma-n anti of the Te Karia folk; if it was found on the Tabiang or Uma coasts it was brought to the Te Karieta uma-n anti. In either case the people of the moiety would take the fish and divide it up amongst the various hamlets, but before doing so they would have to give the village group who brought it a present of food in return. All this custom has importance, since it furnishes an illustration of how all the economic activities of the Banabans necessitating cooperation worked through an elaborate system of kawa duties and rights, dependent for their sanction on the force of custom and tradition. We give below an account of how a stranded turtle would be brought from the foreshore of the Uma district to the uma-n anti at Tabwewa.

30. Cf. also Webster n.d., pp. 39–41, 46, 49.

When the turtle was found it was brought to a house by Uma village called Rawa-ni bong, where the kawa of Te Tarine bound up its head and front ready for carrying, its back being bound by the hamlet of Rariki-n te kawai. Rariki-n te kawai also provided the carrying stick. The turtle was then carried to the uma-n anti of the Te Karieta folk, Te Karawa ititi, Bwibwi-n toora bearing the carrying stick in front and Nang Kouea behind. They were received inside the uma-n anti by the head kawa of the Te Karieta folk, Aurakeia. Two *moimoto* (drinking-nuts) were broken ceremonially and eaten by the Tabwewans and visitors. At the same time a basket of flowers was brought and wreaths placed around the necks of the people of Bwibwi-n toora. A return present was then given and, after much gossip had been exchanged, the visitors returned to their own uma-n anti, Nei Karibaba, where the food was partitioned into three shares by the people of Te Tarine, the first share belonging to the old men of the district,[31] the second to Rariki-n te kawai and Nang Kouea, and the third, known as Te Bukiniwae,[32] to Te Tarine, Bwibwi-n toora and Te Rineaba. These were the five important kawa in Uma, since Bwibwi-n toora was the site of Na Mani-ni-mate's first landing and the first uma-n anti, which was later removed to Nang Kouea. Te Tarine was the head of the uma-n anti and the other two were composed of the direct descendants of Na Mani-ni-mate himself. The rest got what shares they could from the leading hamlets.

The turtle was not killed directly when it reached Tabwewa, but a meeting was held at which the date for the killing was decided on. The first blow was given by a representative of Aurakeia, the head of Te Karieta and the hamlet of the chief of Tabwewa, and the second by Te Maiu, the head of Te Karia. The hamlet of Tekerau had the duty of burning the shell, and the flesh was cooked by North Tekerau and Te I-Namoriki. When cooked, the food was divided by A n te Bonobono into two shares, the head and half the body going to Te Karieta, the bones and the other half to Te Karia.

This elaborate partition of the work involved in any economic enterprise and the sharing out of the results is common to the Banabans and Gilbertese, but with the Gilbertese the patrilineal clan takes the place of the hamlet as the unit for each division of the work. This theme will be elaborated later in articles dealing with the Gilbertese social organization. "The right to ordain the ruoia" refers to the custom by which Tabwewa had the sole right to fix the season for the performance of the amusements and games listed below:

1. *Te itau*, boxing
2. *Te kare-motu*, a stick game

31. This was an unusual feature, which we did not find in other ceremonial partitions.
32. The "end of the foot" or heel. So called as it was supposed to be the remnants after the others had got their share.

3. *Te kakuri*, a game
4. *Te tirere*, a dance
5. *Te kabure*, a dance
6. *Te oreano*, a ball-game
7. *Te katua*, a game
8. *Te kati*, bow-and-arrow shooting
9. *Te karanga*, an exclusively Banaban dance
10. *Te buka*, a dance
11. *Te tie*, swinging
12. *Te kabane*, a game with frigate-birds.

These games comprise all the popular adult pastimes of the island. While many of the games themselves, notably the bow and arrow shooting and the karanga dance, are extremely interesting, they must be held over for a subsequent article. All that we need describe here is their connection with the rights of the Tabwewans over the rest of the island. The chief of Tabwewa and his kawa of Aurakeia would meet in the maneaba and decide to practice a certain game. This game could then be performed by the other village groups. When any village felt themselves to be sufficiently proficient the news would gradually filter through and a date would be fixed for a match with Tabwewa. Once this match had taken place the various village districts were free to compete with each other. The visiting teams would be feasted during the course of the contests but they would be expected to bring presents of food with them.

The Tabwewan right to draw the measuring cord across the land, or in other words to adjudicate on land disputes, was a part of their more general right to settle questions likely to cause trouble on the island. This privilege was only vaguely recognized, and a good deal of tact had to be exercised in its maintenance. The other village groups considered themselves to be free communities and would not permit themselves to be dictated to by Tabwewa. In questions affecting the whole island, however, they were prepared to attend meetings organized by the chief of Tabwewa and, as a general rule, the decisions of the Tabwewan chief would be accepted by the rest.

THE INHERITANCE OF LAND

Both sexes were treated equally as regards the inheritance of land. The eldest son was usually given the largest share of land, but there was no fixed rule, as the parents had far more power than in the Gilbert Islands to leave larger portions of their land to favorite children. The land was generally divided up among the children when they became old enough to fend for themselves, the parents reserving sufficient land for their own maintenance during their old age under the name of *te aba ni kara* (land for the aged). This aba ni kara was divided up after the death of the parents. The formality of apportioning land among children, known as *te katautau*, involved the collecting of the various heirs and walking with them around the parental lands, pointing out to them the boundaries of their respective allotments. Usually each child got his share of both the paternal and maternal lands but often it was arranged between the parents that the children should be divided into two groups, one to receive their land from the father and the other from the mother.

Should a child be adopted as nati [child] he would receive the same share as the natural issue under the title of *te aba-n-nati* (land of the son [child] but, unless he was the only child of his real parents, he would receive none of their land.[33] In the absence of children, real or adopted, an individual's land would be partitioned among his (or her) brothers and sisters or their children, should they be dead. Outside the normal system of inheritance by which it was transmitted to the next-of-kin, land could only pass, in times of peace, by means of one of the customary conveyances mentioned below. Some of these customary conveyances, as will be seen, are in payment for services rendered, while others are in the nature of sanctions by means of which offenders against the community were punished by their fellows.

On an individual being killed by another, two lands would normally pass from the murderer to the family of the murdered man under the general title of *te nenebo* (the blood payment). These lands were called as follows:

1. *Kie-na* (the mat for the murdered man to lie on)
2. *Rabuna-na* (the murdered man's shroud)

The largest land that the murderer possessed would be taken as *kie-na* and the next largest as *rabuna-na*. Should the murderer also possess a canoe it would be taken as:

3. *Bao-na* (the murdered man's coffin)

Land would be claimed by a husband from a man who committed adultery with his wife under the title of *te aba n rau* (the land of peacemaking). The adulterer would usually flee, because if caught he would have been killed. In his absence his land was taken and his house broken up by the wronged individual, whereupon he was at liberty to reappear, as it was considered that his offence had been expiated by the conveyance of land.

On a famine occurring, those who were destitute would go and live with those who had food or were skillful fishermen. These people would look after them throughout the famine and when it was over were entitled to take

33. Cf. Maude and Maude 1931, p. 231. The Banaban custom of *te aba-n-nati* is similar to the Gilbertese one there described.

all their lands under the title of *te aba ni kamaiu* (the land of life-giving). The destitute might continue to use the products of their old land sufficient to maintain them, but in any case the land passed irrevocably on their death.

Should a betrothed boy break off his engagement to a girl after having commenced sexual relations with her, four or five lands would normally pass from his family to hers under the title of *te aba n iein* (the land of marriage). One or two lands would often pass on a boy terminating his engagement even though no sexual intercourse had taken place. Should the girl break off her engagement no land would pass. On Banaba it was customary for betrothals to take place at a very early age, often as soon as the child was born.

Should it be generally considered that certain lands had got into the wrong hands resort could be had to a custom known as *te aba ni butirake* (land of the asking). A girl would bind wreaths on the old man or woman who had obtained the land in question and he (or she) was then compelled by this custom to give the girl a piece or pieces of land. Should there be no good reason for the binding of the wreaths the old man might satisfy the island by presenting a minute plot of land, but should it be general opinion that the girl or her family were the rightful owners of certain lands in his possession he would be expected to give them up with a good grace.

Public opinion would compel a thief, on being caught, to convey land to the owner of the property stolen under the title of *te aba n ira* (the land for theft). The amount of land which passed under this title would depend on the nature and quantity of the stolen articles.

Should an individual kill any tame frigate or other bird belonging to another, one piece of land would be conveyed by the killer to the owner of the bird under the title of *nenebo-n te man* (the blood payment for animals).

Under the title of *te aba n tara* (the land for looking after), land would be given in return for nursing during sickness or old age. The amount of land given would naturally depend on the circumstances of the nursing.

Should an individual be on terms of great affection with someone outside his kindred group he would leave him or her a portion of his lands under the title of *te aba ni karaure* (the land of farewell). It was not considered right to leave more than one or two pieces of land under this title as a token of friendship and should more be devised it would be usually opposed by the next-of-kin.

Finally, should an individual dislocate his or her arm or leg one piece of land would be conveyed to the bone-setter under the title of *te aba n riring* (the land for bone-setting).

This exhausts the conveyances of land customary on Banaba. These conveyances were the chief means by which justice and peace were maintained on the island. Should an individual offend against any social convention for which a transfer of land was considered a fitting penalty, a meeting of his hamlet would be held and the offender ordered to forfeit certain of his lands to the person injured. If the affair was serious and beyond the control of the hamlet a meeting of the village district, or even of the whole island, would be held at which the trouble could be ventilated and appropriate measures for restoring the status quo discussed.

The Inheritance of Bangabanga

To the Banabans the bangabanga or subterranean caves of fresh water, of which there were about fifty on the island, were even more valuable than their lands. Should the food supply run out in a famine they could always catch fish, but if the water supply dried up, as it did one terrible year in the seventies, they were reduced to such desperate expediencies as the sucking of the eyes of flying fishes to obtain a few drops of moisture.

Unlike the lands, the bangabanga were never owned by individuals but always by hamlets. The actual committee who fixed the usage of the water-caves were the *utu-n te maniba* (kindred of the well), the descendants of the discoverer. These were frequently as many as forty or fifty in number. The work of keeping the passage to the well in repair and fixing the large stone that blocked the entrance to each cave in position was delegated to two or three individuals known as *tani kauka te maniba* (the openers of the well). This work was hereditary provided it was satisfactorily performed, failing which a new set of workers would be chosen. The entire hamlet of the discoverer was entitled to draw water from the cave and was known as *te moi n te atibu* (drinkers at the stone).

The procedure of drawing water was, and still is, as follows. The hamlet would approach the utu-n te maniba requesting permission to draw water. The utu in turn would, if they agreed, instruct the tani kauka to roll away the stone sealing the passage. When all had filled their containers, the well would be resealed by the tani kauka.

Conclusion

Many of the customs described in the preceding pages are no longer, or are fast ceasing to exist. The hamlets have disappeared and all islanders now live in the four villages of Tabwewa, Tabiang, Uma, and Buakonikai. Owing to the policy of the government the chiefs have been divested of such powers as they formerly possessed, although their personal influence is still considerable. The islanders are now ruled by a native government consisting of a magistrate, chief of kaubure, chief of police, and scribe, aided by four village police. The rights of Tabwewa have been rendered largely obsolete with the changing of conditions on the island and are seldom now exercised. The sitting-places in the maneabas have long since been forgotten except by the very oldest men and women and the uma-n anti have disappeared, only their sites being remembered. The kouti magic is still, however, performed surreptitiously on the eastern shores, and an enthusiastic revival of the traditional games took place in December 1931, during our stay on the island.

The interests of the younger generation are fast becoming centered around the mission church and the British Phosphate Commissioner's trade store, and their lands are of little importance to them except as a source of income, when sold to the phosphate industry. But in spite of the drastic reorientation of their lives which has been crowded into the last thirty years the Banabans retain a courtesy and independence of thought which makes them one of the pleasantest races to live with and augurs well for their future in the difficult times of adjustment ahead.

2

The Traditional System Revisited

In this chapter I will use the Maudes' work, my own, and some historical sources to characterize the traditional Banaban society in its general cultural setting. In the course of the discussion I will speak of a number of "systems," for example, a ritual circulation system, a descent system, a locality system, a precedence-complementarity system. I am not saying that these systems form a single logical family, but only that using them helps in contending with both the certainties and the ambiguities in the data, particularly the ambiguities. The purpose is to formulate the ambiguities in a meaningful way when the avenue to disambiguation is blocked. In the analysis of traditional Banaban social structure one must consider ritual, descent, kinship, precedence, division of labor, residence, and power. The interrelationship of their lines of distribution constitutes the major descriptive problem.[1]

RITUAL CIRCULATION SYSTEM

I will adopt the strategy of leaving for the moment the question of the precise constitution, the personnel, of traditional social groups. Determining the rule of recruitment is often the first order of business in anthropological description, but there is another problem which is at least as basic: What is really going on here? One way of beginning to outline what is going on in general (I am not really concerned with the details) is to think in terms of ritual circuits. In connection with this I will play out a market and railway metaphor.[2]

1. The following discussion owes much to Douglas Oliver's lectures at Harvard University. My stress on "circulation" in this chapter is a poorly developed amalgam derived from Lévi-Strauss, Parsons, and Oliver, with reinforcement from recent conversations with James B. Watson. Unfortunately, I rethought the material in chapter 2 after the rest of the book was written, and rather than rewrite the balance I decided to let it stand. I apologize for the theoretical inconsistencies, which I hope to remedy in later publications. The discussion here presents what I consider to be a formulation of the descent system superior both ethnographically and theoretically to that in a previous publication (Silverman 1969a).
2. I remind those who think this procedure flaccid of how much has been made of circles, nesting boxes, trees, networks, games, and theater. I suspect that for this data

Let us turn our attention to the complexes of meeting houses, spirit houses, and their associated fields (*marae*).[3] Regard each complex as a ritual distribution center, for the distribution or exchange of symbolic actions between personnel, mortal and nonmortal; a kind of symbolic market with the exchange values (at least in the intermortal transactions) ideally fixed. Each market has its own territory. In one booth (or boti) within the market is the market directorate, with one among them the chairman of the board. In another booth are the managers, with one among them the manager-in-chief. Other booths have people responsible for other things, for example, bringing the fish, or making ornaments for the dance. People in various booths have different responsibilities for the maintenance of the market building. In different markets the job allocations are made in somewhat different ways. For example, the managers may also bring the fish. But the general outline is the same. The booths are graded in prestige, and movement between them occurs in accordance with this order.

Maintenance activities in the market are carried out by those with booths there, and for this purpose goods and actions are exchanged within the market for prestige, among other things. But when certain exotic goods come into the market's territory, they must be passed on to one of the two central distribution centers in Tabwewa. These central markets are Te Karieta and Te Karia, and they have dealings with one another.

Each market is at a junction of railway tracks, which connect them as shown in figure 4. According to some information, tracks run between Te Karia and Buakonikai. The Buakonikai market(s) sends up the exotica to the Te Karia market and brings some things back. The Uma and Tabiang markets send up their exotica to the Te Karieta market and also do not return empty-handed. The two Tabwewa markets get together, at least some of the time, in a kind of supermarket to deal with the incoming symbolic goods.

We can group together activities which involve exotica (greeting visitors and dealing with certain stranded fish and objects) under the term *ritual incorporation*. People now refer to an old phrase, "Banaba is shut," meaning that visitors who appeared on the island without going through proper rituals were dealt with by the spirits of the island. The proper rituals were conducted by the proper booths.

We have seen maintenance as an internal market activity (but an ex-

---

an electrical metaphor would actually be more apt, but I am short-circuited by my limited knowledge of electricity.

3. Here some differences among units are being overlooked in order to make a general characterization. I am also making use of material in the Maude Papers which was not included in chapter 1. Since the relative positions of Te Aonoanne and Toakira are obscure, I only refer to Buakonikai in general.

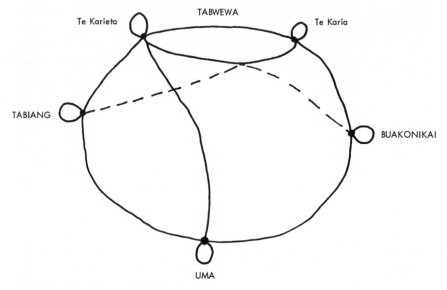

FIG. 4. SOME RITUAL CIRCUITS

ternal activity from the point of view of the booth), and ritual incorporation as an activity which is external in that it plugs the market into a larger system. A second external activity (or more precisely, class of activities) which is also external in this sense consists of *ritual amusements.*

Here we find another kind of two-way traffic involving games and dances, and focusing on the fields. The Tabwewa markets have to open the season for them. Many details of the arrangement are obscure. Briefly, it seems that parties from the Tabwewa centers journey on the tracks to the other markets, and parties from those markets also journey to Tabwewa for the events. The Te Karia people according to one report face in the competitions those from Buakonikai, and the Te Karieta people those from Uma and Tabiang, although in one game Buakonikai, Uma, and Tabiang combine to face Tabwewa.

There is also a track between Buakonikai and Uma along which certain things circulate. Some people now say that a generalized order of Tabwewa-Buakonikai-Uma-Tabiang obtained, and Te Karia and Te Karieta met to decide how messages and the like would be sent to Buakonikai. Some assert that people can go from Tabiang to Tabwewa to claim a special share of the Tabwewa (Te Karieta?) market's symbolic goods. The particular kind of ritual act constituted the "switch."

Let us leave the main line for a moment and return to the markets themselves, the junctions. Each market has a feeder loop linking it with the other stations in its territory. The stations on this loop are the stations of the people of a single market booth or group of booths, some of which may have had local markets of their own. Between these stations and the market, and between the markets, symbolic actions move along the tracks.

All this going to and fro of people, goods, and messages is not organized diffusely. Recall that in maintenance activities, specific booths or groups of booths have specific jobs. The same is true in ritual incorporation and ritual amusements. In ritual incorporation, for example, different booths have different roles to play with regard to the object in question (turtle, driftwood, stranger) at the home market and in Tabwewa. In Tabwewa, people from some of the home booths perform specific actions vis-à-vis people from some of the Tabwewa booths. Thus within Tabwewa itself, Te Karieta and Te Karia act separately or together, and their own booths have specific actions to perform. The same applies for ritual amusements—who plays whom, who does the scoring, and in at least one case, who sets up the markers. All this is determined, and according to an order of precedence.

Thinking again of the booths or groups of booths as stations on the feeder loops, we observe that these stations have feeder loops of their own, which in turn have feeder loops of their own, and on it goes. And the stations along each feeder loop are organized by precedence and by function (or division of labor).

We thus have loops in an organization of loops and things going around them. Certain rituals are conducted in the market by people from one of the loops for themselves, without implicating other loops. Perhaps the general rule is that an activity which is defined as activity of one junction, whether the main junction or subsidiary ones, mobilized the whole system feeding into that junction, thus articulating loop to loop and loop to junction until, for some of the activities, the whole Banaban railway is humming.

This metaphoric description is of course a static one. Some of the apparent inconsistencies within the original data and current reports may arise from the fact that those data are based on different moments in the history of the system, perhaps cycles of the building and closing of stations, the movement of junctions, and even catastrophic derailments.

THE PROBLEM OF DESCENT

My metaphoric footnote to the Maudes' work is intended to illustrate that a complex ritual circulation system existed on Ocean Island in traditional times. To carry the metaphor further: We now have to consider the questions of who had a license in the market, who had a ticket on the train, and what was on the territory.

First, I must correct what is, I believe, an interpretive error in the Maudes' account.

They wrote: "The family was patrilineal and usually patrilocal, though cases in which a man went to live in his wife's hamlet are not unknown." "If, however, a woman married and went to reside outside her kawa she would still consider herself a member of it and would be bound, if called upon, to assist the inhabitants in such matters as preparing food for a ceremonial feast. Her children, however, would definitely consider themselves as members of their father's hamlet." "The male inhabitants of each hamlet were all, theoretically at any rate, descended from a common ancestor and were considered to all belong to the same utu. . . . Each hamlet had a *unimane* (old man) who was the eldest descendant, in the male line, of the founder, and was consulted in all affairs affecting the hamlet as a whole. His also was the privilege of being spokesman for the group in ceremonial dealings with outsiders." "Each hamlet had its own *boti* (sitting-place) in the uma-n anti and *maneaba* of its village district and the descendants of that hamlet had the right of sitting in their boti irrespective of where they were actually living at that time." "Succession to the chiefship passes to the eldest child, either male or female, but should the eldest child be a female, the nearest male descendant or relative will perform the functions of the chiefship until the daughter has a son who can do the work."

The last two quotations suggest but do not entail the major point of difference here. Information from the Banabans today attest to the aboriginal existence of *bilateral* descent units and a form of uxorilocal-neolocal residence (see chapter 13).

It is conceivable that there was a shift in thirty years in people's information bearing on the traditional system. I believe that the confusion arose, however (and Maude agrees) because of the nature of analytic concepts and expectations at the time: descent and residence were not being clearly differentiated from succession and authority. Those who exercise rights of precedence, at least, should live in the hamlet. Ideally, it is men who exercise rights of precedence. The Maudes' informants were, I think, speaking from the perspective of those with seniority in the system, and this gave the appearance of a general virilocality.

The perspective from which the informants were looking at the system would also account for the fact that well-known junior lines are in more than one place missing from the Maudes' published genealogical material. The problem is also tied up with the tendency in some descent unit genealogies for a seemingly unusual representation of male names in the earlier generations—a problem that must await treatment elsewhere in a more technical analysis of Banaban genealogies.

Grimble notes a belief in "descent in the male line" from "chief ancestral heroes," but it is unclear (as is the case at other times) whether he is talking from information specific to the Banabans, or generalizing about the Gilberts (Grimble 1952, p. 46). In the "Sketch History of Banaba" (Grimble Papers), probably written before World War II and almost certainly by Grimble, it is remarked that among the Banabans

> descent may be traced through the female as well as the male line, [and] it is often very difficult to see nowadays why a particular person claims to belong more to one stock than to another. On the whole, the final test seems to be not descent but inheritance. A man claims to belong to the district in which his lands are located, because he necessarily lives near his land. If Tabwewa lands happen to have filtered down through the generations into the possession of a particular person, he will identify himself with the Tabwewa stock, while his brother or cousin, having inherited land in Tabiang, will be equally loyal to the opposing faction.

Actually, this remarkable statement is phrased with caution: "the final test seems to be"; and the question of *membership* is not addressed directly but instead is handled by the more general, "he will identify himself. . . ." On the assertion that "a man claims to belong to that district in which his lands are located, because he necessarily lives near his land," it should be pointed out that a person may own land in all the districts. We do not have the problem here that exists on larger Pacific islands, where inheritance of land (or claims to land) is in far-flung places, and the individual as a practical matter finds it difficult to exercise his rights frequently in all of them. Ocean Island is a very small place.

We conclude from the totality of new and old evidence that birth and adoption, formulated bilaterally, were alternate necessary conditions for membership in descent units. Since in Banaban terms this means blood and either owning land from the ancestor or being in a position of residual heir with regard to such land (see below), we can think of the descent system as a blood and heirship circulation system. The following problems remain: Were birth and adoption *sufficient* conditions for membership in descent units? (This is a problem which occurs in many Oceanic cultures.) In particular, what role did locality and residence play in the definition of units? What was the relationship between the hamlet as a territorial unit, as a descent unit, and as a ritual unit?

We will not be able, unfortunately, to definitively solve all these problems. One thing which points to their partial solution is the fact that, in the local description, an adopter must give some of his land to his adoptee. Thus the locality question is related to adoption, since they both involve land. We will return to this point later.

In order to understand the analytic problems associated with these units, some definitional matters must be raised.[4] Part of the definitional issue, and that which is at the heart of the "bilateral descent controversy" which has recently exercised so many in kinship studies, can be set out as the relationship between categories, units, and groups.

If the only meaning of "We are both descendants of X" is to explain the fact that the people concerned are kinsmen, it does not make much sense to speak of "descent units."

There is a difference, however, when certain people as descendants of a particular person are not only "kinsmen" to one another, but also "speakers in the meetinghouse" or "those with the right to that reef." Something has been added to the relationship: particular objects of solidarity which distinguish them from other kinsmen. I define a *bilateral descent category* as a category composed of the descendants of a common ancestor. A bilateral descent unit is a category in which in addition to being descendants of the same ancestor, the members are unitary with respect to some culturally defined function. A category does not become a unit simply because a common ancestor is recognized. The problem here is the extent to which such functions or objects of solidarity are uniformly distributed throughout the system. Although we are speaking about conceptual units rather than concrete groups, it still could be the case that only one or two such categories have accreted "additional" functions. Then the task is to specify how the system allows for those unique developments. In the Banaban situation there are not just a few isolated units. There is a system of organically interconnected units.

If I know an individual to be a distant "father" of mine, but do not know the exact genealogical connection, an important analytic question is: If I find that connection, will it necessarily add something to our relationship which was not there before? The answer is a feature not only of the degree to which objects of solidarity are uniformly allocated, but also one of international relations. The kinship system of any community may feature descent units, but with marriage occurring with people outside the community, two persons may be related through another community. Thus "finding" the connection would not implicate them in the descent unit system of their own community.

Among Banabans today, the finding of a connection does not imply that

4. My thinking is along the lines of Schneider 1965, and Scheffler 1965, 1966, with some differences in emphasis.

the people concerned are necessarily also comembers of a descent unit, and if this were the case traditionally, then the descent system may have been incomplete. Now there may be an assumption, however, that a common interest in land is implicated. An assertion of common interest in land may be symbolically similar to an assertion of common blood, as we will see. All the claims are never tested, as blood is not tested to see whether people are or are not kinsmen.

We have categories and units, and also groups. I define a *bilateral descent group* as the descendants of a common ancestor, with a culturally differentiated function, where this collectivity "engages as a whole in activities with respect to which decisions must be made from time to time" (Schneider 1961, p. 4). On a partial analogy with Freeman's "kindred-based action group" (Freeman 1961), a descent-based action group would be a group composed of *some* members of a bilateral descent unit or group, who perform differentiated activities together.

Some of the points of analytic vagueness can be resolved by observing the following possibilities of descent categories, units, and groups only:

1. category = unit = group
2. category = unit ≠ group
3. category ≠ unit = group
4. category ≠ unit ≠ group

In the analysis of any one system one has a tangle of problems, if more than one of the above possibilities is realized. Is one talking about conceptual entities or concrete entities? At which level of ramification? At which time and in which place? From whose point of view? For which functions? I do not intend to go through the entire tangle here. Some further aspects of current Banaban information about the old system will be discussed in chapter 14.

In the first possibility the situation is the simplest: The people in the group are the people in the unit, and the people in the unit are the people in the category. This is "pure descent," in a manner of speaking, and comes close to what I call the *ceteris paribus* folk model. In that model, the bilateral descendants of X live on territory Y and conduct a set of ritual activities, Z. The distribution or circulation of descent, people on a territory, and rights in ritual activities coincides.

Where there is an unequal sign (≠), the analytic fun begins. It means that an element other than descent has been added. The personnel on either side of the unequal sign are not the same.

The terms of the *ceteris paribus* equation yield three perspectives from which the traditional system can be analyzed: ritual circuits, descent, and locality. I suggest that when Banabans construct information about the total system, that information is constructed in the *ceteris paribus* frame, within one of the perspectives, or from a combination of them. Some apparent inconsistencies in the data are accounted for by this notion. I will now outline the perspectives. Note two things before we begin. First, by locality or locality system in the strict sense I mean a progressively larger grouping of places. There are lands; some of the lands are grouped into hamlets; some of the hamlets are united in groups of hamlets, and the village district (other than Ocean Island itself) is the most inclusive category. Second, by hamlet coalition I refer to hamlets which participate together in the same activity in the ritual system (for example, Te Karia and Te Karieta is each a hamlet coalition, as are some groups in Uma and Buakonikai; see chapter 1).

From the perspective of the ritual circulation system, one should begin with the ritual circuits which have already been outlined. Relating the circuits to localities, the following can be recognized: intrahamlet ritual circuits (holding small feasts); interhamlet ritual circuits (providing ritual ornaments); hamlet-coalition interhamlet ritual circuits (one Te Karieta hamlet relating to another Te Karieta hamlet in greeting a ship); inter–hamlet-coalition ritual circuits, which might also involve a hamlet which is part of the district but not part of a coalition (Te Karieta and Te Karia calling one another, or another Tabwewa hamlet); interdistrict ritual circuits (Buakonikai dividing food with Uma); the Karia-Buakonikai ritual circuit (bringing in the fish), the Karieta-Uma-Tabiang ritual circuit (playing games).

Then relating the circuits to descent: the links between the participants on the various circuits implicate descent in some fashion. Generally, a common ancestor (founder) is assumed for the descent lines which compose a hamlet, although two ancestors have been reported in some cases. Where a coalition exists, a single ancestor may be stipulated for the respective hamlet founders. That hamlet coalition may be linked to another hamlet coalition because the ancestors of both are siblings, and the two coalitions may be linked to a simple hamlet because its founder is a sibling of the other two. At the same time, however, two hamlets of a coalition may be considered linked through their two ancestors who are siblings, whereas two hamlets of another coalition consider themselves linked because their two founders are siblings, these founders and the previous two being members of the same sibling set of four. Generally, there is a village-district founder, and the members of a sibling set descended from him were hamlet founders, with perhaps the founders of hamlet coalitions in between. These people are ideally related in a bilateral genealogy.

To consider the interdistrict ritual circuits raises an even greater plethora of detail which I cannot consider here (see Silverman 1966). Suffice it say that different accounts involve the political and kinship relations obtaining among the four migrants from Beru who founded four of the village districts; ancient marriages between people (or spirits or spirit-people) of different districts, thus through their issue linking at least sub-units of different districts (although not in an "alliance system" in the kinship theory sense); the transfer of rights from Tabiang to Tabwewa, leaving Tabiang with some claim on Tabwewa (see Appendix 2).

From the perspective of the descent system, one should begin with genealogies, the genealogies of Auriaria and the four who journeyed from Beru to Ocean Island (see Appendix 2). More detail pertaining to this perspective will be covered in chapter 14; the issue will just be adumbrated here.

The descendants of each of the five early figures, at times with the exception of those who were adopted away without receiving land from their natal parents, constitute a bilateral descent category, and categories may be formed in each new generation. The genealogies show the circulation of blood and heirship among the people.

They may be related to localities: Each of the five ancestors lived in a district and various of his descendants founded hamlets. Some or all of a group of siblings founded them. All the descendants do not live in a district or hamlet, but there is no reason to believe that residence was a "one place" thing, that people did not reside in more than one hamlet, either with kin or on their own (or spouse's) land, especially since lands were inherited by both sons and daughters. The members of some lines lived away from the hamlet for a number of generations. Perhaps someone went to live in his spouse's hamlet, his children stayed there or went elsewhere. Some of them, however, may have returned to the original hamlet by living on land to which they had access in the manner just described. They were all still members of the bilateral descent category. Marriage in some cases may have expanded the relationship between descent and locality across village-district boundaries. For example, there is a branch hamlet of Te Karieta in Uma. A Te Karieta person married an Uma person. They settled down in Uma, but the Tabwewa link is maintained. Indeed, members of a single descent category of some depth are living practically everywhere. The misfortunes of physical conflict, however, may have constrained the concrete relationship between locality and descent.

Descent may be related to the ritual circuit system: The children of the founding ancestor had differentiated ritual rights which were inherited by their descendants. Some of their descendants founded hamlets, and for this reason one can speak of the rights as belonging to the ancestor ("X's rights"), his descendants as a descent unit ("the rights of X's utu"), or the hamlet ("the right of Y hamlet"). When these rights were in fact exercised, the units functioned as bilateral descent groups, or at least as descent-based action groups. Any individual might belong to several of these units, since a descent category of which he is a member might be part of more than one descent unit (for example, one descent unit through one grandparent and one through another grandparent). Power plays and other factors complicated this picture, however (see chapter 14), and threw the ritual circulation system out of gear with the descent system. This should not imply that the ritual circulation system was of the social order only. The description of that system is at least that of a system of expectations, and is therefore cultural as well.

From the perspective of the locality system (or in some aspects the "residential circulation" system), one should begin with the localities—for convenience, the hamlets. At any one time a number of people lived there, engaging in the more routine aspects of Banaban life. The hamlet as a group did not seem to have been involved in these activities. The Maudes alluded to the kindred, the family household, and to differentiated roles among kinsmen. Undoubtedly, interpersonal networks were formed among kin, both within and without the hamlet, and kindred-based action groups may have formed too—the "circulation of diffuse solidarity," perhaps.

The performance of many day-to-day activities may not have carried any collectivity stipulation at all. It seems consistent with the orientation of the whole structure to regard the person as a component of the structure. As I explained in the Introduction, by "the person" in this context, I mean the person as a social category or unit in its own right, considered independent of attributions of, for example, sex or kinship—what the fact of being a person implies in the culture.

Many things may have been in the person's domain. With overlapping membership there is an individualizing effect since people's combinations of ties are different, and the person perhaps rises in analytic importance. This is pertinent to a matter we will soon consider: the functions of the system we have described from the point of view of political organization.

One important qualification to this way of looking at the person must be raised, however. In a stricter sociological sense, "resident of Ocean Island" may be a more appropriate label for this component than "the person." It is most likely that with Christianity the person became a more generalized unit. I am operating on the assumption that in daily life on Ocean Island in the earlier era, however, people did think in terms of the person, or individual, as a locus of social meaning.

Let us now return from this detour and relate the locality system to the descent system. The locality was the founder's place, and the founder was the locality's representation. Some of the people living in the hamlet were members of the founder's descent category; some residents were people who married in, and others may have been present too. Indeed, the residents of a hamlet were members of other founders' descent categories. People related to the residents in many ways, including nonresident members of the founder's descent category, no doubt came to visit.

Relating the locality system to the ritual circulation system, we know that life crisis rites brought together, presumably to the hamlet, members of the founder's descent category wherever they lived. The hamlet in many cases was plugged into more inclusive ritual circuits, involving directly those descended from the hamlet founder as a group, including nonresidents. These activities may also have functioned to separate out the hamlet residents who were members of the descent group from those who were not. The hamlet as a locality was thought of as part of the ritual circulation system when it had rights in it. The actual residents of a hamlet were involved in the activities of a number of components of that system.

Important residual problems remain. Hamlets or hamlet coalitions used water caves; were the hamlets functioning here as descent groups, locality groups, or both? Terraces were associated with hamlet coalitions or village districts. Who could go to these terraces? Residents, codescendants, both, anyone? Young men's houses, where they existed, were associated with the village district, and the same problem applies here and for the "old men" of the hamlets and the so-called chief of the village district. Over whom did their limited authority extend? Some implications of this problem will be taken up shortly.

Another critical residual problem concerns the traditional religion. Beyond what is found in chapter 1, only fragmentary accounts of it are available to me. Spiritual entities were associated with some or all of the hamlets, hamlet coalitions and districts (see the discussion of spirit houses, chapter 1). Some of these entities were considered ancestral, others may not have been. Some were embodied in stones; some grave sites were reported as providing the stage for magical activity. Some figures, such as Nei Tituabine, may have been part of a pantheon which transcended particular descent or locality associations. If so, and if the more proximate ancestral figures were regarded as being related to such a pantheon, there is an implication which A. Thomas Kirsch has pointed out: When one is not living on one's home ground, ritual action by an individual can still be meaningful because of the association which can be made between his more proximate spiritual figures and the pantheon.

We do not know the precise form that much of the religious activity took, nor who partook in it; how descent and residence did or did not structure participation in the religious life. I can, however, suggest another metaphor.

Think of the hamlet as a parish. In some forms of Christian church organization the parish has a territory. All the people living in that territory are not parishioners, however. They may be counted in other parishes or no parishes. They may participate in some of the activities of the parish church even if they do not belong to the sect. They may help out their kinsmen in making up the latters' contributions to the church, and they may go along to church socials with their kinsmen (including spouses) or maybe by themselves. If we allow for the possibility that a person can be counted as belonging to more than one parish, and regard descendants of the hamlet's founder as the parishioners, this model might bear some relationship to the reality of the Ocean Island hamlet. Playing out the metaphor one step further: various acts of malfeasance might result in excommunication.

I now want to turn to a specific ethnographic problem relating to descent. One document in the Grimble Papers refers to an event which probably occurred in the prephosphate days, and if so is of extreme interest. The dates suggest that the document in question is by Grimble himself.

In about 1913, the people of the families descended from the ancestors Namanenimate and Anteiati (who call themselves a single *utu*, because the said ancestors made a pact of brotherhood) quarrelled over the rights claimed over a water hole in the district of Uma. The water hole belonged ancestrally to the Namanenimate folk, and to the collaterals descended from Namanenimate's "brother" Na Kainnako. On a point of proper pride the Anteiati people, who really had no blood-relationship with the real owners, refused to participate any further in the use of the water hole. In every other family affair they continued to share as brothers and sisters of the Namanenimate people: they danced and fished and played together as theretofore. Only in the matter of the water hole they seceded.

This lasted until 1922, when a reconciliation was effected. To signalize this a small ceremony took place in the village *maneaba*. On a given day, in the afternoon, the parties to the quarrel, men, women, and children, collected —the one at the northern end of the *maneaba*, the other at the southern end. The senior of the Namanenimate group was a man, the senior of the Anteiati folk a woman. The daughter of the senior Namanenimate man arose with a wreath of flowers in her hand, crossed over to the Anteiati chiefess, and sitting before her put the wreath about her neck. No words were spoken on either side. I was informed at the time that any sort of wreath might have been used, so long as it was sufficiently handsome of its kind.

After the wreath had been adjusted the girl returned in silence to her place.

A feast immediately began. Heaps of food, which both parties had brought with them, were set out in the middle of the *maneaba* and distributed.

The document then goes on, "First share was given to," and tantalizingly ends there.[5]

There are specific points which attract our attention here: The use of

5. Family quarrels, reconciliation: Banaba, n.d., in Grimble Papers (in H. E. Maude collection, Canberra, Australia).

wreaths may have been a wide ritual practice, but one is specifically reminded of "the land of the asking" (*te aba ni butirake*); the role of women is also worthy of note.

The two general points are as follows: First, the document asserts that the waterhole or well, and nothing else, was the substance of the schism. Rights to the waterhole were inherited within one *descent* unit. The "pact of brotherhood" established a *kinship* relationship between the people of the two units, and this relationship, according to the document, was uncompromised by the dispute. The schism was healed, but the dispute dramatizes the distinction between the diffuse nature of kinship, and the specific nature of activities associated with descent. There was a special situation because there was no link between the two units other than the pact of brotherhood between their ancestors.

And this, of course, raises the second general point: the possibility of this sort of thing occurring at all. If the practice was general, it recalls the custom of "the meeting" (see chapter 12), a kind of brotherhood without the blood. Thus not only were birth and adoption, at least, involved in setting the boundaries around kinship units. A kind of alliance existed between two units, making of them a single family, ostensibly because of a *social relationship* between their ancestors.

PRECEDENCE-COMPLEMENTARITY SYSTEM

Recall the *ceteris paribus* folk model: the bilateral descendants of X live on territory Y and conduct a set of ritual activities, Z. We have seen how starting off with each of the three terms yields a somewhat different perspective on traditional Banaban social structure. One of the things which links the three terms, and thus the different perspectives, is the precedence-complementarity system. To formulate this system, however, we will find the descent perspective the most helpful.

At each level in the ritual groupings there was a senior unit and (ideally) a senior person: an order of precedence, framed in a division of labor. And an activity at one level invoked the levels beneath it. Thus if District B were senior to District C, and B has a message to send to C, or a visitor to pass on, or a game to organize, a particular subunit (hamlet or hamlet coalition) of B would carry the message, or whatever, to a particular subunit of C. For B, there was then the question of precisely who in C was the proper person to go to, or which subunit was the proper unit. Assuming that some of the current disputes about who has the right to do what occurred traditionally, it can be easily seen how the position of a unit at any level in this system has to be validated from the outside. Assuming that the norms were institutionalized, it may well have been a very fragile system. In the more complex activities, a dispute at the level of a descent line within a hamlet might have immobilized the hamlet (at least temporarily), and thus the whole system.

If the division of labor involved senority, what principles established seniority? What is the precedence-complementarity system?

Seniority among hamlets in a village district, in the *ceteris paribus* version of Banaban culture, is based on the birth order of their founders. The elder sibling, and thus the elder hamlet, is "the speaker," that is, the hamlet with the right of initiative and supervision. The second sibling, and thus the second hamlet, is "the worker," that is, the hamlet which divides the food in the meetinghouse and carries messages from the first. The other hamlets have more specific rights and obligations, such as cleaning up the thatch and preparing items for games. The Upland/Seashore contrast noted for the two hamlet coalitions in Tabwewa district had some counterparts elsewhere; it is an exemplification of the land/sea contrast (see below).

A right may be vested in a hamlet, but the hamlet does not exercise it in an undifferentiated fashion. There is seniority of descent lines within hamlets, as there is of hamlets among themselves. The principles structuring the different levels are, however, the same.

It was not always the case that the genealogically senior hamlet, or descent line, had the right of initiating. According to local histories, the parent holding a right may have passed by the first child in favor of another. Or the right-holder neglected his rights and obligations, he was ignored by the other members of the group, and his rights passed to the next line. Or there was a conflict solved by violence.

If the senior line is passed by in favor of a junior line, it is disputed whether the switch of rights is final, or whether they revert to the senior line in the next generation. The same problem occurs with regard to sex. In ideal circumstances, the speaker and initiator is a man. If a woman is the elder of a unit which has speaking rights, she should call upon her nearest senior male relative in that unit "to speak for her." In one school of thought, the rights stay where they went, and thus form a rule of patri-succession. In another school of thought, the rights return to the original line in the next generation, as the Maudes indicated. There are cases supporting both points of view. It is possible that this conflict of principles formed the terms of much of the verve of the aboriginal system. Here, two cultural principles (succession by primogeniture, and male authority) bear on the same concrete circumstance, but there is no hard and fast rule for sorting them out, and thus individuals have room to maneuver and to attempt to secure positions for themselves and their own children.

We will have cause at many points to speak of the definition of sex roles. For the conduct of descent unit activities and rights of custodianship over them within a unit, this is proverbially phrased as "the man's right is the

word, the woman's right the wells." Male and female activities are complementary. In some views, in the senior line of the hamlet, inheritance of
the speaking rights is in the male line, and the right to wells and water-caves
is in the female line. In any case, as women can not fish from canoes (and
probably are excluded from some meetinghouse and spirit house activities),
men can enter few if any of the water-caves.

These are rights which are being exercised on behalf of the unit as a
whole. It is what a brother does for his sister, and a sister for her brother.
Although there is a division of rights within a descent unit, all the rights
in a general sense belong to all the siblings, to the unit as a whole. The rights
are in this way vested in the sibling unit (or sibling units), and differentially
exercised within it according to various principles. But at a later time the
rights can be rearranged within the unit. This is at the level of descent units
a replication of the position of siblings as equivalent yet differentiated.

Indeed, the relationship between siblings is the model for the relationship
between the hamlets of a village district, and between the descent lines of
which a hamlet (as a descent unit) is composed. In explaining the hamlet
system to me, one man who was the eldest child in his family made an
explicit comparison: if there were a family affair, he said, he as eldest
would sit inside the house, and his next junior sibling would carry instructions from him to the other siblings outside the house, who were preparing
food and drink for the people assembled. And just as he would defer to a
senior-generation cognate ("My time has not yet come"), the lineally most
senior person in the descent unit may defer to a senior-generation cognate
who is lineally junior. This may also have been the setting for disputes
aboriginally.

I should note at this point that, especially with the possible historical
connection with Samoa (see Maude 1963), it is tempting to rephrase the
interpretative description in terms of a title system. The titles (such as
"speaker"), however, do not seem sufficiently differentiated from the actual
groups to warrant this. I prefer to speak of a precedence-complementarity
system, since this seems to cover more of the terrain of the cultural aspects of
the social system. And it indeed goes further, since the generational and
age roles which are also implicated in the descent organization are at least
now couched in the same terms. The older is responsible for the care of the
younger and has authority over the younger, the younger begins to assume
responsibility and cares for the older.

POLITICAL FUNCTIONS

Ideally, perhaps we would speak of a "power circulation system" to be
consistent with parts of the foregoing presentation. The ideal cannot be

actualized here, and we must be content to try to assess, from available accounts, what actual public power was wielded on Ocean Island, with particular reference to the descent, locality, and ritual circulation systems.

The Maudes referred to the "definite but limited" powers of the village district "chiefs"; I think that *elders* would be a term better suited to their function. The Maudes wrote, "Should there be much sour-toddy drinking or other trouble affecting the island as a whole the chief of Tabwewa would call a meeting of all island chiefs and land-owners to decide on the steps which should be taken to stop it."

It is worthy of note that landowners were included. Grimble records that women went individually into the water-caves (bangabanga), and goes on:

> But no such solo performances were allowed when a drought had lasted for more than four quarters of the moon. Then, in olden times, it was death for anyone to be found loitering alone anywhere near a *bangabanga*: the women did their water-getting all together, at dictated times, each with her strict allowance of coconut shells to fill and carrying a lighted torch, so that her companions could observe her every movement. Precautions of this kind, rigidly enforced before the days of British rule by councils of old men representing all the four Banaban villages, might suffice to eke out the cave supply for as long as two years. [Grimble 1957, p. 36.]

The earliest account of my knowledge which bears on people in power is by John Webster, who visited Ocean Island briefly in August 1851 aboard *The Wanderer*. There was a Banaban nicknamed Tim among the crew, who had been away from his homeland for three years. As the ship approached the island, Tim hailed people on shore and said that the island's "king" would soon be off.

> But Tim, not wishing to be seen by him, concealed himself below. Tim also informed us that there were two Kings or great Chiefs on the Island, and that the one now coming off was not his sovereign, his own King being at the other end of the island. . . . [Canoes came, bearing the so-called king, among others.] Being unable to converse with them, we compelled Tim to issue from his hiding place, which he did with evident reluctance, and appeared very bashful in the presence of the savage monarch. Far more so, indeed, than if he stood before the highest potentate of Europe. Tim underwent considerable interrogation from the King, before we were able to open a conversation with him. They had mistaken the "Wanderer" for a fighting ship, or, as they expressed themselves, for a vessel that killed men; and, on her appearance, had hid themselves in the bush, until Tim's hailing had dissipated their fears. On inquiring the reason why so few canoes came off, Tim informed us that we must first give a present of tobacco to the King, who would then remove the taboo under which they had been placed.

The Banabans did not use sails on their canoes, Webster went on, because the kings prohibited it, since the people might get carried away by currents and winds. "This concern for their safety may be accounted for by the fact that the population is less dense than at the windward Islands, and the two Kings who divide the Island, vie with each other in the number of their subjects." [Webster n.d., pp. 40–42.]

> The population of Ocean Island is between two and three thousand [almost certainly a gross overestimate]. The principal Chief or King is Tapuranda, who, with his son, governs the S.W. end of the Island. The son Tapu-ki-Panapa is the party who boarded us when we first arrived, and is considered as King of the sea. When a vessel appears in sight, he taboos all the canoes, no one daring to go on board until he himself has paid the vessel a visit. On receiving a present, he removes the taboo, and permits the canoes to trade with the vessel. The N.E. end is under the control of another Chief or King, named Tapati, who is less independent than his fellow-potentate. Like at Nikunau, the whole Island is claimed by various individuals—a native's wealth consisting of cocoa-nut trees. [Webster n.d., pp. 45–46.]

The day before *The Wanderer* left Ocean Island, Tapati went to Tim's house to take some of the goods Tim had brought back, and the next morning Tapu-ki-Panapa brought fowls for the ship.

Webester says that the principal village is at the northeastern end of the island, which is unexpected since Tabwewa was generally considered the principal village. However, Webster's reference to the southwest side may be to Tabwewa and Tabiang, and his reference to the northeast side, if he had his directions straight, to a Buakonikai hamlet, although later accounts would make Uma a likelier possibility. Who made the decision is not noted, but Webster observed:

> Thieves here, as on the other Islands, are punished with the extreme penalty of the law. If poor, death is their inevitable portion. If rich, by making sufficient compensation, the matter is settled. Sometimes the delinquents are banished from the Island. They are placed in a canoe with a supply of cocoa-nuts, and sent adrift to perish unheeded, far away on the wide ocean. The art of tatooing is practiced, by priests, who are looked upon as people of considerable importance. [Webster n.d., p. 48.]

This is the only reference we have encountered to priests.

The name of the "chief" who visited the ship is almost identical with one known in a Tabwewa family, and the apellation "King of the Sea" sounds like a reference to the right to board strange canoes or vessels mentioned in chapter 1. However, if Webster's report is correct, the existence of two leading chiefs is something not accounted for in the native traditions which have come to light thus far. The vying for numbers of adherents is reminiscent more of some Polynesian tribal systems.

The reports we are discussing are of course from the period of European contact—during which, among other things, there were large vessels to board. However, competitive leadership may have existed before.

An anonymous visitor in 1875 reports a meeting with the "king," perhaps also someone from a Tabwewa line with precedence or greeting rights.[6] Arthur Mahaffy first visited Ocean Island in 1896, fourteen years after the arrival of the first missionary, and later wrote:

> There are on most of the Gilbert Islands certain hereditary high chiefs, and this is the case on Ocean Island; but I cannot say that their powers are great or frequently exercised, and the whole population of these atolls is amazed at the unique position which Tem Binoka created for himself in Abemama, and which as an absolute autocracy stands, I fancy, alone in the annals of the race.[7]

The missionary Alfred C. Walkup (see chapter 3) was taken up to see the "king" on his first visit, and he wrote in 1896:

> No flag has ever been raised here, and the only government the people know is the will of some of the stronger chiefs. These chiefs have the water caves under their control, also food to a great extent, and now "tabu" the common people from visiting vessels until they have finished their own trading.[8]

Without further knowledge of the traditional religious and economic systems, in addition to the political, it is difficult to interpret this data. Visitors to Ocean Island may have been inclined to inflate what they saw or heard into a chiefly system, but the accounts are too consistent to dismiss them.

Other than religious property, what were the things worth having power over? The possibilities that come to mind are people, land, water, and passages through the reef. Of reef passages there is probably more data available than I have assembled thus far. Control over them would involve some control over fishing, and with foreign ships in the area, access to their goods. Control over land would be the most effective indirect form of control over people. (Large landowners had prestige, but little is known of their power.) If there was power over individuals in a locality, then there was a locality or territory system analytically distinct in power terms from the descent system. The dispersal of an individual's land holdings over the island might, however, qualify the effectiveness of such a base.

Control over water-caves would be particularly salient during times of drought; drought was a recurring phenomenon on Ocean Island. Times of

6. An interesting trip; from jottings of a labour cruise from Queensland to the Equator, in the brig *Flora*, of London, John Mackay, Master, 1875; copy in Mitchell Library, Sydney; courtesy of H. E. Maude.
7. Mahaffy 1910, p. 583. On the general question, see Maude 1963.
8. Walkup, Gilbert Islands report for 1896. ABCFM, vol. 10, no. 31.

crisis may have precipitated a special situation in that large landowners, and those with access to water, had more to offer in return for land or allegiance or both. Information from Grimble and the Maudes also suggests that people with rights of precedence acted politically in times of trouble. Bilateral structures have been celebrated for their structural flexibility in concrete circumstances. The notion of *functional flexibility* may be introduced as a complement.

How did people achieve and maintain power? The factors we have mentioned may well have been involved. Banaban genealogies suggest one means through which followings may have been built up: the intermarriage of people in lines with precedence in the descent system. There was intermarriage between many lines, but among those with precedence, intermarriage may have effectuated alliances and consolidated rights at least for a while.

The most likely situation was that the descent system provided a thread which could be woven with other threads in the achievement of power. Descent-based action groups may have constituted much of the following of particular leaders. The descent system bound people to the past but left room for individuals to maneuver in some fashion, left individual options open, so that there was probably a fluid power situation in any case. Especially considering the recurrent droughts, one might suggest that a social structure to survive under such conditions must have had a flexibility to which the bilateral form and other factors point.

As descent relations may have been used to consolidate larger units of people, they may also have had the practical effect of reinforcing the solidarity of close kin, who were in disputes with other lines or combinations of lines. Indeed, this may have been a general consequence of the operation of the system, deflecting tensions between close kin onto another sphere.[9]

In considering the political aspects of the descent system, one should keep the small population in mind. By the late 1880s, when accounts may be more reliable, there were about 450 people on the island. By this time some Banabans had left on ships, and there was a great drought in the 1870s during which many died. It seems unlikely, however, that the pre-contact population was massively greater than the later figure. Thus those whom outsiders considered "chiefs" may not really have exercised authority beyond a small circle of people, many of whom were junior kinsmen to them anyway.

Given demographic and resource instability, the small scale of the popu-

9. And through the genealogies maintained, the descent system may have cut down on the potential claimants to lands by keeping different lines distinct. In this regard the system may have provided some framework for those who left the island to come back and stake out their lands.

lation, the lack of massive weapons, the wide distribution of lands and of descent unit relationships, the crisscrossing of ties through intermarriage, it is unlikely that any kind of widely based strong regime on Ocean Island could have been a more than passing event. Drought may have favored the fortunes of a few people or groups, for example, the already large land-owners (thus the rich getting richer) and those with more water. Un-fortunately I do not know whether foods could have been preserved to give some people an advantage in the event of drought, or whether large numbers of people lost a significant proportion of their hands and could not get them back.

Comparative material from the Gilberts and from ancient Samoa would illuminate some of these problems. Although it is too easy to invoke "transi-tion" to account for difficult data, it is possible that Banaban social organiza-tion was often on the brink of breaking onto a much more highly stratified level, but the above factors conspired to prevent the leap, not even con-sidering the value system. Perhaps there was a continual struggle and competition to gather up the strands into a few hands, between leaders in villages, or between Te Karia and Te Karieta, each claiming a special legitimacy for itself within the ritual circulation system. Perhaps power could be consolidated for a while and then would dissipate in the competition or for other reasons.

The descent system thus may have had important political aspects. It may have had significant economic functions especially through the owner-ship of rights to water-caves, and the distribution of resources at least through the feasts which probably accompanied many ritual events. The ritual incorporation complex effected some distribution of resources. Un-fortunately it is hard to judge the frequency of appearance of the exotica to be incorporated and their other than symbolic value. If Tabwewa functioned as an entrepôt, some analysts might account for the existence of much of the system by that fact. The goods coming in would have to be exceedingly important, considering the island's isolation.

The kinship system without the descent system could have effected a fairly wide if less orderly distribution of these resources through the rights of kinsmen to ask for assistance from one another. The ritual circulation sys-tem may have *created* a class of goods, the exotica, which were at some point immune from these general kinship claims, since they had to be fed into the circuits. Unless one regards this as a Tabwewa plot, one might make the case (to anticipate the argument of the next section) that the creation of this class of goods functioned to put the concept of obligation or ex-change itself on a more cosmic scale. The major goods are mentioned in a current version of the legend recounted in Appendix 2 as belonging to Nei

Anginimaeao. On the way from Beru to Ocean Island, Na Kouteba saw a timber, a porpoise, a turtle, and an urua fish. Nei Anginimaeao essentially told Na Kouteba, her brother, that those things belonged to her.

We thus have some insights, limited both by the data and my own conceptual apparatus, into the political and economic functions of the descent system (*descent system* will hereafter be used as a cover term to include the ritual circulation system). Given what the Maudes have said, the system clearly had important religious functions, and of course it was tied to kinship. Thus the picture which emerges of traditional Banaban social organization as a whole is that of a *relatively* undifferentiated system in which kinship, political, economic, and religious elements are closely tied together. However, considering the limited scope of the areas of regular involvement of the *descent system*, I interpret its ritual function as the proper one to emphasize.

RITUAL FUNCTIONS

The signal importance of the ritual function is immediately suggested by the fact that the activities around which the system formally centered were not ordinary day-to-day activities. They were special events. The system made them special events. The operation of the descent system was thus largely "contextualized," or limited to a certain class of contexts. To assess the ritual function properly one should consider the organization of the rituals in terms of personnel, the structure of the rituals as symbolic actions, and the total system of meanings which emerges from them. We have already considered some aspects of the problem of personnel; there is no description of traditional ritual action which is adequate by current standards. From the fragments, however, one can make some reasonable if incomplete speculations about the total system of meanings.

With this kind of material it is easy not to see the grove for the palms. Specific actions on the ritual circuits involved many things which were tightly related to the particular state of the social organization at the time. I assume that the rituals were also communicating at a more generalized level. It is not the paucity of data, or comparative knowledge of ritual alone, which forces our attention to this level. Rather than articulating social units which would otherwise not have been articulated, the system created these units, and provided them with a set of meaningful contexts. Thus we must pay close attention to the more generalized level of meaning, for rituals encode messages about the nature of the world and the actor's relationship to it. Whatever else is involved in them, rituals are about definitions, feelings, and interrelations. Let us briefly look at the Banaban system from this viewpoint.

One extremely important set of messages from the rituals was about kinship itself and kinship categories. These are described in chapter 14. The contrasts between generations, between age roles, between different positions in birth order, and between sex roles are dramatized, as are the ranges of variation in their specification. The notion of a single society is articulated. The cosmological contrast between land and sea, and the nature of land itself, is injected into descent unit organization. The spatial and temporal parameters of the local world are defined and interrelated—a local world is created—through the identification of localities and the genealogies which provided some form of chronology. We will see the interrelationship of these things in the remaining half of this chapter.

Between kinship and cosmology there is another area about which the system teaches: the nature of social life itself. Recall the legend of Nei Anginimaeao and Na Borau (see chapter 1 and Appendix 2). What are its implications? In its total setting we see a set of transformations from persons to roles to groups, and then to persons again. A system of roles is created through concrete persons, and a system of groups is formed, but persons interfere with its operation. It is the interplay of person, group, and role that matters, with an uncertain outcome. There is order, but contingency intervenes. One kind of contingency may be a "war," as the Tairua episode is now called. Another may be the nonfulfillment of proper roles— and this is how the transfer of ritual rights from Na Borau to Na Ning is interpreted. Na Borau's own children did not pay sufficient attention to him.

The world that the descent system builds up is one in which one asserts that an organizational ground plan for social life exists, but fluidity or fragility characterize its effective operation. The positions of people and groups change. And relationships must be given tangible form, options (rights) must be exercised, lest they be lost. As one man said, during a recent descent unit dispute: Banaban custom says, if you have a right and do not "touch" it, somebody else will.

In the way social ties are arranged, the value of "Maximize your options" is specified as: "Cast your net wide."[10] The phenomenon of overlapping membership itself is a manifestation of this principle. From a person's point of view, overlapping membership means that he maintains membership in more than one unit. Overlapping or multiple membership is what seems to be emphasized in the system, not cutting off membership, as in some other systems.

10. Lest my intentions be mistaken, I should point out that I am not claiming that these points apply to Banaban society only. They may apply to massive numbers of societies. I am trying to characterize Banaban society, not to set out features distinctive to it.

In the current society, certain patterns of hierarchy coexist with a strong egalitarian ethic (see chapter 10). The expression of precedence is a difficult thing which does not, of course, make of it an any less basic thing. One is cutting down on the options of others. If this was the case traditionally, then the message of the descent system comes through even more clearly. The descent system patterned precedence in the context of division of labor. It stated that this was necessary for orderly society to exist.[11] The "intervalidating" nature of the expression of hamlet rights is in part an exemplification of the intervalidating nature of social activity.

Through the legendary transfer of rights, through the games competitions, and through overlapping membership itself, however, "the first could be last and the last could be first." There was thus a compromise: hierarchy was recognized, but in such a way that the same person could have different status in different units in the same system.

One of the striking features of the Banaban descent system in comparison with some other bilateral systems is that it created and *interrelated* units which ideally comprised the whole island. Why should the people have "bothered" to do so? Here we go back to Durkheim and Radcliffe-Brown. The messages were too important to leave them up to individuals to communicate randomly, and the weight of all relevant humanity was put behind them. Also, the fact that the system was partially oriented to handling "intrusive objects" from the outside placed locally relevant humanity within a wider context.

It may well be asked: Why should a descent system be called upon to bear such a burden? The answer probably has something to do with history (see Maude 1963) and with two of the symbolic bases of that system: blood and land. The descent units are associated with areas of land. *Ceteris paribus,* one is a member by blood or by adoption, and adoption entails the transfer of Ocean Island land from adopter to adoptee. Blood and land are defined as being about the facts of life, and thus the message is stamped with a powerful veracity (see Schneider 1969; Turner 1967).

The Banaban descent system was thus really "about" a variety of things,

---

11. Webster, who visited Ocean Island in 1851, wrote the following of one of the villages: "There is a public building of considerable dimensions in the centre of the village, where the natives meet together when any subject of importance is to be discussed. It is also in these buildings that feasts are celebrated. At such times, every man brings food with him, and exchanges his own supply with that of any of his neighbors, who may possess a similar quantity to his own. The custom is, for no man to partake of the food he himself provides. In front of this building is a clear space, perfectly level, which is retained for purposes of amusement" (Webster n.d., pp. 46–47). This is the only mention of such an exchange system, and for reasons clear to students of exchange and status development it would be an exceedingly interesting one.

including kinship, the kindred, age, space, time, cooperation, exchange, and values, forged in the setting of blood and land.[12]

THE BLOOD AND MUD HYPOTHESIS

From the social organizational aspects of the Banaban system we will turn to a further examination of its symbolic aspects.

The "blood and mud hypothesis" was presented in a discussion of the comparative implications of my paper, "Banaban Adoption" (1970).[13] The hypothesis was an attempt to order material on the symbolization of bilateral kinship in certain small-scale Micronesian and Polynesian societies.

The first element in the hypothesis is the identification of two symbolic complexes which seem to be widely occurring. The first complex centers on notions of common identity, generally symbolized through "common substance," and generally represented by blood. The second is a complex centering on locality or land, represented by rights in land, residence on land, or food from land. *Blood and mud* emerged in the discussion as the rhymed synecdoches for these two complexes. The empirical significance of these two complexes is that they often appear to be involved in the definition of kinship and kinsmen.

The second element in the hypothesis takes off from David Schneider's (1968) distinction for American kinship between kinship as "common substance" (biogenetic substance, blood), and kinship as "code for conduct," a code for conduct or relationship stipulating enduring, diffuse solidarity. Kinship in America means these two things, and kinsmen may be people related through blood only, code only, or both.

The blood and mud hypothesis asserts that the variability in a number of Oceanic kinship systems is a variability in the way these four elements are patterned: the substance complex and the land complex, identity and code.

By introducing land I am not trying to revive the ancient and honorable distinction between kinship and territoriality as alternative modes for grounding the composition of social groups. The point being made is radically different from this simple formulation. The point is to look for the roles that these two complexes play in the very definitions of kinship and kinsman.

---

12. The argument here may seem to suffer from the disease of functional tautology. My defense is to plead for the *economy* of the Banaban descent system: it packed so much into a single complex.

13. The discussion occurred at the Symposium on Adoption, Association for Social Anthropology in Oceania (ASAO), Center for South Pacific Studies, University of California, Santa Cruz, March 1967. The subject was taken up again and clarified at the Wenner-Gren Symposium, Kinship and locality, at Burg Wartenstein, Austria, 23 August–1 September 1969.

There is a limited range of possibilities. At one extreme would be those where relationships of common substance and relationships through the land complex define the status of kinsman in identical senses. At another extreme would be the possibility that one, but not the other, of the two complexes was involved in kinship. Occupying the middle, as it were, of this range of possibilities, would be cases where the substance complex stood for one aspect of kinship, and the land complex stood for another aspect of kinship.[14]

A simple sorting out would be as follows:

Blood : Land :: Identity : Code

And this is part of the Banaban situation. In chapters 12 and 13, Banaban kinship concepts will be discussed in detail. Suffice it to say at this point that central ideas associated with the ideal Banaban construct of kinship are diffuse solidarity, continuity, and equivalence. The descent system is a manifestation of continuity.

The basic ideas are symbolized in common blood and land. Kinsmen are referred to as being "just the same" as one another (see chapter 13). Because they are "just the same," a person can represent his cousin, for example, or his mother at a family gathering (see Silverman 1967b). This sameness of consanguines is conceptualized in terms of unalterable common substance, blood, or common interest in Ocean Island land, or both. By common interest I mean either that a person has a common identification with one of the Ocean Island hamlets discussed earlier, or that a person can envision circumstances in which he might inherit lands which are currently in the possession of even a remote kinsman (if, for example, the line of that kinsman dies out), or both.

The awareness of this eventuality is manifested in the use of the term *kaititi* (*ka-*, causative prefix; *iti*, without issue), which may be translated as "residual heir." When two people, X and Y, are kaititi, this means literally that if X's line dies out, Y will be among the inheritors of X's land, and vice versa. And the term is used as an expression of genealogical closeness. People sometimes say, "We are close, we are kaititi," or simply, "We are kaititi with them."

The point here is that kinship is symbolized in terms of both blood and rights in land. Land functions symbolically in some of the same ways as blood; an assertion of common interest in Ocean Island land is similar to an

14. It should be emphasized that we are not asking at this point the very important question of the degree to which kinship and locality elements are present in the constitution of groups (see Dumont 1964a, 1964b), but the question of the presence of substantial and locality elements in the constitution of kinship.

assertion of common blood. Both land and blood are nurturing (compare Schneider 1969c), "natural," essential, and divisible. We saw in the discussion of descent units that in the *ceteris paribus* version of Banaban culture, membership in descent units is by birth (blood) or adoption. And, as we observed, it is the passing of title to at least one Ocean Island land parcel from adopter to adoptee with the approval of the "close family" that completes an adoption.

To indicate that a person belongs by adoption rather than blood to the family of some other people, one might point out, "He has some land of theirs." Banabans speak generally of land as both the property of the person and the property of the family, but they are not referring to two different kinds of tenure. Title to specific pieces of Ocean Island land is a feature of an individual's distinct social personality, and his social personality as a member of various families.

In giving land to another, one gives him part of one's social personality, and self-perpetuation is important to Banabans. There are cases of adoption where someone is adopted "to replace" someone who has died. The notion of replacement implies that the adoptee receives some kind of title to part of the deceased's share of land.

Birth and adoption as membership and relationship criteria thus entail blood and land. Although one could imagine various symbolic devices for altering the blood (as in some practices of blood brotherhood) Banabans do not make use of them. In one generation, blood is unalterable and cannot be magnified or diminished. Land is alterable and can be magnified or diminished. Blood is an absolute quantity; land is a negotiable quantity. The parent can transfer different proportions of his land (but not his blood) to his children. One of the reasons for this is the children's relative fulfillment of the filial role. Blood and land are both ways of conceptually grounding kinship relationships. Blood and land are also consequences of kinship relationships—through children (blood) and inheritance (land), either actual or potential. The parceling out of land expresses the quality of relationships. Thus as a contrasting pair, blood symbolizes identity, land symbolizes code.

The fact that the passing of land is prerequisite to adoption, and the fact that the parceling out of land expresses the enactment of the parent-child code for conduct, are thus two *related* facts. People point out that the parent has a weapon in his right to devolve his land upon his children. Thus land operates both to transform a bearer of substance (the child) into an enactor of the code, and to transform an actual or potential enactor of the code (the adoptee) into something as close to a bearer of substance as the system allows.

The relationship between substance and land may be inferred from the Maudes' material on land conveyances (see chapter 1). The use of land as a measure is clear enough. One is tempted to see payments for murder as a substitution of land for life or substance. And it is likely that when conveyances were made to nonkinsmen who performed certain services, or for whom special affection was felt, the recipients were seen as having behaved as kinsmen should behave.

The relationship between land and social personality was mentioned above. This relationship is partially expressed in the term *mwi,* "consequence," "remains," "trace." The lands inherited by a person from his father contrast with those inherited from his mother as the male mwi and the female mwi respectively. "There is also his mwi in the Gilberts," is a common phrase meaning that a Gilbertese adopted by a Banaban still maintains his property rights and relationships in the Gilberts. When some Banabans wanted to make it clear to me that certain children (not their own) were just staying with them and were not being adopted, they would say of a particular child, "His mwi is with his parents."

Let us consider this kind of situation. A child is residing with a couple but has not been adopted by them. If this continues for a long time, the child and the couple are participating in a kinship relationship whether or not they are identified as kinsmen. A phrase to denote this situation is that the child has been "in the arms of" the couple. Their coresidence and the nurturance of the child by the couple stand for the relationship or code for conduct. That land has not passed marks that the element of *identity* has not been established.

To recapitulate, the contrast between identity and code is symbolized at one level by the contrast between blood and land. However, in the contemporary culture at least, this opposition can be overcome at a higher level. When the contrast is being made with nurturance and residence as symbolizing code, blood and land symbolize identity.[15] At one level blood contrasts with land as identity contrasts with code; at another level, blood *and* land contrast with residence and nurturance, as identity contrasts with code, and thus:

$$\text{Blood : Land :: Identity : Code}$$
$$\text{[Blood + Land] : [Nurturance + Residence] :: Identity : Code}$$

And the meanings of common substance, blood, may be inclusive of the meanings of both of land *and* nurturance, residence, or other elements which

15. One may want to look at this in terms of the marked/unmarked distinction, some aspects of which are treated in chapter 12.

may be invoked at the time. The field is expansible because the solidarity stipulated is diffuse. And the meanings of land may be inclusive of nurturance and residence.

This point relates back to one made at the beginning of this section. Cultures will differentiate out elements of the blood and mud complexes in different ways. Yet, even in one cultural system, the situation need not be so simple as to entail a single opposition. An opposition at one level can be resolved at another. In this case the opposition is resolved by manipulating the position of land: by opposing it to blood at one level, by combining it with blood and opposing the combination to other elements at another level. And we will see, as the discussion progresses, that this is one of the major functions of land in the symbolic system: it is a means of transformation, exchange, or mediation, between different concepts and domains.

The blood and mud formulation goes a long way, I suggest, toward helping us to conceptualize the residual problem of the relationship between descent and locality in traditional Banaban culture. On this formulation it would make perfect sense for a Banaban to stipulate the exclusion from participation in descent group activities of certain members of the descent category, and even the descent unit. Not living in the locality, for a long term, *on its land*, may have been one of a number of signs in some cases of not paying sufficient attention to the affairs of the group. Not paying sufficient attention to the affairs of the group may have been a specific manifestation of not enacting the code for conduct which membership implied. Thus the place of land in adoption, in inheritance, and in circumscribing participation would all be exemplifications of the same principle. It need not have been the case, however, that this circumspection was uniform. Sentiment, power, or other factors may have warranted some variability. This is to be expected, as we will see in part 4, when the code element is being played out.

THE BLOOD AND MUD HYPOTHESIS: SEX ROLES AND COSMOLOGY

The identification of *land* as a symbolic complex in Oceania leads one immediately into a consideration of *sea*. The contrast of land and sea is one charged with meaning in many Pacific Islands cultures. The land/sea contrast in turn leads one immediately in two related directions: sex roles and cosmology.

Detailed comparative study is wanting on the subject of sex roles. There is a suggestion of a fairly common contrast between the-male-as-fisherman and the-female-as-gardener. On rocky Ocean Island there was little to garden, although this of course was not a restriction on the elaboration of a symbolic system. Banaban conceptions of sex roles pose a complementarity (which we have seen in the descent context) between the male as "speaker" (the figure with authority, and a representative of the female in assemblies), fisherman, and toddy-collector. The female is coconut-oil maker, mat maker and water getter. The water in question was from the highly valued caves and wells briefly discussed earlier, and only women had access to these resources.

Thus the sea stands as the extractive province of men, and the land in itself is unmarked in relationship to it. But it is the male who goes above the land in collecting toddy (an old myth states, "A woman climbs no tree") and the female who goes below the land in collecting water. One may speculate on another contrast: "the word" is at least now spoken of as "moving" from place to place. Perhaps there was a contrast between the word as moving and the caves as stationary, an exemplification of the principle that the man is the "traveler" and the woman the "sitter."[16]

There is still an apparent asymmetry in favor of the male, in terms of the land/sea contrast, which brings up a problem more often explored in patrilineal systems: the relationship between the political and economic powers of men and the reproductive power of women. Relevant to this question is an observation in the "Sketch History of Banaba" in the Grimble Papers, almost surely by Grimble himself. Grimble formulated the view of two major migrations to Ocean Island, also expounded by the Maudes in chapter 1. On the first migrant group, the author wrote: "Another distinctive mark of the culture of these earliest inhabitants was their treatment of pregnant women. When a woman was with child, it seems to have been the custom to bring it into the world by cutting open the uterus, and leaving the mother to die."

We may surmise that this information came from a local myth. There is currently a tale about a figure from another part of the Gilberts who went to Nauru and taught the people there how to bear children; previously they too cut open the uterus of the mother. (Both tales may also symbolize the passage from nature to culture.) A Banaban myth which Grimble collected told of a consummately clever trickster born from a pimple on the forehead of his father (he had ordinary brothers), thus dispensing with the necessity for the reproductive powers of women. (In one version of the myth this trickster was cast from the island by his brothers.)

The existence of special huts for menstruating women; the prohibition on the contact of women with frigate-birds; the fact that it was "important in the

---

16. One may also raise the issue of the individual emphasis in the conception of land inheritance, and the group emphasis in the conception of cave-rights inheritance.

proper performance of the kouti magic to be sure that one did not sleep on the same mat as a woman, or even go near one"; and that "in some of the more arduous types of the kouti magic, for those who were endeavouring to become champions at any pursuit involving intense physical strain, it was necessary to abstain from sexual intercourse for a year at a time"—these suggest some kind of belief in the polluting effect of women, most especially menstruating women, in certain ritual contexts (and the negative effect of sexual intercourse on the development of strength), which as far as we know is unmatched by a complementary belief on the polluting effects of men.

In the descent context there is complementarity between the sexes, but in terms of authority the male comes out on top. In the land context, the Maudes noted that a boy who broke an engagement would often have to transfer land as payment, whereas a girl would not. The asymmetry does remain, however, and the myths may represent an attempt to handle the fact that although descent was bilateral, authority was ideally in the hands of men. In order to clarify this vague area one would have to know more about the structure of these myths both within Banaban culture and within the whole Gilbertese culture area.

The sex role direction from the land/sea contrast has already taken us into the area of cosmology.[17] Another dimension of the land/sea contrast which is suggested by comparison with the Gilberts, and with some older and current Banaban sources, comes close in a Lévi-Straussian fashion to a culture/nature contrast. I have heard the male referred to as "food of the rain, the dew, the sunshine" through his risky and uncomfortable activities as fisherman. In the sea lies threat, danger, and forces which Man seeks to control rationally but cannot overcome. The land stands more for the ordered, the controlled, the human, the intelligent, and if the aboriginal Banaban situation was similar to that in the Gilberts, the mixing of land and sea, and the boundary between them, was charged with a special danger.[18]

It may seem as if we have strayed far from blood and mud, but the route has taken us back where we started. For the contrast between land as a particular and blood as a particular in the context of kinship partially parallels that of the land and the sea as undifferentiated concepts. Blood, land, and sea are all natural, permanent, sustaining, and necessary to life. Land, in

17. I will not go into many further details of the Banaban situation but should suggest that the contrasts indicated may have been mediated by rain from heaven as falling both upon the sea and through the land, both to supply the water-caves and to nourish the trees.

18. I note tangentially that a sun-shower is today called "the rain of death," and there is an expectation that a death will follow. The sun-shower may be considered anomalous because of the combination of rain and sunshine.

relationship to blood, represents the code for conduct which is domesticating and manipulable. Land, in relationship to sea, is the rational, controllable, and human.

THE BLOOD AND MUD HYPOTHESIS: SPATIALIZATION

We have gone from lands to the land, and land to cosmology. The aspect of cosmology which has been tapped is that of its spatial organization. It is time now to consider some aspects of this area in its own terms. For we are dealing with spaces, or localities. I argue here that Banaban culture (and of course some others also—see Hanson 1970) manifested a relatively high degree of "spatialization" or "localization."[19]

Consider the following assemblage of facts:

a. In the contemporary culture, a common form of greeting is, "Where are you going?" or "Where are you coming from?" or both. Actual new information is not necessarily called for: "This way," the direction in which one is walking, or "That way," the direction from which one has come, are satisfactory responses in this phatic sequence. But the communication nevertheless has a spatial focus.

Grimble wrote the following, applying to Ocean Island in 1915 or soon after:

You might contrive to avoid sitting or standing talk, but there was always that bare minimum of conversation you must give to everyone who greeted you. The form of exchange never varied:
Villager: "Sir, thou shalt be blest. Whence comest thou?"
Self: "Sir, [or, Woman], thou shalt be blest. I come from the south."
Villager: "*Aia!* And whither goest thou?"
Self: "I go northwards."
Villager: "*Aia!* And what to do in the north?"
Self: "Just to walk."
Villager: "*Ai-i-ia!* We shall meet again."
Self: "We shall meet again."
Villager: "So good-by."
Self: "Good-by."
    And if you met the same person again on your way back which was most probable at the idle hour of the sundown stroll:
Villager: "Sir, thou shalt be blest. Art thou back?"
Self: "Sir, thou shalt be blest. I am back."
V: "And whither now?"
S: "I go to my house."
V: "To do what in thy house?"

---

19. Hanson 1970 helped me to organize and develop my ideas on localization.

S: "Just to sit down."
V: "*Ai-i-ia!* We shall meet again."
S: "We shall meet again."
V: "So good-by."
S: "Good-by." [Grimble 1952, pp. 43–44.]

b. Grimble is relating a story from the Resident Commissioner, who had unwittingly violated a canon of local etiquette in the same period. When passing between two people in conversation, Grimble wrote, the Commissioner should have stopped "before crossing their line of vision and asked permission to go on. There was a proper formula of words for that: *'E matauninga te aba'* [Are the people offended?] Had he used it, he would have been assured at once that nobody could be the least bit offended. But even then, it would have been proper for him to pass forward with head and shoulders bowed well below their eye line."[20]

Both this observation and the previous ones would apply, with small transformation, today. On passing between people, it may be inferred, one is going into a space which is their space, which is defined by their being in interaction. Other aspects of highly stylized behavior are concerned with space. In a formal gathering, especially in the meetinghouse, people are ranged along the walls, and it is bad form for someone to cross in the middle. It is insulting, except in an intimate context, to reach above another's head without an apologetic request. This is a feature of the near sanctity which surrounds the head but may also be involved in a conception that the space above a person's head is his space and should not be transgressed.

Furthermore, as in so many other societies, space encodes information in the etiquette of status. For example, women of the old school crawl along the floor in the presence of important male guests.

c. There are legends associated with *places.* The coherence of some sets of legends may be only that they apply to the same place; their temporal interrelationship is not salient.

d. The Maudes observed how between leaving childhood and reaching the "warrior grade," boys spent a good deal of their time on seacoast terraces, where magic was performed by men and from which women were excluded. Some village districts had special houses for young men. Menstruating women generally had to stay in a special hut in the household compound.

e. According to current sources, the names of the village districts formed the basis of the directional terminology.

f. Lands had names, some of which were personal names.

20. Grimble 1952, p. 45. The *te aba* of the formula *E matauninga te aba?* which in this context means "people," generally means "land."

g. The relative rank of related hamlets was expressed in the location of sitting-places in the meetinghouse and spirit house, and of course the hamlets-as-descent-units were associated with localities.

I suggest that considered *ensemble*, these facts build up to a picture of the centrality of "place," and the translation of lines of social differentiation into boundaried spaces: from 'the person' (as in some of the etiquette examples) to the descent unit, and the descent unit to the island itself and its people, for a class of descent unit activities was concerned with domesticating, as it were, intrusive objects from the outside.

CONCLUSION

Before the point became common knowledge, beginning anthropology students were told that the nature of culture was such that if you entered the system at any one point, you could, with enough ingenuity, reach any other point—the one-thing-leads-to-another principle. The analysis thus far aspires to go beyond that point. Land in traditional Banaban culture relates directly to concepts of locality, blood, kinship, descent, continuity, rank, value, reward, redress, sex, space, time, nature, nurture, and the person. The route from land to these concepts is a particularly direct one. It is so direct that one may conclude that as a symbol, land functioned as a coordinator, mediator, or means of exchange between the concepts and domains enumerated.

As colonial expansion in the Pacific developed, the major interest of metropolitan powers vis-à-vis the Banabans was in their land, since Ocean Island was covered with valuable deposits of phosphate of lime, convertible into the fertilizer which the farmers of Australia and New Zealand needed so much. Thus the focal concerns of colonizer and colonized coincided in one sense. But their interests progressively diverged, culminating in a phase of intense confrontation politics. And now the Banabans are no longer on Ocean Island, but reside on Rambi Island in Fiji. Through land the people aboriginally ordered the interrelationships among differentiated domains. Now they have two islands, three nations, and two colonial governments to worry about. How this complex situation arose, what its implications are, and how the Banabans marshalled their cultural and social resources to contend with it, will now engage our attention.

PART II

The Transformation
of Ocean Island

3

Christianity, Phosphate, and Colonial Beginnings

INTRODUCTION

During the period 1885–1908, the primary concern of this chapter, Ocean Island was radically transformed. From an island too insignificant to even be included in the Gilbert and Ellice Islands Protectorate, it became the capital of the protectorate. The Banabans were drawn into the networks of the modern world through the activities of a mission, a phosphate company, and a colonial administration, which arrived almost on the heels of one another. Ocean Island became a company town, a social part-system of which the Banabans were only one element. In part 2 the relations between European institutions and Banaban culture will be explored. In their interaction with the people of these institutions, the Banabans began to define and redefine who and what they were in a new and changing way. Even before the dramatic events of the end of the nineteenth and the beginning of the twentieth century, however, the dialectics of Banaban history to which we referred in the Introduction must have begun.

In chapter 1 the Maudes alluded to earlier contacts through the visits of ships (and the presence of European deserters). The figure of one thousand to fifteen hundred as the number of Banabans transported to Honolulu and Tahiti around the time of the great drought of the 1870s is one that both the authors and I now agree is probably a gross overestimate. The details of the drought and the deserters are not publicly broadcast; it is as if they have been blocked out. We know that there was some trade with the ships, and Banabans were taken on to replenish their crews.[1]

There were, no doubt, also occasional visitors, probably castaways, from other islands—native tradition mentions the Gilberts and the Marshalls—

---

1. Some Banabans were reported as having been on the crew of Bully Hayes (Morison 1944). Cheyne, who visited Ocean Island in 1845, reported seventeen white men living there, and Halligon, a visitor three years later, reported seven white men "living peacefully" with the natives (Cheyne 1852; Halligon 1888).

and some strife with Gilbertese. Moss, who was on Ocean Island in 1886 or 1887 reported the following information from Harris, a trader who had been on Nauru for forty-five years:

> About fifteen years ago some Kingsmill natives [Gilbertese] went to Ocean Island and taught the people there to make "sour toddy," by fermenting the sweet liquid which drops freely from the severed green fruit shoot of the coconut tree. Seeing the mischief, the chiefs of Ocean Island made short work of the matter. They gave the Kingsmill visitors their choice, to leave in certain canoes, which were presented to them and take their chance of landing eisewhere, or to remain behind and be killed. The visitors took the canoes and unhappily reached Pleasant Island [Nauru] safely; and that, said Mr. Harris, is how the "hellish toddy" came here. [Moss 1889, p. 144.]

The presence of Europeans and the visits of ships to trade probably gave a new dimension to the traditional right to greet visitors; production for barter with visiting vessels may have introduced unknown changes. We assume that the residence of radically different foreigners in their midst compelled the Banabans to contemplate their social system in a somewhat new, more objective or explicit fashion. Another factor producing the same result may have been the return of Banabans who had left the island.[2]

A remarkable report from 1875 gives a striking picture of the conditions of the times; it comes from a labor cruise of the Brig *Flora.* The reference to the "King" is an indication of developing dialectic.

> On standing off the island for the night, a canoe came alongside, conveying the intelligence that his Majesty the King of Paanopu should honour the ship with his presence at noon on the following day . . . [The "king" came with a hat and shirt. His attendant had been on a whaler to the Arctic Seas, and according to the reporter, came back with tales of his adventures,] when his royal master, finding his services as interpreter indispensible, had him permanently installed Prime Minister.
>
> On making known the object of our voyage, and showing the trade, &c., I was prepared to give them, the old King appeared highly pleased, at once ordering his attendant to proceed with two of the boats and bring off the first consignment, when, as each boat arrived alongside, the necessary trade was sent on shore, thus recruiting during the day sixty people for Queensland. The following morning I went on shore, accompanied by Mr. Kirby, Government Agent, when on landing we were led to the tabu house, where

2. The *Barossa* landed off Ocean Island in 1872, by which time the Europeans had left the island, probably during the last drought. A report of the *Barossa*'s voyage states that "one native spoke English very well, he had served in Whalers and visited America." Report of the proceedings of H.M.S. *Barossa*, dated Hong Kong, 25 July 1872 (Enclosure no. 1 in Chain Letter no. 2216, 19 August 1872); courtesy of H. E. Maude. In 1886 or 1887, Moss picked up a Banaban at Majuro who had been working there, and who hoped to be landed at Nauru and return to Ocean Island from Nauru (Moss 1889, p. 144).

from five to six hundred persons of both sexes were seated, and evidently discussing matters pertaining to our visit. On entering a space was cleared in the center, near his Majesty, whereon was laid a clean mat, which we at once took possession of. We were then regaled with cocoanut toddy . . .

On asking if any more were desirous of emigrating, I was astonished to observe the old King reply, with apparent emotion, telling us, with the tears running down his furrowed cheeks, that in consequence of the dry weather they had nothing to plant, and were wholly dependent on the ocean for a subsistence; and as most of their young men had already gone, should we recruit any more, who would fish for them in their old age? I could press the matter no further.[3]

The droughts were probably responsible for many people leaving the island (including the deserters), although Gilbertese in general are famed in the Pacific as excellent sailors and inveterate travelers. The drought of the 1870s was by all accounts disastrous.[4] Yet throughout Banaban experience the island was subjected to periodic droughts and probably to consequent population reductions. As mentioned above, any social structure that survived must have been a very flexible one. (We cannot, however, rule out the possibility that the traditional social structure did not change in significant ways in traditional times.) The natural environment was a source of great uncertainty. After 1900, and perhaps even before, the social environment was a source of even greater uncertainty.

There is little evidence from the times of how the Banabans actually construed what was happening to them. But Arthur Grimble, who went as a cadet colonial officer to the Gilberts in 1914 and was to become its Resident Commissioner, wrote the following in his charmingly lyrical manner. The old woman to whom he refers may well have been alive during the drought.

> The loving kindness of the Banabans, in common with the whole Gilbertese race, towards Europeans sprang from no feeling of inferiority, but, on the contrary, from a most gracious sense of kinship. Their chief ancestral heroes had been, according to tradition, fair-skinned like ourselves. Au of the Rising Sun with his sister-spouse Tituaabine of the Lightning; Tabuariki the Thunderer and his consort Tevenei of the Meteor; Riiki of the Milky Way, Taburimai the White King, and the woman Nimanoa, the Navigatress—all of these heroic beings, sprung from the branches and roots of a single ancestral tree, were of the red-complexioned, blue-eyed strain called "The Company of the Tree, the Breed of Matang," from which the race claimed

3. From, An interesting trip; from jottings of a labour cruise from Queensland to the Equator.
4. Some material on the droughts and the transportation of Banabans is available, in addition to the references already cited, in Grimble 1957, Wood 1875 (who reports Banabans escaping from drought to Kusaie; pp. 188–89), and *The Friend 1.12.73*, 30:101 (which reports the bark *Arnolda* as having taken twenty-four Banabans to Kusaie; courtesy H. E. Maude).

descent in the male line. The land of Matang, where they dwelt eternally, was the land of heart's desire, the original fatherland, the paradise sweeter than all other paradises, never to be found again by the children of men. Sometimes its forests and mountains might be glimpsed in dreams, but when the dreamer strove to land upon its smiling shores, they faded away before him and he was alone on the empty waters. Yet, though Matang was lost forever, a cherished tradition said that Au of the Rising Sun had promised to return to his children one day, wherever they might be, with all the heroic Company of Matang around him.

So, when white men were first seen in the Gilbert Islands nearly two hundred years ago, the people said (I quote the words of old Tearia of Tabiang, which themselves had become traditional), "Behold, the Breed of Matang is returned to us. These folk are also of the Company of the Tree. Let us receive them as chiefs and brothers among us, lest the Ancestors be shamed." Europeans have been called *I-Matang* and treated always, whatever their faults, with the proud brotherliness due to kinsmen. [Grimble 1952, pp. 46–47]

If this tradition was an ancient and general one, then the people did have an available means of intellectually coping with the situation that was developing in the nineteenth century. If the tradition was a new and general one, it indicates a creative response. There may then have been a way for them to place themselves vis-à-vis the new peoples with whom they came in contact. But soon after the horrible experience of the 1870s, a new means was to become available, and one which promised, perhaps, that sweet Paradise was not beyond the grasp of men.

CHRISTIANITY: LAND AND DIFFERENTIATION

In 1885 the first Protestant missionary arrived on Ocean Island: Capt. A. C. Walkup, a boxer turned missionary-sea captain who belonged to the American Board of Commissioners for Foreign Missions (Boston). Walkup left behind him on the island a Gilbertese mission teacher. For the first time, the Banabans were placed in a regularized relationship with a modern Western institution.

Walkup found a zealous old man who informed him in broken English that he had been to Nantucket and New York on a whaler. The elder (who took Walkup to his house, showed him some clothes, and said he liked clothes and missionaries) escorted Walkup to the "king's" village. Walkup wrote:

> The King listened to us and then asked abruptly and cutely. What good will it be to us? When answered he said the other chiefs and people would be called to deside [sic]. I proposed that they assemble in the village on the beach, where most of the people were collected and decide. In the public assemble [*sic*] after much palavering, they admitted four public sins; viz., Stealing, Quarreling, Drunkenness, and Fornication. They did not seem to

have any appreciation of a future life, or anything in this life above getting clear from the above sins. I told them the Bible would tell them how to do this and more if they would obey its teachings. They accepted a teacher and promised to treat him well and feed him. One man and his wife said they prayed to Jehovah and were christians, for a man from Abemana [in the Gilberts] had been on the island several months and had a book and taught them.[5]

The king-and-chiefs interpretation was clearly by this time established, yet the putative "king" still felt obliged to consult the multitude on such a matter of importance. The pragmatic orientation expressed is striking: according to Walkup, the "king's" major question was what the people would get out of the new religion. Although the statement that the Banabans had no appreciation of future life is inaccurate, Walkup's report suggests an interesting line of thought: perhaps the Banabans allowed themselves to be converted initially to secure a more efficient means toward already identified ends. And if the committing of the "sins" in the religious system was to form demerits for the future, it is conceivable that a new religion was seen as a way of wiping the slate clean. We are conjecturing now on what lay behind the success which Christianity was to have. The association of the religion with the obviously powerful and skilled white man was most likely a factor (thus drawing his power into the circuits), as has been the case elsewhere. Perhaps there was a carry-over from the notion of Matang which Grimble mentioned, and even a promise of its attainability. Another and more profound factor may have been what is today a Banaban tendency to maximize their options.

Conversion appears to have proceeded somewhat erratically, and in the 1930s Maude says, there were a few declared pagans, but by that time the whole fabric of Banaban society had changed.[6] A new, meaningful contrasting pair of social categories was probably established: those who were "people of the church" and those who were not, or Christians versus pagans.

Let us speculate on some general implications of the Christian presence.

5. Walkup, Gilbert Islands report for 1883–85 (August 1885), ABCFM, vol. 6, no. 97.
6. Between 1888 and 1899, American Board figures show from half to the whole population as "adherents." The total population according to mission figures went from 300 in 1888 to 450 in 1899. Annual tabular views, ABCFM, passim. The single school which the missionary set up gave way to four schools probably in 1897, and the number of (male) "scholars" rose from 13 to 154. That year there was a big jump in the average congregation (from 45 to 300); "members" of the church jumped from 20 to 165. (These figures may be for adults; the 1897 figures noted an estimate of 60 "teens.") Seventy-five were received on "profession," and 73 disciplined members were restored, but members dropped to 96 the next year. The number of full-fledged members, probably communicants in good standing, was 107 in 1900, 45–88 between 1901 and 1906, and 144 in 1907. The figures are difficult to interpret fully because more or less stringent standards may have been applied by the missionaries at different times. There is no information bearing on the reliability of the figures.

First, the very activities of missionary personnel, whether they converted people or not, probably brought to awareness and thus systematized the native structure; it could more easily be contemplated as an object. Christianity decreased the embeddedness of the cultural system in the social system. With the literacy gained through the teaching by missionaries, Christianity presented a symbolic system of which any person, in any place, could partake. To accept *or* reject would have required a significant alteration in the native structure. The Banaban religious system was tied to Ocean Island, its land, and its people; Christianity, of course, was not.[7]

The church as a social structure became something far from what had existed before. It introduced a nonascriptively recruited, continuing, solidary, exclusive-membership group organized on quasibureaucratic lines. It brought a theology stressing the individual's relationship to God but defining religious action also in terms of strong groups. There were performance standards for getting into the church organization, although behavior conforming with those standards was probably dogmatically taken as the outward manifestation of one's moral state in what was apparently a strongly Scripture-oriented version of Protestant Christianity. Christianity carried a universal morality, which in the long run was of central importance, as it meant that kinsmen, Banaban, Governor, and Parliament were bound by a single moral system. It offered a unified moral means of envisioning the world as a whole. And that this systematic breaking into the modern world was in moralistic terms is not without its effects today.

Another probable feature of Christianization deserves comment, although there is little direct evidence about it from the times. The Banaban descent system, in contrast to some other bilateral systems, established a program of organization within which units were interlinked in a kind of organic solidarity. *Different* ritual rights, scaled within the precedence-complementarity system, tied the units together. The congregational plan of organization as a social ideal may have represented a radical departure. If the notion of individuals finding their callings was taught by the missionaries and accepted, there was a double shift. First, from the group to the individual as the unit bearing special functions. And second, still further away from ascription as a ground for performing roles. The primary organic relationship may have been to God and his ministers. It is possible that the different village congregations which developed created different

7. Much work on Banaban mythology remains to be done. Grimble collected versions of some myths and published one in Grimble 1923. There is also material in Grimble 1952, 1957. Through the kindness of H. E. Maude I have copies of Grimble's collection and hope to deal with the myths at another time. There is also relevant information in the Grimble Papers and the Maude Papers (in H. E. Maude collection, Canberra, Australia) and some of my own material.

functions for themselves as congregations vis-à-vis other congregations. If they did not do so, then at the group level, as the descent system began to give way to the new religion in many respects, the primary religious groups would have become interrelated mechanically rather than organically. As change proceeded through the years, as we will see in the chapter 14 discussion of the current descent system, the system has become organic, conceptually, but more mechanical, concretely.

The local church was part of an international network, and as religion became more differentiated from kinship, religious roles became more differentiated from other roles. But the idea of Banaban progress—probably a new idea—became linked with Christianization, and Christianization with the church which brought it about. (The *idea* of progress presupposes a tension and thus a marked differentiation between social and conceptual systems.) Banabans contrast the pre- and post-mission phases as the "time of darkness, ignorance" and "the time of light, understanding," respectively.

The content of teaching in the mission schools is not known to me at present. There were at least a few Banabans being educated at the American Board center on Kusaie in the Carolines. The missionaries were apparently looking not for intellects but for moral men and women who would function as exemplary Christians.[8]

In 1896 the successor of the first Gilbertese missionary on Ocean Island was ordained—a sign, no doubt, of what a native could accomplish—and he became head of the local mission. Two Christian Banaban families who had been living on Kusaie returned to help with the mission work after a reported absence of twenty-five years. The next year found Ocean Island with a new stone church and a new schoolhouse. Four families were teaching in four villages, each of which had a new church. A "great change" was noted: of the population of 450, 154 were in school. Books were exchanged for cash and for sharkfins, mats, and coconuts which were to be sold. In 1900 Walkup wrote: "Here is the place where some old men bought, an old edition, but large type, of New Testament, and was having an afternoon school with the pastor to learn to read." The importance of this developing literacy cannot be overemphasized.[9]

---

8. Of one Banaban man the report was: "Mental characteristics—dull. Moral characteristics—very good. Promise for future—average. Remarks—will make a good *preacher*." Of a Banaban woman, it was said that her mental characteristics were average, her moral characteristics good ("not tidy"), and her promise fair. Report of Kusaie school, ca. 1893, ABCFM, vol. 10, no. 7.

9. Channon, Report of the Gilbert Islands work for 1896, ABCFM, vol. 10, no. 31; Walkup, Gilbert Islands report for 1896, ABCFM, vol. 10, no. 31; Gilbert Islands report for 1897, ABCFM, vol. 10, no. 38; Walkup, Gilbert Islands report for 1900, ABCFM, vol. 14, no. 66.

Walkup seemed particularly troubled by "heathen dancing" and the use of tobacco, both of which were proscribed. Tobacco was an offense against cleanliness. Activity was not, however, limited to promulgating Scripture and the simpler virtues. "While looking after their spiritual food and drink," Walkup wrote in his report for 1898, "I wish to help them physically; in fact, I think they appreciate the limes, mangoes, bread fruits and the tank of rain water." The missionary in the Pacific was rarely a totally differentiated religious functionary. The mission teacher may have become involved in exercising a benign influence on local disputes. For 1896: "Of late much sour toddy drinking has been going on and one or more quarrels would have ended in blood, but the teacher arbitrated." An outside agent was truly becoming involved in local affairs. But in 1898 Walkup reports that an "assistant teacher had upheld his wife in a quarrel for land, and the people of the village had asked him not to teach their children any longer." Unless the villagers simply did not like the assistant mission teacher, this may have been a sign of growing religious differentiation, or of the ideal association of mission activities with keeping the peace.[10]

The relationship of the mission to the village is an important one to which we will return. To get ahead of the historical development and to speculate further: An observer in 1902 reported that church services were rotated among the different villages on Sundays. If we recall the case for speaking of the traditional social units in religious terms, we might say that the church "occupied" the higher level localities and for an undetermined period of time operated in some kind of circuit system. The order in which it moved along the circuit may have caused some grief. The villages eventually had both "government" and church meetinghouses, and the church began to take over some of the functions of the descent system. It transmitted basic messages. And if the Ocean Island pattern was similar to that on Rambi today, the church became the new distribution center through which some members of at least one class of exotica were fed: visitors to the island.

The traditional religious base of the descent system and aspects of Banaban culture associated with it were to become undermined. In 1886, for example, a female guide took the missionary into a water-cave, an area customarily restricted to women. In 1900 two women took Albert Ellis, the discoverer of the phosphate, into a cave.[11] (Further aspects of changes

10. Gilbert Islands report for 1895, ABCFM, vol. 10, no. 22; Walkup, Gilbert Islands report for 1896, ABCFM, vol. 10, no. 31; Walkup, Report of touring in Gilbert Islands, 1898, ABCFM, vol. 13, no. 231.
11. Wealth in Ocean Island, *Sydney Daily Telegraph,* 22 April 1902, copy in Mitchell Library, Sydney; 6988, New Hebrides Cuttings, p. 29. Maude observes that there were

have been described in Silverman 1967a.) One can speculate that with the church in some sense co-opting the stations along the main line of the ritual circulation system, traditional activity was refocused on the feeder loops, the units at lower levels. Later phosphate company and colonial government influences were to reinforce this projected development, which is related to the state of the descent system today. Given the "inter-validating" nature of the units within the system, the consequences may have been massive.

Some leading Banabans told Albert Ellis in 1900 that they did not want any Catholic priests brought to Ocean Island.[12] Thus the notion of "Banaba is shut," which was probably tied in with the descent system, may have been accommodated to apply to the Protestant church, and to this day its adherents feel that the lineal descendant (as it were) of the American Board church is the only true Banaban Christian religion. (The American Board transferred its activities to the London Missionary Society in 1917, and in Fiji the latter gave its work over to the Fiji Methodist church.)

The political implications of Christianization were alluded to above. The congregational form of organization for the church is easily generalized to a model for political autonomy. In 1907, after the phosphate mining industry had been in operation for seven years (and Gilbertese laborers had been brought to Ocean Island), London Missionary Society officials observed a "wave of revolt" against discipline and work in the Gilberts. Ellis ascribed it to "swell-headedness" because of wages from Ocean Island. The phosphate company had difficulty getting recruits. The Gilbertese were demanding higher wages, higher prices for their copra, and were boycotting some traders, according to mission sources.[13] The economic change due to the industry developing on Ocean Island was undoubtedly involved. The Banabans themselves may not have been unaware of what was going on in the Gilberts. But another element of unrest, which became intensified, may have been that dissenting Protestants will be dissenting Protestants.

Even as the church moved into a position where it performed some of the same functions as the descent system, the symbolic system was still left dangling. There was a difficult problem of integration. Land no longer could have the same position of ultimacy that it had before. The indigenous focus

---

two meetinghouses, one for the church and one for the village, in the larger villages. The church meetinghouse came first. On visits to the water-caves, see Gilbert Islands report for 1886 (probably Walkup), ABCFM, vol. 6, no. 99; Ellis 1935, pp. 22–23.

12. Diary of Albert Ellis, 10 May 1900, Maude Papers.

13. Goward to Thompson, 22 November 1907; Goward to Dauncey, 25 November 1907; LMS. There had, however, been previous difficulties with traders on some of the islands.

on land was particularizing, as was the concept of Banaban custom, which became elaborated. Christianity pulled in a universalizing direction. The places with which it was concerned were all places, and the peoples all peoples. Indigenous morality had probably focused on kin, age, and sex roles; Christian morality ideally focused on the unity of all men, perhaps more practically on all adherents of the same church. Christianity was inimical to the local references of the aboriginal religion. Even at this early stage the idea of the possibility of realizing on this earth a better world far different from that currently in existence may have been communicated to the people. This would have been one of the most significant changes of all.

A partial solution to the problem of reconciling the particularizing focus of Banaban land and Banaban custom with the universalizing focus of Christianity appeared much later, after the Banabans had been drawn more directly into the commercial and governmental apparatus of the modern world.

MINING AND COLONIAL BEGINNINGS: LAND, MONEY AND AUTHORITY

Some Banabans say that an old missionary prophesied that the rock of their land would be turned into bread. It was, with the discovery of deposits of phosphate of lime by Albert Ellis and his associates in the Pacific Islands Company in 1900.

Ellis and some others arrived on the island, confirmed the existence of the deposits, and signed an agreement with the alleged king of Ocean Island and some "chiefs" for monopoly rights on the mining of phosphate, for an annual rental of fifty pounds "or trade to that value at prices current in the Gilbert Group. Phosphate was not to be removed from land where fruit trees were growing" (Scarr 1967, p. 276). A contemporary source indicated that the "highest chief" signed, but others refused because the land was the people's.[14]

The question of kings, queens, and chiefs will recur below; thus I quote from a pre-World War II document probably by Arthur Grimble. The author had discussed the Banaban legend that on Ocean Island there was an indigenous group centered at Tabwewa, and the descendants of migrants from Beru in the Gilberts (the ancestors of the other village districts) who had divided up the rest of the land among themselves.

> Where the two parties really join issue is . . . on the answer to this question: "What became of Tabwewa when the Beruans divided up the land?"

14. See also Diary of Albert Ellis, 3 May 1900, Maude Papers; Walkup, 18 May 1900, ABCFM, vol. 17, no. 203.

The Tabwewa people claim that their ancestors, being the original stock of Banaba, were not only left undisturbed in their own district by the newcomers, but also as by right assumed the overlordship of the whole place with its inhabitants both old and new. They were in the position of chiefs welcoming the overseas strangers, and hospitably allowing them to settle on the surplus land of the island. But neither then nor thereafter did they lose the sovereignty of Banaba. To support this claim, they refer to the rights and privileges enjoyed by them to this day in respect of the foreshores of the island: Any turtle, porpoise, whale or urua-fish stranded on the beaches or shoals of the island belong by common consent to the Tabwewa folk. If a strange ship arrives, the Tabwewa canoes have the prior right of going to board her, and the Tabwewa families take any presents that may be given by the strangers. These rights transcend all rights of other individuals or families to the various divisions of the foreshore.

The people of the other villages admit that Tabwewa has these rights upon their foreshores, but they argue that they are held as mere concessions of courtesy from the Beruan conquerors. They say that as their ancestors, on first arrival from Beru, sought wives from among the Tabwewans, they could not with any decency make a clean sweep of the island. The Tabwewans were therefore left in peaceful occupation of their own district, and, as a reward for their reasonable spirit generally toward the invaders, were allowed to keep certain foreshore rights which they had always enjoyed. [See chapter 1 for another version.] That they have been allowed to keep them to this day proved no title to sovereignty of the island. As for the Kingship of Banaba, there never was a king.

All the social evidence seems to bear out this statement of the Uma, Tabiang, and Buakonikai people, that there never was a king of all Banaba, as we understand kingship. That is to say, there was never a chief so powerful that he could dictate to the inhabitants in all matters of daily life. Certainly, the Tabwewa family has enjoyed certain privileges which are usually associated with kingship; but it has never in the course of its history been in a position to influence the domestic life of the other village-districts of the island. In all matters connected with land, inheritance, marriage, games, food-getting, and so on, each village has been its own master, has had its own local chiefs [elders], and has gone its own way, uninfluenced by outside authority.

Until the coming of the white man we may therefore regard Banaba as an island divided pretty equally among four [or five] small communities, allied to one another by race and marriage, but politically independent. One of these communities, Tabwewa, has the prestige of being descended from the original swarm that migrated into the island from the west [a Grimble theory]; and it held certain immemorial privileges on the foreshore, which override the local claims of other holders. . . .

It was the coming of the Pacific Phosphate Company which really dragged the question of kingship into prominence, and made a sore point of it.

As recorded above, the Tabwewa canoes had the prior right of boarding all strange ships, and receiving presents from them. So when the vessel carrying the first representatives of the Company arrived, it was a small fleet of Tabwewan canoes which boarded her.

The immediate business of the Company's people was to get in touch with the influential men of the island. The first question they put to the Tabwewans who came aboard was therefore "Who's your King?", or words to that effect. Of course, the Tabwewans produced one of their own chiefs . . . as a matter of fact, this man was not even the senior chief of Tabwewa, being merely the husband of . . . the hereditary high chiefess [a leading elder of the Upland coalition] of that village community. However, he was taken then and thereafter to be the King of all Banaba, and the fact that he, as King, together with four other natives, purporting to represent all Banaba, put their marks to one or two early documents, considerably facilitated the negotiations of the Company in London to acquire a monopoly license to work the phosphate deposit on Ocean Island.

The Banabans soon became aware of the feeling of the white man on the island, that Tabwewa was the home of the kingly line and the center of native politics. Tabwewa naturally enjoyed the mistake, and during the course of years, as the rumour became more and more established (being even accepted semi-officially by the Government), the Tabwewan people began to feel that there really might be some truth in it after all. Uma, Tabiang and Buakonikai contradicted the claim whenever they could, but nobody was sufficiently interested in a matter that seemed so purely academic to go deeply into it; and no concrete case of any importance arose to force the administration to take note of the muddle. Thus Tabwewa has now reached the stage of definitely claiming the kingship of the island.[15]

How the phosphate company obtained its license in London is beyond the scope of this discussion and has been treated by Langdon (1965–66) and Scarr (1967). A few details of licenses and other settlements are set out in Appendix 5.

When Ellis visited Rambi in 1948, the Administrative Officer asked him how he had learned that there was a king. Ellis replied that the captain of his ship had so informed him, but Ellis afterward realized that the man the captain had said was king was not the king. His work was to board ships and see what the captains wanted—this was the traditional right to greet visiting vessels. Ellis also named a chief for each of the four villages.[16]

A. Naylor, who was with Ellis on Ocean Island, wrote in his diary that the "king" at a meeting distributed goods that the latter had purchased, but the Buakonikai and Uma people would accept nothing since they wanted to sell directly to the phosphate company ships.[17] Three days later Naylor convened a meeting in Uma because the Uma and Buakonikai people had indicated some confusion on what had gone on. There may have been actual confusion or even skulduggery on the part of the traditional leaders

15. Sketch history of Banaba, in Grimble Papers.
16. Notes on a meeting between Sir Albert Ellis and the Rabi Island Council . . . 21st September 1948, RIC.
17. Diary of A. Naylor, 19 June 1900, Maude Papers.

involved. They were becoming implicated in activities which the traditional system was not designed to handle. It emerged at that meeting that the "king's" so-called authority was really limited to Tabwewa and Tabiang. Difficulties were created when he withdrew the balance of the company's rental; his purchases went only to Tabwewa and Tabiang people. The report is somewhat unclear here, but the confusion is not. Naylor said he explained the object of the money payment to the "king," and the people seemed content.

There was still more clarification to be made, however. Ellis, who noted that active operations started in late August with seven Europeans and thirty-two Ellice laborers, later recounted that at meetings he held with leading Banabans in September, some of them contested the "king's" right to make an agreement for all the people. Ellis said that after he read and explained the agreement, the participants in a meeting on 18 September 1900 ratified it. The "king" had already received half the amount which had been stipulated, and the Banabans present asked to receive the other half. They got the twenty-five pounds, in trade.[18]

Eliot, a later pro-Banaban Resident Commissioner, wrote as follows:

> The chiefs of the island were feted [in the Pacific Islands Company's ship *Archer*] and a paper was obtained from them giving the company rights to raise and export phosphate from the island for 999 years for the ludicrous sum of £50 a year, or trade goods to that amount (at the company prices, of course). . . . About 1916, when I started to unearth this story, which is now broadcast for the first time, I took statements from three of the chiefs who were feted in the SS Archer in 1900. The company had tried to make out that the chiefs were the representatives for all island land held "in common," and could therefore lease the whole island on behalf of their subjects. Not only in Ocean Island, but throughout Polynesia, every family owns its own land. A chief has no power over any land beyond that of his own family. When it became known on the island that the company's representatives had made some "paper" which was said to bear the marks of their chiefs, the islanders repudiated the document, but the Government gave them no assistance. At that time there was no Government representative on the island. [Eliot 1938; quoted in Langdon 1965–66, p. 45.].

In any event, it is unlikely that the people fully understood the terms of the agreement, nor the terms of the sales and leases of land which went on apace; the ability of the company's interpreter has also been questioned.

Ellis and his crew surveyed the island and kept busy buying and leasing land (after 1902, only leasing was possible). The Banabans surely had clear ideas about land boundaries, but this activity on the part of the phosphate

---

18. Ellis, Memorandum on the land question at Ocean Island, Enclosure in Ellis to Resident Commissioner, 26 April 1911, WPHC Minute Paper 491/09.

company may have fixed the nature of land even more. At the beginning, people were apparently paid in cash orders on the phosphate company steamer, trips to the Gilberts, and later, money. And indeed, to the great complex of which land was the center, the phosphate activity added another element: money.

People were not only receiving goods or money or both for rights to their land, they were also collecting the phosphate rock and selling it to the company. Even the mission teacher, who was at Uma, joined in. Ellis wrote in his diary: "Received a present of fowls and fruit from the teacher; the natives of this village are apparently most anxious to satisfy us in regard to land etc., and probably are jealous of Tapiwa [Tabwewa] village for having received so much of our attention hitherto. There is a great rivalry between the two places, which no doubt will help matters with us." Just after the alleged king and a chief had made the initial agreement, they insisted "that our prospecting party must not stay at the Southern Village [Uma], but must go round to the King's Village; this is owing to there being considerable rivalry between the two places, it being said that the Teacher at South Village was trying to undermine the King's authority."[19] It is also suggested that village rivalries were exploited to motivate people to collect more phosphate rock.

Ellis said in 1948 that he wanted to stay with the Uma missionary, but the Tabwewa people would not allow it. The day after he landed, Ellis noted, Capt. Walkup arrived and told him about the Banabans. Thus the constructs of Banaban culture which Walkup had formed he may have transmitted to Ellis, and Ellis transformed them himself. And by this time the Banabans themselves were probably reacting to those constructs, if only to deny them, as in the kingship-chiefship episodes. But in denial, many surely began to formulate more explicit ideas of what the system was really like. Walkup's own notions were most likely in part derived from what the mission personnel on Ocean Island told him. These personnel were Christianized and perhaps to a certain extent Westernized, and the families who had been on Kusaie in the Carolines may still have been conducting mission work. *Their* ideas were thus formulated against an other-than-Banaban backdrop. And the Banabans themselves were reformulating their ideas in the Christian context. The dialectic was in full swing.

Ellis had told the people that all could work, that they would be paid for their phosphate and fish, that a store would be provided, and even that water condensers would be brought to the island. Especially with the memory of the last drought in their minds, it must have seemed to some as if utopia had arrived. Later, the phosphate industry became much more highly mecha-

19. Diary of Albert Ellis, 11 May 1900, Maude Papers.

nized; the Banabans worked mainly in higher-status jobs and sold fish, and Ocean Island had a hospital and a government school.

Walkup reported in 1900 that the phosphate company "have over a hundred Gilbert and Ellice Island laborers, and the Commissioner sent along a policeman, and laws, to keep them in quiet and good order."[20] It appears, however, that the official native administration was set up by the Resident Commissioner, W. Telfer-Campbell, when the H.M.S. Pylades finally hoisted the Union Jack at Ocean Island on 28 September 1901. The Maudes briefly refer to the form of that administration in chapter 1. Lundsgaarde's recent paper (1968) on the transformations in Gilbertese law makes it unnecessary to go into the details of this system, since at present I have little independent information on it for Ocean Island. An observer reported in 1902 that the "king" and "chiefs" were appointed to represent the four villages, and another chief was scribe.[21]

Ocean Island became protectorate headquarters on 18 December 1907, according to Ellis. Between the hoisting of the flag and that time, the Resident Commissioner visited Ocean Island eight or nine times, for periods ranging from one to two days to three months.[22]

According to Ellis, the "king," three "chiefs" and himself agreed on 1 May 1901 that the fifty pounds of rent should be *distributed to the landowners in proportion to the amount of rock extracted*—a switch from the previous year and one which, as we will see, relates to later claims. The amount was recognized as inadequate as mining proceeded, and when the flag was hoisted, direct purchases stopped (see also Langdon 1965–66). There were rising objections from the Banabans about mining under the original agreement, and on 28 February 1903, Ellis and Arundel, Deputy Chairman of the phosphate company, went to Tarawa to see the Resident Commissioner with a test case of a landowner who had refused to have her land worked. The Resident Commissioner wrote the native government officials that the land should be mined if it was not used for food trees, and mining proceeded. Within a few months the situation was more critical.[23] Arundel wrote to Cogswell, the Acting Resident Commissioner, that the native government officials could not enforce Telfer-Campbell's instructions; the latter had not recently revisited the island. The officials were losing ground, he said, because the power which created their positions was not backing them. Arundel pointed out that the Banabans were laughing at

20. Walkup, Gilbert Islands report for 1900, ABCFM, vol. 14, no. 66.
21. Wealth in Ocean Island, *Sydney Daily Telegraph*, 22 April 1902.
22. Telfer-Campbell operated in the Gilberts most of the time without direct intervention from the High Commissioner for the Western Pacific. See Scarr 1967, p. 281.
23. Ellis, Memorandum on the land question at Ocean Island.

the idea of the Resident Commissioner's arrival; they had frequently been told he would come, but he never did. There was also some trouble between laborers from Tabiteuea and the Banabans. Obviously exercised, Arundel put it up to Cogswell that Ocean Island was becoming the protectorate's greatest income producer, that the company had talked the Banabans into asking for annexation (a Banaban request for annexation is otherwise undocumented), that the company was suffering inconvenience because the land issue was not resolved, and that this was improper.[24]

On Arundel's request, again according to Ellis, Cogswell arrived on Ocean Island on 2 December 1903 and stayed ten days. The Phosphate and Trees Purchase arrangement began then, by which rights to the trees were made over to the company. Discussions for some pieces were dead-locked, however, and when the Resident Commissioner went to Ocean Island he decided they should be worked if no food trees were on them. Telfer-Campbell visited Ocean Island in 1905 and wrote that the native complaints about land acquired by the company were not serious, but showed that the "natives are placing a fictitious value on their land" (Langdon 1965–66, p. 50).[25]

The protectorate administration thus found itself in the position of a party to the operation of the phosphate enterprise. In general, Telfer-Campbell felt that "the protectorate administration, but no other body, was to intervene in most aspects of native life" (Scarr 1967, p. 280) in the Gilberts. Maude has observed that the government assumed responsibility for labor relations and relations between the company and the Banabans.[26] This undoubtedly became more the case when Ocean Island became the capital of the protectorate. If the company had difficulties it did not have to deal with the Banabans as directly as in the past but could take these difficulties to the government, which often decided on issues without consulting the Banabans. This was a shift from the early days when the company's relations with the Banabans were on a personal basis. The traditional leaders, according to Maude, maintained their support for the company even when minor troubles arose. One may conjecture that this was in part because

24. Arundel to Cogswell, 28 November 1903, Enclosure 1 in Acting Resident Commissioner's Despatch No. 40/1903, Minute Paper 26/1900, WPHC.

25. A number of deeds from 1900 and 1901 show individual plots of land being sold to the company for between three and twenty-four pounds, with about two-thirds being for ten pounds or less. All leases but one in these records were for one pound per year (with a term of twenty years sometimes included). Of course, a single individual may have sold or leased more than one plot to the company. Enclosure in Chamberlain to O'Brien, 23 August 1901, 35/01; Reeves to Undersecretary of State, 5 December 1901; WPHC Despatches from Secretary of State, 1901. Enclosure in Reeves to Undersecretary of State, 15 April 1902, WPHC Despatches from Secretary of State, 1902.

26. Except as otherwise indicated, references to (H. E.) Maude's observations come from personal communications and conversations of 1969.

the company through its operations was providing support for the traditional leaders now functioning in a new way. But the objections which arose on the Banaban side indicate that for some, at least, the honeymoon was over.

Maude observes that as things developed, the Ocean Island Native Government was much less of an independent entity than its counterparts elsewhere in the Gilberts. Its major role was to maintain law and order under various government regulations. The Court sessions (see Lundsgaarde 1968) were often attended by a European official, and the European government was referred to in even minor matters. The native government also acted as a channel of communication from the colonial administration to the people.

The Banabans, the phosphate company and the administration were now components of the Ocean Island social field, and their primary mediating link was the phosphate. What of the church in this period?[27]

Mission people were concerned with the possible effects on Christian development of the coming of Mammon to Ocean Island, which they had tried to win for God. One mission writer, probably Walkup, showed an old American spirit (which might have become communicated to others) when he emphatically wrote in 1901 of the consolidation of the Jaluit Gesellschaft with the Pacific Islands Company for the working of both Ocean Island and Nauru, as a *trust*. And later, on observing that the government was collecting taxes in coconuts in the Gilberts: "Some more tea ought to be wasted—this time in the South Sea Islands."[28] There developed, however, a measured cooperation between the company and the mission. The people wanted books, Walkup wrote in 1901, and Ellis said that he would pay for them against credit entries in the passbooks which people now had recording earnings for the sale of rock and fish. "Has not the 'Son of God' commanded that these stones be made bread?" Ellis himself often attended Sabbath services, and work that was not pressing was not done on Sundays. Both Ellis and the company's deputy chairman were religious men. The company built a central church, and Walkup noted in 1905 that company officials respected the native minister, his assistants, and members of the church.

27. Maude has observed that there was a general idea in the Gilberts that the profession of Christianity was compulsory at law. Before Telfer-Campbell's administration, church and state were almost one. Missions may even have organized some form of island government before colonial supervision became closer. It was God's law that was being interpreted. The law of the missions and of the government both came from Europeans and were both interpretations of a common ethical code. How the Banabans fit into this picture at the time is unknown.
28. Manifold letter (probably by Walkup), 15 August 1901, ABCFM, vol. 17, no. 215; Walkup, Gilbert Island report for 1901 (1902), ABCFM, vol. 14, no. 68.

In 1907, Rev. Irving M. Channon, who had been on Kusaie, was considering moving himself and a school to Ocean Island. Ellis discussed the matter with Walkup, and wrote to Channon that they considered Tabwewa the preferred site for Channon's house. Most of the traditionally oriented Banabans lived there, Ellis said—they had not come under the influence of the mission teacher, and would in fact appreciate Channon's presence. But perhaps Tabwewa, the traditional leader in precedence, was holding out more from the church.

All was not rosy, however, in the relations between the company and the mission. Ellis told Channon "that he can only recruit his school on Phosphate Steamers. . . . Mr. Ellis 'hopes to cut off communication from [the Gilbert] group.' A missionary on a Steamer is—Well like Lot in Sodom? 'Not expedient.' "[29]

Company officials probably saw a Christianized population as preferable to a pagan one, although it is likely that they would have preferred a British missionary. It would have been inconceivable for a move such as Channon's to be made without consulting the company.

Mission work went on apace during this period, although the figures for members in good standing were between 45 and 88 between 1901 and 1906, rising to 144 in 1907. (Later figures may include laborers and are thus difficult to interpret.) "With the many hindrances to the spiritual work among the Banaban people," it was observed in 1903, "we find not only Sabbath and midweek and morning and evening services well attended: but also meetings for the children and Seekers [?] on Sabbath afternoons and Thursday with regular chosen leaders at the four villages." There must have been an exhausting pace of religious life, at least for the missionaries. Walkup remarked that Ocean Island was the "only island where all the children are in the schools. In a population of less than 500 some 130 [are] in school, and average attendance on sabbath [is] 250."[30]

29. Walkup to Smith, 17 October 1901, ABCFM, vol. 17, no. 217; Walkup to Smith, 15 April 1902, ABCFM, vol. 17, no. 223; Walkup to Smith, 30 January 1905, ABCFM, vol. 17, no. 246; Ellis to Channon, 12 February 1907, ABCFM, vol. 15, no. 129; Walkup, Gilbert Islands report for 1907, ABCFM, vol. 14, no. 73.

30. Gilbert Islands report for 1903, ABCFM, vol. 14, no. 70; Walkup, Gilbert Islands report 1905, ABCFM, vol. 14, no. 71. By 1905 the mission had established a Woman's Board, a feature of its organization which still survives within the contemporary Methodist structure on Rambi. The board sent a missionary to Butaritari, Walkup wrote in 1905—this probably meant that they paid his stipend through money they raised. The evangelical spirit of the Americans was apparently instituted in their church. The Woman's Board may have been uniquely suited to the Banaban sex-role structure. Church authority was primarily in the hands of men, and the Woman's Board provided a complementary female-based organization oriented to service. I know nothing of the activities of the board, but it may be speculated that it could have served as a tangible object around which notions of female identity were formed. See Walkup, Gilbert Islands report for 1905.

Coming through this scattered archival information is a stupendous fact: in a period of five years, the phosphate operation began, with its people, work, money, and problems; Ocean Island was drawn into the protectorate and a native government was set up; the children were in school. There must have been a massive set of problems for the Banabans to cope with, cognitively and affectively. The people now have three categories: religion, the church (*te aro,* with a general meaning of "way" or "custom"), the company (*te kambane* from English), and the government (*te tautaeka,* with a general meaning of "authority"; or *te tua,* "the law") which they frequently allude to and which specify the important institutions into which they were drawn. The labels can be used as points of chronological reference: certain things happened or certain practices existed before or after the arrival of the church, the company, the government. The three categories are vital parameters of the way in which the Banabans construe their world. Particular missionaries, company officials, and government officers are also remembered as are some of their acts, and the tenures of these people are used as chronological markers, for example "in Mr. Ellis's time." The institutions and their functionaries have entered Banaban culture.

To review and make a few new points: the phosphate company came and a link between land and money was forged.[31] There were some objections to the manner in which the company operated, and with which the government dealt. A little later certain anti-outsider actions were taking place in the Gilberts. Maude comments that there was sporadic trouble in the Gilberts with traders, or between Protestants and Catholics, but no special period of interisland specifically antigovernment actions. It may have been the case that knowledge of actions taken against outsiders elsewhere inspired the Banabans to some degree; they were now undoubtedly much more aware of what was going on in the Gilberts through the presence of laborers.

The descent system, already undermined by Christianity, became implicated both in company and government activities through recognition of representative figures, and the kingship confusion arose. The circulation systems were scrambled. Selling land to the company, and working for it, may have gnawed at the operation of some kinship-related roles as the younger generation was employed. Through all this, the Banabans were probably compelled to think more of what their system was about, and with their recognition as a distinct entity by the company and government, the "community" was on the road to becoming more of an entity than it had

31. To indicate the financial dimension of the change, there are reports that in 1908, three thousand pounds were paid to the Banabans for wages, land, fish, etc. This was also the year that a resident European missionary came, Rev. George Eastman.

been before. Although traditional leaders are often referred to in the documents, the changes which occurred were probably not closely tied to any mobilization of the community by them, but rather a lack of it. In the traditional culture there was flexibility and option maximizing within the system. The mission-company-government complex provided a new arena for this option maximizing to play itself out. And as it played itself out within that arena, the activities in that arena—involving land, money, position—became associated with the notion of the kind of flexibility which the individual should have as a free man. The conception molded to the vehicle.

There is another equally crucial area, about which the data is frustratingly fragmentary. The Maudes observed that there was an ingathering of people from the scattered hamlets into four villages. The formation of centralized villages was the general policy of the protectorate government.[32] Some Banabans today recall that this occurred between 1905 and 1909. According to one elder, people were free to move into the villages in the company's time. Another elder, of Tabiang, claims that people could move into Tabiang village if they had a Tabiang ancestor, but there were many arguments during that period. An old woman recounts that if people did not own land in the centralized village area, they could move onto land belonging to kinsmen if their kinsmen agreed. But special arrangements had to be made regarding the use of trees growing on the land. Some made those arrangements, others still went out to their own land for fruits. This suggests some differentiation between the land and things growing on it and may be compared with the practice associated with "the land of life giving," described in chapter 1.

Yet, on this question of village formation, mission records identify the existence of four villages before the phosphate enterprise and colonization began.[33] What seems likely is that the sites of the villages, at least some of them, were the sites of already existing contiguous and, in the descent system, important hamlets. They became the core of the newly centralized villages, reinforced by the location of the churches, which attained an increasing importance. The conception of the village was partially molded around

32. Woodward of the American Board wrote in 1912 that on Ocean Island there were five hundred Banabans, one hundred whites, five hundred Gilbertese, and three hundred Japanese laborers. He said that the natives were compelled by the protectorate government to live in their four villages for sanitary reasons, to reduce the level of prevalent disease. (He also noted that the mission compound was on the western slope, amid the villages.) Woodward to Chaflin, 5 May 1912, ABCFM, vol. 18, no. 422.
33. "Four villages" are referred to in Gilbert Islands report for 1897, ABCFM, vol. 10, no. 38, although it is not stated that there were no other settlements. Ellis reports the same, on information from the mission teacher. Diary of Albert Ellis, 7 May 1900, Maude Papers.

the church. Assuming a fair degree of movement, however, there might have been momentous consequences. The traditional meetinghouses were organized in terms of descent units related to localities, and individuals lived on their land, or that of their spouses, or both. The concrete relationship between space and traditional social structure was thus broken. Some of the spaces became history. This, combined with the vast input from Christianity and the company-government complex probably also interfered with the normal ramification process in the descent system.[34]

The descent-locality system was probably by this time being pushed into a differentiated symbolic system, with an uncertain relationship to the present and to the individual's status and social personality. And the village as a locality became more highly differentiated from the village district as a descent unit. This took place as the village was formulated within the church, company and government framework. At the same time, some of the functions of the descent system became distributed between the church and the administration. And, as will become evident in later discussion, the "community" became *more* of a self-conscious and political community as it became *less* autonomous. This occurred in a setting in which land, phosphate, and money had become vitally interlinked.

34. The combined effect of centralized village formation and church activity may partially account for the emergence of the idea (if it was not traditional) of a generalized order of precedence, from Tabwewa to Buakonikai to Uma to Tabiang.

4 Opposition and Political Consciousness

Many of the high points and phases of Banaban history which we identify have to do with the phosphate operation, especially with times when there were large leases or changes in the existing system of payment. This mode of conceptualizing the material does not derive from a predetermined analytic interest in phosphate or even in land. It derives from both the general principles which guide this work, and from the concerns of the Banabans themselves. The phosphate history provides some of the points of orientation in the Banabans' sense of their own history, and the political-economic chronology reveals the operation of the essential dialectics of their past.

In this chapter we will focus on the development in the political and religious domains of an orientation toward activism and autonomy; the birth of a Banaban political style which welded together the symbols of God, the government, Banaban land, Banaban custom, and Banaban identity; and a movement toward the codification of a number of important ideas, particularly through the activities of the Ocean Island Lands Commission.

On almost every page one could restate what may be called the "blood and land coefficient." I will not try the reader's patience by repeating it on every page, but ask that it be kept in mind as the very detailed discussion continues. By the "blood and land coefficient" I refer to an aspect of the central empirical hypothesis of this book: Throughout Banaban history, the complex of ideas surrounding land and blood were a constant input to political, economic, religious, and kinship developments. Money and phosphate, for example, must always be seen against the backdrop of land, with all its meanings based in the traditional culture. There was a constant *resonance* of the issues of the day with the basic, highly charged symbols of Banaban culture.

THE FIRST CONCERTED OPPOSITION

We recall that there had been complaints about the company's operation quite early, requiring the intervention of the Resident Commissioner. Be-

106

tween 1909 and the First World War the matter of Banaban complaints had been raised in the House of Commons (see Langdon 1965–66, pp. 50–51). The company wanted more land from the people. The difficulties crystallized into an impasse which marked a turning point in Banaban social and cultural development. I shall hang my description of these events on Scarr's excellent account in *Fragments of Empire* from which I shall quote at length (Scarr 1967, pp. 272–78).

Scarr writes that the company on Ocean Island essentially went its own way in the early period, until the Resident Commissioner moved to Ocean Island. In 1909

the Acting Resident, A. W. Mahaffy, called attention to the question of the Banabans' future on an island which was being gradually eroded by the company's mining operations.

Mahaffy reported that the people now said that when they signed the agreement of 3 May 1900 empowering the company to remove the rock and alluvial phosphate, they did not realize that this would mean the destruction of almost the whole island. Were all the phosphate removed, Mahaffy observed, "it is no exaggeration to say that . . . the island would become perfectly uninhabitable for men—and a mere desert of pointed coral rocks".

Neither the stipulation in the agreement of May 1900 that no phosphate should be removed from land where trees grew, nor the extension to Ocean Island of the general protectorate prohibition on the sale of land to Europeans, had been of any effect; the company had circumvented these by the "phosphate and trees agreements", under which the owner of a block covenanted to the company all the phosphate and trees thereon. The company worked the land and returned it to the owner, "cleared of all phosphate and denuded of trees, and hence absolutely without value"; but the fiction that the land had not been alienated was maintained. Mahaffy estimated that 240 acres had so far been stripped of phosphate and trees or had passed into the company's control with that fate in prospect; another 300 of the island's approximate total area of 1,500 acres consisted of coral pinnacles; and so only about 960 acres were left to support a population of 476 people. In an island so infertile and subject to drought as Ocean, this was not enough. Under the terms of the imperial license, the company was bound to "duly respect the rights of other inhabitants" of the island. Mahaffy could not see that it had the right—as it appeared to suppose was the case—to enforce sales of land which the Banabans were now becoming unwilling to make.

As a result of the removal of the seat of government to Ocean Island, therefore, the administration had immediately become aware that, if Ocean Island was to continue in the occupation of its indigenous inhabitants, the activities of the company would have to be restricted. Later in 1909 Mahaffy's successor at the Residency, Captain Quayle-Dickson, drew up a scheme by which mining would be confined to a clearly defined area, to be bought from the Banabans by the Resident Commissioner in blocks as the company needed it, and the company would make an annual contribution to a fund which would eventually enable the Banabans to buy and remove to another island.

The company was violently hostile to these recommendations.

Quayle-Dickson was thus proposing that the government project itself even more into the situation. He was very sympathetic to Banaban interests but must have found himself in a whirlpool. With protectorate headquarters at Ocean Island, the Resident Commissioner was more directly in touch with both the Banabans and the company. The claims of one were in conflict with the claims of the other. If a Resident Commissioner was interested in keeping the two parties happy, one party being the native landowners and a community under British protection, and the other party being the most productive (and partly British) economic concern in the area, he had a structurally impossible task.

Quayle-Dickson discussed the containment scheme with the Banabans, at least part of the time with them as a group. Mahaffy reports having received a deputation on the land issue.

According to Ellis, purchases of land stopped when Quayle-Dickson said they violated colony law. The law was Section 24 of King's Regulation No. 3 of 1908, which stipulated that the Resident Commissioner should refuse to confirm leases in the protectorate if "it should appear that the land sought to be leased is not the property of the proposed lessor, or that the lease has been unfairly obtained, or that the terms are manifestly to the disadvantage of the native lessor, or that there will not be left sufficient land to support the family, or that the lease is otherwise contrary to sound public policy." But Ocean Island, as usual, came to be viewed as a special case. Ellis wrote to the Resident Commissioner that although the latter had said that the company leases were contrary to sound public policy, it was sound public policy which had dictated the granting of the license in the first place. A memorandum that Ellis was writing would show, he said, that the company had tried to act honorably to the Banabans, and with the government's consent.[1] This company view was not universally shared.

The company resisted the plan for purchases to be made through the Resident Commissioner that Quayle-Dickson had proposed. But even the High Commissioner for the Western Pacific conceded that the company was digging up the island wastefully, with only its own interests in mind, leaving trees on pinnacles of rocks with their roots cut away. These "eyes of the land," he wrote, "are often scattered over the face of the land in such a way that their working prevents access to land less desirable for its phosphates

---

1. Ellis, Memorandum on the land question at Ocean Island, Enclosure in Ellis to Resident Commissioner, 26 April 1911, WPHC Minute Paper 491/09.

and even sometimes . . . prevents access to paths and places and even water-holes almost necessary for the convenience of the natives."

The Banaban response to these visions of their lands can be surmised. As they realized that the whole island was covered with phosphate, they also became increasingly aware of the value of the phosphate. Eliot (1938, p. 139) states that the company "stank in the nostrils of the landowners," and at some time during this period, as an expression of their dissatisfaction, they refused to work for the company.

Either before or during discussions that took place on the containment scheme, one source suggests that the question of moving the site of Uma village arose (whether on company or government initiative is unclear; Rotan Tito recalls that the company wanted to build quarters there). But the villagers refused, apparently presenting a united front on the issue.[2] And this seems to be the transformation which occurred at this time, cul-minating in the deadlock of 1911: The Banabans were recognizing that they had a common interest vis-à-vis the phosphate company and the gov-ernment. A new dimension was being added to the Banaban community as a community, although to what degree is uncertain. Land, as a symbol, had expanded in its area of meaning.

One complication from the Banaban point of view might have arisen from the fact that local government representatives and higher authorities were not always in agreement, and the missionary Richard Grenfell noted that company and government people changed frequently.[3]

There were officials in the Colonial Office trying to get a better deal for the Banabans, in the face of the company's attitude (and the company had influential men in high circles) that the company could do what it wanted on Ocean Island without concern for the consequences of mining to the Banabans, or interference from the government, which may have had no actual legal standing in disputes between the company and the people.

Discussions between the Colonial Office and the company resulted in a proposed settlement which the Banabans refused; they would not "part with any more land, on the grounds that mining was destroying the island which it was their duty to preserve for their descendants. This enabled the Colonial Office to secure better terms. In 1913 it was agreed that the new area of 250 acres should be bought for £40 to £60 per acre and that the Banabans should be paid a royalty of 6d. per ton of phosphate exported as from 1 July 1911."

The new terms were brought out by the new Resident Commissioner,

2. For 1909–10 events, see WPHC Minute Paper 491/09.
3. Grenfell to Barton, 14 January 1915, ABCFM, vol. 18, no. 195.

Edward Carlyon Eliot (see Langdon 1965–66). Eliot, as did Quayle-Dickson, wanted a trust fund and the containment of mining so that the villages would not be encroached upon prematurely. Grimble (1952) said that Eliot won out after "official misunderstanding." Quayle-Dickson, according to Eliot, had been transferred by company pressure (Eliot 1938).[4]

Eliot indicated that he convinced the younger Banabans that the terms he brought would make the community rich; they agreed although there were some holdouts in the older generation. Unless the Banabans did assume that the containment of mining would make the island habitable in the future, or that the island could be rehabilitated, their agreement may have represented a triumph of money over the idea of Ocean Island as their eternal homeland.

> In the circumstances [Scarr writes, the new] terms represented a small victory for the Colonial Office on the Banabans' behalf; but the new Resident Commissioner [Eliot], whose first duty it was to induce the people to accept the terms, soon conceived an intense distaste for the company's general attitude and its acts of petty trickery. It failed to implement, for instance, the agreement extracted from it by the Secretary of State that Banabans should be charged the same store prices as Europeans [the Banabans often had to pay more]. The fact that the royalty was to go into a trust fund, though provident, was a pointer to the eventual outcome that, whatever their own wishes upon the subject, the people would finally be removed to enable the whole of the island to be mined for phosphate.

Rotan Tito, a Banaban leader for some time, has given the following version of the events of this period (written in 1965). I will not assess the legitimacy of the claim; it certainly has a reality as an input to the current political scene, which will be discussed later.

Rotan claims that the buying and leasing of pieces of land

> continued until 1912 when the Company and the Government saw the inconvenience that the Company had to face in taking phosphate from those lands, as these lands did not adjoin its already acquired mining area. The Government and the Company could also see the difficulty that the dissenting landowners who did not alienate their lands were going to face, as their lands would be left isolated in the middle of the mining area and access to them would inevitably be impossible. In the middle of 1912 a decision was made by the Resident Commissioner then Mr. E. C. Eliot (later C.B.E.) that: (a) Sales of land by individuals to the Company should cease; (b) lands which would be required for mining by the Company were to be allocated to adjoin its already acquired lands; (c) all land not within the allocated mining area must be returned to the owners . . .
> In November 1913, a decison was reached between the Government and the Company and they made an agreement before the Resident Com-

4. See also WPHC Minute Paper 491/09.

missioner (Mr. E. C. Eliot) under the Union Jack inside the meeting house at Tabiang village.

Among the terms of the Agreement which Rotan mentions, in addition to the financial ones, are the following:

> There will be no right for any landowner to sell his or her land after the execution of this Agreement. There will be no right for the Company to purchase lands outside the mining area. The Company's limit in digging will be twelve feet. There will be a limit of the export of phosphate from the mining area by the Company which was 300,000 cars, i.e., 300,000 tons (as the landowners did not know what a ton was but they only knew a car which was filled with phosphate from their lands). . . .
>
> There were two families who refused to give their lands on the amount of compensation agreed to by their fellow landowners. The Resident Commissioner with the leaders of the BPC [this is an anachronism] accepted their wish and their lands were left unmined in the middle of the mining area of 1913; they were dug later in 1947 with the approval of the descendents of the original owners and they were fortunate to receive £200 as the compensation per acre and not £60.
>
> The terms of the 1913 Agreement . . . have been verbally passed down to us through our forefathers. It was most unfortunate for us the present generation that our forefathers had unwisely returned the copy of the Agreement to Government for safekeeping. We had since then repeatedly requested the Government to supply us with a copy but they had not given us any . . .
>
> . . . [The] management of affairs maintained from 1913 to 1926 strictly followed the terms of the Agreement, without the introduction of any local executive body for the purposes of altering the terms of the Agreement, until 1927. [See below].[5]

Eliot's style is revealed in an incident recounted by Arthur Grimble, who went to the Gilberts as a cadet in the Colonial service in 1914 and was to become Resident Commissioner. Grimble is referring to the "Where are you coming from—where are you going?" exchange quoted in chapter 2.

> I ventured once in the very early days to tell the Old Man [Eliot] that I found these exchanges a little redundant. He bent his thin dark look on me. "You probably think, Grimble, that you're here to teach these people our code of manners, not to learn theirs. You're making a big mistake."
>
> He only gave one of his curiously narrow-nosed double-barrelled sniffs at my denial, and continued: "Well—I'll tell you something that happened to me not long ago. I carpeted the Tabiang *kaubure* [village headman] the other day to complain to him about the old men's habit of hawking and spitting when they get excited in the native court. I told him he must talk to them about it. My grievance was that a sudden outburst of that kind had drowned my voice when I was speaking to them."

5. Rotan Tito, Review of the phosphate royalty at Ocean Island, August 1965, translated by Teem Takoto, RIC.

"If I had put the thing to him as an offence against hygiene," he continued, "the kaubure would have got on their tails at once, but I didn't. All I talked to him about was the breach of courtesy to me. And this is what he did. He came forward to my desk and laid his hands on mine. Then he looked me straight in the eyes and said, 'How can I speak for you to the old men of Tabiang when you did what you did there yesterday? Even you, who hold us in the palm of your hand?"

It appeared that, in walking through Tabiang the day before, he had passed between two women—the wife and daughter of an elder—as they were chatting to each other across the road. Seeing them in conversation, he should have stopped before crossing their line of vision and asked permission to go on. There was a proper formula of words for that: "*E matauninga te aba* (Are the people offended)?" Had he used it, he would have been assured at once that nobody could be the least bit offended. But even then, it would have been proper for him to pass forward with head and shoulders bowed well below their eye line. His omission of these formalities had been the more astounding to the people because of his exalted rank among them. They had a proverb: "Small is the voice of a chief," which meant, in general, that gentleness and courtesy walk hand in hand with power.

"The kaubure told me all this so quietly," went on the Old Man, "that I felt a fearful bounder. Of course, I asked him to take my apologies to Tabiang, and all was well again. But it was lucky for me he had the guts to talk as he did. Sometimes they don't talk, but keep it bottled up, and then things happen, and they get the blame in the long run when the initial fault was really ours. You may walk round the villages satisfied you're a hell of a fellow, while all the time they're thinking what a mannerless young pup you are–yes, and forgiving you, too, and staying loyal in spite of everything. Let that sink in, and go and learn a bit about them. Yours is the honour, not theirs."

He made me feel as if the brick he had dropped had been mine, not his. [Grimble 1952, pp. 44–46.]

The headman's remark: "Even you, who hold us in the palm of your hand," is as instructive as Eliot's feelings about the people and his comments on their attitudes. A mission source records that once when Eliot was in Fiji, the "Old Men" of Ocean Island wrote to him of an official who was not "keeping the rules," and Eliot returned and removed him.[6] Thus by this time at least the people's sophistication in handling the colonial bureaucracy was increasing.

In relations with the company, Quayle-Dickson and Eliot were apparently exceptions to the general rule. Both colonial officers and the Banabans undoubtedly came to realize that the company was the dominant element on the island. The company had a powerful lobby in London, and local officials on Ocean Island were dependent on the company for the amenities of European existence which the company establishment provided. During this pe-

6. Note by Miss J. R. Hoppin, n.d., Pac. 44, K96Z9, Pam. Bx., ABCFM.

riod the latter had become much more complex, to include Gilbertese and Chinese laborers who made of the Banabans a minority on their own island.

There were other political and related developments in this period which command our attention. A number of Banaban families returned to the island, mainly from Honolulu and Tahiti, where they had been taken by labor recruiters (Ellis 1935). News of the phosphate was spreading, and news of other places must have enriched Banaban culture. Some claim now that their return created no special difficulties; Rotan asserts that those Banabans who were in the church "could not lie," and thus returned their kinsmen's lands. But it is likely that there was some scrambling of land-rights and genealogies connected with their absence. Another element of confusion may have been added to an already confused situation.

Arthur Grimble took Eliot's advice and conducted some ethnographic inquiries on Ocean Island and in the Gilberts which resulted in a useful collection of myths, two popular books, and a number of papers. Grimble's activities might have resuscitated some declining phenomena and probably increased the systematization and objectification theoretically asserted to have been a consequence of mission activity. It is interesting to observe that the author of the myth recounted in chapter 1 attached a note to the 1922 original that there had been agreement on the system of descent unit rights in earlier times, but now there was disagreement.[7] This chord of nostalgic regret may have been a response to changing conditions, but it is equally likely that such a chord would have been struck any time in Banaban history.

In 1920, roughly the same time Grimble was mining the old culture, the phosphate mining began to pay for a school for Banaban boys, thus supplementing mission education. And the British Phosphate Commission came into control of the phosphate. As Langdon notes, the change may not have been much noticed locally, but it was to have tremendous implications: not only were the governments now more directly involved, but the BPC was to sell phosphate to the partner countries, not at a profit, but at cost price. As the Banabans came to see it later, they were subsidizing the farmers of Australia and New Zealand. The groundwork for a further divergence of interests between the Banabans and those with control over them was laid, as was the groundwork for the further complexity of their political dilemma, as they were to contend, at least indirectly, with three governments rather than one (see Appendix 5).

The complexity of life on Ocean Island was increasing. In 1919, according to a mission source, there was a small Gilbertese labor force on Ocean because of wartime shipping complications. The laborers whose contracts

7. Nei Beteua to Deputy Commissioner, 12 May 1922, Grimble Papers.

had expired "have 'downed tools' and refuse to work except at an exorbitant figure."[8] In 1925 there were serious labor troubles, during which Gilbertese laborers struck, demanding that the Chinese laborers be removed (see Ellis 1935; Grimble 1957). This may have colored Banaban thinking about political action; it came two years before the next land controversy. Mission sources report demands against the trading company on Butaritari and disturbances also on Nikunau and Onotoa.[9] Things may have been moving in the Gilberts, although more work needs to be done on Gilbertese history to know whether the pace was actually increasing. As in the earlier period, it is difficult to determine the extent to which this was known on Ocean Island. But as we observed earlier, Ocean Island itself had surely become an important note in the area communications system, given the changing Gilbertese labor force. (There were also a number of intermarriages with Banabans, and many Banabans were probably visiting the Gilberts.)

Let us turn now to developments in the church in the 1909–26 period. The church was not uninvolved with other European elements in the field. Rev. Irving M. Channon, now installed on Ocean Island, figured in the dismissal of some company employees for immorality. And in 1909, he spoke of a community of interest for which the mission was working, and which the company wanted too, manifested by the fact that some European employees were organizing musical services in the native church. One was drilling a brass band in his school, and the white staff contributed for the instruments. Channon was apparently not universally beloved of the European establishment on Ocean Island, but some cooperative activities did take place.[10]

Channon reports that the local managers of the company were helpful in preventing the Catholic mission from coming to Ocean Island, but the London office wanted to maintain a position of neutrality. In 1911 some Roman Catholic functionaries arrived to look after the spiritual welfare of Catholic Gilbertese laborers. Things were not going too well for the American Board. Channon saw the Catholic arrival and Catholic plans (for example, to bring Sisters and to build a chapel) as evidence of his mission's sorry state. A number of Protestant missionaries in the Gilberts were militantly anti-Catholic and provided a heritage reinforced in the native church to varying

8. Enclosure in Arnold to Fleetwood, 11 June 1919, LMS.

9. Arnold, Report of work in the northern islands for 1925, LMS. He spoke of "unrest" among the natives. Around the same time, Bralsford reported that the Chinese-Gilbertese clash had interfered with school and church activities on Ocean Island. Bralsford, Report for August 1925–February 1926 (16 February 1926), LMS.

10. See, e.g., Channon to Barton, 12 July 1910, ABCFM, vol. 18, no. 60; Channon to Barton, 26 March 1909, ABCFM, vol. 15, no. 143.

degrees until the present day. The pace of Catholic activity was reported as decreasing in 1913; then there were two Catholic settlements on Ocean Island, with Sunday evening services alternating between them. Some Banabans converted either through marriage or for other reasons, and the "one church" nature of the community was undermined.[11]

When Channon arrived he found it difficult to get help for various chores, but there must have been a flurry of religious activity with about forty prayer meetings a week for various audiences. New converts (whether Banaban, Gilbertese, or both is not clear) showed a great demand for books, as seemed to be the case earlier: if there were no Bibles or hymnbooks, then readers, geographies, and arithmetics did in their stead.[12] If these books were read, the quantum of knowledge among the people may have radically increased. The Bingham Institute, which was run, I believe, as a school for mission teachers, included work in Bible stories, geography, English, arithmetic, the life of Christ, the early Christian church, dictation, singing, music, and sight reading, and a kindergarten class, with classes four hours a day for five days. In the afternoon most boys worked on the mission station. Six boys fished daily, and their catches were sold to the company; the proceeds went toward their expenses. It is possible that if Protestantism did not build in a general work ethic, it did motivate some people to economic action for contributions, the purchase of books, and education.[13]

Grenfell, another American Board missionary, reported in 1913 the concert of a "native debating society" at which the women and girls of each village dressed in the same way—an indication of the position which the village had attained within the church framework.[14] The debate was on the relative merits of the coconut and pandanus trees. Two people spoke and then the opinion of the gathering was taken. The debaters were usually judged as equal—an unlikely example of the egalitarian ethic referred to in part 1.

The existence of the debating society itself (about which nothing else is

11. Channon to Barton, 12 July 1910, ABCFM, vol. 18, no. 60; Channon to Barton, 26 March 1909, ABCFM, vol. 15, no. 143; Channon to Bell, 6 July 1909, ABCFM, vol. 15, no. 145; Channon to Barton, 12 July 1911, ABCFM, vol. 18, no. 48; Grenfell to Barton, 5 August 1913, ABCFM, vol. 18, no. 136. In 1897 there was a most unflattering reference to the papacy, and the presence of Catholicism was declared to be worse than heathenism. Gilbert Islands report for 1897, ABCFM, vol. 10, no. 38.

12. Channon to Barton, 15 March 1909, ABCFM, vol. 15, no. 38; Channon to Barton, 26 March 1909, ABCFM, vol. 15, no. 143.

13. Grenfell to Bell, 5 May 1915, ABCFM, vol. 18, no. 153. I cannot speculate on the cultural and psychological consequences of the learning of English.

14. Grenfell, A concert in seven languages, 12 May 1913, ABCFM, vol. 18, no. 210.

known) may not be as trivial as it appears. In 1897 the Gilbert Islands School was reported to be using *Robert's Rules of Order*.[15] If a system of rules of order was being followed here, people were being socialized into a view of the world which reinforced certain aspects of Christianity, and with political consequences: the view that people were bound by an objective set of rules and procedures. In current academic parlance, this would be a push in the direction of modernization.

At the debating society concert, songs were sung in various languages, the missionary and his wife contributed a duet in English. Two tattooed old men recited legends. One is impressed not only by a certain cosmopolitanism, but also by the fact that the missionary (at least in his report) did not despise the old men or their tales. Perhaps the strict Old Testamentism of the earlier missionaries had become mollified, and the church was on its way to becoming, in a curious fashion, a conservator of some explicit tradition. One wonders, however, whether the local people could sort out the rationale of which aspects of tradition were acceptable and which were not.

Some church activities involved both the Banabans and the laborers. At this time, the American Board missionaries were working in the northern Gilberts, and London Missionary Society (LMS) missionaries in the southern Gilberts. The two missions had their differences. The southerners were given use of the American Board church. Channon wrote in 1909 that the southerners ran their own meetings (except for Sunday morning), raised their own funds (which were sent to their home churches), and judged and disciplined their own members (under Channon's direction).[16]

For reasons extrinsic to this analysis, the American Board Mission in the region was coming into hard times, and discussions were underway to transfer their work to the London Missionary Society. The situation on Ocean Island pointed up the difficulties of the coexistence of the two societies. In 1917 the American Board transferred its functions to the LMS, which had a somewhat different form of organization and some different behavioral rules. The British hegemony in the region was thus made more complete.

The head of the LMS mission in the Gilberts, Rev. W. E. Goward, was a strong-minded man and a planner. He wrote that the LMS should take over the whole Gilberts group as a special responsibility from Christ. There was some cooperation between the two missions before the transfer, but some Bingham Institute students who went to the LMS school at Beru could not pass the entrance examination, and Grenfell felt that Goward was making things difficult for American Board people on Ocean Island. There was an

15. Gilbert Islands report for 1897, ABCFM, vol. 10, no. 38.
16. Channon to Barton, 26 March 1909, ABCFM, vol. 15, no. 151.

LMS Samoan pastor there for the laborers, and a senior American Board official blamed Goward for telling the Samoan that he was not under Grenfell's jurisdiction.[17]

Goward had put his stamp on the mission. He stated the purpose of mission activity in the Gilberts as living exemplary lives among the people, educating them and their children, training a native ministry and a loyal Christlike church.[18] This was a general congregational position shared by the American Board.

Goward, however, may have been more actively interested in extending the scope of mission activity than was the American Board group. It was part of the work of exemplary Christians. Religion and education, Goward wrote, could not alone raise the people from their poverty. One way to achieve this would be the creation of an industrial Christian mission, with Christians bringing to the people some of the benefits of modern life—benefits which people would see were only forthcoming from the love of Christians. Goward tried to convince his superiors of the worthiness of his plan.[19]

An industrial mission would also have the advantage of being self-supporting. The ideal of the self-supporting church was later echoed by Rev. George Eastman, Goward's successor, but the former noted that the people's poverty made the ideal difficult to realize. Goward's generalized concerns even brought him to consider the mission's involvement in business because the traders needed competition for the natives to get their due, but he was afraid that the LMS would be accused of being missionaries-turned-traders.[20]

Goward regarded his own activism as a contrast to Walkup's American Board organization. Walkup, he wrote, was content to rely on God's Holy Spirit to teach those whom He called and school work was not critical. Goward observed that the two missions worked in different ways, and that what was an essential to one was a nonessential to the other. One issue of difference was tobacco. Walkup had been insistent against its use, which was allowed by the LMS. Channon, who was on Ocean Island during 1908–1913, saw the smoking issue as one interfering with potential cooperation with the LMS. The Gilbertese pastor gave separate communions to the LMS

17. Goward, 13 March 1911, LMS; Grenfell to Barton, 5 August 1913, ABCFM, vol. 18, no. 134; Grenfell to Barton, 14 January 1915, ABCFM, vol. 18, no. 145; Woodward to Bell, 13 November 1916, ABCFM, vol. 18, no. 451.

18. Goward, 6 March 1907; Goward to Channon, 23 November 1908; Goward to Channon, 25 February 1908; LMS.

19. Goward to Foreign Secretary, LMS, 29 February 1904, LMS.

20. Eastman to Lenwood, 13 August 1919; Goward to Thompson, 15 May 1912; LMS.

Southern Gilbertese laborers on Ocean Island, who smoked. There was also a difference in clothing: American Board teachers and preachers wore shirts and trousers. When some American Board students went to the LMS school at Beru, they switched to lavalavas (sulus).[21]

Thus even before the transfer there was a visible difference to the Banabans between American Board and LMS practice, in addition to the Catholic. (A special problem for the LMS was created by the fact that, according to an LMS source, the Catholics permitted and the Government and Europeans encouraged native dancing, of which the LMS for some time had disapproved. Later, "clean" dances became acceptable. The Christmas–New Year season became a focus of dancing activity—perhaps a transformation from the old system to the new calendar.[22])

Although the LMS is regarded among the Banabans as the heir of the American Board, the changeover might have had some consequences for the way in which they viewed religion.

I hypothesize that in some converted communities there is a "flat view" toward the new teaching. A prohibition against smoking is regarded as tapping the same level of ultimacy as a belief in hell. With a transfer of religious supervision of the kind noted here, a new view may arise. It is a view which would distinguish more systematically between areas which are central and areas which are peripheral. Such a view would be another push in the direction of modernization.

What of the LMS and the government? Eliot, the Resident Commissioner at Ocean Island, referred unkindly to the "narrow and prejudiced" native mission mind; at the LMS school at Beru, he said, everything was subordinated to religious instruction. Perhaps through the government more secular influences were making themselves felt in the Gilberts. H. P. Bralsford, from the LMS, noted that when he arrived on Ocean Island there was no religious instruction in the government school. Both he and the Catholic priest argued for such instruction and finally won, with the introduction of one hour per week. Bralsford arranged for the Gilbertese pastor in charge of the northern

---

21. Goward to Thompson, 12 February 1908, LMS; Goward to Thompson, 12 February 1908, LMS; Channon to Barton, 28 July 1914, ABCFM, vol. 18, no. 81; American Board missionaries to the Gilbert Islands, ABCFM Pac. 53, Z9, Pam. Bx. Much work needs to be done on this mission field. I have not yet consulted even all the published sources. For some general information on the missions, see Goodall 1954, Goodsell 1959, Northcott 1945, Sabatier 1939.

22. Enclosure in Arnold to Fleetwood, 11 June 1919, LMS. Grenfell of the American Board had written in 1913 of some unrest on Ocean Island because of the land question between the Banabans and the company. He also noted a spate of heathen dancing which would last beyond the holiday season. Grenfell to Bell, 16 December 1913, ABCFM, vol. 18, no. 138.

villages to teach for the hour. In this way he hoped to reach the older boys whom, he said, did not go to church and did not learn religion at home. Bralsford observed that the LMS-trained laborers had a good influence (from his point of view) on the Banaban community, but the quantum of Christianity in the community was not sufficient for him.[23]

Arthur Grimble, embellished as his accounts probably are, affords us a rare view into Banaban life and the interaction of government, mission, and native attitudes. Grimble is writing of the period around the end of 1921 and the beginning of 1922, when he returned from leave in England and was Acting Resident Commissioner. Grimble will play a critical role in our story soon. I quote him here at length. The "Movement of Clouds" to whom he refers was a Banaban girl with whom he was friendly.

One of my earliest calls after arriving back from England was on Movement of Clouds' grandfather. It was not a social call: I had some official business—I forgot what—to discuss with the old man as headman of Tabiang village. So I planned to be there soon after 3:00 P.M. At that hour, I guessed, his wife and granddaughter would probably be busy shopping (or even busier gossiping with shoppers) at the B.P.C.'s big trade store down at Uma, and he sitting peacefully alone in his brown lodge, just emerged from a refreshing afternoon nap.

But my calculations turned out wrong. Tearia and Movement of Clouds were both at home with him and all three were heavily engaged with another caller. This last was a large, brown mission teacher dressed in the trailing white waistcloth of his calling. He sat cross-legged on a guest mat in the middle of the floor, surrounded by the other three, who listened dumbly, sweating in the languid afternoon heat, while he stated the official reason for his call.

They were so absorbed in his business, nobody noticed me picking my way down the hillside through the palm stems. Rather than interrupt their session, I joined an interested little audience gathered in the shade of a mighty breadfruit tree nearby, and listened in.

It appeared that two village policemen had started the trouble. These interfering fellows, the teacher said, had come snooping round his back premises last night, looking everywhere for a certain pig of his. Having failed to find which in its pen or anywhere else, they had asked him what about it. And when he had replied, *"Kai ngkam!"* meaning he neither knew nor cared, they had said what a pity, and written his name in a book, and told him he must appear before the native court next week on a charge of neglectfully permitting his pig to wander for which crime the prescribed fine was sixpence or, at the option of the convicted party, twenty arm-spans of coconut fibre string. And when he had said how could they accuse him like that of a wandering pig when they had seen absolutely no pig of his wandering anywhere, they hadn't a word to say in reply. And the whole setup was a shame that stank to heaven, anyway, because it was clear

23. Eliot to Lenwood, 23 January 1919; Bralsford, Report for 1924; LMS.

to every Christian that missionaries, together with all the village teachers, pastors and deacons who assisted them, being representatives of the Almighty here below, should by rights be treated as immune from the action of the silly, treacherous, oppressive and altogether ungodly man-made laws for which the headman and his minions stood.

Never had prelate of old, I felt sure, claimed benefit of clergy with arrogance more overweening than this simple, brown lay teacher's. But never, on the other hand, have I heard officialdom's majority views about itself more confidently stated than in the old headman's immediate reply.

"Stuff and nonsense, calamitous gaby! It isn't you missionaries who are above the law . . . it's we of the government . . . we, the lawgivers!"

Yet even in that moment of superb affirmation, the cagey personal modesty of the trained official overtook him. In saying "we," he hadn't meant to claim that he himself made any laws; he paused to explain laboriously, sitting down again; only, being a village headman made him a colleague of the shining company who did so—the resident commissioner and his galaxy of district officers. Now there, if the teacher was looking for heaven-born masters, was a gang worth serving. Why, they walked practically arm in arm with the Almighty the whole day long!

And then his burning *esprit de corps* ran away with his tongue again. If only the teacher could see us at work, he said, the divine play we made juggling our own laws . . . the way we would honour them one day, ignore them the next . . . the way we would add, revoke, twist this way or that, with never a by-your-leave to missionaries, or native governments, or anyone else in earth or heaven, or even to the spirits of the underworld. . . .

Well, if only the teacher could watch us at all these activities, he said, he would realize what truly heaven-born creatures we were. [Grimble 1957, pp. 14–16.]

The wry amusement of the European officer, the attitude of the teacher, the action of the policeman, the identification of the headman, the invocation of the Deity, give a picture of colonial life at the periphery which is not unfamiliar. It is a beautiful vignette which speaks for itself. If the views of the headman in the last quotation are accurately set out, and not expressed ironically, then such views were either not representative or were well on the wane. For the effects of Christianity itself, commercialism, and education were soon to reinforce one another to such a degree that such a statement would be made not in praise, but damnation. And one of the people to be damned was Grimble himself. But that is getting a little ahead of the piece.

Around this time the LMS was considering the formation of island church councils. I do not know when the Banaban one was established, but a council was probably formed in 1919 on Nauru, part of the same mission area. LMS representatives visited Ocean Island on and off during this period. At times there was more concern for activities on Nauru.

The Nauruan pastor had recently been involved in a petition to the

King on certain grievances. He had visited the United States and was locally something of a radical. There was some dissatisfaction with the phosphate royalty on Nauru also, and legal action against the company had been contemplated. Later, at least, there was probably an interchange of information between Ocean Island and Nauru on native political aspirations. The expressed LMS attitude to the situation on Nauru—which was most likely representative of their attitude toward Ocean Island—was that mission teachers should keep out of political controversy, although their responsibilities as citizens had to be recognized. At the time of the Nauruan controversy, the mission head from the Gilberts delivered a sermon taking off from "Render unto Caesar. . . ."[24]

Maude notes that certain European unchristian acts were referred to the company manager on Ocean Island by the mission, but most of the time prudence reigned and confrontations with the company were avoided. In general on Ocean Island, the missions discouraged relations between Banabans and Europeans. Channon was worried about "unsupervised contact" between Europeans and natives, and Bralsford spoke of the Banabans as being "spoiled" by contact with Europeans.[25] In spite of some moves in the direction of cross-racial cooperation, mission policy reinforced that of other European elements: there was a kind of segregation on Ocean Island, with Europeans, Chinese, Gilbertese, and Banabans located in different places. This is not to suggest that as far as residence was concerned any element was very dissatisfied. But the system certainly reinforced the notion of Banaban separateness, which developed into one of Banaban separatism.

In 1919 there were two new Gilbertese mission teachers on Ocean Island, each in charge of two villages.[26] In 1925—the year of reports of "disturbances" in the Gilberts and a strike on Ocean Island—a visiting LMS missionary wrote that each Banaban village wanted a teacher of its own and promised to raise money for his support.[27] The village-mission complex was defining itself. More importantly, however, communications from LMS Beru headquarters to the Banaban church (which presumably had an island church council by now) in 1925 and 1926 indicate that the Banaban church had requested that the balance of the funds it had raised, after its own teach-

24. See Report for 1919 (Beru), LMS. See also Enclosure in Arnold to Fleetwood, 11 June 1919; Eastman to Greene, 1 December 1919; LMS.
25. Channon, Report on work in the Gilbert Islands (received August 1907), ABCFM, vol. 14, no. 72; Bralsford to Lenwood, 8 January 1924; LMS.
26. Enclosure in Arnold to Fleetwood, 11 June 1919, LMS. There is also a report for this year that some church members had lapsed, and that a special problem was created by native dancing, as mentioned above.
27. Levett, Report for 1925, LMS.

ers' stipends had been paid, should be returned for its own use and should not be used to assist teachers on poorer islands.[28]

Thus development in the sphere of religious organization were paralleling the political orientations which began to be manifest in the 1909–13 lands dispute. The people were, more and more, moving in the direction of a mode of activism and an ideology of autonomy—which the very activities of the church, the phosphate company and the government had often unwittingly fostered.

THE SECOND CONCERTED OPPOSITION: LAND, DEFEAT, CODIFICATION, AND THE BIRTH OF BANABAN POLITICAL STYLE

It is beyond the scope of our concerns to specify with greater precision the nature of Ocean Island as a social field. It should be recalled, however, that a complex system was in operation by this time. For example, the company officials were clearly concerned with keeping the mining going efficiently, exporting cheaply, and getting more land when needed, all with the minimum of interference from the Banabans and the local government. At the higher levels, the Banabans had earlier come to be regarded as a nuisance and the government as a meddler. Government officials had more to worry about than Ocean Island but must have been concerned with the maintenance of overt calm between the Banabans, the laborers, and the company, and of course the efficient operation of the company, now a tri-governmentally owned corporation, meant that more money would be paid into colony revenue. The mission wanted to keep Christianity alive and, assuredly in official circles, to keep its hands clean vis-à-vis the company and the government. The Banabans wanted, among other things, more autonomy and more money.

Ordinarily in such a colonial situation one would expect that the local establishment would view its position as more meaningful in an international context than was objectively the case, or than did those in the metropolitan center. The Ocean Island complex was somewhat different because the ties of the element at the periphery were much more direct with the center, and the phosphate was in fact indirectly feeding the Europeans of Australia and New Zealand.

One of the events which would send highly charged impulses all through the network, to Britain, Australia, and New Zealand, to government, com-

28. Minutes of meeting of LMS Gilbert Islands District Committee, 5–6 June 1925, and 1 July 1926; LMS. The Banaban church and the Banaban villages were not alone in an unwillingness to share with other congregations. In general for the Gilberts, this feeling was reported to have abated by 1930. See Eastman to Chirgwin, 11 October 1930, LMS.

pany, and mission circles, would be the refusal of the Banabans to sell more land. The whole raison d'être of the Ocean Island social field would be in jeopardy. And this is what happened.

In 1927 the British Phosphate Commissioners wanted more land. Rotan Tito says that someone involved with the company had warned him that a lands issue was about to arise, and instead of going back to the Gilberts to continue mission work there, Rotan decided to stay on the Ocean Island. Rotan recounts that Arthur Grimble, then Resident Commissioner, told the people to form a committee of two men from each village to deal with land matters. Rotan was involved with this committee. With the obvious divergence of interest between the company and the Banabans, Maude notes, the unsuitability of the native government to represent Banaban interests became apparent, and the traditional leaders, tied in with the company in the early days, were not active. Rotan emerged as a leader of a progressive group which the company recognized it had to deal with. Thus there was a greater differentiation in the social organization.[29]

Rotan and probably some of the others were also church people, and a link between Christianity and the land issue began to form at this time at least. Rotan was a big landowner and had extremely important connections in the descent system. He was born in 1900 and was thus one of the first generation socialized in the phosphate-colonial government-mission era.

In 1927 some Banabans agreed to the price that was offered by the company. Grimble may have had informants on the island and probably lobbied with local people whom he knew. There were apparently some generational differences, with the younger making the demands (see Grimble 1957; a factor may have been that the younger had not experienced the devastation of drought). The capitulation of those who agreed, and the terms of argument of those who disagreed, may have signaled an acceptance among the Banabans of the fact that their island would eventually be almost completely dug up. After the previous controversy the Banabans may have thought that there would be a relatively contained mining operation. Now, the people may have envisioned the devastation of the island and accepted it at least as an inevitability, and at most as a way to get more money to use for the things that money can buy. Con-

29. The limited authority of the native government may to some extent have been usurped by the Lands Committee. But apparently not all of the committee's members were "progressives," and the native government may itself have recognized that the lands issue was outside its purview. A scribe in the native government during the latter days on Ocean Island recalls that the native government had little to do because the people were so law-abiding. This might point to an interesting paradox: the development of experience in some administrative and judicial realms was limited by the people's good behavior!

sumption may have triumphed over the love of the contours of home. The Provident Fund was proposed in 1927 for the purchase of a future home, Maude observes, but the Banabans thought it was a trick to get them off Ocean Island. And there are indications that attempts were made to initiate legal action from the Banaban side, but they were squelched. This was the climate of the times.

Grimble told the holdouts that they would find their lands in the middle of areas where active mining was to go on, and that they should exchange their lands with others so that this would not happen; but a significant number of the people continued to hold out.[30]

If the Banabans still nurtured any illusions about their objective position, they were soon to be shattered. In 1928 an ordinance was passed which would allow the government to resume mining land "in the public interest" when negotiations failed. The documents indicate that the Banabans had approached, in some way, a higher authority—most likely the High Commissioner for the Western Pacific, possibly the Secretary of State for the Colonies. The official quoted back the old price, and the Banabans refused to yield. Trying to manipulate local custom, Grimble pointed out to the Banabans that this official was offended, and if they did not agree to the terms offered, punishment would be considered. Even the breaking up of Buakonikai village (in which Rotan had important connections in the traditional descent system) would be considered, so that it would be empty before the digging began.[31]

Grimble wrote to the Buakonikai people that he was speaking not as Resident Commissioner, but as their old friend and father. (Apparently Grimble was well-liked, except on this issue.) In that role he told them that the "words of life" were to agree, and the "words of death" were to disagree —their land would be taken as Crown land. He wrote that it would be impossible to foretell the limit of land seizing; the price and the digging itself would proceed in an arbitrary manner. If they committed suicide, Grimble told them, he would be sympathetic, but powerless.[32] We will have cause to discuss this kind of language later.

30. Grimble to Kaubure, Buakonikai (in Gilbertese), 24 September 1927, Personal Files of Rotan Tito.
31. Gilbert and Ellice Islands Colony, Mining Ordinance 1928 (no. 4 of 1928). Grimble to People of Buakonikai (in Gilbertese), 5 August 1928, Personal Files of Rotan Tito.
32. Grimble to People of Buakonikai, 5 August 1928. Grimble generally assumed that he knew what was best for his charges; when his charges disagreed, he put it down to "bloody-mindedness." Maude observes that at this time, Grimble "was ill and desparate for transfer and promotion and this he hoped to achieve by a dramatic solution of the Banaban lands tangle—when the Banabans refused to co-operate he was somewhat naturally annoyed." Maude, personal communication 11 June 1969.

The land was resumed, and a price arbitrated—by the British **Agent** and Consul, Tonga, presumably brought up for the purpose, and possibly with the manager of the British Phosphate Commission. The award was similar to the company's terms, which surprised nobody. Appendix 5 sets out some of the terms. Note that payments for surface rights were to go to individuals, but royalties on the phosphate itself were to go into community trust funds.

When the arbitrator from Tonga read the award out to the Banabans, he indicated that the royalty was a question not up for discussion and that the surface price was based on the market value of the land *excluding* any increase in value because of the phosphate.[33]

This separation of surface from phosphate has been an important element in the whole controversy. The funds deriving from the surface and from the undersurface are treated in different ways. The first is regarded as the equivalent in money of the land itself, and the money can change hands only as land can change hands in the official version of traditional Banaban culture (see Maude 1946). Thus the link between land and money was made even more solid, and the government put itself in the position of arbiter and enforcer of custom.[34]

The situation was different with regard to the undersurface. Officials found, not surprisingly, that there was not a special body of native custom relating to undersurface mineral rights. The closest thing was rights to the water-caves, discussed in part 1, and the owners of the rights to the cave need not have been the same people who owned the land above. There was an ambiguous situation until a ruling in 1930 that the money deriving from trust funds should be used for the general benefit of the community, not for the specific benefit of any landowner. In 1931, the High Commissioner for the Western Pacific informed the Banabans that the surface belongs to the owner, the minerals to the government. However, whether payments from those funds were legitimated by the rights of the landowner, or the grace of the Crown, remained unclear. Much remained unclear, and still does. But another axis of controversy was born. (See Maude 1946.)

Although the arbitrator tried to avoid discussion of the royalty with the people, the people insisted on raising the issue. One prominent Banaban

33. Notes of meeting with Banabans, 24 January 1931, Maude Papers. The arbitrator from Tonga stayed with Grimble and was junior to him in the colonial service. The Banabans apparently did not consider this a reasonable course for arbitration.

34. Grimble had spoken against the "degeneration" of the adoption system in the Gilberts and instructed his officers to enforce the "true" system; one could go on at length about the static notion of custom presupposed, and the relationship to adaptability. See Grimble to Acting Senior District Officer, Tarawa, 22 February 1927, Copy in File no. A2, F2/5/5, RIC.

recalled during the discussion that the company first received land in exchange for sewing machines. It was said that Eliot had promised that no more land would be acquired until the land already acquired was worked out, but this promise was now being abrogated. The Banaban interlocutors asked the arbitrator what his personal opinion on the issue was. Here was born a prominent feature of Banaban political style, nurtured by the manner in which some officials behaved (for example, Grimble as paraphrased above). The Banabans suspected—sometimes rightly—that those opposing them were acting on instructions from superiors and in their own minds *must* have seen the justice of Banaban claims. The officials, in turn, would find refuge in their official role, thus reinforcing the Banabans' ideas. Where there were conflicts within various officials, they probably gave off signals to assuage their guilt, thus driving the Banabans on to hope to overturn the decision in question.

Another aspect of Banaban political style is revealed in a Banaban letter of complaint written in 1932, possibly to the Secretary of State for the Colonies. It was pointed out that the BPC had not finished its old area, and this was contrary to a "Covenant" made in 1913, and confirmed by Eliot "under British flags." The British symbolism is being invoked, and the term *covenant* itself is highly suggestive of a religious resonance. The covenant also promised that trees destroyed would be paid for, and the 1931 arbitration did not provide for a special payment for trees on mining lands. The price, the letter said, was arranged between Grimble and the arbitrators; it was neither a buyer's nor a seller's price (the language had become more sophisticated). The company manager would have given a better price if he had not been prevented (see below), they asserted. "So, therefore, please kindly help us by your mercyful arbitration and judgement in front of Our Heavenly God, and in front of His Majesty King George V."[35]

The appeal for personal help expressed in humble language on a strong issue, going up the bureaucratic scale, the invocation both of God and the King (thus acting within the system, by the system's own rules) representing a joining of religious and political symbolism—these became established by 1932. The 1912 land affair joined the Banabans in the idea of a community articulated by an interest in land. The 1927–31 land affair propelled in the direction of a symbolic joining of God, government, and Banaban custom articulated through land. Land was to become the medium of symbolic exchange between these things—in a general sense, land mediated the relationship between a Banaban past, a present embedded in European institutions and an uncertain future.

I will backtrack to consider Rotan's version of some of the events of the

35. Banaban Community to (probably) Secretary of State, 8 August 1932, RIC.

1927–31 period. His version is, again, a significant input to the current political scene.

Rotan claims that after Grimble informed the Banabans of the first offer, the Banabans asked for a royalty not of 10.5d. per ton, but £5 per ton (although they were willing to go down to £2 10s.0d.). A company official came who repeated the original offer and later offered to raise the royalty slightly. The Banabans again refused. The company man was about to make a statement (the suggestion is that it would have been in the Banabans' favor), when Grimble stopped him. Grimble told the people that unless they agreed, the price might go even lower. He then made his "words of life—words of death" pronouncement.

In June 1928, according to Rotan, Grimble told the Banabans that some should prepare to go and look at Kuria, in the Gilberts, as a place of resettlement, but they refused. Grimble was angry when the Banaban delegation told him of their refusal, and he threw them out. The delegation relayed this to the people, and the old men were afraid—they wanted to agree.

There was a great deal of argument until it was decided that they should return to Grimble with the following offer. The price is approved if there is compensation for the trees on the land. Grimble was happy, went off to the Gilberts, and on his return told the Banabans to prepare to sign the agreement. But they asked him about compensation for the trees, he refused, and they refused. The Banabans then said that the matter of land acquisition was over, because the company had much land that it had not mined yet. After this, Grimble forbade games and established a curfew from 6 P.M. to 6 A.M. (there may have been a curfew before at 9 P.M.). There were more refusals later, and then the land was resumed as Crown land. Rotan also claims that the committee representing Banaban interests was told to go to visit the High Commissioner for the Western Pacific with Rotan as its secretary, but there was a last-minute change of plans.[36]

Rotan wrote in 1965 that

> the arbitrators gave the BPC the authority to work the lands where the BPC proceeded by first digging the centre of the island to prepare its way. When the way was ready it began destroying lands without first obtaining the boundaries of each individual holding of the landowners who had refused the proposed land compensation.
>
> We refused to mark the boundaries of our lands, because we did not expect to receive the compensation money and we thought that our lands would be left alone as it had been done to those who refused to alienate their lands in the 1913 Agreement.
>
> Mr. Grimble did not agree with our wish and he gave our lands to be

36. Rotan Tito, personal communication 1961. The possibility of Kuria in the Gilberts as a place of resettlement, to which Rotan refers, had been broached in government circles at least in 1909.

mined. The Company started to cut down coconut trees and dig lands, and we saw, that two pieces of land whose boundaries had not been obtained by the BPC were nearly finished. . . .

We saw this with much grief and anger and we assembled to request the BPC not to destroy our lands while we had not given our consent for them to be worked. Mr. Grimble released the prisoners to accompany his constables and with guns they resisted our approach to the representatives of BPC and he also accompanied his constables.

We were willing to die for our lands at that time, but we respected our elders' word of advice under the Banaban Custom that to shed blood is prohibited on their island.

We followed such advice then with my anticipation and trust in the Sovereign of Britain, that he would readily help us when he is able to hear the true position of the Banabans on their homeland, and that was why we had kept on making petitions.

After that I wrote to our Acting Resident Commissioner, Major Swinbourne, and his secretary, Mr. H. E. Maude, informing them that it was right for us to let them know the boundaries of our individual lands. This was not because we had agreed to the amount of compensation or to their alienation, but simply because of the love for [the lands]. We could not bear the thought of losing them completely when they were going to be worked without knowing their position and compensation value as it was with the lands which had been worked out under the authority of Mr. Grimble's orders.[37]

Disputes over rights in this period apparently did not only involve land. According to a company source, in 1934 (when, incidentally, the government reported that eighty to one hundred Banabans were employed by the BPC as day labor) two women asked if a lease could be arranged for a reef where the Boat Harbor was located. The Resident Commissioner said it was not necessary. In 1937 a man asked about rights to part of a reef, perhaps the same one. He indicated that the rights concerned a certain kind of fish which swarmed there and could not be taken without his permission. The company made a small offer, which it is claimed the government did not confirm. In 1947, it came out that the issue concerned the reef which belonged to one of the village districts, of which the man was a prominent member. There was undoubtedly some misunderstanding on the European side, but there is also the suggestion of a confusion over the translation of traditional rights into modern monetary terms, a confusion which some ambitious people may have tried to exploit.[38]

37. Rotan Tito, Review of the phosphate royalty at Ocean Island, August 1965, translated by Teem Takoto.

38. Notes of speech by Mr. H. B. Maynard to the Rambi Island Council—Ocean Island reefs, 30 September 1948, RIC. On employment of Banabans, see Gilbert and Ellice Islands Colony report for 1934, London, H.M.S.O., 1935. Maude observes that the Lands Commission in 1931 had considered the question of rights to reefs.

I must backtrack chronologically to explore another critical event in the development of Banaban culture: the conduct of the Ocean Island Lands Commission, which the hearing of lands disputes had awaited. The commission conducted its business between October and March 1932. During this period, people's thoughts must have been saturated with land. Lands commissions had been held in the Gilberts, and the procedure was not new. H. E. Maude was Native Lands Commissioner, and the job of the commission was to "enquire into the ownership of all native owned lands on Banaba (Ocean Island) and to codify the native customs of land conveyance and inheritance."[39] The effects of the commission's work were thus to be in two related directions: to deal with specific land claims, and to order the system as a whole.

Four Banabans from each village became members, and the magistrate and chief of kaubure sat as assessors at each village. Maude observes that "two of the elected members of the Lands Commission (for Tabiang) were women," showing that a "knowledge of tradition was already becoming rare. In this case a village could not muster four men in the knowledge of custom which could pass public scrutiny; but they had two very old women who patently knew more than any of the younger generation of men. It never happened in the Gilberts."[40]

Ninety-seven claims were heard. "The vast majority of these claims were either groundless and were unanimously rejected by the Commission, in accordance with Section 7 (1) of the Ordinance, as not being well founded, or were amicably settled by the parties in the presence of the Commission."[41] Thus, as was probably the case with the native court, lands matters were underscored as no longer only being in the hands of the actual owners of the parcels themselves. Banabans were operating with the government to deal with lands matters not concerning their own families. "Altogether 28 claims were rejected by the Commission, either because they were frivolous or because they were clearly based on happenings before the establishment of the Protectorate in November, 1900." The lands system was apparently thus firmly linked to the assumption of colonial rule. "Fifteen claims were withdrawn with the consent of the Commission and 54 claims were settled by agreement between the parties. . . . Besides hearing claims, the native members of the Commission were instrumental in discovering many pieces of land which had been lost by their owners, as well as in settling the

39. Maude to Resident Commissioner, no. 4 of 7 March 1932, Enclosure 1 in Despatch Resident Commissioner to High Commissioner, no. 175 of 27 May 1932, WPHC.

40. Maude, personal communication 11 June 1969.

41. Maude to Resident Commissioner, no. 4 of 7 March 1932. Subsequent quotations on the commission are from this report.

boundaries of lands and in erecting permanent marks where the boundaries had been hitherto in doubt."

Details of various individual land arrangements were secured for the commission, including those concerning adoption. For example, in Maude's lands notes, there is a list of adoptions indicating whether or not the adoptee received land only from his adopters, or from his natal parents also—significant in the normative system for the kinds of relationships applying between an adoptee and his natal family. Genealogical fragments were set out in connection with claims. One claim, which may have been under dispute, concerned the passing of land because of friendship. Some cases which called for a good deal of comment probably involved transfers which were outside the usual parent-child inheritance, for example, where land was given as "the land for looking after" when a person was cared for by others in a more fitting manner than by his own children or grandchildren. The latter may have tried to use the opportunity to return the land to the line. There are a number of records of the division of lands among siblings; perhaps according to some, a number of those lands had passed into the wrong hands. And in another case, maybe under dispute, a man went to Tahiti and left his lands with a kinsman, who gave them back on the first man's return.

Maude recalls that many of the disputes concerned *te moti n un* (a decision in anger), by which a parent gave an unusually small proportion of his lands to a child. This was not considered proper custom, and at times the distribution of lands among siblings could be equalized by transferring more lands from another parent. Although the proverbial position remains today, perhaps the distribution of land was being undermined as an effective parental sanction.

A particular problem which arose was what to do about the lands of Banabans who were away from Ocean Island and had been for some time. The Lands Commission decided on a temporal cutoff point, perhaps ten years. If a Banaban had been away for longer than that time, he was assumed ineligible for lands distribution by the commission. One may interpret this as follows: Enacting the code of landowner, kinsman, and Banaban was established as a necessary condition for lands distribution; identity was not enough.

Some of the boundary disputes involved lands where the claim was made that boundary markers had been surreptitiously moved. Some of the markers were stones. Coconut trees and concrete pegs also marked out lands. When the disputes were under investigation, the elders involved assembled the young people and pointed out the lines. Someone might remember, for example, that a boundary came up from the coast where a certain waterspout was. One way in which the disputes were settled was to split the difference between the two parties.

Some lands the boundaries of which were disputed were magic sites, or groves. A point of prime importance is that they were *not phosphate lands*. The boundaries of phosphate lands had been more or less settled by the company. This testifies to the fact that the importance of land had not been completely enveloped by the importance of phosphate and the economic interests connected to it. Land was still worth fighting about because of the cultural aura surrounding it.

"The various points of native custom with regard to land which arose during the course of the inquiry were settled by the Commission at the time, and at the final sittings the land customs were codified." The various customs were established after a lengthy examination of precedents, with an eye to working out inconsistencies. Thus an explicit, objectified, rationalized normative system was created.

In his report, Maude listed "the customary conveyances that I recommend should be in future recognized by the Administration. They have been read to the Lands Commission and have been agreed to unanimously," the members indicating the Banabans' wish that the rules regarding these conveyances be applied also to cases where "their land has been leased and is now represented by a capital sum or by an annual payment of interest."

There were also a set of "conveyances customary before the coming of the Government but no longer recognized except as establishing ownership prior to the declaration of the British Protectorate." These conveyances (see chapter 1) were the land of peacemaking, the blood payment, the land of life giving, the land of marriage, the land for theft, the blood payment for animals, and the land for bone setting. Some of these conveyances had probably already been in abeyance, and they represent mostly those which were involved in the kinds of sanction activity which the government had taken over.

At the same time, it was stipulated that "the land for looking after" could not be given to a member of the "near kindred," and could only be given when the native court was satisfied that the near kindred had refused to look after the donor. The near kindred for lands purpose was defined as being limited to relatives having a common great-grandparent. This was probably the conventional native definition, but it was likely that those considered or not considered near kindred in many circumstances were so defined by other than genealogical criteria. The role of the near kindred in adoptions was codified, as were other details of the land system. Adoptions had to be formalized by registration with officials.

The attitude of the government at this time may have been the same as that of the people: Some aspects of custom would be maintained and enforced, and other aspects would be dropped, proscribed, or reformulated.

The decision in each case may not have appeared to exemplify a principle, the inconsistent attitude toward custom giving rise to confusion on the status of custom in a general sense. However, it is clear that the implications of colonial government and differentiation for the nature of land as a medium of symbolic exchange were codified.

After the Lands Commission, lands disputes were to be heard by the native court, which consisted of the magistrate as chairman, and the one kaubure for each of the four villages, chosen in village meetinghouses. Especially since the policemen were chosen by the magistrate and the kaubure it would appear that the limited native executive and judicial functions were not clearly differentiated. An appeal was allowed on lands cases from the native court to the Lands Commissioner: the government thus maintained its position of arbiter of matters involving local custom.[42]

Maude observed that those elected to the Lands Commission from the villages were mainly traditional leaders, and for a while they had a resuscitation of prestige as the most powerful native group on the island. Coming as it did on the heels of the 1927–31 phosphate dispute, discussion of traditional lands matters must have had a certain poignancy, and one can imagine alternative principles producing lively debate. The commission "was like a shot in the arm for so many of the old folk. The issues which were raised could be discussed at length in traditional terms which they all (but not the young folk listening in the maneaba) understood. The sheer virtuosity exhibited in arguing out the nicer points of traditional etiquette was a joy to listen to."[43]

Traditional matters were juxtaposed in time, and very likely in mind, with a fight against the modern company and government. An "enthusiastic revival of the traditional games took place in December, 1931," as we recall from chapter 1, which may have been a nativistic response to the phosphate crisis, and which was informed by the activities of the Lands Commission.

Banaban custom was being defined as it was being changed, and as it was being changed certain aspects of the "old culture" were resuscitated which had the effect of propelling the community in a direction of even more rapid political change, since a center of gravity of that custom was land, land had become associated with phosphate and money, and phosphate was a commodity articulating with international business and government. I will refer back later to this apparent and perhaps somewhat obscurely phrased paradox.

Let us pause for a moment to consider some further aspects of the Ban-

42. Most of the otherwise uncited data in this section comes from conversations with H. E. Maude in 1969.
43. Maude, personal communication 11 June 1969.

abans' relations with the government and the company. It was mentioned earlier that the three categories, *the government, the company,* and *the church,* are important categories now in the Banaban cultural system. Maude considers it unlikely that the general category of the government was a central one on Ocean Island. The persons of the Resident Commissioner and other European officials were really the crucial things, although they may not have spoken Gilbertese.[44] Banabans had direct access to the Resident Commissioner and would take up with him matters which on other islands would have been taken up with lesser functionaries. On Ocean there was more of a paternalistic system.

One Banaban who was magistrate for many years had good relations with Eliot, Quayle-Dickson, and Grimble, and they were on a Christian-name basis. As magistrate he was head of the native court, many of the regulations of which were unwritten (also, many government regulations were untranslated at this time); "laws" were thus applied which were probably obscure to those to whom they were applied, and perhaps even to those applying them.

This direct access and paternalism did not mean, however, that there were intimate relations between Banabans and officials. Maude recalls that real social contact with officials, even Grimble, was minimal. The Banabans did not invite Europeans to feasts, for example, in the same way that people did in the Gilberts. The Banabans, while in a social field which included Europeans, may have been drawing a boundary around their customary life.[45]

People also went directly to see the manager of the BPC. The company, Maude asserts, was "indulgent" toward its Banaban employees. The Banabans would not work "in the field"; they regarded themselves as being in a position different from that of Gilbertese laborers, an omen of things to come. Banabans worked in higher capacities, and the company did not apply the same standards to them as it did to others, according to Maude. The picture that emerges is one of a particularism familiar in colonial societies, but this ran counter to certain other trends, which we will take up later.

What of native social categories? The symbolic importance of the British,

44. The Secretary to Government functioned as District Officer. See Grimble 1957, pp. 152–55 on the question of attitudes toward the government; he is only speaking generally of the Gilberts.

45. Maude recalls a resident European government staff of about six in 1931. At the end of 1933, the total population of Ocean Island was reported as 2,074 and was composed of "660 Banabans, 957 Gilbert Islanders, 72 Ellice Islanders, 372 Chinese, 112 Europeans, and one Fijian." Gilbert and Ellice Islands Colony, report for period 1st July, 1932–31st December, 1933; London, H.M.S.O., 1935, pp. 5–6. The Banabans thus only constituted about one-third of the island's population.

the concepts applied to officials and the phosphate company, have been alluded to in previous pages. One may add speculatively that as colonial administration and company activities proceeded, important new categories entered Banaban culture: perhaps *workers* for the company and government; *sellers* of fish and fruit; people *rich* through land sales; *friends* of European officials and employees; *officials* in the native government and on the Lands Commission; those with *knowledge* of the old custom and those without it. There may have been some categorical contrast between conservatives and progressives vis-à-vis disputes with the company and government. The category *Banaban* itself was no doubt becoming more closely tied to certain action implications. And, as before, people who were strong *members of the church* may have been contrasted with those who were not. This is a point sometimes overlooked: the increasing complexity of the total set of categories in such situations of change.

Let us consider the position of the church in this period and a little beyond. It was mentioned above that in 1925, two years before the great Ocean Island lands dispute, there were mission reports of disturbances in the Gilberts. There had also been reports of disturbances in 1907, two years before the first land deadlock.

Rev. George Eastman, the head of the LMS operation in the Gilberts, referred in 1928 to a general self-assertion against authority, both mission and government. He wrote that giving Gilbertese more responsibility in the church was good in principle, but it was difficult especially because of the infrequency of visits to train church councils. European supervision was still considered necessary. The people, however, were to outrun their principals. (The head of the school at Abaiang in the Northern Gilberts went so far as to refer to a "spirit of Bolshevism" there in 1930; the students even asked to be paid to clean up the station. It should be noted here that not only were there Gilbertese laborers with LMS backgrounds and LMS pastors on Ocean Island, there were also Banabans who were trained in LMS schools.)[46]

Rev. Percy Hannah was at this time responsible for the spiritual oversight of both Ocean Island and Nauru. Hannah wanted to run the church affairs of both islands directly under the London office rather than through the LMS Beru headquarters because, he said, of the nature of available means of communication. This underscores the special position of Ocean Island within the colony. Its ties with the metropolitan center were more direct than were those of the other islands. It was of course the capital, but it was the capital in part because of the nature of those ties, which centered on the phosphate. This position was critical for the Banabans' development.

46. Eastman, Report for 1928; Report of the Northern Islands for 1930; LMS.

There was a mission teacher in each Banaban village, in addition to the Ellice teacher responsible for the spiritual welfare of the LMS laborers; the latter was probably head of the Ocean Island Church Council. The LMS District Church Committee sent a letter to the council in 1930 reminding the teachers that they had to report to Hannah on matters of importance. One may reasonably make the assumption that at least the committee felt that the teachers had not been reporting to Hannah on matters of importance. Hannah spent most of his time on Nauru but did make visits to Ocean Island.

There was serious trouble in the Nauruan church at this time, related to the antiadministration activities of a pastor, to which we referred before. Some Banabans today are aware of the activities of that pastor, whom they regard as having stood up for his people. Maude observes that there was constant communication between Ocean Island and Nauru, and that Rotan and the Nauruan pastor were friends. The Nauruans were learning things which they had not been officially taught, according to Hannah—about murders, divorce, strikes, and gambling among Europeans—from newspapers which found their way to Nauru. This was related to what he said was a decreasing respect for Europeans. The same may have been true on Ocean Island. In 1939 Rev. Clifford Welch, a visiting LMS missionary, reported that after a new church was opened on Nauru, the Banabans decided that they wanted one. Nauru was apparently a model of great importance to the Banabans from the days on Ocean Island.[47]

During the 1927–31 lands dispute the LMS pastors and teachers were "sane and helpful," according to Hannah, with the exception of one man— probably Rotan. Being sane and helpful most likely meant, minimally, keeping out of the fracas. This probably represented the official mission point of view, as was the case on Nauru. But at the same time Hannah relayed the information that the Banabans wanted to run their own church, and they felt that the Ellice man in charge was an outsider.[48] This may well have been a continuation of the same notions which lead the Ocean Island church earlier to request control over the funds they collected, an antecedent, perhaps, of the idea of the legitimacy of control over phosphate funds. Thus the solidarity that was being expressed in the political sphere continued to be paralleled by developments in the religious sphere.

I have no data, unfortunately, on the participation of Banabans in the

47. Hannah to Phillips, 28 September 1929; LMS Decennial report 1920–30, Gilbert Islands and Nauru Mission; Minutes of meeting of LMS Gilbert Islands District Committee, July–August 1930; Report of message from Hannah, 1 December 1931; Hannah to Chirgwin, 26 January 1932; Hannah to Barradale, 18 September 1928; Welch, Circular letter, Ocean Island, 26 May 1939; LMS.
48. Hannah, Report for 1931; Hannah to Chirgwin, 16 November 1931; LMS.

Ocean Island Church Council. Welch remarked later for the whole region that both religious and civil life were controlled by a gerentocracy.[49] Perhaps some aspects of church activity were reinforcing traditional age concepts, while other aspects were indirectly undermining them. Given the general nature of LMS organization, it is likely that even if many Banabans were not on the church council, they at least exerted pressure upon it. Church meetings in this period, as before, dealt with offenders against church discipline.[50] As the Lands Committee provided experience in dealing with Banaban political-economic issues, the organization of the church must also have helped develop ideas about autonomy.

Another church activity which may have propelled some in the direction of being more modern men is reported later at the LMS Beru school. Missionary and other types of plays were produced—including that great political drama, *Robin Hood*. A version of the *Merchant of Venice* was adapted, with the main theme of "a pound of flesh."[51] Such plays may have given people experience in empathizing with roles which were removed from their direct acquaintance, a point which Lerner (1958) considers of great significance in the transition from tradition to modernity.

Welch was one among those who was concerned about making the activities of the church more relevant and lively to the people. He bemoaned the fact that in the Gilberts there was a "harsh sabbatarian discipline," and the difference between right and wrong was not properly handled. This may qualify our interpretation of the effects of church transfer. The churches administered the rules of the Old Testament, Welch said, with a few people having a "glimmering" of the grace of the New Testament. "They are under the law; not under Grace." He even suggested that pastors participate in clean dancing to liven things up. Elsewhere Bible stories were incorporated in dancing, thus purifying the dances, and Biblical history was expressed "in a living and understandable way."[52] Eastman was concerned that the elderly mission teachers on Ocean Island had "little appeal" to the boys and younger Banaban men, a situation perhaps ameliorated by the arrival of three new teachers in 1938.[53]

The Empire Day celebration on Ocean Island in 1939 closed with native dances, and Welch told the people to conserve their native arts and crafts. Special hymns were sung from each village, and the high point of the meeting

49. Welch, Report on a visitation of the Gilbert Islands, 1 June 1940, LMS.
50. Hannah, Report for 1933, LMS.
51. Miss Pateman, Annual report 1934; Levett, Annual report 1936; Levett, Annual report 1937; LMS.
52. Welch, Report on a visitation of the Gilbert Islands.
53. Eastman, Annual report 1936; Eastman, Annual report 1938; LMS.

was the presentation of collections taken from the villages for the year's work.[54] A competitive aspect may have been added early to village-church activity on Ocean Island, and it provided much of the verve of church life, as it does on Rambi. This competitive aspect, one can speculate, was an important factor in the church's success. For although it was not proper to give advertisements for oneself, it probably was proper to give advertisements for one's village and its success.

The association of church activities with public holidays had become a fixture of Banaban life, partially integrating the political and religious institutions into which the people were tied. The use of native dancing also yielded a resonance from the traditional culture, and thus there may have been an attempted ritual tying up of things in one paternalistic package—the Empire, the church, and custom, in rites of colonial legitimation.

In 1934, some Europeans joined in a combined Christmas service in the company chapel. As was probably the general case in such affairs, each Banaban village and the Ellice people sang a song or hymn. Perhaps the church was in a limited way providing a framework in which people of diverse origins might join on occasions of transcendent meaning, if on a paternalistic basis, and which at the same time gave tangible formulation to the ideas of both a separate Banaban identity and of the village as a meaningful unit—in a religious setting.

How the Catholics fit into this picture is obscure. Hannah abjured the notion of popes because "the Church is the people, in Christ." But at the same time there was a reaction by some missionaries against the anti-Catholicism which existed—a call for love, not hate.[55]

The Jubilee of Christianity on Ocean Island was celebrated in 1935 to mark the progress of the community into the modern Christian world. A Banaban today recalls that the people were told to wear white rather than black lavalavas to symbolize their transition from "the darkness" into "the light." The Resident Commissioner and his wife attended the service, and the colony police paraded. The first hymn the Banabans learned was sung on the spot where the first missionary landed, and a man who was on the mission ship from which they landed recalled the events of that day. Banabans at the affair spoke of the "great changes" which had taken place since

54. Welch, Circular letter, Ocean Island, 26 May 1939.
55. Hannah, Annual report 1934; Miss Pateman to Chirgwin, 18 July 1931; Spivey to Chirgwin, 26 July 1932; LMS. The theme of separateness and combination was also represented in the mode of collecting money. In 1941, for example, the Ocean Island Church Council decided on a collection, separate from the usual May drive, in which Banabans, Gilbertese, and Ellice Islanders joined forces. Welch to Goodall, 1 March 1941, LMS.

1885, and Eastman, who went for the occasion, wrote: "From being a be-nighted, poverty stricken herd of pagans, they had been raised by the Gospel to a self-respecting and generous Christian community, and by the develop-ment of the Phosphate industry they had become comparatively speaking a well to do community not unmindful of their duty to help their needy brethren."[56]

The church was of course not the only source of the transition from dark-ness to light. I cannot assess here the role of increasing education in the com-munity. There must have been a growing sophistication in financial matters, critical for the phosphate issue, and knowledge of what was going on in other parts of the world.[57] The Banabans flocked to the cinema, according to Maude, and its importance cannot be overemphasized.

While this growing sophistication was taking place, and while the com-munity was being reminded of its emergence from the darkness into the light, vast and reverberating changes had been occurring in the definition of land rights, *inter alia*, which must have been difficult to understand. Given the importance of land in the Banabans' structuring of the world, they must have been faced with cognitive and affective problems of massive propor-tions. The church might have been looked to as a source of stability, even while it too was responding to general structural trends. But there was to be little respite, since new developments were to occur to which the Banabans again had to respond, with their redefined personality, social and cultural resources.

---

56. Eastman, Report for 1935 (January 1936), LMS. They contributed twenty-six pounds for work in a "needy field," perhaps manifesting a greater degree of charity than before, or at least the ability to raise money for such an occasion.

57. On the mission schools on Ocean Island, Welch remarked critically that the school and church should be the center of interest of the native community, but the people saw the school as the responsibility of the teacher and his wife. He also said that women were lagging behind men in education (Welch, Circular letter, Ocean Island, 26 May 1939). I note in passing a comment by a European teacher at Beru that as Gilbertese wealth was generally measured in land, the word *acre* was being added to the vocabulary. Miss Pateman, Report on education in the Gilbert Islands, 21 Novem-ber 1933, LMS. The word had no doubt long been in the Banabans' vocabulary.

5

Codification and the War

In this chapter we will focus briefly on four things which occurred rather closely in time: the introduction of an annuity system which codified the relations between blood, land, locality, and Banaban identity, and thus continued the codification process discussed for the Lands Commission; the formation of a Cooperative Society, which extended to the realm of economic organization previous developments which had occurred in political and religion organization; the consideration of the purchase of a new island in Fiji; and the trying times of the Second World War.

CODIFICATION CONTINUES

A new arrangement regarding Banaban funds was under consideration in the government in 1936. A proposal (of undetermined nature) was made to the Banabans in early 1937, and it met with a disquieting response. The proposal was probably some earlier transformation of the annuities scheme ultimately agreed upon, and some aspects of which are indicated in Appendix 5.

At a meeting in the Tabiang meetinghouse, a number of old men were present on government invitation to have the proposal explained to them. The representatives went off to discuss it with the people and replied to it by saying (with Rotan as their spokesman) that the government's intentions were good, but that the community wanted the direct distribution of royalties to landowners, and that the landowners should be free to do whatever they wanted with them.

This was a rejection of the ideas advanced by the government in the 1930 and 1931 decisions: that payments from the undersurface should be used for the benefit of the community as a whole. Thus, the community stand that welded around land, and what solidarity came with that stand, did not go so far as to entail the putting of monies into a collective pool to be used for the collective benefit. The fact that people owned different amounts of

139

land was still recognized. The Banabans apparently did not then (and they certainly do not now) accept the logic of the surface-undersurface distinction. The individual owned land, money came from that land, and the individual should get the money from that land. Collective action was thus in part oriented to the securing of individual rights as defined by the Banabans through the translation of land into money, the practice established in the earliest company times.

This orientation, however, introduced a certain strain in Banaban political thinking which is still present: Where do the boundaries of the domain of the community as a community, and the individual as an individual —particularly as a landowner—begin and end?

There is some indication that the government proposal involved the payment of a uniform annuity. An agreement was reached whereby there would be both a general annuity, and a bonus to *landowners only*, those in the 1913 and 1931 phosphate mining areas. The bonus would be scaled according to a person's total holdings but with an upper limit of £10 (see Appendix 5). The settlement thus combined features of a recognition of both the identity of Banabans (qualified in a manner to be discussed shortly), and of their differentiation as individuals with different amounts of land.

The government had proposed that payments be made only when a stipulated minimum tonnage export of phosphate was achieved in one year, but some Banabans concluded that the amount was far more than that necessary to pay for both annuities and the services for which Banaban funds were used. A decision then came down that the availability of funds would determine whether the payments could be made. It was then that agreement was reached; only Rotan and two of his children dissented. In order to prepare for the first distribution, the government locally had to bring together information on landholding and births since 1913, thus again fixing certain information.

One particular problem came up at this time which is of central interest to us: the status of people who were not full-Banabans. It is not clear whether the initiative for considering them in a manner distinct from the others came from the government or from the people. The colonial administration recognized the need for an annuity to support a native resident on Ocean Island but simultaneously recognized that a part-Banaban—thus a person who had land rights in the Gilberts (or elsewhere)—could derive his support from those rights when in his other home locale. There was also the consideration that people from elsewhere might cut into Banaban funds, through an *ad hoc* adoption, or in some other way. In collaboration with Banaban elders, the administration in 1937 produced a set of nineteen rules.

The rules stated a determinate relationship between kinship, land, and locality, and all but the first must be set out:

"2. Natives over 15 years of age are to be regarded as adults for the purpose of the payment of the annuity.

3. Children of a full-Banaban and a half-Banaban ('itera') are to be regarded as full-Banabans for the purpose of the payment of the annuity.

4. Children of two half-Banabans shall be regarded as half-Banabans.

5. Children of a full-Banaban and any non-Banaban shall be regarded as half-Banabans.

6. Children of a half-Banaban and any non-Banaban shall be regarded as half-Banabans.

7. The Resident Commissioner reserves the right later to define the status of half-Banabans in consultation with Banaban representatives, for the purpose of the payment of the annuity, if such definition shall appear to him necessary owing to later weakness of consanguineous ties. [In the Gilbertese version, the last section would be translated more correctly in the following way: ". . . if it appears that the true Banaban blood is becoming weak."]

8. No payment shall be made to the relatives or dependants of any full or half-Banaban, who shall die during a six-monthly period, either in respect of the whole or part of that period.

9. Children born during a six-monthly period shall be eligible to receive their share of the annuity at the date of payment next following their birth.

10. Full-Banabans shall be eligible to receive the annuity no matter in what island or country they may be resident at the time of the payment.

11. No half-Banaban, whether adult or child, shall be eligible to receive the annuity during his or her absence from Ocean Island.

12. (a) A half-Banaban who returns to Ocean Island before the payment of a share of the annuity, shall be eligible to receive his or her share of the annuity, the payment of which next follows. No specific period of residence prior to the payment of that share of the annuity shall be necessary.

(b) If, however, the Resident Commissioner is of the opinion that the above-mentioned rule, 12(a), is being abused, he reserves the right to impose a residential qualification for half-Banabans returning to Ocean Island to obtain their share of the annuity.

13. (a) In future, only a native adopted as 'te nati' [child] by a full-Banaban shall be regarded as a full-Banaban and shall be eligible to receive the annuity as such.

(b) Such an adoption shall be held to imply that the native adopted has renounced his or her rights to his or her lands elsewhere, with the exception of those lands given as 'te iria' [the accompaniment].

(c) Should this form of adoption be, in the opinion of the Resident Commissioner, abused, (it being customary only to adopt one 'te nati'), His Honour reserves the right to limit the number of natives adopted by one family as 'te nati,' who shall be eligible to receive the annuity.

14. A native adopted by a full-Banaban under any recognized form of adoption other than adoption as 'te nati' (i.e., tibutibu, i-taritari, i-mamane and te nati-ni-kauatabo) [grandchild adoption, sibling-of-same sex adoption, sibling-of-opposite-sex adoption, and a form of child adoption in which the child is regarded as still a member of his natal family], shall be regarded as a half-Banaban for the purpose of the payment of the annuity, and shall be eligible to receive his or her annuity as such, but only if land has passed from the adopter to the native adopted.

15. Any non-Banaban adopted as 'te nati' by a half-Banaban shall be regarded as a half-Banaban for the purpose of the payment of the annuity and shall be eligible to receive his or her share as such.

16. Any non-Banaban adopted by a half-Banaban under any recognized form of adoption other than adoption as 'te nati', shall not be eligible to receive any share of the annuity.

17. In order to entitle a native adopted as 'te nati' to the receipt of the annuity, the adopter must sign a written declaration at the time of the adoption to the effect that the adopted native shall receive a portion of the adopter's lands, not less than the maximum portion due to any of the adopter's natural issue.

18. In order to entitle a native adopted by a full-Banaban under any recognized form of adoption other than adoption as 'te nati' . . . to the receipt of the annuity, the adopter must sign a written declaration at the time of the adoption specifying the actual piece or pieces of land which he is passing to the native adopted.

19. Any native to whom land has passed or shall pass, which has carried or shall carry with it the right to a landowner's bonus, shall be entitled to receive the same irrespective of whether he or she is a half-Banaban or non-Banaban, provided that, in the case of an absentee

landlord, the bonus will only be paid to a caretaker duly appointed to receive it on his or her behalf."[1]

It has already been indicated that with the coming of Gilbertese laborers and increased communications in the area, many Banabans married Gilbertese. Although I have not yet counted heads, it is likely that most Banabans today have at least one Gilbertese parent or grandparent. This does not mean, however, that the Banaban gene pool was completely closed aboriginally. The genealogies indicate that some Gilbertese married in, and some were adopted. But by the time these rules came into force, the Gilbertese presence was dramatically different.

The first thing that should be noted about the rules is what is implied by Rule 19 in contrast with the others. For the landowner's bonus, the right was carried by the land rather than by the person, although a "caretaker" provision is made. This is directly tied to notions in the descent system. For the annuity, the right was carried by the person, but could depend on land conveyances.

The rules stipulate two categories, full-Banaban and half-Banaban, without indicating how one originally decides whether a person is a full-Banaban or a half-Banaban. If one could be a closer or more distant kinsman according to the amount of blood one shared with another person, one could apparently also have been more or less of a Banaban depending upon how much Banaban blood one had. I repeat that I do not know the origin of the writing-in of this distinction. The Banabans might have become more concerned with drawing lines around themselves.

The 1937 rules defined *full-Banaban* for annuity purposes as the natural child of a full-Banaban with a full- or half-Banaban, or the adopted child of a full-Banaban if the adopted child's land rights from his adopter were already insured, and his only lands from his natal family were "the accompaniment," a small parcel or parcels of land which symbolized a limited continuing relationship with the natal family. (The adoption system is discussed in detail in Silverman 1970, and I will only allude to it briefly here.)

The rules defined *half-Banaban* for annuity purposes as the natural child of a half-Banaban with a half- or non-Banaban, the natural child of a full-Banaban with a non-Banaban, the adopted non-Banaban child of a half-Banaban (with the assurances of land transfer), or a person adopted in one of the other forms by a full-Banaban, if land had already passed. The distinction between different forms of adoption, and their relation to full- and

---

1. Banaban rules—adopted 1937, Enclosure in letter from (signature undecipherable) for Secretary, WPHC, to Holland, 1 February 1947. File no. F. 76/3/4, RIC.

half-status, represented a transformation of aspects of the kinship system into the community societal system.

Full-Banabans and half-Banabans, as defined, were also subject to different residence qualifications: the full-Banaban could be anywhere at the time of payment and get his annuity; the half-Banaban had to be on Ocean Island. In many circumstances, the Resident Commissioner reserved the right to change the regulations, in consultation with Banaban elders, if it appeared that the blood and the money were dispersing too widely. It is quite clear from the rules that blood could go anywhere, land was as good as blood if the holder did not have significant land relationships elsewhere, but land was not quite as good as blood if he did. The non-full-blood had to validate his status by being on Ocean Island itself. Thus was the relationship between blood, land, locality, and Banaban identity defined. And the general codification represented by the Lands Commission continued.

The full-Banaban, half-Banaban terminology was carried through in the *Ocean Island Regulations, 1939,* which stipulated that a native other than a full- or half-Banaban, unless he was a missionary, teacher, or a person assured of employment, could not land on the island without a permit signed by the native magistrate. The boundary around the community was reinforced.[2] The regulations—which I will not discuss in detail, since their period of applicability was so short—also regulated the proper care of children and the aged, dancing, feasting, and public order. Custom in a revised form had moved again into a partially differentiated legal system. And we note again that only certain aspects of custom were transformed into the legal system, the transformation perhaps giving them a certain permanence, and giving judicial authority the right to apply sanctions for their enforcement. Custom was a thing to be drawn from, and it became clear in the lands issue that government and indigenous interpretations of applicable custom did not always coincide, although the interpretations of one had been conditioned by the interpretations of the other. On many matters the government probably applied a modified standard of "public good" to sort out "positive" and "negative" custom. Custom as a moral force was thus given authority. But the government did not thereby secure for itself an unquestioned legitimacy as the appropriate sorter. One man's public good is another man's oppression.

A COOPERATIVE BORN, AND A NEW ISLAND CONSIDERED

In 1940 an event of paramount importance took place: the formation of the Banaban Cooperative Store, financed by a deduction from funds, and

2. I am unaware, however, of the manner in which landing on Ocean Island was previously administered.

supervised by the Banaban Welfare Officer.[3] The cooperative movement had been proceeding in the Gilberts, and a report had been issued on the Nauruan cooperative, which had been doing its own importing and exporting according to government sources. Rotan was a moving figure in the cooperative, and Maude observes that it provided an outlet for the more progressive elements in the community. A Banaban today recalls a time when the store had overstocked a particular item, and the people were pressured into buying it after the distribution of annuities. All business had previously been in the hands of the BPC, which for an undetermined length of time had a two-price system: higher for natives, lower for Europeans. The Banaban store was an economic unit with political overtones. The changes which had been occurring in political and religious organization were now replicated in the economic sphere. The importance of the store will become apparent when we discuss the early days on Rambi.

In 1940 there were also new proposals from the BPC on the acquisition of 230 further acres of mining land, including £175 per acre for surface rights, and 1s. per ton royalty, with the Provident Fund to increase over time to £250,000. The Banabans agreed in principle, but were dissatisfied with the plan for cash payments; they asked the BPC general manager to advance their case. The war was to delay consideration of further acquisitions (see Maude 1946).

The matter of acquiring a new island was also broached in 1940. At a meeting probably with the Resident Commissioner, the Banaban Committee asked for an increase in the annuity and bonus and also asked for the approval of purchasing a new island to plant with coconuts because of the "increasing poverty" of Ocean Island.[4] Probably through government sources, the people had been informed of the availability of Wakaya Island in Fiji, and they wanted to go and inspect it. The committee was asked whether a permanent or partial resettlement was contemplated. They replied that they did not want to give up their rights to Ocean Island but wanted to move back and forth at will. A little later they identified a government official as the "Adviser" whom they wanted to go with them (a man who apparently had an ability to influence Banabans); they recognized their inability to handle the difficult problem on their own. Fiji was cited as the locus because it was within the Empire and governed by the High Commissioner for the Western Pacific. (It was governed by the Governor of Fiji, but for many years the Governor and the High Commissioner were the same

3. See Maude 1953. Maude suggests that "Welfare Officer" was a revised title for the local District Officer.
4. Notes of Meeting of His Honour with the Banaban Committee, 23 May 1940, Personal Files of Rotan Tito.

man.) The Western Pacific High Commission was the next step up in the colonial bureaucracy, and Rotan Tito tells that the real reason behind this move was to be closer to the High Commissioner, to facilitate the presentation of Banaban grievances. The move was also to realize a decision made by the "old men" in Eliot's time.

In their letter, the Banabans noted how Ocean Island was being gnawed, and that the present generation was beginning to forget native crafts. "We feel sorry that our descendants will consequently be compelled to habituate European ways of living," and they wanted to revive native cultivation and fishing, "like our custom before." It was also noted that Wakaya was near trading stores, so that European goods were available when wanted.[5] I cannot judge the extent to which the letter was framed in a manner directed to appeal to European officials, but this combination of two things—remaining distinctly Banaban, and having the benefits of modern, Europeanized life—became a major theme in Banaban culture. The people probably did not realize the difficulty of simultaneously maximizing these two goals.

With the threat of invasion upon them, European government and company officials, with a few exceptions, departed from Ocean Island in 1942. One can speculate on the effects upon the Banabans of their abandonment by the establishments which had presented themselves as their protectors.[6] One of the officials who remained, the Gilbertese-speaking District Officer C. G. F. Cartwright, continued discussion of another island. By this time Rambi Island in Fiji, which was owned by Levers, was injected into the deliberations. An inspection by the Banabans was now impossible. Wakaya was pointed out as being smaller and less fertile than Rambi. Banaban sentiment, however, was apparently in favor of purchasing Wakaya, as an investment. Later, the Western Pacific High Commission purchased Rambi only,

---

5. Banaban Community to Secretary of State; Enclosure in Banaban Community to Resident Commissioner, 7 June 1940, Personal Files of Rotan Tito.

6. Some known events of interest occurred earlier. In 1940, the Banabans contributed £12,500 from their funds to British war funds. Dickes, Memorandum—Banaban Trust Funds, 6 June 1940, Personal Files of Rotan Tito. They reminded the British Government of this fact in their request for approval of purchasing an island in Fiji. Rev. George Eastman noted that in 1941 the Banabans contributed to other war funds and decided on a voluntary levy on church members to help the LMS in its time of difficulty, especially because of the London bombing. He reported a new Young People's Movement in the Ocean Island Church, "The Children's Guild of Banaba," which raised money to help the situation in the Gilberts. There had been letters from the Gilberts asking for assistance: the war interfered with the sale of copra, the major resource in the Gilberts. Rotan appears to have been instrumental in the Guild, perhaps an indication of a growing solidarity among younger people. See Eastman to Goodall, 9 October 1941, LMS.

with invested Banaban funds, since Wakaya was considered too unsuitable as a locus for resettlement.[7]

Japanese forces landed on Ocean Island in August. Eastman wrote that the Japanese stopped the work of the LMS teacher but allowed four Banabans limited church work. The Japanese activity thus may have reinforced Banaban ideas on autonomy. During this period Rotan may have consolidated his position of leadership. He argued to get more food for the people from the Japanese.[8] To his significant positions in the church and the descent system he had added that of being a leader in the lands controversy. Now he again showed courage.

Captured Japanese documents indicate that the occupiers tried to plug the existing system of native administration into their own. Each Banaban village was under a chief, and the chiefs were the old village kaubure. There were also chiefs of the BPC and government settlements. The Banaban magistrate became General Village Chief.

The village kaubure were supposed to function as links with the villagers. They were, for example, to be informed of births and deaths, which would then be reported to the Japanese administration. There were regulations on rationing, acquiring food and fish, and supplying the Japanese with items they wanted, and labor. The Banabans report that the Japanese commandeered whatever they wanted, and women were hidden in the middle of the island to remove them from the conquerors' path.[9]

In July 1943 a serious food shortage on Ocean Island developed, and the deportation of the Banabans began: to Kusaie in the Carolines, Tarawa in the Gilberts, and Nauru. By common agreement the group at Kusaie were the worst off, suffering greatly from malnutrition, and the people at Tarawa fared better, in part because they were sheltered by the Gilbertese there.

People left without many of their possessions, and other things were either commandeered, destroyed, or lost. Among these were treasured family genealogies and land records. The records of the Lands Commission disappeared.

One could go on at length about the privations of the wartime experience,

7. Maude 1946. Minutes of meeting of Banaban committee with G. J. Bridges and L. W. Cole, 20 February 1942; Announcements of C. G. F. Cartwright to Banaban Community, 11 March 1942, 15 March 1942; Personal Files of Rotan Tito.

8. Eastman, Report on mission to Gilbert & Ellice Islands Colony, 27 February–12 March 1944, LMS.

9. Dances were to be provided for certain occasions, and the new regulations included one forbidding the wiggling of the thighs in the dance. Japanese documents include a diagram of native administration. See also directives from Japanese commissioner to village chiefs, 1942–43, Maude Papers.

including hunger, forced labor, beating, bombing, and death. The events of the war are often recounted today. But perhaps one of the things of prime importance was that in spite of it all, the community survived. Some say "God looks after the Banabans," and their sheer survival was one testimony to this fact. People recall how they had to trick and steal to get food; breaking the rules was justifiable because of an unjust situation.

Detached as the Banabans were from the people, places, and structures which had provided a framework for their lives, their survival speaks of a vigorous adaptive flexibility. One of the factors contributing to that survival was probably that Christianity, like Banaban blood, was transportable.

The Australians took Ocean Island in October 1945. The government stated that because of the destruction there, it could not be occupied by a native community for two years. The officer whom the Banabans had selected before the war as their adviser went to Tarawa and collected the Banabans from their various places of exile (some were caught, or had been living, on other islands in the Gilberts). The people were asked whether they were willing to go to Rambi. After two years they would decide whether to stay there or return to Ocean Island. The government would foot the bill for transportation. On inquiring, they were told that the resettlement would not compromise their interests on Ocean Island. Land had not been forgotten. The community was not unanimous in its enthusiasm, but the proposal for the move was accepted, and on 15 December 1945 they arrived by ship at Rambi, about sixteen hundred miles from Ocean Island (see Maude 1946).

6

The Transformation of Banaban Culture

An almost microhistorical presentation has been unavoidable, as I indicated in the Introduction, because of the time factors involved here. There were fifteen years between the arrival of the first Protestant missionary on Ocean Island and the advent of both phosphate and colonial control. (For that matter, there were only about ten years between the last disastrous drought and the appearance of Christianity.) Between the beginning of the commercial-governmental complex and the first significant lands negotiation: nine years. From the solution of that dilemma to the beginning of the next, in which Banaban lands were resumed: twelve years. From the resumption to the introduction of the annuities-bonus system: six years. From then to the Second World War: four years.

We have seen, in the period under discussion, a number of things. Christianity was introduced and with it a greater degree of *religious group differentiation*. Christianity brought a set of implications deriving both from dogma and religious organization, set within a universalizing framework. Phosphate opened the island up more concretely, linking land and money, and dramatizing the ambiguities in the position of traditional leaders, some of whom found themselves in a native government which was created after the assertion of colonial control. A system of four centralized villages was established and reinforced by church and government administration. This system further distanced descent and locality-as-residence. The separateness of the Banabans as a people was also reinforced, and an association was formed between that separateness and the Protestant church. Concepts were forming and reforming around new factors in the social field.

Unhappiness with land arrangements and realization of the island's eventual destruction crystallized into a concerted opposition to the phosphate company and the government when the latter acted in the company's defense. Banaban land as a resource became closely identified with the Banaban people, and the creation of "common funds" gave them a corporateness which they had lacked before. Education, and ethnographic inquiries, simul-

149

taneously underscored and objectified the traditional structure, and increased sophistication in dealing with new structures.

A second set of land negotiations crystallized a developing progressive element and brought the situation to a point where the power which the people still had over their lands was lost. Some *political group differentiation occurred*, with strong economic relationships. Undersurface rights were asserted as not belonging to the landowner at all, and funds from them were to be used for the community as a whole rather than for the individual landowner. This was a stipulation which was to be resisted as contrary to the cultural meaning of land, as seen within the setting of an individualism fostered by religious and other kinds of change. A "political style" was formed that linked the Banabans' position, the nature of the Empire, and the universalizing ethical system of Christianity. Almost simultaneously, the Lands Commission codified the inheritance system, with the implications which this had both for kinship and for the objectification of traditional culture, and a revival of one of the aspects of traditional culture occurred.

This codification continued as a new annuity-landowners' bonus system was introduced, which raised the question of the relationship between the Banaban collectivity, Banaban identity, Ocean Island as a locality, and land as a locus of inalienable individual rights and community membership.

The rapidity of changing circumstances may have placed a constraint on an orderly social and cultural transformation, and a burden on individuals to work their own transformations. But as we look backward from the phosphate-focused summary just concluded, to other domains, and look forward to the rest of the Banaban historical experience up to the crisis of the war, certain tendencies or directions become evident. The text has been peppered with them; I will try to bring just a few points together here, with apologies for repetition.

The historical consequence of developments in the church and trouble in the Gilberts, with some of the more dramatic events of Banaban history, suggests both that the kinds of things described were not localized to Ocean Island, and that the church was a setting in which the movement toward an idea of *autonomy* and *solidarity* was crystallized. Even if local European missionaries did not enact the formal ideal of self-governing, self-financing, and self-propagating churches, enough became communicated, and enough was inherent in the nature of the kind of Protestantism taught, to have the effect noted.[1] The church was a domain more subject to local control and more responsive to local circumstances. The cooperative store, formed just before the war, and in competition with the BPC store, was an even more

1. This is of course conjectural, and in part a "reading back" from events cited.

direct manifestation, a tangible formulation to define concepts. It represented some measure of *economic group differentiation*, with strong political relationships.

This manifestation may have been sparked by the Nauruan cooperative, and it seems reasonable that there were lines of communication with Nauru other than through the church, so that the use of external models increased. The guides for action were no longer coming only from the inside.

As noted, Christianity presented an ethical system ideally binding on all men. In religious, political, and economic units (I make an educated guess) there was somewhat of a shift toward performance orientations, although the company may not have applied the same standards to all. Thus developed an increasing universalism, and universalism is notorious for its "spreading effect." It should be remarked, however, that a shift toward such standards does not just happen automatically. The shift may be represented in different degrees by different members of a community, and it may produce some strain between those who apply them and those who do not. And people can have the idea that the criteria for judging a person's activity in a role should be the adequacy of his performance, and they can have the idea that generalized standards of capability, rather than birth, should be used in selecting people for certain positions. They can have these ideas without being clear, in their own minds, on what those standards are—for example, on what counts as an instance of an adequate performance. It is a reasonable guess that a condition such as this was the case in the latter days on Ocean Island.[2]

At the same time as this process of increasing universalism was underway, with its source in European institutions, a two-price system was in force in the company store and a limited segregation was applied on Ocean Island. Thus there was a contradiction within the colonial structure. But the Banabans themselves had an interest in the maintenance of particularistic definitions because of the phosphate, and no doubt also for the gratification of being a landowner, *inter alia*. The contradiction from their point of view was partially resolved by their ultimately judging their interests as being legitimated within the framework of a generalized morality.

It is quite clear also that a valuation on a high level of consumption of European goods and services developed early and increased. Even in the

2. That universalism was not galloping is indicated in a recollection of Maude's, which relates to the identity of kinsmen which we discussed in chapter 2, and to which we will return in part 4. "I was constantly finding somebody's brother or cousin on duty [in the police force]," Maude recalls, "and wearing A's uniform, because A was sick or for some reason wanted to knock off for a week or so." Maude, personal communication 11 June 1969.

early phosphate days people enjoyed store food. At the same time as this value on modern consumption developed, there developed a concern for the conservation of Banaban identity, which was in part defined by a custom which had nothing to do with the consumption of European goods and services but did involve food.

The relationship among these elements is informed by the phenomenon of *increasing objectification,* postulated as a consequence of mission and government activity. The distance between the individual and the system progressively increased. An explicit notion of custom was written into official regulations and supported by some European activity. At the same time, given the assumption of many of the functions of the descent system by other institutions, individuals and families probably elaborated and systematized their own versions of that structure in different ways, particularly of those aspects erratically practiced or practiced not at all.[3] People reformulated ideas about their own positions in that structure.

This brings us right back to blood and mud. Blood and land as symbolizers of kinship in general continued right through. Assuming, however, that the major aspects of the traditional culture described in part 1 were in fact institutionalized in the traditional society, the descent-ritual circulation-locality complex was probably being pushed into a differentiated symbolic system. This system, as indicated earlier, had an uncertain relationship to the present and to the individual's social personality. (Recall that some people had moved from their defining spaces.) Through the phosphate days the system, in a refined form, was partially historicized. People could say: "This is what it was like in the days of our ancestors." But there was still a skirting of the issue of what it had to do with the present. It undoubtedly served identity functions, and operated as a set of subjective status categories. And the meanings from that system must have constituted a continuing input to the whole phosphate issue. The phosphate issue had resonances from the center of traditional Banaban culture.

One likely feature of the entering of the complex into a more differentiated symbolic system, a feature related to the redefinition of localities on the island, was the transformation of hamlets into categories with more of a conceptual and less of a concrete aspect than before. The implications of this will be discussed in chapter 14.

---

3. As Rotan Tito observed to me, after the phosphate enterprise began, company ships were not handled by the "right to greet visiting vessels," and the main harbor was at Uma, not the traditional center at Tabwewa. Maude observed in 1932 that the full-fledged feasting of a visitor (*te kairuwa*) had last been performed in the first decade of the century. It may be noted here again that, similar to the situation in the Northern Gilberts (see Lambert 1963), the ramification process in descent units was probably interfered with by village consolidation, enforced peace, and legal codification.

At the same time as constructs of Banaban custom were being elaborated, constructs of a modernized society were being elaborated, with the dimensions specified by the tendencies discussed earlier. Here we return to the notion of external models. These external models (of, for example, the Nauruans and the British) not only informed the constructs of a modernized society. As the traditional symbolic forms which set out the parameters of social action became less closely related to social action and aspirations in their specifics, the external models may have moved in, as it were, to occupy that more direct relationship. As one set of constructs became more highly generalized, another set of constructs developed within the culture. By definition, the less generalized set was interpreted in the light of the more generalized set, but their exact relation was problematic.

There was obviously some institutionalization of the new constructs of a modernized society, as political, religious, and economic developments indicated. But given the nature of the colonial system, these constructs could not be fully institutionalized. In the resettled situation there was more of an opportunity to build a social structure, with consequences which will be set out.

As further background to that discussion, it is clear that a critical factor to elucidate is the way in which the community was conceptualized as a community. Had the "modern revolution" in Dumont's sense (1961, pp. 36–38) occurred? Had the idea of a nation developed (see Dumont 1964*a*), with a territorial focus and with individuals as its basic constituents?

The answer may be more in the negative than the positive direction, although the material is ambiguous. The differentiation between individual-as-individual and individual-as-landowner may have been incomplete. The functions of land as a medium of symbolic exchange had become elaborated. Not only did land function to order the relationships among differentiated elements within the traditional sector of the system, but it also functioned to order the interrelationship of that sector with the "modern" sector.

Perhaps the situation can be clarified by a comparison with Schneider's discussion of nationality, religion, and kinship in American culture, an expansion of some points made in *American Kinship* (1968).

In American Culture, one is "An American" either by birth or through a process which is called, appropriately enough, "naturalization." In precisely the same terms as kinship, there are the same two "kinds of citizens," those by birth and those by law. And indeed it would not be hard to show that the same three categories are derived from these two elements as three categories of kinsmen are derived from those elements. There is the person who is by birth an American but who has taken the citizenship of another country; there is the person who is American by naturalization but not by birth; and there is the person who by both birth and law is American.
What is the role of a national? To love his country, his father- or mother-

land. Loyalty and support for his nation and all those who belong to it. Patriotism in the extreme of "My Country Right or Wrong" is one statement of it. But even where it does not take that particular form, loyalty to and love for one's country is the most generalized expression of diffuse, enduring solidarity [Schneider 1969a, pp. 120–21.]

Drawing on both current definitions and the 1937 annuity rules cited above, we observe: One was a Banaban either by birth or through adoption, which entailed the transfer (assured or actual) of Ocean Island land. There was the person who was by birth a Banaban but with a special status if he had land rights on other islands. There was the person who was a Banaban through adoption but not by birth, also with a special status if significant land rights were held elsewhere. The special status had to do with place of residence. Then there was the person who by both birth and residence was a Banaban (it is inconceivable to have Banaban blood and not Banaban land). Thus the paradigm follows fairly closely, with the important quali- fication that "naturalization" in the societal system was only possible as a consequence of adoption in the kinship system, and adoption in the kinship system to have this implication was only possible through the transfer of land.

As for generalized expressions of enduring, diffuse solidarity, we have some documentary indications, but the data is too incomplete. The major contexts in which such a solidarity would have been called for involved, again, land. As some people contemplated the future, however, such a notion probably crystallized (and the war gave them a heritage of common suffering). It may have been part of the conception of the Protestants. This brings us to religion and the following discussion by Schneider:

> With Christianity [in contrast with Judaism], as is well known, the criterion for membership shifted from birth to volition. That is, in the most general sense, one is a Christian by an act of faith and not an act of birth, and correspondingly conversion to The Faith becomes a very different matter and a real possibility since it takes only an act of will to effect.
> But this view leaves out two very important facts. Being a Jew is not simply being born a Jew. There is a code for conduct which is linked to the fact of birth. What is true is that it is the act of birth which has the quality of the defining feature, and so the other element tends to be easily overlooked. And it is here that the parallel between kinship and religion in Judaism is quite clear, for in both there are those two features, relation- ship as substance and relationship as code for conduct; the substance element is bio-genetic, the code for conduct is one of diffuse, enduring solidarity.
> Although the shift from Judaism to Christianity seems to drop the con- dition of substance as the defining feature and rest it entirely on the commit- ment to code for conduct, this is not really so. Certainly there is a shift away from the particularistic, bio-genetic, criterion of substance as the defining

features. But the shift entails a re-alignment so that commitment to the code for conduct becomes paramount as the defining feature, and the sub-stantive element is re-defined from a material to a spiritual form. It is the triumph of the spirit over matter that is at issue here. Closely linked to this is the prominent place given to love as a symbol, to the spiritual aspects of love, and to the spiritual aspects of creation as against its rather more narrowly material or bio-genetic aspects in Judaism. [Schneider 1969*a*, pp. 122–23.]

Among the Banabans, needless to say, Christianity did not differentiate out of Judaism. It was imported. But the general line of argument holds. Schneider is making the point that in America (at least), "the domain of religion may well be structured in the same terms as kinship and nationality," in terms of substance and code.

In the Banaban situation, the contrast between identity and code is symbolized at one level by the contrast between blood and land. Yet, at least in the contemporary culture, to repeat what was stated in chapter 2, the opposition between blood and land, both symbolizing unity, can be overcome by a contrast with nurturance and residence, symbolizing code. Nurturance and residence are not things but continuing acts; they are more literally code-like. And the meanings of blood may be inclusive of the meanings of both land and nurturance, and residence, as the meanings of land may be inclusive of the meanings of nurturance and residence. Land again is the mediating link. Out of this complex the revised descent system, the new village form, Banaban identity, and a plan for a new island were differentiated; into it Christianity was injected.

If the correct transformations are made given these symbolic differences, Schneider's paradigm can be applied to the Banaban case. Thus we are right back to one of our early analytic points: blood and mud, identity and code, and the ways they are distributed against one another.

PART III

Testing Out
on Rambi Island

7

Arrival, and the Integral Model Explored

INTRODUCTION

I concluded part 2 with the statement that we had returned to one of our early analytic points. Where do we go from here? The basic problem is really where did the *Banabans* go from there?

With the traditional Banaban situation we were dealing with a structure that is relatively undifferentiated—in comparison with many other traditional Oceanic cultures, and certainly in comparison with what the Banabans were to become.

I described events and processes which separated aspects of the system which had been more fused together. Out of the kinship-descent matrix more positively differentiated domains emerged. Land and blood were the symbols keeping the different domains in some kind of interrelationship, and with the exception of the new village, the different domains as pure domains, in Schneider's sense, were similarly structured. If I understand him correctly, Schneider contrasts the pure domain, in which one is concerned with the symbol or symbols which provide distinctive features, with the conglomerate domain, in which nondistinctive features occur (which may be, or presumably are, distinctive features from other domains, for example, age in kinship).

To coin a phrase, Man does not live by pure domains alone. Man conglomerates. And one of the problems of the Banaban people was to set boundaries of the pure domains and establish the mode of conglomeration.

The problem of the conglomeration of domains at the cultural level is parallel to the problem of the differentiation and integration of structures at the social level—the problem of who should do what in which capacity, and how the whole thing fits together, if at all. As in the Banaban case, where a system of priorities has not been institutionalized, the problem assumes a greater magnitude: the relationship, for example, between the solidarity of co-nationals and the solidarity of kinsmen.

This was one of the problems of the Banabans, poised on the shores of Rambi Island. Both the cultural and the social problem may be encapsulated under the terms *differentiation-integration*. Differentiation-integration is an analytic problem for any cultural and social system. The difference for the Banabans (although certainly not for them alone) was that this was, and is, an urgent real problem with which real people had to contend in real circumstances—not *tabula rasa* but in the context of the historical process delineated in part 2, and in the context of the natural and social constraints of the situation.[1]

The reader is referred back to our discussion of the testing out process in the Introduction. We have identified this process as the major means through which the Banabans are coping with their situation on Rambi, thus manifesting the dialectic between conceptual and social form. There were many fragments in Banaban culture waiting to be articulated. This condition, which was related to both the plugging of aspects of Banaban society into the Ocean Island structure, and the rapidly changing milieu, may have put great pressures on individuals to try and construct their own syntheses of what had happened to them, what was happening to them, and what might happen to them. The modern world had taken the people on a roller coaster ride for which the tracks and the shape of the cars were not of their own making, although they could choose to look in one direction or another. The roller coaster had now deposited them on a new island.

IDENTITY AND LOCALITY: THE INTEGRAL MODEL

When the people of Ocean Island arrived on Rambi, they found themselves in an environment radically different from that of their homeland. Rambi is nine times as large, six times as high, and five times as wet as Ocean Island. Ocean Island is 160 miles from Nauru to the west and 240 miles from Tarawa to the northeast. Rambi is within sight of the eastern coast of Vanua Levu, Fiji's "second" island. An hour's trip on a slow launch takes one to the villages along Buca Bay and the road to the government headquarters town of Savusavu. The island of Taveuni is three hours away, and from both there and Savusavu planes fly to the colony capital at Suva.

Although Fiji is politically and commercially more highly developed than the Gilberts, Ocean Island since the discovery of phosphate had been a much more cosmopolitan place than Rambi. For the Banabans, the change from the status of a special community of landholders, workers, and

1. See Parsons 1964, 1965, 1966; Eisenstadt 1964; Bellah 1964, 1965.

small-scale market producers, on an island thriving with industrial activity, to the status of copra cutters and gardeners in the bush was a comedown. The outlook now especially of those old enough to remember Ocean Island is that of the large landowner living in exile whose estates have been nationalized.

Banaban life on Ocean Island had been intimately connected with administrative, commercial, and religious institutions which were parts of larger networks of control. This was to become the case in Fiji also. But the war and the move essentially *unplugged* the substructures of the community from those institutions. The Banabans probably anticipated the unplugging in the context of the autonomy values developed earlier. Their experience was not far different, however, from that of peoples newly decolonized, in that there was no single agreed-upon plan of organization to implement the generalized conceptions. Nor was there an institution, other than the community as a whole, with a clear legitimacy to conduct that implementation.

One of the more immediate problems was whether to stay on Rambi at all. Even when the decision was made to stay, however, the larger problem remained unsolved, in the sense of a generalized consensus. The larger problem may be stated very simply as the relationship between Ocean Island and Rambi, or the relationship between the Banaban people as a people and these two localities. At the beginning, would they stay or not? Would some stay but the majority return to Ocean Island, to await the exhaustion of the phosphate? Would the people return and Rambi be leased out to others, and the Banabans resume occupation later? With the decision to stay, was Rạmbi "figure" and Ocean Island "ground," or vice versa? To what extent would attempts be made to take the models of the way certain things were on Ocean Island (lands subdivision, for example) and institute them on Rambi?

"Territorial consciousness," (Dumont 1964*a*) was no doubt increased by the distance from Ocean Island. It could be contemplated as a whole object, and in such contemplation, as Dumont (1969) points out, certain features are ignored and other features begin to be welded together into a more consistent picture. As the Rambi generation grew up, there was little opportunity for direct reality-testing of the images of Ocean Island which were under construction.

"Ocean Island," however, did not become only a historical picture. People kept in touch with developments there. A Banaban representative went to look after their interests vis-à-vis the phosphate company, and there were other sources of information. Comparing Ocean Island and Rambi became a general activity. Rambi's size, water resources, agricultural potential, and proximity to the bright lights were seen as positive attributes. But Ocean

Island had more activity, more immediate European riches, and it was home. It was also where the phosphate was. And from the first year, uncertainty about the manner of the sale of remaining phosphate lands, uncertainty about the manner of ownership of Rambi, uncertainty about what ownership was, complicated the picture. *Uncertainty* was the key word.

The government's intention was clear: the Banabans should stay on Rambi. There are Banabans and others who do not look upon that intention as arising from an interest in the community's social future. They see it rather as arising from a desire to have the Banaban thorn removed from the administrative and commercial side. With the Banabans more than a thousand miles away, the peaceful exploitation of phosphate would be enhanced. In any case, whatever the motives, government actions were oriented to committing the Banabans to Rambi as their homeland (see Maude 1946).

Two very specific points must be made before we see how the Banabans coped with this extremely complex situation. The first is the presence of an officer who eventually became known as "Banaban Adviser," and had some of the powers of District Officers elsewhere. The first Adviser was the man selected by the Banabans before the war.

The second point concerns the internal complexity of the population on Rambi. When the Banabans arrived, there were some Fijian and Solomon Island laborers there associated with the old copra operation, but with a few exceptions they were soon to leave. The real problem involved the composition of the migrant group itself. Population statistics are presented in table 1 (adapted from Maude 1946).

TABLE 1
POPULATION OF THE RESETTLEMENT GROUP

	Banabans	Gilbertese	Total
Men	185	152	337
Women	200	97	297
Children	318	51	369
Total	703	300	1003

The Gilbertese present were a mixed group from several points of view. Some were married to Banabans, others were friends from Ocean Island or friends made during the war. They were from different islands in the Gilberts, and many had kinship connections with one another. Some also were related to Banabans through Gilbertese ancestors of Banabans.[2]

---

2. A Banaban may recognize relatives on his "Gilbertese side" if he has a Gilbertese ancestor. Some part-Banaban, part-Gilbertese families who had been living in the Gilberts have joined the Rambi community at various times.

There had been, of course, many Gilbertese laborers on Ocean Island—they actually outnumbered the Banabans. But their position generally created no particular problem of status which the Banabans had to solve. On Rambi the situation was radically different. On Rambi the Gilbertese were in a limited sense in the same new boat as the Banabans, and the number of Gilbertese men was only slightly smaller than the number of Banaban men. The statistical order of magnitude of the problem was to diminish over time, but the cultural order of magnitude was not. The Banaban (Settlement) Ordinance (no. 28, 1945) defines the *Banaban Community* as "the natives hitherto living on Ocean Island and such other persons as may now or hereafter be accepted as members of the Banaban community in accordance with Banaban custom." It was not entirely clear, however, what Banaban custom was applied to such a circumstance. In 1949, the Banaban Adviser was concerned over the implications of the definition as it regarded lands, rate paying, and the holding of local offices. He may have been reflecting a community concern at that time. A 1957 ordinance amends the above definition to include "any member of an aboriginal race indigenous to Micronesia and Polynesia who is ordinarily resident on Rambi Island." The Micronesia-Polynesia clause is a genuine reflection of the composition of the population, and it was probably also designed to avoid certain administrative complications which would have arisen from the inclusion of Fijians. A 1965 ordinance, to which the Banabans assented, defines *member of the Banaban Community* as "a descendant of the original indigenous inhabitants of Ocean Island, of the whole or of the half blood, illegitimate or legitimate, or a person who is accepted as a member of the Banaban community in accordance with Banaban customs."[3]

I will return to the implications of the presence of Gilbertese. I merely want to note here that a new problem had to be handled, and that problem was one of the definition of the community itself. Since many of these people were married to Banabans, there was no doubt that they were part of the community in an analytic sense. The issue was their being or not being part of the subjective community, and of their rights in specific matters. The manner in which this was a problem relates to the differentiation of kinship from nationality, or of two kinds of nationality: an Ocean Island nationality, and a Rambi nationality.

The initial attempt at a solution of the Rambi organizational problem, as I interpret it, was an integral model. Some of the political and economic lines were designed by the Adviser, with inputs from other governmental

3. Banaban (Settlement) (Amendment) Ordinance, 1957 (no. 15, 1957); Banaban Lands Ordinance, 1965 (no. 31, 1965).

sources, and Rotan was also a critical figure at this time. The religious aspect, which may have developed slightly later (although its origins are old), very much involved Rotan and the adherents of the LMS. By "the integral model," I mean a general idea that the Rambi community was to be organized into a single system of which the Island Council was the political instrument, the Banaban Community (or Cooperative) Store the economic instrument, and the Protestant church the religious instrument.

These organizations were to be instruments of the Banaban community as a community. This was a testing out of a generalized notion of solidarity. The integral model was one from a range of possibilities suggested by the encounter between Banaban concepts (in the context of a history of partial differentiation) and the problem of building a society on Rambi. The notion was of course being tested out in a field positively different from Ocean Island. One of the many important differences was that on Rambi more areas of life *could* be regulated by the people themselves. The pattern of work activity is an example. There was no phosphate company setting hours and wages, although on Rambi there were obviously many external constraints (for example, the copra market and the mode of copra marketing).

The organizations which were the units of the integral model were intimately tied in an overlap of top personnel, and the question of their differentiation was the question about which much of succeeding Banaban history focused. For the integral model ultimately failed. The process of differentiation and creative elaboration which allowed this model to originate in the first instance could not be contained, and other things were being tested out too. The model presupposed the primacy of the value of group solidarity. It presupposed that people would subordinate their other commitments, that they would violate the option maximizing principle. They did not.

Soon after arrival, a meeting of heads of families was held, which agreed to the formation of an island council. The heads of families were to elect annually a chairman and seven councillors (Maude 1946). Three councillors would be appointed by the chairman, in consultation with the Adviser. The system became effective after the government passed the Settlement Ordinance; until that time, members of the old native government from Ocean Island were asked to act on a temporary basis. Rotan was unanimously elected chairman of the new council. There was also to be a deputy chairman. In the Adviser's conception, the appointed councillors were to be more conservative elders. It was already in the wind that the council might take certain actions which needed a brake.

The original plan might have been almost a ministerial one; the chief of police was a member and had the policemen under him. A chief of elected councillors was responsible for schools and medicine. The island magistrate was a member, and thus the differentiation between the political and legal systems was incomplete.

The proposed island court, to adjudicate under local regulations, could not function until the Fiji Government took legitimizing action. The plan was for the magistrate to preside over a court consisting of two appointed and four elected councillors, with the island Scribe (also a member of the council) and the chief of police acting in some capacity.

According to Maude (1946), probably writing from the Adviser's reports, the people wanted the Banaban Cooperative to handle commercial affairs. The cooperative was ultimately responsible to general meetings of family elders, and all Banaban families belonged. The co-op manager was elected by the elders. Rotan was elected to this post also. On his request, the co-op's accountant became a nominated councillor and deputy council chairman. The co-op was organized with a manager, deputy manager, and accountant, and overseers of the three major plantation areas which had been worked by Levers. The overseers were responsible for the central driers that had been left, and a staff of copra cutters, planters, and cleaners.

During the meeting at which this entire format was laid before the people and approved by them, a Banaban elder asked what constituted family groups, the heads of which were to serve as electors. The Adviser replied that he knew that there was a complex kinship system involving marriage, locality, and historical associations, but that here economic considerations should be paramount: those who ate over one fire constituted a family. The proposal was approved, and the Banabans probably considered that it was being left up to them to decide the actual composition of the relevant units.

The society was thus formally constituted as an association of families linked by Banaban identity, which elected a council and the management of a cooperative society. The religious picture will be discussed later. Partially differentiated political, economic, religious, and kinship systems were placed into interrelationship with one another.

At the meeting, which might almost be called the Banaban Constitutional Convention, the Adviser asked if the people would agree then to permanent settlement on Rambi. The people replied that they wanted to await the next and final lands agreement with the BPC, the payment of back annuities, and the solution of other financial matters.

8

Two Crucial Decisions

THE DECISION TO REMAIN

There was no smooth, easy transition to a local government operating with a European official at its side. The aftereffects of the war may have been involved here, both biologically (there was much sickness) and psychologically; I am unfortunately not competent to judge these aspects. Physical distance may have increased conceptual distance from the system; the war was the first time that the community, although divided, had been away from Ocean Island en masse. Circumventing or secretly breaking Japanese rules could have developed a more manipulatory attitude toward outside authority in general. The humiliation of the British could have had implications too.

The first phosphate payments that came on Rambi appeared to be lower than they had been previously because of deductions for currency exchange; this was one cause for dissatisfaction. For a few years there were reported incidents of lawlessness, from a people who before the war and after the initial period on Rambi had a reputation for being law-abiding.

What was interpreted as antiadministration behavior began to focus on the Adviser. The Adviser's demeanor offended many Banabans, and he may have expected too much too fast. A group of prominent Banabans petitioned for his removal. In connection with this the District Commissioner visited Rambi and informed the people that a new Adviser had been appointed, a man who had been a schoolmaster on Tarawa. It is worthy of note that a number of officials in Fiji had worked in the Gilberts, and over the years the Banabans used these contacts, which probably did not enhance the notion of a universalistically oriented bureaucracy—not that that notion would have been correct everywhere.[1]

1. See Maude 1946. Kennedy to Macdonald, 8 June 1946, RIC. Minutes of meeting at Rabi Island to meet some of the elders at their request, with District Commissioner, Northern, 13 June 1946, Holland Papers (in H. E. Maude collection, Canberra, Aus-

The District Commissioner raised the question of whether the people wanted to stay on Rambi or not. Their response demonstrated uncertainty about the ownership of Ocean Island and Rambi, and the position of Banaban funds.

Two events of paramount importance occurred in 1947: the decision of the Banabans to stay, and a putatively final lands transfer with the BPC.

The decision to stay was connected with the approval of a document, the Statement of Government Intentions regarding the Banabans on Rambi, known in Gilbertese as the agreement, or covenant. The Statement presupposed that a majority of Banabans wished to make Rambi their home. On 10 and 11 May, a secret ballot referendum was held on Rambi, while the Resident Commissioner of the Gilbert and Ellice Islands Colony (acting for the High Commissioner for the Western Pacific) and the Acting Assistant Colonial Secretary, acting for the Governor of Fiji, were present. Their joint presence reflects the fact that the Banabans were at that time still partially under the jurisdiction of the Western Pacific High Commission (full transfer to Fiji was effected in 1949).

In April 1947 there had been a new proposal from the BPC, signed by a number of prominent Banabans "for the Banaban landowners of Ocean Island." But further meetings were held in August on this subject. It appears, then, that there was *(a)* acceptance of the lands proposal, *(b)* acceptance of the Statement and a ballot on staying on Rambi, and *(c)* further discussions of the lands proposal.

The sequence is important since observers agree that the lands settlement was a precondition for the Banabans' making a decision to remain. The lands proposal will be considered in the next section.[2]

The Statement assured that acceptance of Rambi would not affect rights to Ocean Island lands, and that the titles to lands no longer used would revert to the Banaban owners. The government realized that the protection of these rights was critical to the Banabans. Except for a small government reserve, the ownership of Rambi would be vested in the council on behalf of the Banaban Community resident on Rambi. Note that residence was a significant factor in the definition. The council would handle matters of land tenure and inheritance.

---

tralia). Kennedy, Handing over statement, Maj. D. G. Kennedy, D.S.O., handing over to Maj. F. G. L. Holland, O.B.E., G.M., 13 August 1946, RIC.

2. On one copy of the Statement of Intentions (RIC), the date of the signatures is given as 12 March 1947. I assume this was an error; it was probably May rather than March, especially because the voting took place on May 10–11. There is the possibility, however, that I am in error. Statement of government intentions . . . , 12 May 1947, Holland Papers. Also Gilbertese version, RIC.

The Banaban Royalty Trust Fund and the Provident Fund were to be amalgamated into a single fund, the Banaban Fund, the proceeds of which were to be used for the benefit of the Banabans on Rambi—except for the annuity, the receipt of which was *not* contingent upon such residence.

Management of Banaban funds was placed in the hands of the Banaban Funds Trust Board, with the Adviser as chairman and not more than five members of the council elected from it as members. The board, first elected in 1948, was to deal with annuities and other financial matters relating to Banaban funds and to submit yearly accounts and statements of estimated expenditures for the following year to the Governor or his designate for approval. (In practice this designate was the Colonial Secretary, but in 1959, legislation replaced him with the Financial Secretary—the Banabans were becoming more integrated into the Fiji administrative system.)[3] The accounts and estimates would be submitted first to the council for approval and then forwarded to the government by the Banaban Adviser. The government maintained a veto power over expenditure: an important issue, as we will see. Annuities would follow the 1937 lines unless the board recommended a change and the Governor approved.

The board was to deal with the Landholders' Fund, investing its capital, and the rights of landholders in the fund were to be the same as those over lands, according to Banaban custom. Any decisions on that fund had to be approved by the Governor. The land-equals-money equation, as part of a codified Banaban custom, was thus reasserted.

The Statement noted the Banaban request that capital could be withdrawn from the fund for permanent improvements to Rambi land, with the Governor's consent. There was, in fact, a general wish by the Banabans to get money into the individual's hands, expressed in a demand that the capital and the interest of the fund be divided among the owners. This was regarded as contrary to custom and allocated money from the undersurface was in general considered as communal property by the government. The government, again, put itself in the position of maintaining custom when people wanted to change it. Undoubtedly, this was not the only element; officials were afraid that the people would fritter the money away.

There was, however, a curious logical position. The Banabans apparently pointed out that the provision based on the land-equals-money equation might have been viable on Ocean Island, since keeping funds in the bank

3. Banaban (Rabi Island Council) (Amendment) Regulations, 1959 (Legal Notice no. 125, 1959).

was in part directed to making sure that the people would have a source of support after the exhaustion of the phosphate. Now that they owned a new island, they would devise land there according to Banaban custom, and so the money should be subdivided, because there was a physical replacement for Banaban lands. Many still considered a much smaller amount from the royalty desirable for Rambi use, but others noted that Rambi's needs could be handled by taxation. The government held the line. It also held the line on the questions of distributing most of the money to individuals.

The government did, however, accept the request for withdrawal for permanent improvements, with approval by the Governor. Legislation for this came into effect in 1949; in 1958 it was legislated that the board could pay out money for purposes approved by the council and confirmed by the Adviser.[4]

The Statement affirmed that the Banabans on Rambi were subject to the laws of Fiji, including those on taxation, and were eligible for normal government services. The Banaban Adviser was to be affirmed as an officer of the Fiji Government, appointed to advise the people on matters of social and economic advancement. He would be paid from Banaban funds, and his tenure could be varied by the Governor.

The proposals may have been more liberal than had been expected, and arguments referred to above that were directed to receiving more control of funds proceeded.

But the Statement *was* signed, by a number of prominent Banaban men, including councillors, as representatives of the Banabans. Almost all of those over eighteen voted by secret ballot on whether to make Rambi their homeland or not; 85 percent said yes, and 15 percent no. Even though it was recognized by some in government that further demands would be made in the future, and the actual work of building had not progressed as quickly as would have been desirable, the vote may be interpreted as a vote of confidence in the resettlement scheme.

I noted above that the 1946 meeting on organization was perhaps a Banaban Constitutional Convention. One might now want to rephrase it as a compact. The Statement of Intentions became a kind of constitution. That is why I have dwelt upon it at length. The Statement in its entirety was not, however, enacted into law, although some of its provisions were to find their way into law. Some of its provisions were also to find their way into controversy. Each such statement or concession becomes the focal point for

4. Banaban Funds Ordinance, 1949 (cap. 111, 1956 series); Banaban Funds (Amendment) Ordinance, 1958 (no. 34, 1958).

new clarifications and new demands, and they are of the type predictable from the tendencies or directions formulated in part 2.

THE 1947 LANDS SETTLEMENT

In 1947, the BPC proposed to acquire the remaining phosphate lands on Ocean Island.[5] The lands were in two groups with a compensation for surface rights of £A200 per acre in the first group and £A65 per acre in the second group. New land leases were also to be written, and the royalty would go up to 1s. 3d. per ton. After the lands were worked out, they would revert to their owners.

The terms were more generous than those proposed in 1940 and included a new feature: the lands would not be surveyed in detail, but would be "located approximately" with the help of a party of Banaban landowners who would travel to Ocean Island. As a reward for complying with the speedy process the BPC would present a gift of £7500 for the landowners to dispose of as they saw fit. Later, according to the Adviser, the council on his advice decided to distribute it in proportion to the individual's acreage. Although the council had a role here and was also involved in completing the lists of owners, areas, and values, the original meeting to consider the settlement was with Banaban landowners. The settlement was approved and signed by both councillors and some other prominent figures "for the Banaban landowners of Ocean Island."

The settlement was apparently approved with an ease which contrasted radically with previous instances. The gift, improvement in the terms, the promised trip, and the reversion clause were probably part of the story. Another element may well have been that the focus of action for the righting of wrongs was shifting to the government (see below), and people did want to see one thing settled in a manner which materially embodied their conception of themselves as Banaban landowners who lived, however, on Rambi Island.

The acceptance of the proposal for "approximate location" may be significant as representing a greater generalization in the concept of land. As a locus of rights and value it did not change. But in order to fulfill that function, the precise contours of lands did not need to be established. The

5. Sources for this section include: Memorandum of agreement . . . , between Banaban landowners and the BPC, 10 April 1947; Notes of meetings with Banaban landowners, 5–7 August 1947, and with members of Rabi Island Council and the Banaban Committee, 8–9 and 16 August 1947, signed by H. B. Maynard, representative, BPC, 11–13 August 1947; Handing over statement of F. G. L. Holland, Banaban Adviser, Rambi, 31 January 1949; Holland Papers.

very fact of the absence from Ocean Island should have had something to do with this. The lands were not there to be seen.

Almost four hundred Banabans made the voyage back to Ocean Island—most of the adult community. Tales are now told of the delights of Ocean Island that the voyagers experienced on that trip, especially the lower prices for European goods. But all returned to Rambi, and thus the way of life which could be envisioned on Ocean Island did not have a dramatic pull.

The boundary marking *(te tautia)* is an important chronological marker to the people. It stands after the arrival on Rambi as a point of reference. In sorting out the events of the early period, people say that things happened before, during, or after the boundary marking. Although the trip back to Ocean Island did not induce people to stay there, it did serve to recharge the Banaban-ness of the Banabans in several ways. There was, for example, a section of one hamlet in Buakonikai known as a special place. Ancestral skulls were located there, and disaster befell outsiders who conducted certain kinds of activities on the site. Many Banabans tell of how during the boundary marking, some members of the hamlet anointed the skulls with oil and left offerings of cigarettes.

A young man of Uma village referred to another incident, which was more generally known. Nei Tituabine is a spirit recognized as, among other things, exercising some protection over Ocean Island. She is particularly noted for meting out justice to Gilbertese who do things wrong according to Banaban custom; I have heard her jokingly called a "policeman." This is part of the "Banaba is shut" message, and concepts from the traditional religion were adapted to relate to the new identity position of the people.

Some still see Nei Tituabine in dreams, where she appears as an old woman carrying a basket, signaling death. (She is the familiar of a particular hamlet in Uma.)

The young man's story was that when the people returned to Ocean Island, Nei Tituabine appeared to members of that hamlet and said: "So you Banabans are not all dead. I have been looking for you." She came back with the people on their ship. After the return, the health of the community improved; before, there had been many deaths. The improvement was Nei Tituabine's work. Ocean Island had come to Rambi.

Not everyone made the trip; some relied on their kin to specify their lands, and disputes arose from this practice. Kawate Maibintebure, a renowned local composer, composed a song about the event, part of which is as follows:

We are going,
We are going,
We are going,
The time has come.

The boundary marking on Banaba;
Where is my land?
This is my land.
My grandparent says
This is my land
But I don't know.
I am a child,
And have just been born.

We are going,
We are going,
We are going,
The time has come.

The boundary marking on Banaba;
Where is the boundary?
This is the boundary.
I really don't know
The boundary
But I hear that
Miss What's-her-name and Mr. So-and-so
Are next to me.

This is a sardonic comment on how people, especially younger people, had to rely on their elder kin for information about land, and that the trustworthiness of their information was open to question.

The time had come in more ways than one. It was after the return from the boundary marking that people really began to disperse from the tent settlement at Nuka (which is often likened to a wartime encampment), and form the villages which were to become named for those on Ocean Island.

9

The Integral Model Examined: The Banaban Community Store

In the largest context, we may view the social system of Ocean Island as having been differentiated for the production and export of phosphate. The Banabans' place within that social system was a complex one which has been explored in earlier chapters. The Banabans participated in institutions of the modern world, but they neither exercised significant control over those institutions nor, with the exception of the cooperative and the church, developed the complex of parallel institutions found in other, larger colonial societies. And the Banabans had confronted new ways of life which they saw before them more as individuals than as a community.

On Rambi the question of the nature of the community as a community became a more immediate one. There was more of an opportunity for parallel or self-consciously nonparallel institutions to develop. The larger context, however, was different. From the point of view of the Fiji system, islands such as Rambi were differentiated for the purposes of copra production. The Banabans were thus objectively faced with a double problem: the place of Rambi within the Fiji system, and the nature of differentiation within Banaban society. Given the nature of internal differentiation, we will have to refer back and forth between activities and concepts involving different domains. In this chapter we will focus briefly on some aspects of the cooperative organization, which was uniquely suited for the immediate and crucial role it was to play in the development of Banaban society on Rambi Island.

The differentiation problem may be illustrated by a controversy which occurred early and was apparently far from trivial. There were some cattle on Rambi, and the government regarded them as community property since the island was bought with community funds. When slaughter was approved, the Adviser's plan was for the meat to be sold by the co-op; the proceeds would be kept in a separate account and then deposited for the purchase of studs. In 1946 the deposit was not made. (Some Banabans considered themselves free to kill wild cattle at will in the bush. Their view, at least as more recently expressed, was that because the cattle were community property, individual members of the community were free to do what they wanted with them.)

By 1949 the "cattle debt" had been paid by the co-op, but there was more slaughtering, and the council apparently told the co-op that it could keep the proceeds. The council indicated to the Adviser (then the second one) that all the Banabans belonged to the co-op, and the council was the representative body of the Banabans, so there was really no difference between the council and the co-op. The Adviser tried to explain that the council was a political structure and the co-op an economic structure, but the councillors thought the matter academic. The same reasoning was applied when the council did not consider it necessary for the co-op to repay an earlier loan from community funds.[1]

It will be recalled that the co-op was formed shortly before the war on Ocean Island as a Banaban institution in competition with the BPC. On Rambi it initially may have had the legitimacy of being a Banaban institution not tied in with colonial structures. It was associated with Ocean Island but not with any of its sublocalities. The co-op on Ocean Island, according to Maude, was a vehicle for some of the more modern elements in the community. On Rambi it attracted some people who had had training on Ocean Island, and along with the small island office, it provided training for some in modern economic methods. Indeed, the co-op later fed personnel into the council: many of the younger people who were elected to the council fourteen years later had been schooled in the cooperative society.

By this time the co-op and other institutions were probably reflecting a growing orientation toward performance standards, although, as was explained earlier, the Ocean Island colonial setting appears to have been structured so that the development of universalism was blunted. And much of the performance-oriented activity on Ocean Island was involved with institutions which pointed away from, rather than in toward, the local community. On Rambi the situation had a potentiality for change, since there was a larger area of action within which performance standards could be internally applied, and the government was not the same local particularistic presence. Given the nature of both phosphate and the copra economy, however, internally oriented and externally oriented activity are difficult to disentangle.

The problem of lack of clarity about what counted as an instance of an adequate performance may have been somewhat ameliorated by giving positions of responsibility to people who had worked for the government or

---

1. See Kennedy to Macdonald, 8 June 1946, RIC; Kennedy, Handing over statement; Holland, Handing over statement.

the company on Ocean Island. There was at least an external judgment of adequacy of some kind. Rotan occupied a special position, as we have seen before. He was an original organizer of the co-op, a religious leader with a history of fighting for Banaban rights, and during these fights he had acquired more information about the whole phosphate picture than anyone else was assumed to have. He had tried to improve the people's position with the Japanese. He also had important credentials in the descent system, although those credentials were to prove to be a burden as well as an advantage. He is also one of the most skillful politicians I have ever encountered, with a locally recognized ability to "speak gently" with the old men and sway them to his point of view. (By his own report, one of Rotan's motivations in building up the co-op on Rambi, in addition to the objectives of keeping the community viable and together, was to keep external merchants out.)

Although the management of the co-op, as the council itself, was entirely composed of Banaban men, Gilbertese could have a place in its activities. The co-op, like the LMS church, was thus an explicitly Banaban institution, but one which could at least attempt to overcome the distinction between Banaban and Gilbertese by involving the latter in its activities. The complexion of the co-ops had changed by the time I first arrived on Rambi in 1961. But at that time Gilbertese did serve on the committees of the four village cooperative societies and also worked in the cooperative stores.

The cooperative was the major instrument of immediate organizational continuity between Ocean Island and Rambi. It was also the major instrument in the continuity of Rambi itself, since it handled the copra plantations which had been worked by Levers. This became especially important after the end of the one month period during which the people received rations, while most of them were living in tents in the area of Nuka.

Nuka is on the northwest coast. Some people began to disperse along that coast; their copra was sold green at Nuka, where it was dried. A copra work-force was at the two other plantation centers, one on the south coast, one on the east coast. These workers received daily wages and rations. Later the workers' return depended on the amount of copra they produced; the sense in which the people were acting as employees of the co-op was thus reduced.

In the earliest period, only the central copra driers left from Levers' old plantations were used. This placed a constraint on the settlement pattern, since the green nuts had to be delivered to one of three locations. Some time in the period 1946–53, a few people began experimenting with a homemade drier which eventually took the form of oil drums used with burning coconut husks. The idea caught on, and the dispersal of the people was facilitated. Cutting copra for sale was the major economic activity at the time; it was reported to the Agriculture Department in 1953 that little work was underway on plantation clearing, fence building, cattle controlling and gardening. The Banabans did not take to the notion of agriculture as their primary productive activity.[2]

On the retail side of the co-op's operations, a system was in practice which eventually became one of great concern both to the government and some more commercially minded Banabans. At the beginning there was little money in circulation, and the co-op extended credit. The stores began to operate as exchange centers, where purchases were made against wages and other sources of income. The Banabans were reported to treat the store as if its goods were common resources to be used when needed.[3] Without sufficient money in the early days, Rotan recently said, the people simply had to live on credit. "Without food they would have died. Now there is life and activity." These reasons justified deficits in the store's trading account.

Outside traders must have become more insistent to have their bills paid, however, and Rotan told the people that the only solution was to work the debts off in copra. In 1952, £18,000 was paid in this way, but the co-op apparently later decided to credit the people for the copra they cut, thus creating another debt. There was also a system by which part of an individual's cutting was deducted for the payment of debts. This notion was not universally accepted, and some copra was sold off the island to avoid the reduction, thus worsening the store's position. The council suffered because expected funds were not being transferred from the store. By 1955, an island rate and school fees were supposed to be paid from copra, the money going from the store to the council, but the system apparently broke down.[4]

From 1950 to 1955 there was no resident Adviser on Rambi. This was part of the problem. The third Adviser was transferred to be District Officer, Taveuni; Rambi was still in his domain, and he did visit it. There are indications that the Banabans had wanted a resident Adviser. Some of the reasons for this will become apparent later. The most immediately relevant one is, I suspect, a rather familiar constellation in which people rely upon an outsider to make certain kinds of decisions which they would like made but cannot explicitly formulate.

The fourth resident Adviser arrived in 1955, and arranged C.O.D. rather than credit shipments of goods to the island. Buying on credit decreased, but people were still selling a good deal of copra outside the co-op. Eco-

2. See Maude 1946. Kennedy, Handing over statement; Agricultural Officer, Northern, to Director of Agriculture, 1 July 1953; RIC.

3. This is one of many interesting points made in an unpublished economic study of Rambi written by Carleen O'Laughlin *circa* 1955.

4. Information from conversations with A. F. Grant while Banaban Adviser, Rambi, 1961. Banaban Adviser to Colonial Secretary, 10 January 1953, RIC.

nomic behavior was clearly being seen as something differentiated from group solidarity. The Adviser saw the need for a system of rules to regulate the sale of copra, so that the debts which remained could be cleared up and the council's local financial base secured.

The solution related to the registration of the co-op in the Fiji cooperative system, with its attendant regulations. This matter was broached at least as early as 1948; the council apparently accepted but then changed its mind. The maintenance of the credit system was probably involved in the decision, but another element may have been that of Rambi autonomy, especially as this occurred (see below) at a time when a request for political independence had been made.[5]

In 1957, however, with the co-op in bad condition, registration in the Fiji system was accepted. There were four cooperative societies, one in each of the four villages which had by that time become established (see chapter 11). The existence of the villages was undoubtedly related to acceptance of registration, since the co-ops were tangible institutions which could express and shape the idea of the village itself.

The experience of the Banaban Community Store points to something which became evident in later economic and religious experience: Opposition to the external system, or internal disputes, may be expressed through activities of stores or churches. But those activities tie the local institution in with the broader Fiji system, which applies different rules of credit and credibility.

In 1957 and 1958, government ordinances and regulations were passed which gave a new footing to the economic and political structure of the island.

Legislation enabled the council, with government approval, to fix a compulsory cess on copra and require individuals to take out licenses to cut copra, the proceeds going into a Rambi Island Fund. The cess had first to go for the payment of debts, however. Copra could be sold *only* to one of the four village co-op stores, the price being fixed by the store manager with the Adviser's approval. And the council could fix the areas in which people of the different villages were permitted to obtain their nuts.[6]

A factor in the situation which I have not yet mentioned is that by this time the Banaban Community Store was having some competition, from a

5. Holland to Chief Secretary, WPHC, 9 November 1948; Chairman, Rambi Island Council, to Administrative Officer, Rambi, 3 January 1949 (Enclosure in Holland to Chief Secretary, WPHC, 9 November 1948); Notes of address of Chief Secretary, WPHC, to Rambi Island Council, 3 January 1949; Holland Papers.
6. Banaban (Settlement) (Amendment) Ordinance, 1957 (no. 15, 1957); Banaban (Copra) Regulations, 1958 (Legal Notice no. 6, 1958); Banaban (Copra Cess) Regulations, 1958 (Legal Notice no. 7, 1958); Banaban (Rabi Island Council) (Amendment) Regulations, 1958 (Legal Notice no. 8, 1958).

co-op with a proportionally large Catholic membership, which had branches in Uma and Tabwewa villages. The mixture of religion, politics, nationality, and economics which this sort of thing represented will be taken up later, but a few points may be made now.

Rotan was the leader of the one community-one church faction. The Catholics, many of whom were Gilbertese, refused to accede. The fact that many were Gilbertese put them at a special disadvantage in the local situation. The Catholics today have a roster of grievances about the discriminatory action taken by the council and the LMS majority during this period. Even if a minority church in such a situation is arguing for the differentiation between religion and politics, one of the few courses of action open if it is to maintain itself is to act politically. The political component of the whole social field thus expands.

The Catholics may have found themselves in a position vis-à-vis the council similar to that in which the Banabans found themselves on Ocean Island vis-à-vis the BPC and the government. The Catholics were not alone, however. There were others who were dissatisfied with the way the Banaban Community Store was being run. They opposed the copra *corvée* for the paying of debts, and probably also (it was certainly the case later) objected to the very mixture of religion, politics, nationality, and economics.

Just as the Banabans on Ocean Island founded the co-op as a move in opposition, a rival co-op was founded on Rambi in 1956 as an instrument of opposition. By 1947, the government reported, half of Uma village was in this society.

A leader of the operation was a Gilbertese Catholic, who said that the majority story that it was a Catholic plot was untrue; some of the instigators as well as the members were dissatisfied Protestants. He reports that a Banaban elder chose the name of the society, which was the name of a channel on Ocean Island which was calm even when others were rough. It was a safe shelter in rough times. As part of the society's safety plan, some money was to be put aside to use in case a lawyer was needed. In 1958, a delegation from the society journeyed to Suva and protested the new regulations which deprived them of the right to deal in copra, but without success.

By the next year the society's activities decreased, and it was reported that the wives of most of the members were buying shares in the Tabwewa and Uma village societies. Its members were also buying elsewhere. It soon fell apart. There were debts too, including those of Protestants who bought there. But part of its point had been made, since by this time the "integral model" had been displaced.[7]

7. See Fiji Department of Cooperative Societies, File, Rabi General (File 10.34), and File, Nauniname Cooperative Society (File 10.41). I did not, unfortunately, have time to research adequately the files bearing on the cooperatives.

There was an elaboration of distributive units; private stores had arisen. Some of them were organized by kinsmen with a few affines and friends or others interested on purely economic grounds. The kinship component was one of their problems, because it is difficult to refuse credit to your kin. The stores rose and fell, but the very fact of this elaboration of economic activity is significant. The new thing was being tested out in many ways. The co-op maintained its copra monopoly, but especially in the string of settlements on the west coast, Tabwewa, Nuka, and Uma, there is a livelier retail trade.

The failure of the integral model was marked by the multiplication of economic units, sectarian difficulties (and, as we shall see, the multiplication of sects), and even challenges to the authority of the council. Elaboration, testing out, and the maximization of options marched together.

The objective of autonomy was not, however, to be forgotten. There is evidence that in 1961 the village societies wanted to combine and deal with overseas suppliers rather than with the Suva traders. There was in fact an amalgamation of the societies, on government advice, but at last report the villages wanted to revert to the previous state of affairs in which their stores were independent, for reasons which need not be detailed here. There was still talk, however, of the island's getting its own ship, so that even the Fiji shipping companies could be avoided.

10

Banaban Identity and Community Action

The integral model failed; what arose to replace it?

The model failed in that it was not institutionalized in the social structure of the community as a whole. Rather than being replaced, it was displaced, both physically and conceptually. The village of Buakonikai was the physical displacement. People went there who wanted or could at least live with an integral structure.

Generally the model was not replaced in an absolute sense; few things in Banaban culture are. They linger, in a manner frustrating to the analyst who is searching for clean lines (see discussion in Geertz 1965). The lingering is, however, a reflex of the raison d'être of such models in the first place. They are "creative responses" to the problem of order in a disorderly situation. Even when they are tested out and found wanting, they are kept in reserve for future reference. The nature of the lingering pieces is conditioned, however, by their cultural as well as their social environments. It is going to take many pages to outline that conditioning process.

The phenomenon of lingering, holding things in reserve, is a way of keeping personal and organizational options open, and this has a resonance with the nature of the kinship system in general and the descent system in particular, as we will see in part 4. The total picture represents the people's stance toward history.

Rather than continuing to work from the past to the present (to 1964–65), I will take off from the present and fill in some of the blanks of the past en route. This seems the most effective way of getting to the final analytical outcome, and I beg the indulgence of readers more lineally oriented. We will contend with the problem of what being a Banaban means.

As will be recalled, one is a Banaban by being born a Banaban or by being adopted as a Banaban and receiving Ocean Island land. The solidarity entailed in being a Banaban is regarded as enduring and nonterminable although there are certain shifts which we will come to shortly. The unit of

Banabans itself is also seen as enduring, or rather properly enduring. There is of course the possibility that its existence can be threatened by the full integration of Rambi within Fiji, the loss of rights to Banaban lands, or the disappearance of Banaban custom. The Banabans believe that these eventualities must be actively deterred. The focal concerns which make Banaban solidarity on Rambi meaningful are Banaban custom, Ocean Island phosphate, and the governance of Rambi Island. I say "on Rambi" because in Suva, for example, there may be diffuse relationships between people because they are Banabans—a generalized solidarity similar to that found by many conationals traveling abroad.

I will attend briefly to Banaban custom (*te katei ni Banaba*). The feature shared by those things classified as Banaban custom is that they are behavioral norms held to have been current in the Banaban past (on Ocean Island): current not in the sense of having been "obeyed" by all people at all times, but in the sense of being norms. It embraces historical Banaban norms, and historicity is one of its important characteristics.

Some aspects of Banaban custom are regarded as currently appropriate, and some are not. The notion is akin to that of heritage, or tradition. All Banabans are considered parties to this tradition and more than that, the only parties to it. It is not changeless (certain changes are held to have occurred within it), but only those people whom it in fact distinguishes and defines as a people have the right to arbitrate its applicability or reformulation. The protection and exhibition of that right in face of challenges perceived as emanating from government policy, and the prevention of cultural dilution which might result from uncontrolled immigration to Rambi, constitute part of the *code for conduct* of being a Banaban, and part of the domain of Banaban solidarity.

One evening at a performance of traditional dances, the Banaban Methodist minister said, "There are two things that hold our people together: the custom, and religion." In operation, both custom and religion are at least as divisive as they are unifying. But what is important is that there is the idea of a body of custom regarded by the people as their own, and their own to dispose of. There may be, and are, bitter arguments about whether custom devolves upon Group A or Group B the right to do something, but there is the conviction that there should be a correct solution, and that it is a Banaban solution.[1]

The context of the application of this idea of custom, as we have indicated before, is that both the people and the government have not clearly

---

1. This is ideally speaking. Doubts have developed about whether a pragmatic solution of disputes can be found; see chapter 14.

specified the criteria by which certain customs are good and others bad (except in some cases of conflict with Christian dogma), or the criteria which should be used to decide what custom is. The government, for example, claims that custom is being enforced in the insistence on communal holding of funds (which the people dispute) but suggests that custom be changed so that centralized planning can be developed. If we look at the government's behavior, there is an objective inconsistency, unless the principle of consistency is simply that of the authority's decision at the time of what it is expedient to do on grounds which may transcend the future and interests of the Banabans.

The current position of the phosphate issue may be introduced by a piece of political oratory delivered by Tengata Tenanai, an island council member from Uma village, at a welcome celebration on Rambi for Mr. and Mrs. M. J. C. Saunders. After the departure of the last Banaban Adviser, the question of employing a lawyer to advance Banaban phosphate claims, and a Banaban Adviser not responsible to the government, was broached. Saunders, a partner in the Suva legal firm of William Scott and Company, visited Rambi in connection with these positions. The council approved his appointment to both, the reaction of the government not yet having been ascertained.

The councillor speaking was the Catholic catechist, and the Catholic choir provided the songs as indicated. The speech and verses were delivered in Gilbertese and interpreted to the guests of honor by the Banaban Methodist minister. Although the latter was not acting in a religious role, the ecumenical spirit is well worthy of note.

> A pitiable girl was born on the island of Banaba. She was in the charge of a chief whose chiefdom was large among the chiefs. When she grew to womanhood, the chief chose a husband for her, a young man favored among the chief's group. She was not long in staying with her husband and was abandoned, and was taken with the sickness of wanting to marry.
>
> She was given her second husband and they were also not long in living together, as she was frequently deserted by men. After her fifth or sixth husband, her way of being abandoned continued and she was about to appear, as it were, haggard.
>
> What should happen but that she was now attacked by the sickness which is the sickness of separation, or the sickness of love; she didn't eat much, didn't sleep peacefuly, and only cried continually.
>
> During that period of separation she composed a sad song which was her lament, and these are some of its words:
>
> (Choir):
>
> "How unfortunate I am,
> As I loved a boy who was bound
> By his many lovers there."

(Women only) Chorus:
"How sad I am in this thought of mine.
Perhaps I cannot achieve it—
As I feel within my love for you;
As I have learned from you."
The chief was angry and didn't concern himself again with obtaining a husband for her; her parents were ashamed to arrange her remarrying as she was always deserted, and she still wanted to marry as she said she lived more comfortably in marriage than in single life.
She set about to look for a husband, as the chief refused to get one and her parents were angry too as they disapproved her marrying, and this was the thing weighing upon her: "I am past my prime; perhaps men are about to despise me, but I should find my lover by persistent pleading." There was also a song which she composed, and sang while on her way to find a husband, and here are some of its words:
(Choir)
1. My setting out and my journey
   Are to search for the flower of my heart;
   When will it be found?
   Perhaps it will come through pleading.
(Women only) Chorus:
   How sad I am in this thought of mine.
   Perhaps I cannot achieve it—
   As I feel within my love for you;
   As I have learned from you.
2. I will sail my canoe back and forth
   On the other side of Britain,
   For I want to know what you think;
   You are just about to be revealed
   As one who lied to me from your very lips,
   And your heart so far away.
   The husband of Miss Abandoned has now been found: Mr. Saunders, the lawyer from Britain.
   The story ends there.

The interplay between the male councillor, the mixed choir, and the women members of the choir was beautifully staged. The fact that the "pitiable girl" is a girl sets up the structure for the marriage allegory, which is salient because the spouse is someone who is acquired rather than inherited. There is an inversion, because in Banaban marriage it is the man rather than the woman who is supposed to take the initiative. That she is a girl also suggests her defenselessness and need for care and protection. And furthermore, Ocean Island is referred to by the people as "the woman's land," because of the people's disinclination to violence in contrast with some Gilbertese, who "love to fight."

It is ambiguous whether the "pitiable girl" is the Banaban community or the island council. The author said it could be either, but perhaps the council was more appropriate as it is the unit which has a role in considering the Banaban Advisers who were the succession of "husbands." The council acts, however, as a representative of the community. How did this legal position develop?

In 1948 the Adviser had proposed adult suffrage and a secret ballot. The council first saw this as meddling with Banaban autonomy but then accepted the plan. Family heads were thus no longer the electors, but individuals. In 1951 regulations were passed which affirmed the secret ballot, and any member of the Banaban Community resident on Rambi over twenty-one years of age was qualified to vote or nominate. The magistrate could not be a member; thus the political and legal systems were further differentiated. The Banaban Community legally included some non-Banabans (see above); thus the council was representative of the Rambi population rather than Banabans only. A regulation taking effect in 1957 reduced the council membership from ten to eight; this may have been the time when the four villages became the electoral units. Each village now elects two members to the council.[2] Whether the "pitiable girl" refers to the people or the council, the condition is certainly one calling for pity, both the Banabans pitying themselves, and their calling upon others to pity them in their plight. The Advisers were sent by the government allegedly to help the people, but they were "bound" by their superiors to do what they were told, however they felt personally, to prevent the people from obtaining their due in money from their land. And the fact that the people were "abandoned" also invokes a sense of dependency.

Maude recalls that it was not the government's intention that the Banaban Adviser be an advocate for Banaban political-economic aspirations. The Banabans, however, have interpreted the position differently. In their view, the advising that they most urgently need is on those political and economic aspirations, and if a man is paid by them, he should work for them in the manner that they see fit.[3]

The Banabans had taken steps in the past to modify the Adviser's position, which, having become that of a man in the middle, is an impossible one. The steps were in the same direction as the present effort. In 1948 the council wanted the level of government control over expenditure to end with the Adviser as chairman of the trust board, and they also wanted

2. Banaban (Rabi Island Council) Regulations, 1951 (Legal Notice no. 6, 1951); Banaban (Rabi Island Council) (Amendment) Regulations, 1956 (Legal Notice no. 103, 1956).

3. I am not sure of the details of the Banaban Adviser's salary. It is possible that the council pays the government, and the government pays the Adviser. From the Banaban point of view, however, this would make no difference.

to free him (in what manner is unclear) from the Fiji government. When the second Adviser was due to retire, the council noted to the government that it paid the Adviser's salary and would prefer an Adviser who would stay there a long time, and in addition to him, a lawyer. It was later requested that the board's chairman be selected by vote, thus depriving the Adviser of that automatic status. In early 1949 the Chief Secretary of the Western Pacific High Commission stood ground on the Statement of Intentions: the final appointment and tenure of the Adviser were up to the Governor. He said furthermore that a lawyer could be hired but not on a permanent basis. This was the matter coming up again now.[4]

One of the significances of being a Banaban is being a present or future holder of Ocean Island land. It is a consequence of the principle of classification and the inheritance system. In political discourse, *Banabans* and *landowners* are often used interchangeably. There are certain entailments on land concerning the rights of near kinsmen, but any discussion on land matters can leave no doubt that the Banaban regards plots in which he holds title as his own. Being a Banaban entails having Ocean Island land, and having Ocean Island land is generally taken as presumptive evidence of being a Banaban. Even with regard to a person whose descent is obscure, if one asks, "Is he a Banaban?" one may meet with the reply, "He owns land on Banaba, doesn't he?"

All Banabans thus have an interest in what happens to phosphate mined on Ocean Island land. The rock belongs to the owner as much as a pumpkin planted on it. The British government, however, the "chief" in the councillor's tale, does not concur in this view of land ownership, as I have outlined in detail. New fuel for the controversy was added when the Banabans discovered that whereas they (by then) were receiving 2s. 8d. royalty per ton of phosphate, 23s. 0d. went into Gilbert and Ellice Islands Colony revenue. The Banabans regard this disparity in returns as fraud, and legal arguments about rights of taxation and the difference between surface and undersurface mining rights as deception. (This latter distinction is even questioned in a legalistic fashion: since the phosphate is continuous from the surface downwards, the distinction between surface and undersurface is meaningless.)

Proceeds from the phosphate, wherever they go, are in discourse called "Banaban money" or "our money," and if they are "ours," we should get them. In 1948 the council wanted a record of all expenditures from Ban-

4. Rotan Tito for Rambi Island Council to Chief Secretary, WPHC, 8 November 1948; Rotan Tito for Rambi Island Council to Administrative Officer, Rambi, 27 October 1948; Notes on address of Chief Secretary, WPHC, to Rambi Island Council, 3 January 1949; Holland Papers.

aban funds on Ocean Island, including money given to the government "for damage done to Banaban lands." They asked for the distribution to land-owners of the royalty which went to the government in lieu of rent. There were also claims against the BPC, which was alleged to have gone back on promises made earlier. There was a fair degree of confusion about previous agreements, which some may have tried to exploit, and others to explicate.[5] Once when the council asked for copies of agreements, the BPC denied that there was an actual 1913 agreement (see part 2). Some gov-ernment correspondence in the Banabans' hands referred to a 1913 agree-ment. To put it mildly, people did not know where they stood.

Not only were there attempts to secure back revenues. In 1948, the council indicated that it wanted assistance from Ocean Island rather than Fiji revenue. If money had been diverted to the government to pay for Ban-aban services, now that the Banabans were on Rambi the same should occur.[6]

The local agents of British government, having taken the community in its charge, are committing an offense against not only the Banaban land system, but also against the Christian justice in terms of which they purport to rule. The Advisers who were sent were involved in the plot, came and went without helping the people in the task which is the paramount business of the Banaban community, the righting of this wrong. All this, of course, is as the Banabans see it.

The "chief" and "parents" in the councillor's presentation, in this case the British administration, were pictured as neglecting the best interests of their child. This kind of imagery occurred at other times, for example, when it was stated that the administration claims to be "father of the people" and should behave as such. What is emphasized here is a just responsibility. The term was actually used that way in the greeting to Saunders, the lawyer. Assuming his appointment, one Banaban speaker proclaimed that Saunders was now "father of the Banaban," and, bringing the identity of the spouse-pair into political imagery, his wife (also present)

5. During the meeting between Ellis and the council in 1948, Rotan asked Ellis to talk about the history of Ocean Island and early dealings with the company because some young councillors did not know the history. Ellis gave some information about the early days, and Rotan then asked for details about the money. Holland's question about the kingship, referred to in chapter 3, may indicate that descent controversies were looming at this time; see further discussion in chapter 14.

6. Chairman, Rambi Island Council, to Administrative Officer, Rambi, 8 July 1948, Personal Files of Rotan Tito. Notes of speech by Mr. H. B. Maynard to Rambi Island Council, 14 September 1948, RIC. Chairman, Rambi Island Council, to Ad-ministrative Officer, Rambi, 27 October 1948, Holland Papers. Maynard to Coode, 11 April 1949, RIC.

was "mother of the Banaban," and that there was no one else occupying those positions.

Grimble (see chapter 4) had referred to himself as the people's old friend and father. The Resident Commissioner in the Gilberts, and some of the Advisers on Rambi, were each known as the Old-Man, a term of generalized respect also applied to elder kin.

The implications of this complex are clear: the government had put itself in the position of father. It occupied that position in the law. But it was not enacting the proper, just code for conduct which fatherhood stipulated. This, perhaps, is the price of paternalism.

The idea was mooted that after the departure of the last Adviser, no new one should be hired, that the people could handle their affairs themselves. The child had come of age. Doubts arose, however, about whether the people were in fact capable enough. The European could not be fully trusted, but a Banaban was no match for a European in arguing about phosphate with other Europeans. Thus the Banabans developed the "sickness of separation," and with it the fear that, because they had been instrumental in the retiring of two Advisers in very unhappy circumstances and because there had been stories spread about how difficult the people were, they could not find a replacement.

The British administration could not be relied upon to do the job and might disapprove the plan of having an Adviser independent of it. So they took the initiative themselves, the girl braving the anger of parents and chief to plead for another husband. Pleading, appeal on the basis of justice against injustice, might work after all.[7]

The phosphate-lands issue is something which non-Banabans, nonlandowners, cannot be expected to understand, or to advance unless they are moved by considerations of abstract justice. They may, of course, be paid for pleading the cause. White people ought to be so moved, but they can be reached by the forces actively seeking to deprive the Banabans of their patrimony. Universal truths are involved here as they are only in religion, among Banaban solidarities. We will pick this up later: the sense in which the phosphate issue *is* religion.

The denial of Banaban land rights, or rather the Banabans' perception of a denial by the Gilbert Islands administration or anyone else, is one of the most provocative acts which can be committed. It is almost equivalent to denying that Banabans exist.

7. The verses in the piece were adapted from another song. The last stanza, it was explained to me, is not an aspersion on the integrity of the lawyer, but an allusion to the kind of thing a girl does when she is checking up on whether the words expressed during a rendezvous reveal the true feelings of her lover.

Reaction to this threat is evident in two lyrics. Such lyrics and speeches as we are considering are some of the means through which the Banabans articulate their concerns to themselves and to others.

The first is a warm-up song for action dances, and it is said to have been composed long ago on Ocean Island, which indicates the prescience of the composer or of the spirit who taught it to him in a dream.

> It is said
> That you will blot out Banaba;
> You are pretentious,
> But hunting for protection.

"Blotting out Banaba" is denying Banaban land rights. While acting as though he had achieved his end, however, the offender is trying to cover up his tracks because he fears exposure. This was interpreted to me as relating to recent magazine and newspaper articles about the Banabans, a product of a campaign to secure publicity for the Banabans' plight led by Rotan's son, Rev. Tebuke Rotan, and the lively interest of the *Pacific Islands Monthly*. The publicity campaign is founded on the idea that if the world knew what was happening, Banaban grievances would be redressed.[8]

Following are the lyrics to an action dance composed on Rambi:

> How astonishing, really astonishing,
> What is said about the Banabans!
> Perhaps Britain doesn't properly know us.
> Banaba is truly our land;
> It is *our* earth the B.P.C. takes out
> To the World.
> *Aué*! It is our heritage!
> Where are you? Where are you lost?
> *Aué*! It is no affair of yours!

The lyric requires little interpretation. It *is* an interpretation. "What is said about the Banabans" alludes to the government contention that it can decide for itself the fate of the phosphate money. The government behaves, in the native view, as if the land belonged to it rather than to the Banabans, and through the route of native symbolism, the denial of land rights is almost a denial of individual existence.

The "astonishment" derives from the fact that the government could be doing what it is doing. It must be "lost" somewhere, for if it knew the true facts, it would not be doing what it is doing. Perhaps lesser functionaries are hiding things from their superiors. For government is fundamentally just.

8. See, for example, *Pacific Islands Monthly* for September, October, and November 1965 and January 1966. See also the *Fiji Times* for 21 September 1965, 22 November 1965, and 18 December 1965.

Or it might be. Many Banabans are hovering at a point where their commitment to the fundamental justice idea is in total uncertainty. Others have already made the break and see the United Nations, charitably viewed as a world court dispensing justice, as the only recourse. Thus *they* have not abandoned a notion of generalized justice but have moved its enforcer one step up. Others have given up entirely or almost. And this is precisely the point: *People do not know what to think,* and in many respects in not knowing they are behaving rationally, given the information at their disposal. And some of the demands for action, including the most radical, may very well emanate from a deeply felt desire to see reality encode *something* which can act as a vehicle for the individual's inchoate thoughts and feelings.

Still operating on the old lines, the council went progressively up the administrative scale. When they talked to the Colonial Secretary and he said they could not have more money at once, they assumed that the Governor surely did not know what was going on. When they saw the Governor, and he more or less said the same thing, then it must have been the Secretary of State for the Colonies in London who did not know what was going on, and they tried to arrange a meeting with him. If only Parliament knew, or the Queen. . . .

The fundamental justice orientation is related to a belief held by many that not only will right be done, but that it will be done *soon*. This has implications which will be discussed below.

When a high Colonial Office official recently went to Rambi to discuss Banaban demands and British attitudes, he was reliably reported to have said that the reason why the people were not receiving more money was that it was inexpedient. The British government had to administer the Gilbert and Ellice Islands effectively—there are twenty times as many people there as on Rambi—and the phosphate profits were their major source of revenue. This of course reinforced the holy crusade aspect of the case. Furthermore, when some government officials meet with Banabans, they communicate on two levels: the level of official policy, and if only through innuendo, the level of personal opinion, and the personal opinion is that the people perhaps really should be getting more money than they are (this point was also raised in part 2). For them, their own careers and the values of effective administration—the greatest good for the greatest number—and the values of individual property rights are in conflict, and this conflict communicates itself to the people and helps shape their attitudes.

When Sir Albert Ellis, the discoverer of the phosphate, visited Rambi in 1948, Rotan said, "We feel pleasure that the hand of God was in your going to Banaba and finding the phosphate and your long association with the Banaban people." Rotan's son, the Methodist minister, later became actively involved in politics, and during one sermon raised the question of the legitimacy of his action: What did a preacher have to do with it? He did not become an activist, he said, because of a concern with raw money: it was to see that Evil did not triumph in the world. Rotan's address to the visiting Colonial Office representative is instructive in this regard. He opened with a prayer, thanking God for the opportunity to meet with him, and asking God's help. He went on:

> [In] your arrival among us there are things which are both very unfortunate and very precious. I say unfortunate, for us and for you, because: (a) Sixty-five years after the destruction of our land, you have just come to see us and find out about us; (b) We have been on our new island for twenty-five years, and you have just come to see us; (c) We have been asking you to help us for thirty-eight years [since the 1927–31 affair], and you have just come to hear from us.
>
> I say before you, and before the Council, that your arrival today is something very precious, for we are like the person who was lame for thirty-eight years, and sat by the healing pool of Bethesda waiting for the waters to move, but could not step in because there were other people before him. But when Jesus came to him, he made him whole. And we are the same as the lame man: we have been waiting thirty-eight years, from 1927 to 1965.
>
> Therefore we say that your coming to us is like the arrival of Jesus to heal that lame man, who is ourselves, the Banabans.

Thus Christianity informs and supports the issue, and the strength of the issue derives from the fact that it is grounded in the two explicitly recognized bases of morality: God and the Banaban custom.

The same cultural logic which gives to the Banabans the sole right to dispose of their money also gives them the sole right to decide on the future of Rambi. The achievement of autonomy is another interest with respect to which the Banabans, as Banabans, are solidary. Attitudes toward colony taxation and various (almost all) government proposals indicate that insofar as there is a constituted authority to which the Banabans are responsible on Rambi, it is the Rambi Island Council.

In 1948, the council actually asked for "independence." It asked that it no longer be subject to the Fiji or Gilbert and Ellice Islands government, but that the council take over administration and control Ocean Island and Rambi taxes "with the Governor at Suva." Exactly what the latter phrase meant is obscure to me. It may have been obscure at the time. "We rejoice," the council wrote, "when we submit our request for independence because you (the British government) are truly the givers of Independence." The Governor of Fiji and the Chief Secretary of the Western Pacific High Commission visited Rambi independently and said flatly that independence was impossible. It was contrary to the Statement of Intentions, which gave the people more control than they had before, and with which they should be satisfied.[9]

When the independence request was made the council apparently had the model of Tonga in mind, although the Adviser pointed out that the British Agent and Consul there had the kind of veto power which the Banabans were in fact resisting.

The external model which came to predominate was that of Nauru; in part 2, I indicated certain interconnections between the Banaban and Nauruan scenes. What was believed to have been happening on Nauru gave shape to the idea of Banaban autonomy which was being tested out.

Nauru lies to the west of Ocean Island, outside the Gilberts, and is a phosphate island worked by the same company that works Ocean. It is (or rather was at the time of research), however, an Australian trusteeship, not part of a Crown colony as are both Ocean Island and Rambi. The Nauruans are represented as living a modernized Oceanic *dolce vita*. From their phosphate royalties they receive large individual payments. It is said that people have well-paying jobs, own automobiles, dispose of only partly worn clothes, practically throw money away. It is a place where, as it were, the cargo has arrived. The Australians give scholarships for study in Australia, have offered to buy the Nauruans a new island for resettlement with everything prepared on it, and furthermore find them an entity to contend with. The Nauruans have been active in articulating and defending their interests. The Nauruan case had come before the UN and delegations had been there. The Nauruans have hired experts to help their case, and had made moves in the direction of independence (since successful).

The Banabans have been taking some political actions on the Nauruan model. They regard their own original situation as identical with that of the Nauruans; anything the Nauruans get, they should get too. The Nauruans represent what they *should* be like, materially and politically, and would be like if they were not prevented from being so. The condition of the Nauruans is in fact a sanction which they try to apply against the British. That the Nauruans have succeeded is an indication of the rightness of their own case.

Autonomy is a statement about the relationship between the community and the outside. With regard to the inside, the definition of contexts of responsibility is less clear. The ambiguity, as noted above, is in the question of where the domain of "Banaban" ends and where the domains of other social units, including the individual, begin.

9. Chairman, Rambi Island Council, to Administrative Officer, Rambi, 30 June 1948; Notes on speech of the Governor at Rabi, 3 August 1948; Holland to Chief Secretary, WPHC, 9 November 1948; Notes on address of Chief Secretary, WPHC, to Rambi Island Council, 3 January 1949; Holland Papers.

It was observed in part 2 that collective political action was being designed to achieve the recognition of individual rights more than to achieve something material for the collectivity as a collectivity. The extent to which there was to be an individual or a collectivity orientation was problematical. The situation on Rambi crystallized into a dilemma for which the Banabans were culturally unprepared. The reasons why they were unprepared and the reasons why it was a dilemma are interlocked.

On Ocean Island the government and the phosphate company provided a structure of equipment and services many aspects of which were valued by the Banabans. These things were part of what modern life means, and in them Rambi was lacking. Unsuccessful attempts to get help from Gilbert Islands revenue were noted above. When approached, the Fiji Government indicated that Rambi was eligible for what other islands in Fiji received, but no more. The BPC was approached with partial success (see below), but on some matters a situation developed wherein the Fiji Government tried to put some of the burden of responsibility on the BPC, and the BPC tried to put some of the burden of responsibility on the Fiji Government. The fundamental responsibility was placed with the Banabans, and it is for this that they were unprepared. They had to build much of the Rambi infrastructure themselves. If they wanted to recreate the accouterments of modern life, they had to do it on their own. Since the accouterments were essentially givens on Ocean Island, they did not have to contemplate the institutionalization of some of their values. Rambi, as an undeveloped island, was a new situation. To organize a system of transportation, supply electricity, and build buildings, individual action was insufficient. The analogy with some newly decolonized states is clear, and the problems of what to do with Rambi and what to do with Banaban funds are fused.

These problems are illustrated in a bitterly divisive controversy which occurred in 1965, and publicly involved three issues: what to do with present funds, how to get more, and the position of the Banaban Adviser. Pertinent to the discussion is the fact that the money from royalties was forecast to end by about 1985, when the Ocean Island phosphate runs out. Lack of clarity on the exact time when phosphate operations would cease has been one factor in the lack of a sense of real urgency which government officials felt should be there.

It will be recalled that royalties are paid into the trust fund administered by a board which prepares yearly estimates of expenditures which, after the approval of the full council, are sent on to the Fiji government for approval.

It will also be recalled that an annuities-bonus system was set up in 1937. In 1947, the Banabans wanted to remove the distinction between full- and half-Banabans. This was done, and the residential qualification was extended to include both Ocean Island and Rambi. The council furthermore wanted to abolish the residential qualification entirely, abolish the general annuity, and put that money together with the land bonus money and have the latter's distribution reflect more accurately the size of the individual's landholdings. This was a revival of prewar proposals and was presumably focused on the idea of the land, rather than the individual, as defining rights.

Annuities were paid, however. The government was not particularly in favor of these payments because it wanted to insure that the people would stay on Rambi, and that the community would have a financial base for development spending. The Banabans were not particularly in favor of the annuity for the reasons indicated. Perhaps from the government point of view, approving the annuity was a lesser evil than approving the council proposal. The government may have feared that disallowing any such payment would be interpreted as going back on previous promises, and the ire of the Banabans would be incurred. From the Banabans' point of view, getting the annuity was a lesser evil than getting less money directly into the hands of individuals.

My data on what happened to the bonus and annuity in the succeeding period is shockingly incomplete, and the issue does relate directly to the controversy under consideration. The matter is of general significance because decisions on such questions—Who gets the annuity? Who pays the island rate?—are more than minor questions of detail. Such decisions are boundary-defining ones, defining a boundary around the Banaban community or the Rambi community. And the decision has a feedback to the conceptions of the community itself, especially when those conceptions are ambiguous.

Some time after 1949 the annuity was apparently eliminated in favor of an expanded landholders' bonus. Some local sources said that there were annuities which went not only to Banabans but also to resident non-Banabans, and that this caused a great deal of argument at the time. What does seem clear from the muddle and a few records is that prior to 1965 the council decided not to distribute the annuity and bonus at all, but rather to use the money for building and other projects. These included the building of concrete-block houses on a matching contribution basis with the BPC, which had made certain offers of assistance for development in 1960.

The controversy referred to was brought into the open in a community meeting, where only Banabans and the Adviser spoke. Some councillors and others had said that the Adviser was acting in a high-handed manner (incorrect both for an Adviser and a European), by ordering rather than advising, and not respecting the council. He had also incurred the ire of a number of church people because of his atempts to disentangle the use of board money and paid time for things which seemed to be more in the service of the Methodist church and Rotan's supporters than of the community as a whole.

Those who organized the meeting, operating in part through church channels, wanted the annuity and bonus reinstated. The Adviser said that this was a foolish course. Additional grants and royalty increases had been given by the BPC after their commissioners had seen that the money was being used for development, and after the Banabans had agreed that it would not be distributed. The land on Rambi, he argued, was poorly developed, and the money should be used for improvements before it stops.

The board prepared the 1965 estimates without the individual distribution. The full council refused to approve them and said the annuity must be included. The Adviser said that the whole council had no authority to amend the estimates, and an impasse was reached.

At the meeting, Rotan said that of the money in hand, two-thirds should be distributed to the people. The BPC, he said, would contribute more toward development, and some of it was really the responsibility of the Fiji government anyway. The annuity money was the people's money because it came from their lands, and thus they could decide about it at that meeting: whether they wanted the annuities or not. Even if there are unjust restrictions (the risk of government veto), they must declare what they want or risk getting nothing.

One of his few opponents, an Uma councillor, said that there was an agreement which had to be respected, that the people were not free. Rotan denied the existence of such an agreement and intimated that perhaps it was an understanding reached between that Uma councillor and the BPC, and thus not binding on the people.

The majority sentiment was that people were in difficult economic circumstances *because* they were not getting their rightful share of phosphate profits and had a right to "their money," from which only some were receiving advantages through wages. Therefore, as much as possible should be divided up, and more obtained from the outside. The minority suggested that dividing the money at hand and getting more were incompatible; a tractor driver argued that although the wages were not going to everyone, the recently constructed road was walked upon by everyone, and everyone would get houses. This, however, did not get him very far. The new road and the new houses, which are being built by local labor and partially with local funds, are to the people tangible signs of "progress." There is a fair amount of pride in them. At the same time, people critically compare them with what they know roads and houses could be like and feel that construction should proceed faster, better equipment should be available, and construction should ideally be paid for by the BPC or the government. It is not that the Banabans are trying to get something for nothing. The something that they are trying to get, in their view, properly belongs to them.

One of Rotan's frequent comments is, "We did not come to Fiji to be workers on the land, but to get our money," by being closer to lawyers and centers of political power. This is the dominant concern of the Banaban people as a people. Money from one's land is the greatest material sign of being a Banaban in Fiji, as opposed to being something else. The cooperative development of Rambi, especially to the older generation, is not the same. Working on the land does not have the same valuation that it does elsewhere. *Owning* land matters more. Banabans share an interest in the maximization of the money from this land, for themselves as landowners rather than as a group.

It was the money from Banaban lands (invested royalties) which bought Rambi, thus insuring the right of Banabans to be there, and which is being currently used for development. This is not the ideal situation. The corporation was set up against the background of government insistence that it could pay the dividends only to the corporation, and reserved the right to veto decisions made by the board of directors.

The people believe—and there is almost no division here—that it is their right to decide about "our money," and about how Rambi, purchased from that money, should be run and also to exclude from a role in the decisions those who own no share. Furthermore, these rights must be periodically reasserted lest they lapse, even if attention must be deflected from the investment of community-funded time and energy in tasks recognized as worthwhile, such as the replanting of coconut trees (most of which are old).

For what is interpreted as a situation of poverty, there is on the one hand the attitude, "Why doesn't the council do something about it?" and on the other, when there is a plan for doing something about it, "What right would they have to tell me what to do?" The general stymieing effect is obvious. As a consequence of the fact that the level of political naiveté is decreasing, and of other facts, this view is losing ground. There are some now trying to mobilize support for community action in development who a year before regarded such proposals as near treason. But the situation is confused. Another problem is that almost any government proposal is regarded as a potential threat to Banaban autonomy, the arguments being similar to the money-means-control, or once-in-never-out variety familiar in the United States.

I will probably write a microanalysis at another time of the meeting at which these issues were aired. It lasted ten hours, and ended with a film. It was a great catharsis, during which the meanings and problems in meaning of many of the categories which organize the people's social thinking were articulated: Banaban and Gilbertese, landowner and nonlandowner, wage earner and copra cutter, kinsman and nonkinsman, membership in different churches, individual and collective responsibility, progress and stagnation, and others. Of special note are two related things. First, there was some feeling that the distribution of annuities might indeed result in "misfortune," but if that were the case, the people would all be unfortunate together. Second, when it was suggested that signatures be taken on each side, the suggestion was resisted. When the climax approached, people wanted to get the decision ratified quickly. (Some might also have been afraid of the information being used against them. A proposal for a plebiscite also met with failure.) The decision had to be represented as one emanating from the people *as a people*. The showing of hands was a more collective act than the signing of a document, and there would be no division made eternal on a piece of paper. As one young man put it with great feeling, "We want to see the power of the Banaban community!" And indeed, they were in the process of defining the Banaban community, as they decided for the distribution of money and against the Banaban Adviser.

The community discussion was a *maungatabu,* a kind of town meeting, grounded in custom, the decisions of which are binding. It met on 27 November 1964. The power of the Banaban community apparently did not receive sufficient external response between that time and 14 April of the next year, when the people took up arms.

During most of the intervening period I was absent from the island. The *Pacific Islands Monthly* reported that the Banabans' resentment over their situation

> finally came to a head on the morning of April 14 when between 300 and 400 men, armed with spears, knives and clubs, marched to the public hall on Rabi intent on violence to attract attention to their plight.
> At the meeting the Banabans decided to:
> Kill several of their countrymen who had supported the Banaban Adviser.
> Burn down the Banaban Adviser's house and office, and deport him across the narrow strait to Napuka on Vanua Levu, with a warning that he would be hurt if he returned to Rabi.
> However, before these acts could be carried out, a radio message brought District Officer Hughes speeding to Rabi from Savusavu, and he and others, after arguing with the armed men all day, finally persuaded them to lay down their arms.
> In doing so, Mr. Hughes promised to ask the Fiji and GEIC Governments

and the Western Pacific High Commission to treat the Banaban situation as one of urgency and gravity.[10]

Later, Rev. Tebuke Rotan told a news conference in Sydney that

> the meeting . . . decided to kill the one man supporting the adviser, and . . . [Tebuke] had stepped in and forbidden any killing.
> "They nearly speared me then, because I had disobeyed their custom," explained Tebuke. "We had all clapped three times to agree with the decision, you see. But I was a member of the church, and there wasn't to be any killing. They said they would agree, so long as we got rid of the adviser."[11]

Local accounts of the April event vary somewhat, but the outline is clear enough, and the interplay of notions of custom and of the church displayed themselves. The Banaban community had been finally driven up to the point of taking collective action outside the law. And the Banaban Adviser did not remain for another term, for a variety of reasons.

In his Sydney news conference, Tebuke said that the Adviser "was a very nice man. We had no quarrel with him."[12] This illustrates one of the difficult problems of the time: the differentiation of the man and the office. The arguments against the Adviser were against both his behavior and the nature of his office. The two matters were almost inextricably tangled. After the April event, some who had spoken vociferously against the Adviser began to reformulate their statements to convey the impression that there was nothing against the Adviser personally, but the dispute was with the office, which should be in the service of the Banabans rather than the government. It is interesting to note that Tebuke, along with a number of others, sometimes refers to Rotan (Tebuke's father) in political contexts as "the chairman" (of the island council). At the meeting which voted on the future of the Adviser, the bonus, and the annuity, Tebuke made a point of saying that he was not following his father on kinship grounds, but it was a matter of justice. The differentiation is an unstable one, and critics of officeholders frequently accuse them of acting on the grounds of other solidarities (kinship, religious, village) or sheer self-interest. Perhaps in such a small community with overlapping ties of different kinds between individuals, a clear differentiation of office and man is difficult to effect in practice. This is not, of course, a problem specific to even small societies.

We will now lead into another problem of differentiation raised several times: the ambiguity and need for clarification in the boundaries of the community domain itself, with particular reference to the council as its ac-

10. *Pacific Islands Monthly*, vol. 36 (September 1965), no. 9, p. 16.
11. *Pacific Islands Monthly*, vol. 37 (August 1966), no. 8, p. 19.
12. Ibid.

tive instrument. The council's position raises the question of *legitimacy*. We will then lead from a discussion of that problem into a more general discussion of Banaban values.

Every member of the Banaban Community over twenty-one has the right to be an elector and to stand for election to the council. To date, however, only Banabans have been elected, and as far as I know, only Banabans have ever stood for election until the most recent one. All the members have also been men. Men are properly the people to hold public responsibility, to do the talking in official capacities, to take the initiative. They are also expected to know more about matters of finance and government than women. When I jokingly suggested to some people that Rambi should try a council composed entirely of women, they replied that the women would be at one another's throats after a few minutes; men can consider matters more calmly. When I suggested perhaps one woman, they said that the men would not be able to get a single word in during the meetings. Women are, however, much in evidence at political meetings, asking questions and expressing opinions. A few are quite influential.

Authority traditionally resides not only with men, but also with old men. Some of the oldest men were members of the first council. In 1964 members' ages were: 64, 49, 41, 40, 40, 34, 33, 28. Only the chairman, who was 64, qualified as an "old man." Although people ill-disposed toward the council may point out that one cannot expect reasonable action from it because it is composed of children, and the chairman himself may try to squelch another member by saying that he was born yesterday, there is a general recognition that certain skills, particularly the speaking of English, are now required of councillors, and that the younger, more educated people are the ones who can deal with Europeans with less risk of being fooled. The old people simply do not understand the modern world, some say.

The generation to which all councillors but one belong is that known as *rorobuaka; roro* means "generation," *buaka* "war, fight," and the local etymology is "the generation capable of fighting." Traditionally, one hears, these were the fighters, taking orders from the elders. Now they are taking the initiative upon themselves.

A recently formed unit is the Rorobuaka Society, which began, and is still located, in the Methodist church. Some of its founders and leaders saw one of its functions as informing the council of any popular dissatisfaction with council decisions and also undertaking activities on behalf of the community which the council could not because of its link with the Fiji Government (such as inviting foreign consuls and United Nations officials to Rambi to learn the Banaban side of the phosphate dispute). It also had overtones which suggested a threat to the legitimacy of the council itself. Although the majority of the people on Rambi are Methodists, and this group claims to speak for the Methodists, there is some objection even from Methodists that church and state should not mix to that extent, that when they mixed in the past, Banaban solidarity was threatened. Some of the initiating membership had specific grievances relating to the Adviser, the bonus, the annuity, and the behavior of countrymen who were not on the side of the majority. The formal aims of the society seemed vaguely defined, within the general framework of a religious service group and a political pressure group. Through social action the group will clarify its position to itself. Original proposals to expand it into an all-island group have not gotten off the ground. The society has branches in each village, and one has taken the name of the Banaban Democratic party on the analogy with political parties elsewhere.

The suitability of the rorobuaka generation for leadership comes from two recognized factors. First, it is the generation of fighters, and the Banabans see themselves as engaged in a fight. Second, that generation is presumed to have a greater understanding of modern conditions, and to have the education to be better qualified. Yet again, precisely what the proper qualifications are is a matter of some obscurity.

Maintenance of public order and control of certain services, such as immigration, health, education, and transportation, are recognized as being located in the community domain. There is a set of regulations passed by the council and approved by the government which draw from old Ocean Island and Gilbert Islands regulations, Fiji regulations, and purely local concerns. One of the council's responsibilities is setting these regulations out. The council receives money from, among other sources, the island rate, which (with certain exceptions) men between eighteen and sixty must pay; a cess on copra; and licenses to cut copra. Councillors also sit on the lands court which registers transfers and attempts to resolve disputes.[13]   •

13. See, e.g., Banaban (Settlement) Ordinance, 1945 (cap. 110 of 1956 series); Banaban (Rabi Island Council) Regulations, 1951 (Legal Notice no. 6, 1951); Rabi Island (Cultivation and Burning of Land) Regulations, 1956 (Legal Notice no. 96, 1956); Rabi Island (Animals) Regulations, 1956 (Legal Notice no. 97, 1956); Rabi Island (Infectious Diseases) Regulations, 1956 (Legal Notice no. 98, 1956); Rabi Island (Buildings, Villages and Sanitation) Regulations, 1956 (Legal Notice no. 99, 1956); Banaban (Settlement) (Amendment) Ordinance, 1957 (no. 15, 1957); Rabi Island (Buildings, Villages and Sanitation) (Amendment) Regulations, 1957 (Legal Notice no. 80, 1957); Rabi Island (Animals) (Amendment) Regulations, 1957 (Legal Notice no. 81, 1957); Rabi Island (Cultivation and Burning of Land) (Amendment) Regulations, 1957 (Legal Notice no. 82, 1957); Rabi Island (Infectious Diseases) (Amendment) Regulations, 1957 (Legal Notice no. 83, 1957); Rabi Island (Miscellaneous Offences) Regulations, 1957 (Legal Notice no. 84, 1957); Rabi Island Regulations (Application) Order, 1957 (Legal Notice no. 85, 1957); Banaban (Copra) Regulations, 1958 (Legal Notice no. 6, 1958); Banaban (Copra Cess) Regulations, 1958 (Legal Notice no. 7, 1958); Banaban (Rabi Island Council) (Amendment) Regula-

As I noted, the extent to which reponsibility for general well-being lies with the council is not clear. The council's responsibility to pursue the phosphate and autonomy goals relates to the other issues, since there is the general feeling that if everyone had his financial due from phosphate, most things would take care of themselves. It is a muddle.

There are, however, problems of legitimacy even here. During the meeting at which Saunders, the lawyer from Suva, was greeted, these problems arose. A Seventh Day Adventist, long an opponent of the Methodist political ingroup, rose to ask whether there was no way in which the landowner could make his voice heard in the selection of legal or Banaban advisers. This man's village councillor answered from the podium that any of his constituents was free to speak to him at any time, and if there was one in the audience who was ever denied a hearing, he should identify himself. The Seventh Day Adventist was rather outmaneuvered by the reply, but the point was one which was well understood, and not new. After the meeting, a friend commented that the Adventist had raised the question at the wrong time, but it was something "in the minds of all landowners": perhaps, in some matters of collective interest, especially those involving phosphate rights, which almost all matters do, the landowners as a group should be consulted. Although the council is elected, it is not elected only by Banabans, and it may be out of touch with the views of the landowners.

Through its power over the allocation of community resources, such as vehicles and the working hours of its employees, and its role in the assignment of land for houses, gardens, and churches, the council touches upon the domain of every kind of social unit on Rambi. Some of the details of this are irrelevant to the present analysis, and others will be treated elsewhere. But relevant at this point is the council's role in actually defining, for certain contexts, the boundaries of social relationships and their domains. With regard to kinship, for example, it was a council decision to prohibit new adoptions of Gilbertese by Banabans, and the council and magistrate are involved in what shall be considered the near kindred, whose consent is required to legalize an adoption. It is the council which is charged with deciding whether a religious group may build a school, or how many churches it may have. It is the council which defines the boundaries of garden land assigned to each village. These concerns extend into adjudicating the relationships between social units, both positively and negatively, as when it

---

tions, 1958 (Legal Notice no. 8, 1958); Banaban (Rabi Island Court) Regulations, 1958 (Legal Notice no. 9, 1958); Banaban (Settlement) (Amendment) Ordinance, 1965 (no. 32, 1965); Banaban Lands Ordinance, 1965 (no. 31, 1965). I wish to acknowledge the assistance of Mr. M. J. C. Saunders who identified these regulations. Saunders refers to a 1952 regulation which I have been unable to track down. See also Land Court minutes, RIC.

was decided that if visiting dignitaries were greeted in the traditional Banaban manner, or traditional sports played in the traditional way, all involving descent group rights, the amount of argument among the relevant groups might lead to violence, and so the council itself assumed the functions of direction.

Coupled with this definitional and adjudicative involvement in social relationships, there is a progressive disinvolvement from other aspects of them as solidarities. A significant process occurring on the island is the halting and erratic establishment of an independent domain of community political activity, in dissociating community matters from religious matters and others; for example, there is a discussion on whether sects should put up candidates for council elections; on whether the diffuse obligations of support for kinsmen apply in community matters.

But there remain certain anarchic tendencies in community political thinking, a disinclination to recognize the virtues, as it were, of the social contract. This is part of a generalized value which opposes the taking of orders from, or the overt expression of authority toward, anyone not being in such a position through kinship, age or sex. It was manifested in the question of one man: "Would we be freer if we had no council?" The problem of *legitimacy* of a binding decision-making entity is a troublesome one.

I will conclude this section by picking up one strand just played out, weaving it together with others which have already been mentioned, and producing a few new loose ends.

The term *community matters* is a Banaban term. There are also family matters, church matters, and village matters. Communal, kinship, religious, and village units are the most important collective structural components of the society. There is no one kind of unit, however, which is so dramatically multifunctional that an entire sociological analysis could be pegged on it. The kind of integration that obtains in many respects is what Schneider and Roberts (1956) call "ego-oriented" rather than "group-oriented." The person is at the center of a complex of ties different from those of other persons, but the *kinds* of ties for most people are the same.

Certain functions are unambiguously in the domains of the units mentioned. Families arrange marriage ceremonies, villagers arrange what to do with a meetinghouse, churches choose their elders. There is also a formal overlap among these domains with regard to certain activities (for example, both the church and the family are concerned with marriages), and this is one of the ways in which the system is glued together.

Then there are the ambiguities in all the domains, in their functional boundaries. Certain things are supposed to happen but their domain allocation is unclear: the role of the churches in elections, for example.

This kind of domain ambiguity may be a general feature of structures of this kind in societies of small scale. Social units try to shore up their solidarity, or extend their membership, or both, by drawing on other kinds of solidary ties: churches work through kinship networks, for example, or kinship units work through churches. For this kind of thing, however, they pay a price. The price is that the use of other kinds of solidary ties makes the user particularly sensitive to divisiveness which relates more directly to those other kinds of ties than to itself: a dispute among kin, for example, can split a church. The social unit is in a position of trying to have its cake and eat it too, but this is very tricky.

Domain confusion may thus be an endemic feature, but it is also a feature of the resettlement and wildly changing situation in which the people find themselves. Certain things are supposed to be done which did not have to be done in the old days. Certain things *can* be done which could not be done in the old days. Yet it is the nature of the case that there are not clearly established routines for accomplishing these things. Many Ocean Island routines are not viable in the Rambi situation. Copra cutting and fishing carry more regularized routines, but these touch on relatively internally oriented activities—subsistence—rather than more clearly externally oriented activities, which are of such importance to the people, and the articulation of those routines even with larger internally oriented concerns is not entirely clear.

The response that one finds is what was mentioned earlier: testing. Families, churches, villages, elaborate ideas of what they might do (form a store, put up a candidate, have a cooperative cleaning campaign) and are not sure of whether they can do it, or even whether they really want to do it. So they try to do it, try to give tangible form to their ideas of what they are and what they might be—*action to disambiguate concept.* Since the social field is composed of a number of units testing out, people may find that a retreat is necessary, or desirable, or both, because a collision is in process. They may then begin to reformulate their ideas of what they are and what they might be. This is a very simple model, but it accounts for a bewildering variety of data.

The social units which are relevant to this process and to the cultural and social structure include one which was mentioned in chapter 2: the person. The person qua person has certain obligations and certain freedoms, as do other cultural units of social structure. But it is true that the domain of the person, and his area of freedom, are not as clearly specified as are those of other units. The person's domain is partially a residual one in terms of freedom and includes those things which are not already allocated to other social units. This aspect would fall within Levy's (1962) category of individualism "by default" rather than "by ideal," with the exception of certain concepts derived from Christianity.

I have introduced the term *freedom* because the Banabans do. There is a strong and general value on freedom, and social obligations are often felt as oppressive. Beyond the domains of kinship, age and sex roles, as noted above, a kind of nervous egalitarianism prevails, and even within those domains the acknowledgment of authority is not lightly felt. Those domains are the ones which tap most directly into the culturally defined facts of life, and they are also the domains within which the relationship between social identity and behavioral norm is more firmly bound.

The person as a unit is testing itself out also, attempting to define its domain. Again, this may be a constant feature of certain structural forms. This feature is also upgraded by the whole direction of Banaban history and the kinds of changes which have taken place.[14]

When action of a novel kind is to be undertaken, the burden of proof is on the group to show that it is not interfering with the freedom of the individual; it is not upon the individual to show that he is not compromising the solidarity of the group. In directing many community political activities, native politicians often *apologize* to their constituents for the exercise of leadership, for limiting their personal freedom. There are strong arguments about whether some task should be assigned to any group, or whether it properly resides in the domain of the person.

In summary: The person is a unit alternative to and complementary with other units. Also, it is persons who belong to other social units, and membership in those units establishes social identities for the person. Someone is a Methodist, a member of X village, a Banaban, and so forth. He is also a person, and when these social identities are stripped away, person-ness, as it were, remains. The recognition of this has certain normative consequences, as Read (1955) has argued in his paper contrasting Gahuku-Gama with Christian morality. Since the Banabans are Christians, many of his observations apply to them. Certain kinds of behavior are enjoined between human beings as human beings, or persons. The people contrast people with animals and can critically compare them. "He's just like an animal," is a statement meaning that someone has exhibited behavior inappropriate to human beings. Not all disapproved behavior calls for this kind of condemnation; one can also point out that a person is manifesting European rather than Banaban behavior.

There is a premise that, fundamentally, people do not like to be led, and that except in a few well-defined areas, it is presumptuous, if at times

14. One may note in this regard that although the churches stress group organization, both the theoretically voluntary nature of church membership and the multiplication of positions of church responsibility are "individualizing" in nature. The descent system was also individualizing, but in part through multiple membership, which is not a feature of the religious membership system. For a discussion of part of this problem in evolutionary terms, see Carroll 1966.

necessary, to try to direct their activities, to compel them to behave in a particular way. This is reflected in the appearance that so many groups give of being in a state of imminent dissolution.

People react to their sense of this not with joy but rather with a kind of sorrow: c'est la vie, and isn't it dreadful. This is quite instructive. People have images of what groups should be like; they can and do lecture on the virtues of cooperation, group solidarity, and continuity. These are general values, but so too are the values of freedom of the person and equality. Banabans can speak from a group or custom frame of reference, or an individual frame of reference, and produce different statements thereby. On the one hand, people are referred to as being bound in every move; on the other, as being as free as birds.

The situation is encapsulated in a Gilbertese formula which concludes some songs and can be uttered when a child sneezes: "health, peace, and precedence." "Being desired" is sometimes added to it. The problem is that seeking after individual precedence may be incompatible with peace. The term for precedence (*te tabomoa*) here, the only term I know in Gilbertese which has this meaning, was never spoken in my hearing in another context. It may be that a very threatening area is being tapped.

The people recognize that envy is one of the major disconcerting factors in their lives—it is in their nature as Banabans, and they have been unable to overcome it. It is freely admitted, for example, that many will oppose the supporting from community funds of the higher education of children who are not their own, because those children and their families will rise in prestige. This is the dark side of the formal ideal of egalitarianism. It is a bad thing which threatens the progress of the community, but it is recognized that individual and family considerations are difficult to transcend. And just as behaving in a certain manner for the benefit of a group or conformity to an explicit norm are sufficient explanations of behavior, so is self-interest.

As is the case in some other societies, I suggest that here an attempt to resolve the conflict between individual prestige-seeking and egalitarianism-group solidarity is made by channeling the culturally defined ambitions of individuals into group activity. Pride in the group is a legitimate form of public expression, whereas pride in the concrete individual is not. Churches manifest this most directly, but villages and the community itself do also. The reflected-glory principle leads to competitive activities between groups, which require organization. Organization in turn requires the distribution of authority, and there will thus be people in authority. These people, however, are liable to the accusation of seeking their own prestige, which may indeed be true. For them the situation is a very tricky one, and a high degree of political and rhetorical skill is called for to navigate in it. If this skill is not consummate, there is dissension, and the effective operation of the group is compromised. This in turn leads to frustration as the channel for expression dissipates.

People are often unwilling to take steps which would permit groups to be as they are supposed to be within the group frame of reference. There is a genuine and basic bind in social values: between group solidarity and individual freedom, between individual freedom and prestige-seeking, between obligation and free will (compare Reay 1959). One of the implications of this bind, as we have suggested, is that the leader is subject to the quite realistic fear of imminent condemnation. It is a hard insult to accuse someone of being pushy, pretentious, trying to put himself above others *(kamoamoa)*. Many shrink from leadership because they do not want to take the risk.

The inability to maintain united group action is seen as a major source of difficulty in coping with current problems, including the problem of effectively dealing with outside authority. No one is satisfied with the present economic and political state of affairs, and for this state of affairs, the people blame primarily the government. Yet there is a sense in which they also blame their own nature. This relieves the individual of personal responsibility for the dilemma (compare Campbell 1966) by partially placing the burden of guilt upon the community as a whole. At the same time, one of their major concerns is the maintenance of that community as a distinct and autonomous entity within the colony of Fiji, and they define their uniqueness in terms of a valued common custom different from that of other groups in the Colony.

There is thus, an ambivalence in the attitude that the people have toward themselves. This ambivalence and the value conflicts are reflected in the disjointed nature of political expression over time. One finds both an ironic shrugging of the shoulders and a hitting out at the representations of local and outside authority. One of the consequences of this is that administrative officials cannot build up a set of coherent expectations about community behavior, and they at times react to events on the island in an ad hoc way. This in turn means that the members of the community cannot build up a set of coherent expectations about administration behavior, and this vicious circle only exacerbates the sense of inability to cope with major problems.

Where such an inconsistency of values exists, one naturally looks for an operational resolution in terms of contextual separation, or ranking; in the political domain, perhaps institutionalization through political parties. The Rorobuaka Society may be a nascent indicator of the latter situation. But to repeat, the problem here is that the differentiation of a distinct domain of community matters is a process now underway. In precolonial times there was apparently little genuinely collective Banaban action. The creation of the Banaban community as a corporate entity was basically a response to the requirements of colonial administration and to the requirements of dealing with the phosphate company. A paternalistic government and company provided many of the things the people must now provide for themselves, if they want them, and made many of the decisions that the people are now faced with making for themselves. Thus a clash between the ideas of collective and individual responsibility had little opportunity to occur in concrete situations, since such situations occurred but rarely.

At several points I have parenthetically remarked that aspects of the Banaban dilemma are not distinctive to the Banabans. Individualistically oriented readers may find that responsive chords have been struck. Anthropologically minded readers may see other societies being described. Far from claiming that the Banaban situation is unique, I suspect that we can now specify a certain type of society within a logical range of types, although I will not go into a long excursus on this here. I must point out, however, the following: An individual may feel a conflict between individual and collectivity orientations. If he assents, however, to the legitimacy of a differentiated structure which has binding decision-making powers on a broad range of issues, that conflict has a very different "environment" than it does in the situation where he does not so assent, or where there is no such structure. And if he is not actually faced with having to make decisions with real implications for whether a road will be built, a cooperative strengthened, or a planning campaign instituted, *for the whole society,* his articulation with the real social world is different from that of a person who does. The average Banaban, and perhaps the average person in other small-scale societies injected into the modern world, is being called upon to act in a context in which the implications of his action have more immediate structural consequences for his society than do our own individual actions for our society.

Much of Banaban social behavior is most comprehensible if we assume that they are trying to formulate a cultural paradigm of social structure with the following elements: (1) Christianity (universalizing) and custom (particularizing) as bases of morality; (2) principles of social classification and subdivision (for example, communal, religious, village, kinship, age, sex) which provide categories to make social action comprehensible and ground the constitution of social groups and networks; and (3) the person.

There is constraint, not only because of the fundamental nature of society itself, but also because of the value on freedom and the testing out of domains.

Freedom is one cultural label for the value on maximizing options. Any system, of course, defines a range of options. (Note that I am not speaking here of individuals manipulating out of a primal self-interest; I am speaking of the system definition of interest.) One may perhaps contrast systems which emphasize the filling of a niche rather than the juggling of alternatives. But even in the first case, there is a range of options, and one can imagine a value on keeping much of the range alive. It may be argued, therefore, that adducing a value such as "Keep your options open" does not get one very far. How far it gets one depends upon the *level* of the value system which is involved.

At one level, options X, Y, and Z may be means toward a single end. At another level, options X, Y, and Z may be ends. One may rationalize X, Y, and Z as a system, that is, one may institutionalize priorities among them, or institutionalize a set of principles for the assignment of priorities. Or one may not. If one does not and furthermore regards concerted movement in one direction as excluding the possibility of other directions, then one has a serious case of option maximizing at the highest level. This is, I suggest, the Rambi situation.

We have alluded to a number of Banaban values: the maintenance of diffuse solidary ties; community autonomy and the conservation of cultural identity; solidarity and continuity; a high level of consumption of modern goods and services; religious salvation; and personal freedom, equality, and repute. These are code-for-conduct meanings of the symbols of blood, land, custom, progress, God, and the person. The codes for conduct, however, are not only codes for conduct in the logical symbolic sense. They are *commitments*.

There are two problems. The first is how to actualize some of the commitments. For example: what kind of action is appropriate to attain group autonomy? One of the ways in which the answers to such questions are sought is in looking to the experience of other communities: external models. The second problem, and one that is more fundamental, is that of ranking, of structuring these commitments. And with more of the Banabans' affairs under their own control, as we have observed, this has become a serious problem plaguing the council, so much so that action in many spheres becomes relatively stymied. There is a demand for action, but, I suggest, a retreat from ranking, and for many things ranking is necessary for action.

Obviously a number of these ends became defined in the mission-colonial period. The colonial situation was not conducive to a rationalization of ends, for reasons which are clear from the structure of the Ocean Island social field: the lack of local integration, the failure to develop a legitimized decision-making body, the blocks to institutionalization, and the consequent lack of necessity to face up to potential contradictions. I do not think, however, that the value of "Keep your options open" developed as a *response* to

the colonial condition. It existed in what had been a relatively undifferentiated society with a relatively ego-oriented structure. Then its field of
activity, as it were, became that of a dependent unit, a unit in a colonial
structure. And the value was nurtured by uncertainties about what kinds of
action superordinate authority would take.

In concrete situations, people do of course rank among ends. A *pattern*
of ranking is not institutionalized. My colleague A. Thomas Kirsch has suggested two related consequences of such a system. First, people need not
make the same judgments (or have the same expectations) about the consistency of behavior as they do in a more rationalized system. Second, there
is a different attitude toward the implications of having made a particular
choice at a particular time: an attitude of "conditional acceptance." One
is not heavily committed to a choice; decisions are not as perpetually binding. Thus the exercising of one option does not exclude others.

One may term the entire situation one of "fluid commitments." There is
a quality of tentativeness to social life, a lack of positive expectations about
the long-term behavior of others. These are qualities which I felt on Rambi,
and which I believe the Banabans feel.

Another phenomenon which this value may illuminate is that of *gossip*.
The social and psychological functions of gossip have received some attention by scholars in recent years, and their conclusions apply to the Rambi
situation. An additional function may be this: People must act, and people
must act on the basis of expectations about the behavior of others. Where
there is not a consistent, highly generalized pattern of expectations, the
most one can do is try to assess the current dispositions of others, even
while recognizing the tentativeness of such assessments. Gossip is a means
of providing an on-going source of information for such assessments.

Other than the highly general value of option maximization, what are the
instruments of the integration (if in some aspects limited) of Rambi Island
society and culture?

The primary instruments of structural integration are the person and the
island council. The primary instruments of action integration are activities
which involve a multiplicity of ties and symbols drawn from different domains (to this we will return later).

The primary instrument of symbolic integration at this level is the interplay between the person and the symbolic complex focusing on land. Land
encapsulates notions of the individual as an individual, as a member of
families, as a Banaban. It is something personal and perpetual. And through
the phosphate issue, as before, it unites group interest with self-interest,
and orientations to the past expressed in custom—the assertion of conceived
traditional values—with a commitment to a modernized future. Winning

the case, from the Banaban point of view, would allow for the maximization of all options.

In the Conclusion I will take up further aspects of this line of argument. At this point, however, the following may be said: We recall that as structures differentiate, values must be pushed to a higher level of generality if the substructures are to function more adaptively. There are some indications from current Banaban history that certain things are becoming more highly generalized. The focus, however, on land, and thus on phosphate, is at an extremely high level. The normal specification process that one might expect for other values has been blocked by this focus.

In subsequent chapters we will see applications of the theory of Banaban structure posed in this section.

11

People, Lands, and Localities on Rambi

We have discussed in some detail the concept of Rambi as a whole, and how it is related to the concept of Ocean Island as a whole. Only incidentally in the discussion of the Banaban Community Store and the council did the question of places on Rambi arise. We will be concerned now with some aspects of the formation of villages as localities, the establishment of the village domain, and the subdivision of the lands. The interplay of notions about Ocean Island and about Rambi will again be manifest.

The four villages are named as they were on Ocean Island: Tabwewa, Uma, Tabiang, and Buakonikai. Nuka, which is between Tabwewa and Uma, and was the site of the original settlement, contains the council's headquarters. One occasionally hears it jokingly referred to as "the town." For some activities, such as intravillage competitions (which may be rehearsals for intervillage ones) and various projects for which food must be provided, the villages may be divided into geographic sections. Physically this is reminiscent of the old Banaban model—differentiated sections of a village district—but it is devoid of the descent aspect.

There are nineteen small hamlets located in coconut plantations. A few are permanently occupied by a core and floating population; others are occupied periodically. (In early 1965, during the school holidays, one-fifth of the people were living in the hamlets.) The villages and plantation areas lexically contrast. The larger of the plantation areas have for some time been assigned to a particular village, for example, Tabwewa people have the right to collect coconuts in Ntaku and Nasau, Uma people in Matuku. The non-assigned areas are open territory.

The first stage of the lands subdivision, giving one acre of coconut land to every member of the Banaban Community, has been completed in Buakonikai and Tabiang, is underway in Uma and has not yet begun in Tabwewa. The villages are thus in different stages of a directional process, and we will look briefly at some history to explicate it.

At the time of the arrival on Rambi, it will be recalled, the plantation areas were worked through the co-op, workers first receiving daily wages and then money according to the amount of copra they cut. The dispersal from Nuka picked up after the return from the Ocean Island boundary marking, which was after the decision to stay. By 1949 clusters had formed in the neighborhood of the old Levers' driers, and the council was formally considering the founding of villages to correspond in some fashion with the Ocean Island villages. By 1949 also the Banaban names had begun to displace the old Fijian names for the areas. The Banabans were inscribing themselves on the landscape, and the landscape in themselves.[1]

Around 1957, the site of one of the clusters around a Levers' copra drier, which was becoming Tabiang village, was moved. The new place was more pleasant, and also there are indications that there was a religious split, with more of the Catholics staying in the old area, which became a hamlet. In Buakonikai, the location of houses has for a long time been regarded as temporary. The people consider their present site not entirely suitable and are waiting to pick out a better (but nearby) one. This has delayed the building of concrete-block houses there. The residence situation has been in flux.

The geographic interrelationship of the villages which formed was not the same as that on Ocean Island, although some apparently had that in mind. On the question of continuity of personnel between the Ocean Island villages and the Rambi villages, I have a mass of data not yet converted into patterns. People were officially free to go where they wanted. To some their residence on Ocean Island or their identification with a village district descent unit or both were apparently sufficient to motivate them to go to a particular place. To others these factors were not. In fact, the series *kain* (person or people of) *Tabwewa-kain Uma-kain Tabiang-kaini Buakonikai* refers either to the Rambi village with which a person is identified, or to the Ocean Island village where an ancestor is supposed to have lived. Thus someone may be *kain Tabwewa* vis-à-vis Rambi, but *kain Tabwewa* and *kain Uma* vis-à-vis Ocean. When asked why they live in a particular village, some will say, "We have always been people of that village; we lived there on Banaba." Others will say, "We like it," or refer to the proximity of the central school, rich coconut land, or other factors, including those of kinship and religion.

The village occupies a rather peculiar position. It was observed in part 2 that both the administration and the church defined the reformulated village as a significant unit. In pre-European times, the spirit house was a sacred

1. Holland, Handing over statement; Coode to Colonial Secretary, 27 September 1949, Personal Files of Rotan Tito.

center and the meetinghouse a perhaps more secular center for the village district, in general. It may even have been the case that the meetinghouse reflected more directly the nature of the village district as a territory, and the spirit house reflected more directly the nature of the village district as a descent unit. The historical material unfortunately does not allow for a conclusive statement. With the coming of the mission and the government, there were village meetinghouses and church meetinghouses. Although significant as a unit of organization, the village may have been more an artifact of the administrative and religious systems, in the context of their being transformations of the descent system.

Insofar as a domain of village matters has been established on Rambi, it is composed mainly of two sets of functions: those derived from its position in relation to the community and the council, and those derived from custom. I shall reserve most of the discussion of the latter for chapter 14.

The villages as units are most vivid in athletic competitions and dance performances (generally also competitive), activities associated with the idea of the meetinghouse, which take place on colony-wide holidays, the anniversary of the arrival on Rambi, the greeting of distinguished visitors, and a number of other occasions. When the village athletes or dancers win or lose in a competition, it is the village which wins or loses. The teams represent the village; some of the games are traditional ones, and we are dealing with a transformation of the ritual game aspect of the descent system.

More materially significant are the electoral, educational, and business aspects of the village domain. Each village elects two councillors, and the councillors are channels (but not the only ones) between the village and the community. Tabwewa and Uma share a school in Nuka (the last two years of education there are, however, for the children of all villages), and there are schools in Tabiang and Buakonikai. Elected parents' committees attempt to raise money for the school. The schools are in the difficult but familiar position of being creatures of both the council (which makes some regulations governing them) and the villages, each at times trying to convince the other that the other has the financial responsibility.

We have already referred to the village cooperatives. Before the recent amalgamation, each village had a cooperative store, spoken of as "our cooperative," but with a membership formally distinct from that of the village.

The Banaban Cooperative Association, Ltd., into which the four societies were amalgamated on the advice of officers of the Fiji Department of Cooperative Societies, found itself in difficulties during its first year. The headquarters store was charged with monopolizing the best and the most goods, and in part because of unpaid debts, no dividend could be paid. The people in villages with few debts saw no reason why they should suffer in not receiving dividends because people in other villages suffered from fiscal irresponsibility. There was also general feeling that each village store should order its own goods and be independent of central administration. The popular phrase was, "The cooperative should return to the village," and at least on the retail side, this may be done. One of the relevant elements in what may be interpreted as a contest of solidarities in which the village won is that the cooperative was an institution removed from the village and tacked on, as it were, to the community. The situation was watched to see whether the change would be economically beneficial, and it was not. Part of the feeling probably derives from the fact that the co-op is the most tangible continually functioning institution involving all the villagers. It is an institution which gives shape to the idea of the village itself. The teams serve the same function.

The identification of the co-op with the village does not, however, prevent people from conducting transactions outside it. To the dismay of some officials, many people (who are co-op members) are large customers of small private businesses, and some of the most active people in the co-operative movement have stakes in those businesses. Thus the profit of the co-ops is reduced. The question of credit is involved here. It is easier to run up large credit balances with some private stores than with the co-ops. Through dealing with more than one retail unit one can cast wide one's credit. Some of the private operators are shrewder purchasers than the co-ops. But the economic sphere also demonstrates one dimension of the "Maximize your options" principle well: it might be called, "Hedge your bets."

On Ocean Island traditionally the meetinghouse embodied the village. Some say that the villages are not yet true villages because there are no true village meetinghouses in them. The Methodists in the villages have built religious meetinghouses, and these from time to time play the role of village ones. But they are not "real meetinghouses, the body of the village." The village lacks its true center. Land for a village meetinghouse has already been reserved in Uma, and there is talk in Tabwewa of giving the church meetinghouse to the village; the church's new meetinghouse has just been completed. Queen Elizabeth Hall (the name bears noting) in Nuka serves as a meetinghouse for the community as a whole. It was there that the two meetings discussed in the last chapter occurred.

The village meetinghouse is the tangible point of contact between the two components of the village domain. To this we will return.

The Rambi Catholic church is located at the south end of the Nuka area, within the Uma village boundary. At times in the immediate past, the Catholic choir and dance group has represented Uma at occasions involving more than one village. At some athletic competitions, primarily intervillage affairs, the Catholic group fields a team itself against Tabwewa, and in official greetings, performs on its own. With or without whom the Catholics perform is interpreted as a commentary on the state of village solidarity at the time. The Methodist-Catholic split is regarded as primarily responsible for the inability of villages to cooperate, as villages, in some activities. In Tabwewa and Uma it is also a split between competing descent units. In this sense, it is kinship and religious loyalties which split villages, not villages which split *them*.

At a recent Uma by-election, certain governmental electoral instructions were interpreted as indicating that the four organized sects should nominate one and only one candidate each. The four organized sects on Rambi are the Methodist (which took over from the LMS), the Roman Catholic, the Seventh Day Adventist (which was the first "new" sect on Rambi), and the Pentecostal church (the second new sect). The Methodists are by far the largest sect, and the Seventh Day Adventists and Pentecostals have small groups of adherents.

The notion that the sects should put up candidates was seen by some as a logical step; by others, as an incorrect mixing of religion and politics. If we look at individuals, we see that commitment to differentiation is uneven. Nomination by religious groups is more than the acceptance of sectarian grouping as a means for the communication of information (such as councillors explaining decisions at church meetings). It would be a recognition of the ineffectiveness of the village in meeting its own responsibilities.

All social units on Rambi are sensitive to developments in others. One encounters the interweaving of unity and divisiveness for which social structures of this kind are celebrated. The village may be particularly sensitive because it does stand as a unit without very much of an independent functional existence at this time. A few years ago the council called for the formation of small village committees. The Buakonikai villagers put forward their existing large committee of old men, but the other villages appeared to have difficulty in realizing the idea—an idea which may have called for a degree of organization inappropriate to the village.

The lack of a strong independent functional existence for the village is not the only reason for the strong sensitivity of the village to developments in other domains of the social structure. Another reason takes us back to one of the basic features of traditional Banaban culture: spatialization, the inscription of lines of social difference on the ground.

This is becoming manifest with the churches. Around the Catholic church in Nuka there is a small group of houses occupied by Catholics. The northern half of Tabwewa is regarded as being more of a Catholic place than the southern half. Some Seventh Day Adventists have gravitated to the area around their church. A small settlement has grown up around the Pentecostal church's headquarters; some live there permanently, and others come from elsewhere especially on weekends.

To varying degrees the villages and their populations bear local stereotypes: Uma people are contentious; Tabiang is small but beautiful, and a quiet place of the old and young; Buakonikai is strict, collectivist, Methodist, and the people are concerned with gardening; Tabwewa, Nuka, and the northern edge of Uma are livelier and reflect the presence of more modern, individualistically oriented bureaucrats, skilled and semiskilled laborers, and the income they receive.

The one large village which manifests a lively "village feeling" is Buakonikai, where village and congregation have become fused. There is a sentiment that the villages ought to act in a solidary fashion, but other lines of cleavage compromise that solidarity drastically. The village must apparently be shored up by other solidarities to make it a going concern. The solidarity in Buakonikai is widely admired, but even some Methodists regard it as having been bought at too great a price: the dedifferentiation of village and congregation, and the introduction of a strong regime.

Buakonikai is the only village with a village meetinghouse now, which doubles as the Buakonikai Methodist church, and thus indicates well the identification of church and village there. Although not used in geographical reference, Buakonikai's alternate name is New Buakonikai (*Buakonikai ae Bou*); the name is used in the village anthem with which Buakonikai generally begins its participation in intervillage dance competitions.

By decision of the elders, with Rotan as the moving force, Buakonikai is supposed to be an exclusively Methodist village; most of its members signed an agreement setting up *Te Bonnano* (Unanimity), the Methodist village-church organization, binding its members to decisions of the committee of elders. The old custom of precedence in the meetinghouse was abandoned in favor of organization by church positions, they say, because it was seen how the custom leads to arguments which divide the village. (Religious arguments may do the same, of course, but life was made uncomfortable enough for members of other sects, or highly individualistic Methodists, so that they either joined or left.) The name of the meetinghouse is The Joining, which symbolizes both the coming together of all willing people in the village of Buakonikai and the coming together of the two village districts (large descent units) which formed Buakonikai.

In combining village with religious solidarity, Buakonikai is unquestionably the most solidary of the villages. The people spend, for example, as much as two days per week in the leveling of the hill for the new church. This could "only happen in Buakonikai."

The original vision of an integral model has to some extent been implemented in Buakonikai. It was possible because it drew a sufficient number of people willing to rank one commitment above others (but not all others— see below) at the collectivity level: the commitment to religious salvation and to leading a publicly Christian life within a church-dominated community. Buakonikai is a living exemplar of what has to be done to achieve the kind of community solidarity which in a generalized fashion is valued.

The people of the village have not withdrawn from the rest of the island, nor are they constant proselytizers. They can operate outside their village on other rules. They have not closed off other avenues.

Although the quality of life in this village is different from that of life in the other villages, the elements of which its structure is composed are not different in their nature. What is different is how the elements are hierarchically combined (compare Geertz 1959). The situation there, however, is an extreme form of a tendency perhaps inherent in religious commitments —they can "break out" to essentially dedifferentiate the structure.

It is not only that religion defines itself as that element tapping the highest degree of ultimacy and that the churches are the only substantive units without overlapping membership. It is also that the religious model of organization, at a time when models are in need, is the clearest and most neatly worked out. Furthermore, the church, as a symbol, means progress, the transition from the pagan "time of darkness, ignorance" to the Christian "time of light, understanding."

In Buakonikai, the Rorobuaka Society (see chapter 10) was recently formed as part of a Methodist church drive to form such societies in all villages. The idea for it was brought back by the local Methodist minister, Rev. Tebuke Rotan, from a church conference in Samoa, where it was presented as a way to organize the active men of the village on behalf of their church, in raising funds and participating in building projects. As indicated earlier, its quick development on Rambi had political as well as religious aspects, and it was envisioned as an island-wide pressure group with village branches.

When Rotan, the senior Buakonikai councillor, in his role as elder of the Methodist church, called a meeting in Buakonikai and told the rorobuaka of the village that they should set up a society, there were many questions on what it would do, answered generally in terms of helping the church, and vague allusions were made to political parties. Some of the people protested that they were satisfied with the leadership of the old men of the village and did not want to compromise the status of Te Bonnano, the village organization led by the old men. Rotan said that Te Bonnano "would not be broken," and perhaps it was time that the younger men participated more fully in the leadership of the village.

The society, when formed, began to assume more of the functions of the old men's committee than, it seemed, was intended, and the "consultation with the elders" that was mentioned at the time of its formation was quietly dropped. Its decisions were considered more strict, trying, and hastily arrived at than those of the elders, who "know how to make considered decisions that please the people." One old man, a power on the Elders' Committee, returned from observing a meeting of the Rorobuaka Society shaking his head and chuckling. They have to talk endlessly, he said; everyone has his own opinion and will not defer to anyone else; someone proposes a task requiring a great deal of work and money, and others will not object as they fear being called pusillanimous. The younger men were testing themselves out as a group.

To raise the Buakonikai church's part of the Rambi Methodists' contribution to a Fiji-wide Methodist celebration, the society decided on a community copra-cutting excursion which practically denuded the area of coconuts. There was much grumbling, but it was more private than public. The Buakonikai contribution was the largest from Rambi, and the contribution from Rambi was reported to be the largest from the smaller islands. People were acting for the good name of the village, for the island, and for God. Fund raising is a crucial part of religious activities. It demonstrates the sacrifices that one makes for a total commitment. Giving money to the church and the pastor may be similar in nature to some aspects of "merit making" among Thai Buddhists (see Kirsch 1970). The pastor and the church are tangible representatives of divinity and are links to a dogma which may be imperfectly understood. Channeling money to them is thus a religious act of extreme importance and may also help the individual assure himself that he really is a Christian, that the pagan past, which in fact crops up here and there, is really dead.

The coming into power of the younger group in Buakonikai is not something I totally understand, but the following may be relevant. There is still a notion, realized in some places at some times, that the elders are the proper custodians of the meetinghouse, those who should supervise the internal concerns of the village. Some of the images of what is required in village leadership in general contrast with those of what is required in dealing with "the outside." For the village, the calm deliberation of the elders in things emanating from custom is more acceptable. Custom's domain is a familiar one which familiar forms of organization can handle. For dealing with the outside, the time of deliberation has ended. The fight is on.

It is difficult to effect the kind of solution where the elders focus on the village and the moderns mediate the village's relationship with the community and the central political-economic crisis. The meetinghouse itself is an institution *interrelating* the villages as well, and thus involving the community domain. The crisis is in part generated by interpretations of custom. In the Buakonikai case, furthermore, the validity of the gerontocracy was grounded in custom ("You must listen to the elders" is an oft-repeated injunction from Banaban custom), but the conception of the village (its religious exclusiveness) and the operation of the meetinghouse (in transcending the descent element) in the denial of custom. The explicit orientation of Buakonikai leaders—to wipe out divisive and bad old customs and maintain only the good ones—cannot be smoothly realized unless there is consensus on what the good and bad customs are, and the orientation itself opens the door to a general challenging of existing organizational models. The same point applies to the point of view of the government and church on Ocean Island.

The situation is thus fraught with contradictions, and the kind of action taken represented one response to those contradictions.

The tumultuous interplay of village, church, and kinship (we will have more to say of the latter in part 4) is another manifestation of the testing process. How far can you push a church? How far a village? In the Buakonikai case there was the advantage of Rotan. There is also the advantage of the relative isolation of Buakonikai from the other villages, which perhaps makes the maintenance of at least a surface of consensus a more urgent task.

I noted above the double reference of village terms but have not yet broached the question of which people are considered "people of" the villages.

In discussing community, we were able to make a very simple statement about what the distinctive features of Banaban are. Those things which constitute the domain of Banaban solidarity define what behaving as a Banaban is, and the different functions implicate the same people. The relationship between identity and code for conduct is relatively clear.

The situation is more complex for the village. If Tabwewa is holding a dance, the participation of people who hold land in Buakonikai but live in Tabwewa is just as natural as that of people who hold land in Tabwewa. A person can be a member of the Uma electorate, dance with Tabwewa, and garden with Buakonikai. For a long time, with registration of neither village nor housing land, the matter of who is a member of what must have been one of reasoning: He who behaves as a villager is a villager. But life has become more complex; that complexity involves the land subdivision.

The question of how Rambi land would be subdivided arose at the beginning, but uncertainty about settlement and concern with grievances relating to phosphate and autonomy deflected attention from the issue. It is also reported that there was not much real agitation for private ownership.[2] This would seem surprising, given the place of land in Banaban thinking, but it is less surprising if we assume that the concern with individual pieces of land was linked directly to Ocean Island and was a little later to become generalized to include Rambi land.

As early as 1949, the Adviser submitted alternative plans to the council. The first was to divide Rambi lands equally among Banaban landowners and to operate on the assumption that funds and their proceeds had compensated the larger holders. Faced with having to make a response, the Banabans probably invoked both the Ocean Island syndrome and economic advantage. The bigger holders disapproved of the scheme, and the smaller holders, possibly out of shame, were reported as having little to say, at least in public. The Adviser then proposed two divisions, the first equal, the second unequal, the aggregate to be in proportion to Ocean Island holdings. The problem with either the first or the second plan was that they required surveys, which are costly operations. A third plan called for beginning with a squatters system, and the council reacted favorably but had too many other things on its mind to follow through. The 1953 lands ordinance stipulated that land was to be held according to Banaban custom, which would give the people (and the government, if it were to step in as arbiter) a certain degree of freedom but provided no guidelines. Alienation of land outside the community (except to the Crown) was, however, forbidden.[3]

I do not know what went on in the succeeding period, except that the villages were forming, people had squatted, and lists of occupants of housing land were prepared. Some permanent houses were also being built. With the partial exception of the hamlets in the copra areas and some individuals, the basic pattern which emerged was that of the compact village. The copra areas provided some release from what was otherwise life in relatively compact villages.

In 1959 a survey was contracted for, and in 1960 the Adviser again

2. Banaban Community to High Commissioner for the Western Pacific (via Administrative Officer, Rabi), 7 March 1947, RIC.

3. Holland, Handing over statement; Banaban Land Ordinance, 1953 (cap. 112, 1956 series).

broached the problem of coconut land and housing sections. He laid out a number of alternatives and combinations of alternatives on coconut land: Divide all the land according to the proportions of landholdings on Ocean Island; divide half the land according to the proportions on Ocean Island and the other half equally among Banabans alive on the day of voting; divide all the land equally among Banaban landholders; divide all the land equally among Banabans alive on the day of voting; leave the matter up to the large landowners and elders of the villages.[4]

By this point, because of the political developments which had gone on and were going on, the solution of the lands problem called for a general confrontation of the problem of who the people were.

The central problem is in precisely what way Rambi represents Ocean Island. Rambi land in a certain sense *is* Ocean Island land and is Banaban land, since it was phosphate funds which purchased Rambi, phosphate funds come from Ocean Island lands, Ocean Island lands are owned by Banabans, and those lands are of both different acreage and different productivity in phosphate. Two issues apparently crystallized.

The first issue was whether among Banabans the land should be divided equally or in proportion to their holdings on Ocean Island. The second issue was whether or not resident Gilbertese (who are members of the "Banaban Community") would be allotted land. Both equal division among Banabans and allotment to Gilbertese seemed contrary to custom. Was Rambi, then, to replicate Ocean Island or to be a transformation of it? In a sense, were persons or Ocean Island landholdings to be "mapped" onto the new island?

Unfortunately, I lack precise data on the politics of the decision. The compromise solution was that the subdivision should have two phases. The first phase would be in the areas presently planted in coconuts, one person–one acre, including Gilbertese. (Coconut land was surveyed into one-acre blocks, and housing land into quarter-acre blocks.) Gilbertese were, after all, permanent residents of the island, and it was only kindness to "grant them their living." The Banaban-Gilbertese distinction is maintained, however, in the assumption by some that if a Gilbertese should die without issue, his plot would either be given to his surviving Banaban spouse (through whom his position in the Banaban Community is generally conceived) or revert to the council. In a similar case applying to a Banaban, the fate of the land would be decided according to the principles of the Banaban land tenure system (where the land does not pass to the spouse, but to the nearest consanguines).

The second phase of the subdivision would be in the bush land, among

4. Grant, A talk about Rabi lands (draft), to Banaban Community, 20 April 1960, RIC.

Banabans only, and in proportion to their holdings on Ocean Island. This was the solution, but the "Banaba firsters" still often point out what they see as the inequity of a solution whereby a Banaban with holdings on Ocean Island hardly larger than a floor mat, married to a Gilbertese, with eight children, would get ten acres of decent land in the first phase, whereas a small family of "true" Banabans who are land rich on Ocean Island might get only three.

As the subdivision proceeded, it appeared that the council was applying a certain qualification to the general principles, also applied in the distribution of annuities in 1965. Banabans living outside the colony of Fiji, and not outside because they were on a temporary job or being educated, were excluded from both. Shortly before I left Rambi, one of the Tabwewa councillors told me that two part-Banaban, part-Fijian families, who were listed among those eligible for the Tabwewa subdivision, should be removed from the list. These families own land elsewhere in the colony, live there most of the time, and are considered to have become Fijianized. When the question of the exclusion of nonresidents from the annuity and subdivision was brought up in one informal discussion, some people objected that it was unfair: they were Banabans, landowners, and had as much right to the Rambi land and annuity as anyone else. The councillor maintained, to the agreement of many people present, that they did not pay the island head tax, were thus not contributing toward the maintenance of the island, and should not receive the benefits of that maintenance.

Thus, as the situation develops, something is being added: those people are Banabans because they have Banaban ancestors, but this is not sufficient to warrant their inclusion in the Rambi community. Because they are Banabans, they have a certain right, but they have failed to exercise that right, and they thereby lose their claim. They are Banabans but have not been acting as Banabans. The community may be in a sense disinheriting its errant members. The identity/code paradigm of Banaban kinship and inheritance was being generalized to apply to the Rambi community, as it had been generalized to some extent on Ocean Island to apply to eligibility for certain critical benefits. Recall the decision of the Lands Commission and the annuity rules.

It is the village which acquired an important function in the lands subdivision. The subdivision is being executed in the village context under the direction of the village councillors, with the participation of a local council-appointed surveyor. When there is a dispute on the location of housing or garden land, the councillor alone, or with a general village meeting, is called upon to resolve it if the contending parties cannot. It is likely, however, that certain disputes will be carried to the lands court, which was legislated in the 1965 Lands Ordinance, and which consists of the magistrate and four council-appointed assessors. An appeals procedure allows disputes to be carried to the Commissioner, sitting with the Adviser. This ordinance vested Rambi Island freehold in the council (which had become a corporate body), in trust for the benefit of the Banaban Community.[5] Some disputes might be brought up to the council itself.

In the Uma subdivision, the first stages of which I witnessed, it was quite clear that the distribution of Uma land—how the assignment of people to plots would progress; where exceptions to the council guidelines of one man-one acre would be made—was first a village responsibility, *bain te kawa* (a village matter). Although the distribution of land on the basis of holdings on Ocean Island is supposed to take place later, in Buakonikai and Tabiang some people were tentatively assigned lands which it is said they had already planted, as equivalents of their Ocean Island lands.

The intention of some councillors, under expert advice, was that the members of one family would hold their land in contiguous blocks in their village, for reasons of agricultural efficiency. It was also mooted that families reside on those lands, but most seem to prefer the sociality of village living. Although the desirability of contiguous holdings was suggested, people were free to declare where they wanted their own and their children's land. Some have divided their children among more than one village to emphasize, make use of, or keep up *(kabonganaa)* their connection with that village (the assumption being that an ancestor lived there on Ocean Island). They say they will "have a place to eat" if they should want to take a holiday in another village. This is similar to the idea that it is good to have close relatives in another village because one would have a place to stay there.

Some spouses have taken their garden plots in different villages, either alone or with their consanguines. A child may be entered in the register of another village on his own, or perhaps with a grandparent there. A few people have already declared their intention of having their one acre (first phase) plot in one village, and their "land from Banaba" (second phase) in another. Thus, whereas the village was a garden-land holding unit under the earlier Rambi system, under the new system all people normally resident in one village will not own land in it, and concomitantly, people not normally resident in a village will. This is more nearly the old Banaban pattern and is recognized as such. "It may be better farming to have your lands together, but custom dies hard."

The Uma people decided on a method of their own, and individuality is supposed to be an old trait of Uma people. It was decided at a village meeting

5. Banaban Lands Ordinance, 1965 (no. 31, 1965); Banaban (Settlement) (Amendment) Ordinance, 1965 (no. 32, 1965).

that, still within the framework of the one man-one acre principle, first one acre would be assigned to each quarter-acre house plot, as close to it as possible. There is not enough land in the village area proper to go around, and people said that it would be ridiculous to have to go miles to your land in the plantations to get a coconut for dinner.

Although everyone is entitled to one acre, and the assumption is that these are individual lands, where subdivision has occurred the land has not (yet) been listed in the names of individuals. In Buakonikai and Tabiang, where the first phase of subdivision has been completed, and in Uma, where it is underway, in the lands book the code numbers of the allocated lands (corresponding to the numbers on the survey map) are listed under the English entry "Names in the family," which is itself under "Head of family." The head of family where a Banaban is married to a Gilbertese is generally the Banaban (a feature of "nationality"). Where both are Banabans, it is generally the name of the man (a feature of sex roles in marriage). The relevant matter here is that the family is allotted the number of acres corresponding to the number of names, and it is expected to decide itself who gets which acre. For the purposes of garden-land ownership, the village confronts these families as units; it is subdivided into them. The family is what the people involved say the family is. A person may live all the time with his parents in Tabwewa but for lands subdivision be listed with his grandparents in Buakonikai. Or he may be listed by himself.

Allocation of village housing land presents both similar and different problems. The original idea was that each married couple would be allotted a quarter-acre section within the village area proper (not in the outlying hamlets) and would be entitled to one cement-block house built on it (from the construction program jointly financed by the BPC and the trust fund). If an unmarried person's parents had died, the eldest of the sibling group would receive title on behalf of his siblings.

A problem that subsequently arose was whether, when both spouses were Banabans, they should both receive plots (it was acknowledged that they should share one house), perhaps even in different villages. As someone put it, "Are not both spouses landholders?"—on Ocean Island. And another, "If the section was registered in my husband's name, and he died and his family turned me out, where would I go?" The council, in an ingeniously indefinite solution, voted that a Banaban spouse could be granted another housing section if he wanted one, if there was enough land in the village.

The problem here is, Who is entitled to housing land in the village? How is the village structured for this purpose? A house plot should go to an individual who is *oinibai* or *toronibai,* which in other usages mean a real, valuable, genuine, or useful thing. In this context I will translate it as re-sponsible entity. A responsible entity here is: (1) a married couple and their unmarried children, if any; (2) a married person; (3) an unmarried person or the unmarried members of a sibling set both of whose parents have died; (4) an unmarried person or the unmarried members of a sibling set with one surviving parent who has remarried and has had children with the second spouse; (5) a person not a responsible entity by the preceding criteria, but who was willed a particular house.

I cannot fully explicate the responsible entity concept without going into the details of kinship concepts. I will, however, outline the position now and repeat the points in context in chapters 12 and 13.

Although marriage does not terminate a person's relationship with his natal kin, a new social identity is conferred upon him. Siblings in one sense constitute a unit, but they are differentiated by their affinal relationships. Thus the unmarried members constitute a responsible entity, and it is gen-erally assumed that the junior siblings will be "under the eldest."

The case of remarriage is classic. A person ought to treat his spouse's children by a previous marriage as his own. If he does not, it is reprehensible but understandable. If there are children by the new marriage, the child from the first should get a housing section of his own, with his siblings, since there "might be trouble" with the step-parent, although it is still said that the parent is really the responsible entity. The step-parent may favor his own children; that is the explicit reason. The code is there, but the sub-stance lacking. Even if the step-parent is kin to the deceased parent (the ideal case), the situation does not change. Substance is present, but the person's own children complicate the picture by introducing a potentially qualifying solidarity.

The solidarity of spouses is similar to that of consanguines in its diffuse-ness, but there is added an element of impermanence. Thus two quarter-acres can be allocated for spouses: there is always the eventuality of separation, death, or divorce, and an ambiguous position for the surviving spouse vis-à-vis the family of the deceased spouse, who could exercise control over the housing section. The position thus reflects both the status of landholder in the community system and the fact that marriage confers a distinct social personality upon the individual.

Thus notions of both nationality and kinship are being inscribed in the subdivision. Land reflects nationality and kinship identities, which them-selves are formed through land or blood or both, and marriage. And the subdivision thus far has shown the operation of the "Keep your options open" principle: through the compromise solution which is giving land to both Banabans and Gilbertese; the compromise plan to give Banabans some land equally and some land in proportion to holdings on Ocean Island; the decision of the members of a significant number of families to distribute their lands over more than one village; the decision of the council ideally to allow a house-plot for each Banaban spouse.

There is talk now of closing the villages, meaning that no new names will be accepted for the allocation of garden land on the one man-one acre principle. People who have declared their intention of taking their house plot in one village would not be permitted to transfer to another. The only discussion of how this land would pass from one person to another has concerned, as far as I know, inheritance. People (again, to my knowledge) have not thought out the implications of the arrangement: A distinct set of people would hold garden land in that village, and only the children of a holder would be garden landholders in the village. Among the members of a sibling group, for example, those born after the closing would have no land under this kind of distribution. If this arrangement is followed through, a number of problems might arise, for example, what would happen if a person moves from one village to another, because of either inclination or marriage? (One may speculate that people might exchange lands, as apparently happened from time to time on Ocean Island.)

The question of how the second phase subdivision will be conducted, however, that of "land from Banaba," has not yet been answered. Thus the village would be closed in a very limited sense.

The one matter where a substantive definition of village membership is called for is the electoral function. When I asked some people about who could vote where, they pondered the matter and pointed to the case of one woman living in Tabwewa who took her garden acre in Buakonikai and voted with Buakonikai; "That must be the principle." Another woman, who lives in Tabwewa but has her garden acre with her father in Buakonikai, said, "I can't even vote in the Tabwewa election," and represented this as an understandable but troublesome piece of red tape. A councillor, when asked about who the villagers were who were entitled to vote, said those who had land in the village. When I mentioned that someone might have a housing section in one village and his garden acre in another, he replied that the housing section would be definitive. This is, of course, incomplete, since a person over twenty-one who is not a responsible entity does not have a housing section yet is entitled to vote. In another instance, when it was said that a certain man who had Uma ancestors but was living with his wife in Buakonikai was going to take all his land in Buakonikai, some Uma people commented, "He is now wiped off Uma."

I doubt if the comment would have been made, however, by the man in question. We have been speaking about elections, but the village is more than an electoral unit. For a long time, with registration of neither housing nor garden land, as stated above, the matter must have been one of reasoning: Someone who behaves as a villager is a villager. From the point of view of the village, there is a unit with certain functions. But the people implicated in those different functions are not necessarily the same. For each function, and thus for the analytic status of the relationship, the grounds for participation have been self-declaration. The ambiguity in the relationship among the functions (for example, land ownership, or what kind of land ownership, and right to vote) has the same import as the failure of the attempt to have a family take its house and all the lands of its members in the same village. From an individual's point of view, he has relationships with a number of villages through different functions. The emphasis in the concept of the village is in bringing these functions into line; the emphasis in the concept of the person is extensional and option maximizing. Both the village and the person are testing out.

The elements with which a cultural paradigm of social structure is being formulated (see chapter 10) specify this condition. There is a dialectic between the person frame of reference and the group frame of reference. The "state of the system at the time" is the form that the dialectic is taking. Since the elements are testing themselves out, in an environment of other elements testing themselves out, the situation is unstable but analytically comprehensible.

Some things are, however, becoming codified. Filiation has been combined with something else as a criterion for the granting of land and annuities on Rambi. Permanently living on Rambi, enacting the code, maintaining the relationship, has been identified as a precondition for sharing in boundary-defining functions.

Similarly, taking one's land in a village seems to be emerging as a precondition for voting in council elections. The formal constitution of the village domain is in large measure a reflex of council activities. As things develop, landholding may become more of a distinctive feature of the village domain. And Ocean Island landholding and Rambi Island landholding are being systematically interrelated through the set of transformations with which we have been concerned.

From the group frame of reference, the emergent constellation seems to be: Ocean Island landholding and Banaban identity define one another. Banaban identity plus Rambi residence in the case of Banabans, or Rambi residence as approved through a legal transformation of Banaban custom in the case of non-Banabans, entitle one to land on Rambi. Some kind of landholding in the village entitles one to participate in one of the main boundary-defining activities of the village. A code element combines with an identity element to produce a new identity, which in turn combines with another code element to produce an identity in the process of being defined. In each case, the adding of a criterial element is a response to an attempt to give tangible institutional form to the identity.

The theoretical point with which we have been wrestling in this and preceding chapters is essentially as follows: It is far from satisfactory to describe Banaban social structure in terms of a classic who-what model, where certain classes of actors are associated with certain classes of activities. The boundaries around the classes of actors and the boundaries around the classes of activities may be ambiguous. People may disagree on those boundaries, or on the relationships between the classes of actors and activities. Activities performed, in the dialectical model, may come to shape the boundaries around the classes of actors and the relationships between actors and activities, but in the context of a continuing process of reshaping. Furthermore, as we will see in chapter 14, consensus may be lacking on what a legitimate performance of the activity is, and as we have already seen, on what a competent performance of the activity is.

The long-run prospect, one suspects, is not for a rigid resolution of these ambiguities. The process of shaping and reshaping may be permanent. And rather than the emergent applicability of a tight who-what model, one suspects the possible applicability of a model which will specify ranges of variation of acceptable activity. Thus, beyond a minimum of what a family or a village must do, there will be a range of things that it might appropriately do. But even here, one must leave room for the existence of substantive disagreements. For a colonial subsociety with limited control over its own fate, in a changing environment, this may in fact be the most adaptive solution.[6]

6. The remarks in the preceding two paragraphs were largely suggested by the written comments of Prof. Amélie Rorty of Douglass College, Rutgers University, which were addressed to an unpublished paper by the author.

PART IV

Kinship, Descent,
and Affinity

12

The relationship of blood and land to identity and code has been a recurring element in our discussion: the situation in the traditional culture (one operates as though there were a kind of baseline simply because of lack of data on changes in precolonial times), and the implications for those concepts of the dramatic transformations in the Banaban experience. Some aspects of the relevance of those concepts for an understanding of Banaban kinship and descent were set out in part 1. We have also from time to time alluded to the connection between kinship and developments in other domains. It is time now to confront more completely (if tediously) the Banaban kinship system in its own terms. Our starting points will be vocabulary in this chapter and ritual in the next. The analysis to be presented will also join the points made in preceding chapters as preparations for a look at the descent system as it functions on Rambi.

UTU

With a few erratic exceptions, I have eschewed the nonparenthetical use of native terms in this book. In this chapter there will be many native terms, since the question being addressed is one of native terms. Some excursions into conjectural etymology will even be made. I should note first that when I speak of Gilbertese as the language, I mean Gilbertese as spoken by Banabans.

At this point I will not go into a theoretical discussion of kinship terms, but rather allow points to emerge as the data is presented. One point, however, should be clear at the outset. Careless usage at times makes some pose an opposition between terms and behavior. This is a false opposition, since terms represent a particular kind of behavior: labeling behavior. In talking about terms we are talking about how people behave when they label or classify.

The focal term of this chapter is *utu*. Generally when I have used "family," or "kinsmen," or "kinsman," these have been translations of *utu*. And this usage of mine reflects something of the concept.

One can label a person as utu: "He is my utu." One can label a set of people as "that utu." And one can label a kind of behavior as utu. The word *utu* thus combines certain aspects of what in English we call relatives, family, and kinship. This is one of the things which makes the analysis of the term somewhat complex.

Another complicating factor is this: From the point of view of an individual, there is not a single set of other individuals whom for all times and in all contexts he labels utu. At the level of distinctive features, utu contrasts with things which are not utu in a consistent fashion. But the individual does not divide the social world into two context-free sets of people, so that utu could line up in one place and not utu could line up in another, and it is not because an individual capriciously changes his mind from one moment to the next about which people are and which people are not his utu. Someone who at one time is utu is at another not utu, or, if not utu, then "my utu, but . . ." or, more interestingly, "he is not my utu; he is the utu of other people." Every individual in the society is regarded as the center of utu. Some people are your utu, and also the utu of other people who are not your utu, and this is relevant to your behavior toward those people.

There are other complicating factors. A Methodist may speak of the "utu of Heaven," but not regard his coreligionists as his utu, and in fact contrast utu matters with church matters. A Catholic will refer to his priest as "the father," but not regard the priest as his kinsman. Indeed, a person may refer to his mother's sister's husband by the same term as he uses for his father but not regard the former as his utu either. And when one chants, "Our Father who art in Heaven," there is something interesting going on.

The final complicating factor which I will mention is the key to the problem, the answer to which, of course, was given many pages ago.

One of the meanings of the suffix -*na* is "to use or treat as one's." "Lamp," for example, is *taura*. If I *taurana* a lamp, I use it as my own, or appropriate it. If I *utuna* someone, I behave toward him in a manner appropriate to kinship. (Kinship terms can be used in this way also). The verbal usage could indicate a situation where people who do belong to the same utu do not behave as utu to one another ("If she doesn't want to utuna me, that's fine with me," one man said of a kinsman who did not invite him to a family gathering), or where people who are not otherwise utu do behave as utu to one another.

For the marriage of the son of the Catholic teacher from the Gilberts (the son was acting for his father while the latter was away in a hospital), Catholic adults were called upon to present gifts of money. A man commented, *"e utu te aro,"* which, to preserve the flavor, may be translated "the church family-s."

As with the English "family," and similar terms in some other cultures, utu can be used to label a nonhuman category, such as a family of plants. And "to divide into groups" can be *koro-utu* (*koro,* cut, divide). In all the usages of utu for people, either one or both of two features are present. These features are alternate necessary conditions for utu to denote, and they are: (1) common identity (connection by common substance or adoption), and (2) a code for conduct which stipulates a relationship of enduring, diffuse solidarity; or kinship connection and kinship behavior. Utu means these two separable things.

Kinship connection or identity, and code or behavior, contrast with others. For example, "friends" lack a connection by substance or adoption (land), and "friendship" is contingent rather than enduring.

Out of these two elements, identity and code, are formed notions of both who is a kinsman, and what kinds of units are kinship units. We will look first and in a little detail at how people are and are not labeled as "my utu"; this is more apt than starting with units, since it makes the relationships among those units clearer.

The identity and code elements are separable but can also be combined. The manner in which they are separated or combined reveals one of the most consistent features of Banaban kinship labeling if not of labeling in general: marked versus unmarked categories (see Greenberg 1966).

Before we begin looking at identity, it should be observed that the adopting of either the identity or the code framework explains much of the surface variation or apparent ambiguity in usage. Let us examine a few dramatic examples. If a child has been adopted by another and has received no land from his natal family, he has "gone away." He is now somebody else's utu. It is recognized that he may have strong feelings toward his natal family ("the blood loves its own"), but the normative code is not there any more. The incest prohibition remains, but not the complex of enduring, diffuse solidarity. That child is a child to his natal parents by identity but not by code. It is thus perfectly reasonable for those parents to say that the child is their utu, that he is not their utu, or that he is their utu but has been adopted—yes, no, or maybe, depending upon which element (or elements) is being invoked.

Consider people who are utu and whose children have married. They have become affines. The code of affinity is different from that of kinship. They are utu in the identity sense and not utu in the code sense.

The other possibility is of course perfectly realized in the case of the spouse: the substance-land complex is missing in a direct sense, but the code is present. Thus it is perfectly appropriate for a person to say that his wife is his utu, or, "she's not my utu, she's my wife!"

The absence of code in the presence of identity, or the absence of identity in the presence of code, may specify a person as not utu, somebody else's utu, or "my utu but . . ."

The initial statement about identity stipulates two types of identity, or rather two modes of identity origin: blood (*te rara*) and adoption (*te tabetabe*). To emphasize blood identity with a person, one might say, "He is my blood." One might say of a person, "He's not the blood, he's adopted," adding, perhaps, "He has some land of ours." Blood utu in contrast to adopted utu may be referred to as "real utu."

Although there are thus two modes of identity origin, and a complex of possible phrases dealing with them, the two categories are also structured in a marked/unmarked relationship. Adoption is marked vis-à-vis non-adoption, and in this context "blood" is the descriptive label for the unmarked category. Thus a member of an adopting utu may say of their adoptee: "Yes, he is our utu, but he is adopted." Or, "No, he is not our utu, he is adopted." Or, "He is not our utu, he is so-and-so's utu."

Land, which is prerequisite to adoption, was discussed earlier as a means both of transforming a bearer of substance into an enactor of code and of transforming the code into something as close to substance as can occur. Thus within identity a feature related to code defines the marked category.

Identity is something which is either present or absent. It is also something which, between two individuals, there can be more or less of. A second contrast which derives from the definition itself concerns distance. There are distant utu and close utu. This transcends the question of adoption. Adoptive kin are close or distant according to the position of whoever it was who adopted them. The Gilbertese terms for distant (*raroa*) and close (*kaan*) are the same as those for spatial location. But they are not the same as those for intensity of relationship as is the case in English. The image here is genealogical. Although genealogy does not exhaust the domain of Banaban kinship meanings, it is part of them. One can label a kinsman, a kinship connection, or the utu-as-a-unit as distant or close. Or, one can compare people as being either closer or more distant than others.

The boundary of distance is not firmly fixed. Whatever the boundary is which is invoked at a particular time, those beyond the boundary may be indicated as "not utu," "not the real utu," "outside," or "utu but distant." Thus in this context, distance and closeness are structured so that distance is marked and closeness unmarked. Although the distance being marked is genealogical distance, there is a general expectation that the intensity of the relationship will vary with genealogical distance.

Sometimes the boundary is invoked to separate lineal from collateral kin. At other times, the relationship of two people is described by the phrase "Their grandparents were siblings." For example, once the Rorobuaka Society at Buakonikai decided that all available copra would be cut in connection with a Suva church camp. Someone proposed that those people who were soon to be involved in the heavy expenses of the marriage of their utu should be exempted. People agreed that "only the true body" should be exempted. This developed, most distantly, to include those whose grandparents were siblings.

The feature of distance, which is a derivation from the distinctive features, also specifies a usage which is almost synonymous with utu. The term *koraki,* when applied to an individual, can be used in a sense identical with that of utu. *Utu* is a term occasionally heard for "class" in general; *koraki* is a term frequently heard for "group" in general. As with utu, there is a verbal form (*korakina*) which means "to behave as kinsman." Although I did not make a count, I suspect that koraki can carry with it a suggestion of greater distance, so that a person would be much likelier to refer to his child or brother as utu than as koraki. It is not fortuitous that, frequency aside, *utu* is also a general class term and *koraki* a general group term. The verbal forms are, as far as I know, kinship specific.

Koraki is the term used in a kind of insult that I only heard in jest. It is used in a manner similar, perhaps, to ways in which "mother" occurs in American. For example, if someone says to me, "I will beat your ears" (which is obscene, as are similar expressions applying to the head area), I might reply, "The ears of your koraki!" Or, in joking, a particular item may be mentioned, and someone will interject that it is the item of "your koraki!"

We have, then, the identity element marked by adoption and by distance. In both cases there are code-like connotations. We have already observed that identity in the absence of code, or code in the absence of identity, may lead to the "Yes, but . . ." complex. Identity plus code is the great unmarked category of Banaban kinship. We will now look a little more closely at the code element, insofar as it is involved in how people define other people as kinsmen.

As there are different modes of the origin of kinship identity, there are different modes of the independent origin of kinship behavior. There is some fuzziness of interpretation here probably because of incomplete data.

One mode is the meeting (*te bo*). It is a term which first applies between very good friends with a continuing relationship which arose in a particular circumstance, such as a trip together, or unusual acts of kindness. The acts of kindness were unusual because the people were not utu. The special feature of the meeting is the expectation that the relationship will not die with the people who formulated it, and it may even extend laterally beyond the initiators to their close kin. The social personalities of the people concerned are what "meet." Sometimes this is described as, "We *bo-koraki*." They meet but do not combine, which is what is symbolized in blood and land. The relationship is a step short of adoption and might end in an adoption.

As adoption could be plausibly interpreted as mediating between identity and code if more than one level of contrast is considered, the meeting mediates between adoption and marriage. Ideally speaking, adoption transcends a generation, and the identity element is present. Marriage does not transcend a generation, and the identity element is absent. The meeting transcends a generation, and the identity element is absent.

People related through the meeting may be utu, and fall under the general rule that code-only utu can be marked or excluded vis-à-vis identity-plus-code utu.

Marriage presents a special problem in this context. The problem is not the existence of marriage as one of the modes of the origin of kinship behavior, contrasting, for example, with the meeting. The problem is the relationship between marriage and another mode, coresidence. It is ethnographically inexcusable that such an important problem should not have a decisive answer.

Of the people who are a person's utu at some level, the person's spouse is the only real kinsman by marriage. His spouse's kinsmen are not *his* kinsmen in their position as spouse's kinsmen (although, as we shall see, he does use terms for them, some of which are kinship terms).

Let us hold this point in mind for a moment and turn to another. The more or less permanent residents of a household, who are almost always related through identity or marriage links, are often labeled "an utu." Let us say I am the elder male in a household which includes my wife's nephew. He is not my utu because he is my wife's nephew. But I may regard him as my utu because of the kinship behavior between us.

The problem, then, is this: Do we have two cultural categories which are modes of origin of code contrasting with the meeting—marriage and coresidence? Or do we have one category, coresidence, which is divided into two subcategories—spouse and a residual class? The residual class would be unmarked, yet the situation does not fit well into marking theory, as I understand it, since the marked category would not be subordinate to the unmarked category.

I am inclined toward the interpretation that we have one category, coresidence as a special case of code, and that the marriage relationship is the primary exemplar of that category, or a synecdoche for it. The major ground for this is that sexual relations alone are not sufficient for two people to be regarded as spouses. When there has been a church marriage, the problem is much less ambiguous. When there has not been a church marriage, it appears to be coresidence which transforms a "girlfriend" into a "spouse." There is also an etymological or morphological suggestion. In informal discourse the most common label for "my spouse" is *buu* (*bu*, spouse; *u*, my). An alternate one is *kainabau*. *Kain* is "a person of"; *aba* is "land"; *u* is "my"; thus, "a person of my land." Coresidence in this interpretation would be the most strictly kinship aspect; sexuality will be treated later.[1] Another thing which undoubtedly inclines me toward this interpretation is how nicely it relates to the blood and mud hypothesis.

It is the intersection of the person perspective and the unit perspective which creates some of these analytic problems. What, then, of units?

Any collection of people related by kinship behavior or kinship identity can be labeled "an utu." In the case of "the utu of Heaven," there is a spiritual element (see chapter 6). In the other cases there are material or behavioral elements. The descendants of a common ancestor (through substance or adoption) are an utu. It is more likely for the members of a hamlet (*kainga*) to be so identified than the members of a village district.[2] They have more substance and place identification in common. Although they can be labeled collectively as an utu, this does not mean that they all utuna one another. Some of its members may have become affines of one another. This matter will be taken up in more detail in chapters 13 and 14. The utu in this case can be labeled "people of the hamlet" (*kain te kainga*), and at the furthest limit, which can include the village district, as *te baronga*. The latter is a term which can be used in the general sense of "group." A few English-speaking Banabans, however, possibly as a consequence of mission translation, translate it in the descent context as "tribe."

In the named descent unit context, the utu is *utun* X (the utu of X) where X is the founding ancestor. In the kindred context, the utu is *ana utu* X (*ana*, his, her, its), where X is the relevant person. The form used in the named

---

1. There is another way of referring to the spouse, with a vague comicality to it: in the first person possessive, as *au bai te mane* (*au*, my; *bai*, thing, object, property, right; *te mane*, the man) and *au bai te aine* (*te aine*, the woman). Similar English usages might be "my man" or "my woman." Utu or not utu, the relationship is clear.

2. On Rambi, *kainga* is the most common label for the Ocean Island hamlet, which is termed *kawa* in chapter 1. Kawa is not unheard now, however, and there are references to kainga in the Maude Papers. If both usages were traditional, perhaps kawa came to be applied more consistently to the modern-era villages on Ocean Island, and kainga came to be applied more consistently to the traditional hamlets. The old village districts, however, are also called kawa now.

descent unit context is the same as that for the things of a place, or the parts of a body.

The kindred is also labeled an utu, or alternatively a koraki. The kindred is distinguished from the descent unit not only by the different use of the possessive, but also by the fact that baronga is not used for the kindred. (The identity/code rules apply for the kindred, and relationships through the meeting may or may not be included in it.)

The residents of a house, as we have already discussed, may be an utu. The problem of marriage occurs again and brings up the problem of utu vis-à-vis whom, which will recur in the context of terms below. When a man and wife speak of "our utu," they may mean themselves and their children (and perhaps grandchildren). In this sense a person can label his brother, his brother's wife, and their children as "another utu." What ego is recognizing is that his brother is now also a kinsman of someone (his wife) who is not ego's kinsman, and who has claims like ego's. In calling them different utu, the person is not asserting that he and his brother are no longer utu, nor that from another perspective both of them are no longer "one utu."

The elements of identity and code, then, distribute themselves out not only among individuals, but also units of individuals which are kinship units.

Kinship Terms and Terms for Kinsmen

The overall structure of kinship terms derives from the structure of utu.

I will now turn to a componential analysis of a set of terms (see Goodenough 1964). The analysis assumes a genealogical grid. In chapter 14 more will be said of genealogies. At this point I note that te riki is a word which refers to a genealogy. Riki also means "grow, originate," and the genealogy of a person is rikina, which connotes his origin, the growth of his utu. Te kateiriki (katei, to make stand) refers to the act of reciting a genealogy, or to the genealogy itself. In recitation it may be said that X procreated (karika) Y, or that Y is his child, was born, or came forth.[3]

"Ancestor" is used for people in earlier parts of the genealogy. There is a word for "generation," referring either to a genealogical generation or an age grouping. A person's descendants are his "issue" (kariki), "contents" (kanoa) or utu. A person as part of a genealogy may be called a "head."

Thus a componential analysis has a cultural reality in that the notion of a genealogical grid has a cultural reality. As is clear by now, however, it is not the only cultural reality in kinship, and I shall soon indicate where the limitations of the genealogical model are.

---

3. It is possible that the form of genealogies in the Bible has influenced the local style.

Under analysis are the "obligatory" distinctions made among kinship positions in the genealogical grid of identity, when one asks, "What is he (she) to you? (*Raam?*)" The forms are in the first person possessive singular. "Obligatory" is actually a very tricky word, since in a certain context, in response to a certain question, a long relative product may be the obligatory kind of correct response. I will also indicate certain usages which do occur but which are not common as responses in this frame, and putting them into the lexical set would give the analysis a complexity which it does not deserve.

TABLE 2

COMPONENTIAL ANALYSIS

	1	2	3	4	5
a. tibuu	1.2	2.2			
b. tamau	1.2	2.1	3.1		5.1
c. tinau	1.2	2.1	3.1		5.2
d. natiu	1.2	2.1	3.2		
e. tariu	1.1			4.1	
f. maneu	1.1			4.2	

1. Similarity of generation between ego and alter
   1.1 Same generation
   1.2 Different generation
2. Number of generations between ego and alter
   2.1 One generation difference
   2.2 More than one generation difference
3. Seniority of alter's generation in relation to ego's
   3.1 Alter's generation senior
   3.2 Alter's generation junior
4. Similarity of sex of alter and ego
   4.1 Same sex
   4.2 Different sex
5. Sex of alter
   5.1 Alter male
   5.2 Alter female

The terminology as presented in table 2 is of a "Hawaiian" or "generational" type. In his own generation, ego distinguishes by relative sex: between people of the same and of opposite sex. In the first ascending generation ego distinguishes by absolute sex: between males and females. Otherwise only generation is distinguished, with a grouping of those more than one generation distant.

There is one feature of such a system which deserves special comment.

The children of holders of a certain position are labeled by the same term as the initial holders. Thus:

child of x : child of y : : x : y

It is thus not only generation that is stressed, but also the continuity through time of the terminological relationships as they stand.

I shall sacrifice purity for economy and convenience by using the following glosses, within double quotation marks, for the terms in table 2.

a. "grandparent" and "grandchild"
b. "father"
c. "mother"
d. "child"
e. "sibling of same sex"
f. "sibling of opposite sex"

This lexical set is encoding certain information about equivalence and continuity, notions which are central to the concept of utu. Alternate usages, however, suggest that those notions are measuring sticks against which the intrusion of other elements can be gauged.

Some of these usages are of the marked/unmarked type. Most prominent is the prefix *ai-*. One of the meanings of ai- in other contexts is "like a . . ." (for a case similar in some ways, see Eggan 1960). Thus, for example, *tamau* ("my father") and *ai-tamau*. There is an alternate way of making constructions with ai-, and that is by using the series *irou, iroum, irouna, iroura, iroumi, irouia* (by me, by you [sing.], by him or by her, by us, by you [pl.], by them, respectively). For example: *ai-tamau;* or *ai-te-tama irou,* "ai-the/a-father by-me."

Ai- marks collaterals from lineals and is a manifestation in the terminology of marking by distance in utu itself. Father's brother, for example, is both "father" (*tamau*) and "like a father," (*ai-tamau*), or rather there are two kinds of male consanguines in the first ascending generation: father (who may be termed "my real father"), and those who are like a father. This is consistent with the kinship symbolism as a whole. Those people are "the same as my father" because they share common blood (or land) with him. They are like a father in that their role toward me is similar but not identical with that actually expected of my father. They are not responsible for me (nor I for them) in the same way as my father is, and as they are for their own children.

Another usage qualifies the initial point in another direction. *Au karo* is a common alternate for "my father," and "the karo" is the usual contrast with "the mother" when obligations or attributes of "the father" and "the mother" are discussed, as in sermons. Au karo, however, can also mean "my parents," thus combining the father and the mother, who otherwise are kept separate, as their identities are separate. "Fathers" and "mothers" are both authority figures, but the former more so "since they are men." The husband is in general the appropriate representative of the couple. Thus we have "parents," and mark for femaleness.

If *au karo* for both parents is to be taken as a cover term, perhaps "my grandparent" for more than one generation of distance should also be taken as a cover term. (The problem is similar to that of "cousin" in English: what one does with first, second, etc., and once removed, twice removed, etc.)

"Grandparent-grandchild" reciprocals for generations more distant than two are rarely used, and the remoter ones are not universally known, or people are uncertain. These terms are *tibutoru* for three generations removal; *tibumamano* for four; *tibutaratara* for five. These are, then, marked in relationship to *tibu*. There are some folk etymologies of these terms which explain them by the progressive incapacity of the people in the categories as they ascend.

Another set of terms reflects some of the same principles we have been discussing. These terms are: *mama* (or *ama*), "mother"; *baba* (or *aba*), "father"; and *kaka,* "grandparent." The terms are primarily used in address by youngsters, and in reference by youngsters and by others in their presence. Often the female title *Nei* (Miss, Mrs.) is used before mama and kaka. I recall hearing the male title (which would be *Nam* or *Tem* before *baba*) used rarely in this context. In many contexts the use of the female title is more general than that of the male title. This may be the same order of phenomenon as marking for femaleness.

The only other kinship term generally used in address is *tama* (father), for God (*tamara,* our father) and the priest (*te tama,* the father). Otherwise personal names, with or without the male or female titles, are used in address (or such usages as, "You over there!").[4]

The hierarchical nature of the relationships is suggested by the fact that

4. I must confess here what is probably the most serious and least excusable gap in my ethnographic material: I did not conduct systematic research on personal names. There is no question but that the names of ancestors constitute a pool which is drawn from. Biblical names appear on the genealogies soon after the arrival of the mission; some people may have taken on biblical names. I recall a comment or two that one can ask a friend to name one's child, and one report that a man in naming a kinswoman dropped the first syllable of his own name. It would be particularly neat if kinship, religion, and the person formed the three basic parameters of name-giving. But on the question of the relationship between the people who can "assign" the right to name, the namer, the named, and the name itself, I must maintain an embarrassed silence.

there are no specific reciprocals from senior to junior generations; there are also no complementary terms for siblings. *Kaka* is not used for a "grandchild" by a "grandparent." Thus a distinction is made that is not made by *tibu*. Between "grandparents" and "grandchildren" there is the conventionally liberal relationship, but the junior still respects the senior. The terms do not generally take the possessive, which suggests that they are titles.

These terms are among the first that a child is taught. (There are other baby talk reduplicated monosyllables.) A man may tell his child to "take this to mama," the mama present being the child's mother or, perhaps, mother's sister. The father is thus invoking the child's relationship to that other person. As the child gets older, the terms used by him are in general limited to his real parents or to someone acting *in loco parentis*. There can be variability of usage here in the following sense: An older man may address his mother as mama, or by her name, and refer to her to others as *tinau* (my mother), *tinara* (our mother), or by her personal name.

Let us consider an example of the *in loco parentis* case: A young woman of twenty-one was brought up by her mother's sister and the latter's husband. Her own mother had died, and her father left the family. She calls her mother's sister mama and her mother's sister's husband baba. The latter once pointed out to me, in commenting on how the girl was "like my child," that she referred to him, rather than to her real father, as baba.

The paradigmatic marking problem concerns the label *tari,* which I have been glossing as "sibling of same sex." We will soon see how this is used in the general solidarity sense of "brother" in English, and how a compound is formed from it with a meaning equivalent to "brotherhood" in English.

There are two descriptive phrases in which tari means "sibling." They are: "Their grandparents are (were) siblings" (*A tari tibuia*) and "their spouses are (were) siblings" (*A tari buia*). The sibling relationship is thus combined in one label. "Opposite sex-ness" would appear to be marked. This calls for some exegesis.

The highest equivalent solidarity should obtain among siblings, who should care for and love one another irrespective of sex and age. Between siblings of the same sex there should prevail an open, free relationship not obtaining to such a degree between siblings of opposite sex. The latter have complementary roles, as has been indicated in the discussion of the traditional descent system. This is the manifestation in the kinship domain of ideas from the sex domain, as some of the things about parents and grandparents are manifestations of ideas from the age and authority domains.

Siblings of the same sex, however, can also argue with one another publicly as no one else can. A man should fight only with his "brother." They are, after all, "just the same," and will get over their anger in time.

Equivalence and substitutability apply to some degree to the utu as a whole. For example, when a man is ill or disinclined to go to his job on a construction project, he might feel he can send a kinsman to replace him. But siblings of the same sex are more substitutable than others. An anecdote will underscore this. I was having dinner in Benaia's house, and dinner was to begin without Benaia. I asked where he was, and someone jokingly replied, "Benaia is *there*," motioning toward his brother.

Lineal relatives are more "just like one another" (*ti te bo*) than collateral relatives. People in the same generation are more equivalent. Among lineal relatives, siblings are more like one another than others. Among siblings, siblings of the same sex are most like one another. The kinds of solidary behavior implied by utu in general are expected to be manifested more particularly among "real utu," and more particularly siblings, and it is in this sense that the sibling relationship is the model for the utu relationship as a whole.

It is interesting to note in this context certain usages with regard to closeness, which partially repeat a point made earlier. If I want to emphasize the closeness of the connection between two people, I may say, "They have but one mother," or "Their fathers are siblings of same sex," or "They have but one grandparent." One step beyond that, it is "Their grandparents are siblings." This line is one conventional formula for closeness, and it roughly defines the unit within which sexual relations constitute incest and within which marriage is prohibited. Beyond this line, the indication of the relationship is more complicated. A relative product string may be used, but it may be used for any relationship. Or, going a little further back, let us say the relationship in question is between two living people, X and Y. One may hear: "There was A, and his sibling of opposite sex, B. X is *te kanoanimane*, and Y *te kanoanaine*." *Mane* is "male, man" and *aine* is "female, woman." *Te kanoa* in other contexts means "contents" and is used here for "descendant." Thus a pair of siblings of opposite sex (in this example) is identified; one person is identified as "descendant of the man" and the other person as "descendant of the woman."

To return to the main point: The marking problem for tari is tied up with notions of utu identity, sex, and authority, if only in the denial of the latter two. The tari relationship is kinship at its purest.

Kinship, however, does not always exist at its purest. As the sexual differentiation of siblings can be overcome in the manner described, it can also be negated in another direction. A terminological set indicating birth order is another alternate set of descriptive terms. I will first present the terms with the article:

te karimoa	the first born
te karimwi	the later born
te bina	the last born

Thus:

karimoau	my elder sibling	*au karimoa*	my eldest child
karimwiu	my younger sibling	*au karimwi*	my younger child
binau	my youngest sibling	*au bina*	my youngest child

I do not think binau is generally used; rather, te bina is. The youngest child is in a double proverbial position: his position within the sibling set is the most junior, and he may lose out in certain distributions from the parents. Yet he may also be their favorite. Te bina thus sometimes carries a joking connotation. As a joke, or as an insult, an alternative to te bina can be used: *te bukinikoro*. Sabatier (1954, p. 158) has a relevant discussion: "*peti* of the pandanus fruit: stringy remainder of a pandanus fruit section after sucking (used as food). *te riki ni peti:* pandanus sprung from a *peti;* fig. twerp (insulting expression); syn. *te buki ni koro*" (italics added).

There is another term in this series, *te karinuka* (the middle born), that is, the second of a group of three siblings. I did not hear it used except with the article.

Thus within one's sibling set, or among one's children, birth order terms can be used to make distinctions not otherwise made. These terms can be used with other possessives, for example, "our eldest child," where the married couple is the point of reference; "our youngest sibling," where the sibling set is the point of reference.

Simple ordinals can also be used, and there are other expressions (for example, *te ikawai,* the eldest). For children and grandchildren one can specify sex by adding the words for "male, man" (*te mane*) or "female, woman" (*te aine*), for example, *natiu te mane* (my child the male).

Some of these further specifications relate to a situation in the sibling set which is the result of the intersection of other domains with the kinship domain. First, elder has authority over junior. Second, male has authority over female. We have already seen some of the problems created by this intersection in the descent context. With regard to the sibling set the problem is the same. On the one hand, the eldest is in the highest position (and thus the plan for the eldest of the unmarried members of a sibling set to hold title to house plots on behalf of his siblings in certain circumstances). On the other hand, the (eldest) male is in the highest position. Upon inquiry, people produce varying statements about what is involved in sibling set authority. This is because of domain intersection and the absence of an absolute rule about priority of domain.

Is the *karimoa-karimwi-bina* set a set of kinship terms? Perhaps they are borderline cases between kinship terms and terms used for kinsmen. More firmly in the latter category are old man (*unimane*) and old woman (*unaine*). These are not only age-descriptive terms but also generalized terms of respect. They invoke a role. A person may refer to an elder relative by them, or an old person may so refer to his or her spouse. With "my" it is generally the elder relative. Yet it is significant that these people can in some sense be classed together.

CODE FOR CONDUCT EXPLORED

I have already discussed the verbal usages of utu and koraki. All the kinship terms listed in the table can also be used verbally by suffixing *-na*. The meagre discussion of kinship roles in the preceding pages was not introduced to demonstrate a correlation between labeling behavior and other kinds of behavior. The labels, among other things, *mean* those roles. The same applies to affinal labels, to which we will soon turn. The verbals allow one to quickly specify the situation where one individual is genealogically connected to another as, for example, "child," "sibling of same sex," and "brother-in-law," but the *role* they happen to enact is that of brother-in-law-ness: "He is 'my child,' 'my sibling of same sex,' and 'my brother-in-law,' but I 'brother-in-law him.' "

Most of the usages of the kinship term verbals concern adoption. For example, if I were to ask you whether or not you were *natinaki* (*nati,* child; *-aki,* passive suffix) by your father, you would probably reply, "No, I wasn't natinaki; he is my real father." There is a larger sense, however, in which the verbals signify the role in general. The point is that it is the context of adoption which generally calls for the giving of information of this kind.

I will give two examples of the more general usage, and one of a closely related usage.

1. At an informal gathering of young men, there was much mutual bantering, as usual. People were joking about a particular man, L. One of the young men present was L's sister's son, F. F did not have very cordial feelings about L, who had actually been adopted away but still maintained relations with his natal utu. Joining in the fun, I interjected as if in criticism, "You are joking about F's 'father' [*ana karo F*]!" F said smartly, "He is not my 'father.' I do not treat-as-father L. He is the 'father' of other people!" (*Tiaki au karo. I aki karona L. Aia karo tabemang!*) Another echoed the

last phrase, "He is the 'father' of other people," with a rising voice, communicating, as part of the whole humorous situation, "Look what he's saying!"

2. A mother and daughter were arguing. The daughter's husband had recently died, and the daughter (according to the second-hand information I am using here) wanted to marry another man. Her mother disapproved. She was thinking of the children, whom another man might not look after properly. The daughter had brothers who could help her, and besides, the man she wanted to marry was her father's "sibling of same sex" rather closely. The daughter persisted in her wish, and during an argument said to her mother, "I don't want to treat-you-as-mother [tinaniko], and don't call me your child again." The mother replied that it was fine with her, but that the daughter should remember that they were her words, not the mother's. She asked her daughter to leave the children with her before she went off to live with the man, but the daughter refused.

3. A young man was asked from outside the house whether his (widowed) mother (the form reported was "your old woman") were at home one afternoon. She was not, and had been away from home a good deal lately, as if she were a heedless young woman "on the make." To "Where is your old woman?" her son replied, "Not my old woman, my 'sibling of opposite sex!' "

It is in fact the interplay between the classifying and role-designating meanings of kinship terms (see Schneider and Roberts 1956) which gives the point to much kinship humor. Kinship humor will be treated more extensively in the context of affinity.

We have already observed "the utu of Heaven." Another usage is "the utu of Christians." Methodist preachers often address their congregations as tari (recall the unmarked sibling usage). God is 'our father," and the Catholic priest is "the father." (The priest can also be referred to as "our father," or as "your father," but here the possessive particles are used rather than the suffixes: thus for these examples, ara tama or ami tama rather than tamara or tamami.) Members of the Pentecostal church refer to one another by sibling terms (a practice introduced, I think, by the local pastor trained on Viti Levu). A minister referred to "our tari" (tarira) who had suffered during a recent hurricane, thus expressing solidarity with and compassion for them as equals. We saw in remarks to the visiting lawyer and his wife the use of "father" and "mother of the Banaban" for them. The council chairman was once called "father of the community," and a councillor, "father of the village." These are usages for unequals.

Religious usages can combine the identity and code elements, or the classifying and role-designating functions. God is the Creator Father, and the priest is the point of contact with Him. As "children of God," people are "siblings." In other usages the role-designating function of kinship terms is used, and the code element of kinship is being invoked. The actual term used may reflect differences in sex and equality or inequality (see Schneider 1968), before God or among men. Even before affines. And that is why a person could say that the eldest male in a sibling set is "like a father," and should be treated in that way.

From the listed kinship terms, another lexical set is formed by reduplication and in some cases the use of the reflexive prefix *i-*. These terms delineate the different kinds of adoption which are possible. At a more general level (and this is consistent with the *-na* usages), the sibling terms of this set are used as "brotherhood" is used in English. (The terms are *te i-taritari* and *te i-mamane.*) Many is the sermon or other gathering in which the trio of friendship, sibling-of-same-sex-ship, and sibling-of-opposite-sex-ship, or only the first two, will be declared as the right and proper relationship obtaining between the people present, or between all people. Love (*te i-tangitangiri*) may be added. The language of solidarity, obligation, cooperation, and, in some ways, affect is very much the language of kinship. They are what kinship relationships are about.

TERMS AND AFFINITY

They are not, however, what *kautabo* (meaning in-laws, or the in-law relationship) is about. There is no general term for "affines" in the anthropological sense, which contrasts with utu. The term *kautabo* (and its partial alternate *butika*) comes closest. People who are "not my utu" in a particular context can be glossed by the many forms we have indicated. Or they may be termed *iruwa* (strangers, guests, foreigners—generally, outsiders), or called not my (our, their, etc.) *rao* (companion, friend; "not our *rao*" is used in the sense of "not one of us"). *Kautabo* is a contrast, however, with the general idea of the utu relationship.

The Methodists of Uma village were hosts for a week to a visiting Gilbertese pastor and his family, and gave them food and entertainment. He said to the group, "We come to you as our utu, our 'siblings of same sex,' and 'siblings of opposite sex,' not as the kautabo or the butika." Some terminological aspects of kautabo will be considered shortly. The point here is that kautabo is proverbially a relationship of tension and reserve (and there is a verbal, kautabona). What the pastor meant was that he came as "one of the family," not demanding special attention, and of essentially the same nature as the village congregants. He was expressing solidarity and affection with them.

Some affines are referred to by kinship terms, others may be, others are not at all. Some affines are referred to by terms which cannot be considered kinship terms, since those terms are not used for kinsmen. They are terms, however, which class together people who are kinsmen of one another on the basis of their kinship relationship with one another. Perhaps these terms should be called kinship-linked terms. To approach this problem we must reconsider the married couple, whom I will call "the couple."

The word *te tanga* can be used in the sense of "a troop." Much more frequent is its use for a couple. In oratory connected with marriage rituals, "the new couple" is a phrase heard over and over again. In informal discourse, it is heard most frequently in the form *tangaia X ma*. I will have to go a little more into the structure of Gilbertese to explicate this crucial usage.

In usage, *ma* (and) is a word of delightful vagueness, and there are similar terms elsewhere in Oceania. When used after the name of a person, and at the end of a sentence, its meaning is closest to "and his crowd." For a married couple, using it is something like transforming "Michael" into "The Michaels." Ma in this sense is not restricted to kinship. If there is a church event of some kind and I ask if "William ma" came, since William is the Methodist pastor of Uma village, the question will be taken to mean William and other functionaries of the Uma church.

In the context of utu identity, ma can be used to specify a diffusely bounded set of kin. For example, one way of suggesting the kinship connection of a person is by saying that he is "the utu of Alfonso ma," or even "the 'sibling of same sex' of Alfonso ma." One does not go through a complicated genealogy, and one may not even know it. Ma expands from the person named, in the context given

The third person plural possessive suffix is *-ia*. *Tangaia* would have a literal meaning of "their married couple," and thus *tangaia X ma*. X is the name of either the husband or wife. It is more commonly the husband: the man as representative figure of the couple, a feature of sex roles as exemplified in the marriage context. The English analogue would be if there were a married couple where the husband was named Alfonso, and the wife Margaret, and one commonly referred to them as a pair as "the Alfonsos," or "Alfonso's couple." (Less frequently used is *tangan X* [*-n* is the third person singular possessive], which means X's couple.) Thus, if people are talking about who came to a party, they might say *tangaia Alfonso ma, tangaia Tom ma,* and so on.

The first person plural possessive suffix is *-ra* (our), and the second person plural *-mi* (your). *Tangara* (our couple) can be used in reference. *Tangami* (your couple) may be spoken to either one or both of the spouses, signifying both of them as a unit. Husband and wife are being classed together as a single unit. It is from this fact that the understanding of affinity proceeds, and the structured tension between the solidarity of consanguines and the solidarity of spouses, to which we will return.

The unity of the couple has a counterpart in terminological usage in general. When terms are considered appropriate to use, there is a general rule for their minimum obligatory form: If x, and spouse of x is y; then if y, spouse of y is x. Stated in another way: Where alter is ego's x, and alter's spouse is ego's y; when alter is ego's y, alter's spouse is ego's x. Or, x's are married to y's. Thus the spouse of a "father" is a "mother," and the spouse of a "mother" is a "father." The spouse of a "child" is a "child." The spouse of a "sibling of opposite sex" is a brother-in-law," and the spouse of a 'brother-in-law" is a "sibling of opposite sex." In the last example the system contrasts radically with the American. The couple acts as a unit, each half defining the other. One might term this the "pattern of spouse-pair terminological uniformity."

There is another conjunction of a terminological pattern with a cover term which is of extreme interest. *Te kanoanikainga* (*kanoa,* contents; *kainga,* hamlet) is a term I did not hear often, and it means "spouses of the utu." It sets off the utu from those who marry to it and does not go beyond them. One woman explicated the term as follows: "We are *iruwa* (strangers, guests, foreigners—generally, outsiders) in the hamlet." Another said that those people married to the utu were all called one thing because "they have the same position," vis-à-vis the utu. The utu here is the kindred. (A couple of times, the term was given as an alternate for the other terms used for spouse's "sibling's" spouse; see below.)

One might expect that, since there is a setting off of the kindred from those who marry to it, the terms used for those who marry to it would be different from kinship terms. Exactly the opposite is the case. The general rule ("correcting" for sex) is:

$$\text{spouse of x : spouse of y :: x : y}$$

where x and y are reciprocal consanguineal labels. Thus, assuming that it is considered appropriate to use terms, a man can refer to his wife's sister's husband as "sibling of same sex." His wife and her sister are "sibling of same sex" to one another. A woman can refer to her husband's brother's child's spouse as "my child" (the term between her husband and his nephew). They are not utu, but they can use kinship terms. They are using kinship terms in their role-designating aspect, and the relationship between them is specified as a reflex of the kind of relationship between the members of the utu into which they have married. This pattern is closely related to that of spouse-pair uniformity. All the patterns which I shall specify are intertwined. That is why I do not call them principles, since principle would suggest that they are different variables acting in combination.

Recalling a previous pattern, we thus have, with appropriate transformation for sex:

child of x : child of y :: x : y
spouse of x : spouse of y :: x : y

The centrality of the existing consanguineal link is thus "ratified" in two directions: as defining in perpetuity the terminological relations between descendants, and as defining in the present the terminological relations of co-affines.

In generations other than ego's, kin, spouses of kin, and kinsmen of spouse are classed together by the kinship terms, which can be marked by the prefix *ai-* as is the case for collaterals. For example, my father's brother, my father's sister's husband, and my wife's father can be *ai-tamau,* and similarly for *ai-tinau, ai-tubuu,* and *ai-natiu.* Thus a person and his spouse are in a similar position with reference to senior and junior generations. A person refers to members of his spouse's utu, in different generations, by the same term as his spouse does. And correlatively, members of the utu refer to spouses of other members of the utu, in different generations, by the same term as to that consanguineal of opposite sex. Thus, allowing correction for sex:

in different generations, spouse of x : y :: x : y
(or, in the other direction) y : spouse of x :: y : x

The terms are designating the kinds of roles which should be played. Toward spouse's elder kinsmen the spouse is to behave with respect, but this respect is not as qualified by the intimacy of the utu relationship. We will have more to say on this problem in the next chapter.

The protagonists in a little joke will, I think, set the stage for the remaining discussion. First we have Nei G and her daughter Nei H. Then we have Nei P and her husband Q. Nei G is "child" to Nei P. They live near one another and interact frequently; both are old women with a highly developed wry acerbity which is characteristic of many Banaban old women. The connection means that Nei H is "grandchild" to Nei P, and Nei P is "grandmother" to Nei H. Nei H has cultivated some of her mother's wit. Q is Nei P's second husband. It was not a church marriage. Q is an almost constant comedian.

One day, Q and Nei H were on the launch returning people who had spent some time out in the copra areas to their villages. As P and Nei H were about to disembark, P gave his sack of laundry to Nei H and said, "Take this to Nei *Kaka.*" Nei H replied, "Pfui! I refuse to kaka-you!" This was very funny.

Kaka, it will be recalled, is the "grandparent" term in the set used in address by children and some older people, and it is used in reference to children. (The English equivalent might be someone telling a child, "Take this to Nana," where Nana is grandmother.) It is thus conceivable for Nei

H to address Nei P as kaka. Having married Nei P, Q becomes "grandfather" to Nei H. He was jokingly invoking his position of seniority vis-à-vis Nei H, by invoking their link. The use of the baby-talk term fixed it firmly. Nei H, however, was meeting him on his own terms, as it were, and used kaka in a verbal form for the purpose. Q could be thought of in a grandfatherly role toward her. This is in the code sense not the substance sense. But even in the code sense, the nature of the marriage probably introduced an ambiguity that could be played upon.

It is through connections in ego's own generation that one finds the use of distinctly affinal terms. Two of these terms class together spouse's "siblings of opposite sex" with spouses of "siblings of opposite sex." These terms are *butika*, between men, and *kainuma*, between women. The nearest English glosses would be to think generationally of butika as "brother-in-law" between men, and kainuma as "sister-in-law" between women. The third term, *eiriki*, classes together spouse's "siblings of same sex" with spouses of "siblings of same sex." Since these terms are self-reciprocals, as are sibling terms, in the same generation:

$$\text{spouse of } x : y :: y : \text{spouse of } x$$
$$\text{spouse of } x : y :: \text{spouse of } y : x$$

Before we perform an exegesis on these terms, another must be brought back into the discussion: *kautabo*. It was observed earlier that the term can be used somewhat in the general sense of "affines" or "in-laws." For example, at a marriage it may be said that the bride's (or groom's) utu "kautabo among themselves," that is, her male side and her female side act as kautabo to each other. A less abstract and more common usage is that between the "fathers," "mothers," and "grandparents" of spouses: "co-parents-in-law," or perhaps "co-seniors-in-law." An alternate of kautabo in this sense is butika, which is also "brother-in-law" between men, and this begins to indicate the problem of relationship between utu created by marriage. Both utu are in a general sense kautabo of each other. The people who are kautabo in particular are the senior, responsible generations of the utu, one aspect of the authority of which is the granting of rights over their "child" and "grandchild." Kautabo are also butika, and it is in the generation of the spouses that the relationship of butika is carried through, but by men, who as males, represent the claims of the utu.[5]

5. The terms *kautabo* and *butika* as general in-law terms may occur differentially in different parts of the Gilberts, and it is possible that the present Banaban situation is in part a product of varying usages from different islands entering the Banaban vocabulary. Research in Gilbertese terminology may clarify this point.

It is possible to interpret some of this data in terms of the marked/unmarked

Kautabo proverbially visit only on special occasions (at least for some time before and after the actual marriage), show great reserve, and are loath to make requests of one another. This behavior is the opposite of utu behavior. The relation of reserve is also manifested between "brothers-in-law." In the relationship of butika we have men with authority over the same woman, and "interest" in her reproductive potential, for different utu. They should cooperate but take care not to express authority over one another. A man should "support" his "brother-in-law": "Your brother-in-law is the first person to fight for you," people say. But it is in its formal definition a tense relationship and one must take great care not to offend one's butika (in contrast with the brother relationship). I support my sister's husband because my sister is "with him"; my wife's brother because I am "holding" something which is his, as well as mine. An argument between "brothers-in-law" may break up a marriage. The butika, in that generation, represent the claims of the different *utu* over the same woman. As if they had read Radcliffe-Brown, the people recognize that there is a potentiality for conflict that must be held in check.

The relation of kainuma is somewhat similar, but there is not the same tenseness, and the authority position is reversed: kainuma are subject to the authority of the same man. They too are of the different utu but are women; not the protectors, but the protected. The term *kainuma* is not used in normal conversation to the same extent as *butika*. It is not a relationship that draws much comment.

The relationship of eiriki is opposite to that of siblings. A person's eiriki is one with whom and about whom he can make rude remarks and can refer to as "spouse" humorously. We will take up this joking relationship in detail in the next chapter. Suffice it to say here that if a person dies and has had children, it is considered appropriate for his or her sibling to marry the surviving spouse, "to care for the children." Since the children are already "child" to him, it is expected that he would be more likely to treat them well than would someone from outside his utu who may neglect them in favor of

---

distinction. Thus, for example, butika are "in-laws," and are "brothers-in-law" in contrast with "sisters-in-law" and other categories. Similarly, kautabo are "in-laws," and are "co-seniors-in-law" in contrast with "brothers-in-law," "sisters-in-law," and so forth. One could then go on to discuss marking by sex and generation. This interpretation is complicated by two suspicions (which I regret are only suspicions). First, the usage of butika in its general sense, as compared to the usage in its specific sense, may be more consistently in the *plural* possessive form. Second, kautabo as used in both its general and specific senses, as compared with the terms which would contrast with the specific usage (for example, "sisters-in-law"), may also be more consistently in the plural possessive form. It is possible that the historical problem makes these terms a little difficult to analyze structurally. It is far from surprising, however, that the marked/unmarked distinction should show its utility in the affinal terminology.

his own children. It would also insure that the in-marrying spouse's land "stays in the utu."

The term *eiriki* is the usual contrast with *butika* and *kainuma* when one is discussing terminology. But as far as I observed, it is not generally used in normal conversation. Eiriki as a role is much more narrowly defined than the others, and when a joke is to be made, the alternate "spouse" expresses even more directly the implication. When a genealogical point is to be made, it is better expressed by relative products ("his spouse's 'sibling of same sex,' " "the spouse of her 'sibling of same sex' "). The sexual connotation is probably what keeps the term in abeyance: a clear indication of the prominence of the role-designating meaning of the term.

Thus siblings of the same sex in one sense present a united front to the spouse of one of them. Both butika and kainuma represent claims of different utu, but with butika, being men, there is the authority problem as well. As indicated above, this helps us to understand butika as an alternate of kautabo. The kautabo relationship is carried to the next generation by the men. It is men, rather than women, who are considered the most appropriate spokesmen for an utu. In the next generation still, the ties are those of consanguinity, among the children. My butika, kainuma and eiriki are "father" and "mother" to my children. The relation of affinity works toward its own extinction.

At this point it may be helpful to have a brief morphological or etymological look at these terms. *Ei* is a bound form meaning spouse. It is used with numerical forms to produce words similar to the English "first husband" (or wife), "second wife" (or husband), and the like, and with the possessive particles: "my first spouse" (*au moan-ei*), "his second spouse," (*ana kaua-ei*). This may be the same *ei* as in *iein,* "to have sexual relations, to marry" (*i-* is a reflexive prefix).

Riki means "more, again"; thus eiriki.

Kain is "a person, member, inhabitant of," and *uma* is "house." Kainuma may thus carry with it the suggestion of coresidence, as eiriki carries with it the suggestion of cohabitation.

For butika the situation is quite complex. In Gilbertese, *bu* is a polyseme, and it is particularly tempting here to push interpretations too far. We have noted its use with the possessive suffixes for "spouse." With the possessive particle, it is an uncommonly used term for "kindred." This is particularly suggestive, especially as Sabatier (1954, p. 190) gives one of the meanings of bu as "to come or go out, to come or go out again, to bud," as a derivation from *buta,* "to remove, to take away."

In myth translations, Grimble has translated *te bu-n-anti* (-*n,* of; *anti,* spirit) as "the breed of spirits."

Katika means "to pull or make taut" (*ka-* is the causative prefix).

Sabatier (1954, p. 229), in addition to the in-law usage, gives the following for butika: "pole with a strip to detach the fruit of the pandanus," and in verbal usage as "to meet" (this is without the suffix -*na;* with the suffix, it means "to brother-in-law").

Thus butika in one direction may carry with it the suggestion of detaching or pulling away, but also meeting. This would be singularly appropriate for the affinal meaning: the brother-in-law is one who can pull away one's sister or one's wife and is one with whom a relationship exists. Bu itself may have a general sense of movement beyond an original point. Beyond this point I cannot honorably go. Needless to say, a study of Gilbertese morphology would be very useful.

Certain terminological ambiguities reflect the nature of affinity. For such positions as child's spouse's siblings—sibling's spouse's parents, and sibling's spouse's siblings, the general pattern is that there is no term. But the use of certain terms is feasible. I asked an old woman how she would refer to her daughter's husband's brother. She thought for a while, and then said, perhaps kautabo. I asked a young friend how his sisters would refer to his wife's mother. He replied: "Perhaps 'mother,' but you should really ask my mother. She would know the right word." Sibling's spouse's siblings are either definitely nothing at all, or the same as sibling's spouse. The general problem here is the relationship between the unity of spouses, and the unity of utu, and more particularly, siblings.

The use of sibling terms for co-affines (a specification of the rule, spouse of x : spouse of y : : x : y) presents a similar problem. Some responded that there was no term. But if there are terms, they are the sibling terms. The alternate norms are not about which term would be appropriate, but whether any term at all is appropriate.

For the child's spouse's sibling—sibling's spouse's parents and sibling's spouse's siblings problem, the local explanation of why terms could be appropriate is of the same nature as one of the reasons why you could refer to your mother's second husband's relatives by kinship terms. On the one hand, you are "showing your respect." On the other, the relatives of your stepfather "could come to your house to see him." Comments on the affinal usages are of the latter type. If your sibling's spouse's parents saw you, they might call you to their house. If you are visiting an island in the Gilberts where there are relatives of your child's spouse, they will look after you. The use of the terms makes sense when the role is being played that is meant by those terms. The possibility of their use is related to the possibility of the roles being played. The possibility of the roles being played is a product of marriage. Relationships between kinsmen's affines and affine's kinsmen express both the continuing interest of each utu in its members, and the recognition of the claims of the other utu.

With these affinally linked people, the emphasis, to repeat, is on the role-designating rather than classifying functions of terms (Schneider and Roberts 1956). The ambiguities point to this since it is not their genealogical position which is problematic, but their roles. When terms are used, it is because a certain role is being played or its possibility envisioned, and the usages recognize the unity of siblings, the unity of spouses, or the general contrast between utu and kautabo.

The affinal terminology indicates not only the contingent nature of the relationship between utu, but also the unity of the utu relationship itself, since the consanguineal pair is the unit through which the position of co-affines (the spouses of consanguines) is defined.

This takes us back to the initial observation about the spouse, who is either not utu, because identity through blood or land is lacking, or is utu, because code is present. For those linked to me through marriage, if there is death, separation, or divorce, unless some relationship continues, terms are not generally used. If my sister gets divorced from her husband, or she dies and he remarries, without a relationship, he is no longer my "brother-in-law."

Although one places terms such as these in a list in a single form, they are not of course uttered in a single form, and this is important for an understanding of use. For example, if you casually ask a man how another man is related to him, he might use the plural possessive, such as *tarira* (our sibling of same sex), or *ai-tarira*. The implicit vis-à-vis here is the sibling set. The full set of possessive particles and suffixes is:

au	*-u*	my	*ara*	*-ra*	our
am	*-m*	your (sing.)	*ami*	*-mi*	your (pl.)
ana	*-na*	his, her, its	*aia*	*-ia*	their

A question may be phrased in the same way. "She is *ai-tarimi,* isn't she?" One often hears people referred to as *ara koraki* (our kindred).

There is, however, another implicit vis-à-vis: the couple. One can say *natira* (our child) vis-à-vis the couple or the sibling set (that person would actually be "child" to both). Or, one can say *tinara* (our mother) vis-à-vis the couple to refer to the mother of husband or wife. Especially for more distant consanguines, the "our" usage is very common. It is also common for kautabo, and butika in the sense of "co-senior-in-law." For it is the role of these people vis-à-vis the utu as a whole that is important. The individual participates in the relationship as a member of an utu. The two bonds, consanguineal (particularly sibling) and marriage, define the two vis-à-vis.

Roles are being played in relation not only to individuals, but also to utu and couples. The use of Banaban kinship terms actually suggests a tendency toward "pluralization."[6] With notable frequency a person will refer to another person's relationship to him by using an "our" form (for example, "our sibling of same sex," as above), and the relationship between two people will be described by a third party in a "their" form (for example, "their sibling of same sex"). Perhaps one of the points being made is that relationships do not only involve individuals as individuals.[7] The pluralization phenomenon may represent an application of the group frame of reference discussed in chapter 10. The phenomenon recalls the ma usage discussed earlier in the present chapter (for example, "William ma," meaning "William and his crowd")—this usage would appear to be consistent with the co-occurrence of the group frame of reference and the person frame of reference (the latter yielding the ego-centered character of many aspects of social integration).

The significance of the role meaning of terms can be approached from another direction. The same people can often identify more than one terminological relationship between them, because they are related in more than one way. For example, two men may be in the genealogical sense both "father: child" and "sibling of same sex: sibling of same sex." Or they may be both consanguines and affines of one another, so that they are "sibling of same sex" and "brother-in-law." People say that the closer connection tends to be emphasized, but often they do not know which is the closer connection. When people who are utu marry, their "close utu" proverbially behave as affines rather than as utu, but here, as in the preceding cases, people can settle into a role relationship that they are more comfortable with, or behave in different roles at different times. Multiple options can be kept open.[8]

6. This label emerged in a conversation with Harold W. Scheffler at Yale University in 1969.

7. Perhaps it is a point that needs making, e.g., a person signals (or it is signaled to him, or signaled in general) that he is not appropriating a kinsman to himself alone.

8. There is some feeling that in older times, kinsmen who became related as affines ceased more systematically to behave as kinsmen to one another. If this is true, then behavior in this area has changed. It is possible that people would have such an impression because of the increase in population. There are more people, perhaps with more distant connections, whose behavior would be an input to such an idea. Another alternative hypothesis, which is not inconsistent with the population idea, is that the notion of change is a reflex of the general tendency to see the past as more orderly than the present, to see "lines" in the past as having been more clearly drawn. This notion may be a product of the general experience of change. Alternatively, it may always have been the case.

USE AND INFORMATION

Knowledge about kinship relations is not, of course, confined to kinsmen. If I see that X went to tell Y that X's child was about to marry and that Y should come to discuss the matter, it is a reasonable conclusion that X and Y are utu. It is not a certainty, but a fair probability. There are other circumstances which might account for it, but the usual circumstance is kinship. An illustration will combine this point with the preceding one.

A certain woman, Nei D, is "sibling of opposite sex" to my friend S (a young married man). S told me that Nei D's husband, E, is "sibling of same sex" to him. He knew this to be true because his (S's) father told him so. I asked S if E was aware of it. He said that E must know it, because "it comes out in conversation." The way it came out in conversation was in certain kinds of joking. This is "brotherly" behavior. Without that link, they would be "brothers-in-law" only, and that joking is not brother-in-law (between men) behavior. Friends might behave that way, but these men were not friends, and one was almost twice the age of the other.

If one knows the genealogical ties between two kinsmen, one can formulate a categorical relationship, although one cannot predict role behavior absolutely. When one knows that two people are kinsmen, one can infer that their descendants and full siblings are kinsmen. Knowing that two people are kinsmen of a certain type (that is, the kin term), one can infer the types of categorical kinsmen their children are, even if the connections between the original pair are totally obscure.

In general terms, one has knowledge about social identities by being told (for the identity of another—by that other, or a third party), or by inference from observation or knowledge of another identity (of the identified person himself, or another). It is by a combination of "direct report" and "inference" that one knows who is what.

I will give an illustration of the kind of process I mean from a time when I was an unwitting participant in the situation, again involving S. A certain wedding was imminent when a man, B, arrived at the house of the family of the bride. He was representing the groom, and they were discussing various arrangements for the ceremony. Some people had commented at another time that the groom's mother had been adopted by B's parents. (All these people on the groom's side are Gilbertese.) After the wedding, I was trying to sort out the relationships of the participants. I sent S (who had a Gilbertese father and a Banaban mother) to the groom's mother to ask her about any relationship to B.

When S returned from the interview he looked rather distraught. He said that B's parents had indeed adopted the groom's mother as their daughter. I knew that S and B were "siblings of same sex" and participated in a kinship relationship (although the precise genealogical connection was unknown). I asked S if the groom's mother were thus his utu too. By that time I had assumed she would be, and that S was upset because he had not contributed to the marriage of his kinsmen. His statements verified the interpretation. He said, however, that he did not really err, because he did not know. They had not been in a kinship relationship. Now he knows: she is his "sibling of opposite sex." When I asked him if he thought the groom's mother knew of their connection, he said that she must, because when you come to a strange land, your kinsmen tell you who your mutual relatives are. This added a certain poignancy to the event because the groom's mother was an "outsider" to the island, and with a reduced circle of kin had to rely more upon them.

One can thus reason, if probabilistically, from category to category, from role to category, and from category to role.

One learns which categories apply between whom in part from hearing the categories used. I will very briefly address the question of some of the contexts in which kinship terms occur. First, there is socialization. Small children can be asked by the parents or others, "Who is your father?" "Who is your mother?" much in the manner of the first catechism. To my enduring regret I did not do much work with small children.

Second, there is the simple context of directing attention to another person. "Give this to your sibling of same sex," who might be sitting on another side of a room.

Third is asking a question: "Where is your mother?" More information might, however, be needed. One evening a teenage boy came into a store, and someone asked him, "How is your Old Woman?" He looked perplexed. "Which Old Woman?" he replied. "Your mother," the man responded. His mother had been ill, and the boy then communicated the information that she had just died.

Fourth is simply report, which shades into narration. "And he said to his father . . ." "And he gave that sibling of opposite sex . . ." Narration may include quotation. "Then the boy cried, Mama!"

Fifth is address, for the Mama-Baba-Kaka set. Although there are no reciprocals in address from the senior to the junior generation, a mother may croon to her babe in arms, "My child, O!"

Sixth is correction: in a narration, where someone says, "And he gave that sibling of opposite sex . . . ," someone might reply, "Not his sibling of opposite sex, his child."

Seventh is identification. A person is "placed" by naming known kin.

People on Rambi sometimes point out that the population has grown so numerous, the people are now so fertile, that one does not know everybody. Often if a strange young person is walking on the path near a house, someone inside may say, "Who is that young man?" Another may reply, "X's child." His village may also be mentioned, but the primary placing identification, the one bearing the most information, is kinship. There is an erratically functioning intervillage telephone system on the island, and one young man was using it. He identified himself to the person who picked it up in another village as "Rewi's child."

Eighth, because this information does have such a high semantic load, there is the context of explanation and justification. This can occur in rituals which will soon be discussed, for example, where I present a gift to you as "your gift through your mother." Or if a stranger is spending a lot of time with an islander and someone wants to know why, the reply might be, "Her koraki from Tarawa; her mother." This is enough information to reduce the puzzle.

Finally—although one could go on further—there is the invocation of the relationship in a more direct sense, either positively or in criticism. Thus: "Our Father who art in Heaven," and the use of sibling terms in the church or to invoke a wider solidarity. Or, a woman handing their child to her husband, "Take your child." Or, "His own father, and he struck him!"

THE PROBLEM OF HISTORY

Until this chapter, my discussion has been historically oriented. The problem with kinship terms and affinal terms is the lack of historical data. On Rambi I was engaged in trying to untangle the subtleties of contemporary usage and had little time to devote to working with old people on possible changes.

In the Grimble and Maude papers there is, however, one incomplete list of terms from an old Banaban woman. Grimble obtained much information from her and also included in his notes some limited genealogical information from her, with terms listed under names. It is not clear whether the terms given were those in contemporary usage, or whether the inquirer was looking backward. The information is of very limited value but is difficult to ignore.

For consanguines, "father," "mother," the sibling terms, "child," and "grandparent-grandchild" appear to be as we have discussed them, although there is incomplete information in the genealogy. The differences concern affines. The "reciprocal term used between parents-in-law" is *rao-ni-kabo* (companion-of-causing-to-meet). If this term was in general usage, the shift to *kautabo* would not be one of distinctive features. Influence from Gilbertese may have occurred.

"Husband's sister" is *kainuma,* as now; there is no information for a woman's brother's wife.[9] Spouses are *bu* or *kainabau.* "Wife's brother" is butika, but there is no information for a man's sister's husband. On the term list, "wife's sister" and "husband's brother" are given as eiriki (as now), or *nga-ni-bu.* On the genealogy there are notes to the effect that nga-ni-bu applies to "real" opposite-sex siblings of spouse, but eiriki to more distant ones. Sabatier (1954, p. 622) lists one of the meanings of *nga* as "community of origin, kinship."

A later genealogical fragment from Maude shows butika (in the sense of "brother-in-law" between men) and kainuma, as now, and nga-ni-bu between siblings-in-law of opposite sex. If nga-ni-bu was general in its usage, then Banaban Gilbertese has lost one term, coming closer to what appears to be the general Gilbertese pattern. If the distinction was one involving distance, it has been replaced by the possibility of using *ai-* in this context also. Without the loss of nga-ni-bu, the pattern of spouse pair terminological uniformity would probably not be as absolute as it is now. There is unfortunately no information on terms for spouse's sibling's spouse, so this line of argument cannot be carried much further.[10]

A much more serious matter is that of terminology for affines one generation removed. Wife's father is "father," husband's mother is "mother," and a child-in-law of the same sex is "child." *Tinaba,* however, is indicated as a reciprocal between wife's mother and daughter's husband, and between husband's father and son's wife (compare Lundsgaarde 1966, p. 83). Tinaba, then, is a kind of counterpart in proximate generations of eiriki in the same generation. This is true both of the attributes by which the distinctions are made, and in one sense of the sexual aspects meant by the roles, which will be taken up in the next chapter. If it was in general use, its falling into desuetude may be a result of the same process by which eiriki, although known, is not frequently used except in certain contexts. This is religion having an effect on kinship terms.

I am not undertaking here a comparison of Banaban kinship or terminology with contemporay systems in the Gilberts; I feel I should await the

---

9. Grimble wrote that in the Gilberts, *kainaba* is used for the husband's sister of a woman, whereas on Banaba *kainuma* is used (Grimble 1933, p. 4 n. 5).

10. Perhaps nga-ni-bu was marked (for closeness) and eiriki was unmarked. Then the change has an interesting aspect to it: the unmarked category (eiriki) was retained, and marking for distance (the possibility of using *ai-eiriki*) replaced marking for closeness (nga-ni-bu). For whatever reason, this would also be a change in the direction of consistency within the terminological system.

expected publication of materials by Lambert (1963) and Lundsgaarde (1966). I will only note my general conclusion that terminological variation concerns affines rather than kinsmen. If the reports of Banaban terminology from the first third of this century are generally accurate, then the changes which have occurred have been in affinal rather than consanguineal terminology. We have noted that the greatest contemporary variation—in the sense of the existence of alternate norms—concerns affinal rather than consanguineal (or "identity") terminology. This suggests an enduring, and in the Gilbertese cultural sphere widespread, kind of labeling behavior centering on features of common identity. This may well be an enduring part of Banaban culture.

It is not only labeling behavior which encodes general information about kinship. Certain rituals do also. The Banabans do not only utter their categories. They dance them. We will turn to this after one final observation about terms.

We have seen the use of kinship terms for nonkinsmen, and the use of nonkinship terms for kinsmen. It seems surprisingly difficult to say exactly what a kinship term is. It comes to the point where one cannot say, "Here is the vocabulary which has to do with kinship, and here is the vocabulary which does not." The reasons are simple and interrelated. One has the interplay between the identity and code aspects. Also, and perhaps more fundamentally, what is stated in kinship is more diffuse than what is stated in other domains. Thus the domain is particularly magnetic in two senses. First, since kinsmen are also persons, and since kinship relationships become implicated with other relationships, the domain "attracts" elements from other domains: age, sex, status, for example. And second, since the domain is diffuse, it sends elements out to combine with other domains. Although the distinctive features remain the same, this implies that the surface realizations of kinship behavior have the possibility of variability and change, so that the compilation of things like final lists is in the nature of the case impossible.[11]

I spent a good deal of time cogitating on the nature of Banaban kinship terms in my cottage in Nuka toward the end of my stay on the island. Next door lived a young couple, the husband of which considered himself one of the most modern-minded people on the island. Often my cogitations would be shattered when he sang out to his wife, in perfect English, "Sweetheart!" Perhaps he was trying to tell me something.

11. In order to establish these points clearly, it would be necessary to systematically compare usages in different domains, e.g., the range of alternatives and variation in usage about kinsmen, religious functionaries, and politicians. In the field I was compulsive about noting down kinship usages, but alas much less so about others.

13

Kinship and Ritual I:
Consanguinity and Affinity

FAMILY GATHERINGS

In this chapter we will be concerned with "family gatherings," primarily marriage, and the implications of some of the messages about affinal relationships encoded in family gatherings.

Banabans themselves direct one's attention to some of these gatherings as displays of custom in operation. The gatherings are "cultural performances" (Singer 1959), both for the nature of kinship and for Banaban custom in a more general sense. This applies particularly to the set of gatherings which define certain points in the individual's development: first birthday, first menstruation, marriage, and death. Marriage is the paradigmatic cultural performance both for Banaban kinship and Banaban custom. One reason is that it is the only regular gathering in which descent units are operative, as gift-giving and gift-receiving entities. This aspect of marriage will be treated in the next chapter. The gatherings are among the things through which people give tangible form to their concepts of kinship, and through which those concepts are themselves formed.

First birthday, first menstruation, marriage, and death are regarded as a kind of core set. There are also other occasions when kinsmen beyond the members of a household may gather for a defined purpose. For example, they may gather to greet a kinsman who has been absent from Rambi for a long time or one who has come from the Gilberts. One set of kin had a birthday party for a middle-aged man. Another held a celebration when a baby's umbilical cord fell off. This latter family had strong Gilbertese connections, and people thought that perhaps it was a Gilbertese custom.

A young girl adopted a Gilbertese man as her brother, with the consent of her family who said they would give him land. The family sponsored a celebration of the adoption. At that occasion, a Gilbertese elder of well-known rhetorical abilities proclaimed that the utu of Nei B "should know" C "as her sibling of opposite sex, her older sibling [*karimoana*] or her younger sibling [*karimwina*]," and that the utu of C "should know" Nei B as his "sibling of opposite sex, his older sibling or his younger sibling." Not only was the adoption itself being commemorated; the nature of utu and siblingship were being defined.

There is another kind of gathering which I only witnessed once, and on which I did not make wide inquiries. Although there is only one case, it dramatizes well many of the things we have been discussing.

There had been a breach among siblings, particularly between a woman and her sister. But a reconciliation was finally planned. At the reconciliation were the siblings who lived nearby, and a neighbor family also related to them. I went with that family, the wife of which (who was the person related to the siblings) said to me, "We are the only ones from outside"—kinsmen, yes, but outside the sibling set. The meeting was at the house of one of the disputing women, the younger sister.

The only others present, in addition to the spouses and children of those mentioned, were kautabo. The kautabo were the parents of the boy engaged to the daughter of one of the brothers; they came with their son. Before they arrived, leading the elder sister, a mat was placed on the north side of the house, and someone whispered, "Te kautabo!" The brother's daughter and her fiancé sat in the center.

The sisters did not speak at first. Then the mother of the fiancé somewhat uncomfortably announced, "We have something to say. If there has been any error, please forgive it." Then the small talk began.

The woman with whom I went told me that the brother had said that the elder sister should come to the house for the reconciliation. The younger sister was angry, but the elder was led by the kautabo. "The kautabo are the ones who bring people together." It was the kautabo who spoke. If the elder sister had spoken, they knew that the younger sister would be angry. But she could not be angry if it was done by the kautabo.

Here one is bringing an outsider in to try to achieve what an insider could not—but a very special kind of outsider. The spokeswoman was not the mother of the fiancé of either sister, but rather, of their common brother. And she and her husband were kautabo to all the siblings. Disputing with a kautabo can wreck a planned marriage. The younger sister would thus not only alienate her brother, but would also compromise a relationship which was central to the continuity of the utu as a whole.

The existence of these occasional gatherings, which also occur of course among ourselves, is structurally just as important as the existence of the core set. The expansibility of the field of kin unit activities is a parallel to the expansibility of the field of kin terms. The functional definitions of kin units (with the exception of descent units) are diffuse. They allow of a wide range of variable and even innovative behavior without compromising the nature of the system. They are in fact reflexes of the nature of the system.

What I term the core set, however, does inform those other possibilities, in that, among other things and to varying degrees, it articulates the nature of kinship itself. It is in this sense that those gatherings may be considered rituals. They are important not only for those who participate in them. Others know they are being carried out and may discuss them informally. The news of a gathering travels quickly. Just as the kinship relations among people who are not one's kin are a significant input to one's knowledge about kinship and one's behavior, so too are the gatherings.

Considered ensemble from the point of view of kinship, the core gatherings (each member of the set to different degrees) involve statements which can be organized into a system of intersecting planes structured in the following way:

1a. Defining a person or persons in new or revised roles, or the circumstances leading to such a revision;
1b. Defining the nature of roles, or the circumstances leading to transitions;
2a. Defining specific ties between specific people;
2b. Defining the general nature of those ties;
3a. Defining the integration of specific ties between specific people;
3b. Defining the nature of the integration of ties;
4. Defining the event as a special kind of event.

The b functions and the fourth are the most generally ritual components.

To take first menstruation as an example: Members of the girl's family assemble and bring presents of coconut oil, cloth, food, and money. Coconut oil and cloth are things within the female province. Food is for the meals which mark any significant social occasion. One has not only commensality, but also (especially in gatherings when the group is large) the cooperation of people in preparing the food. It is what kinsmen do to "help" one another; they are behaving as kinsmen in an undifferentiated fashion, except that there may be some sexual division of labor. The money helps pay for everything.

While the family eats and amuses itself for the first two days, in the model form, the girl is withdrawn on a Spartan diet. She sleeps little and occupies herself in the making of sennit and mats, with a few old female relatives watching over her. She is dressed in the old form of leaf skirt, and her breasts are exposed. The big meal is on the final day, when she joins the party dressed in new clothes.

The rite marks the fact that the girl has become a young woman and is soon to be eligible for marriage. People say that before governmental restrictions, girls married one or two years after first menstruation. The rite also demonstrates that her parents have successfully brought her up to the point where she is a young woman, a performer of female roles.

The rite articulates a certain definition of the female role: not what women actually do most of the time or even any of the time, but "young femaleness" uncomplicated by other things (see Gluckman 1962).

We will have more to say about gifts in a moment. The kinsmen who come and present gifts, or who send gifts through proxies, are stating the existence of a relationship between them and the girl, or rather her parents. At the same time, both to them and to others who know of the event, participation, gift giving and "working for your utu" state in general what utu-ness is about. It is a tangible representation of the utu being an utu.

The coming together of the utu of the father and the mother, for an event centering on the child, states the relationship of specific affinal and consanguineal ties, as is the case in all such family gatherings. And their coming together states, for all to see (or at least know about) the general nature of the relationship between utu and affinity. This will be explored later. Briefly now, we may state it as follows: In the utu there are connections of identity and of relationship; of equivalence and differentiation; of sharing and exchange (compare Wagner 1967). In affinity, there is the transformation of relationship (marriage) into identity (the child); of differentiation (between husband and wife and their utu) into equivalence (vis-à-vis the child); of exchange (between the utu of husband and wife) into sharing (vis-à-vis the child).

In the other gatherings of the core set and some noncore gatherings, religious functionaries participate and thus define the integration of specific ties (kinship and religious) between specific people, and the mutual relevance of kinship and church domains. In the case of first menstruation the situation is more complex since there is a general feeling that the Protestant churches find this ritual to be inconsistent with Christianity. Even here, however, church functionaries may appear. In one Pentecostal church family, the parents were not going to sponsor a first menstruation, but their utu took the matter into their own hands.

This brings us to the fourth kind of statement. Of the core gatherings, first menstruation and marriage in particular have what I call a heavy "meta-ritual" component. What I mean by "meta-ritual" is that one of the basic messages being communicated is: "Look! In spite of certain changes which have occurred in our culture, we are performing such-and-such a ritual which is a transformation of such-and-such a traditional ritual." When one participates in a ritual with a heavy meta-ritual component, one participates in a ritual in part *about* the ritual which the meta-ritual is purported to be. It is in this sense that many aspects of first menstruation and marriage are cultural performances of the custom.

One may speculate that the symbolic elements, such as coconut oil and the leaf skirt, are designed not only to support the messages which make the first menstruation rite, for example, so similar to other *rites de passage* (separation, privation, reintegration, and the like). The symbolic elements are also designed and redesigned to support the message: We are holding a ritual which is a thing of Banaban custom. One may speculate further that, especially with incomplete records of the referent rituals, one direction that the ritual structure may take is that of generalization. In this context, by "generalization" I mean that both the structure and the content of rituals appropriate elements which come to be considered as suitable to any ritual in the society. In Banaban rituals the exchange of cigarettes and matches between guests and sponsor may be a manifestation of this process. It is not that cigarettes and matches are regarded as traditional, but that they come to be distributed widely over the behavioral class of events. This is also true for the presence of pastors. At the same time, however, there is a recognition of the transformation of specific elements, for example, the substitution of money for food in marriage exchanges.

Not all people hold first menstruation gatherings, although all know about them. They are called *te rara* (the blood, menstruation). Not all people hold first birthday celebrations either, although they are more common for the first child. The same sets of messages, except that involving the significance of menstruation itself, are present here. The first-birthday celebration may have been introduced by the mission in the early part of the century. It is also regarded as custom, but not in the same historic sense as first menstruation. Here, the first year of life has been successfully negotiated; parenthood and grandparenthood have been affirmed.

I am not going to dwell on the details of death, nor on the paraphernalia or the specifically religious components of events in the core set. Such detail would take us into the systems of four different churches, and symbolic elements from cakes to coffins to conceptions of the Holy Family. That will have to await another time. It is important to note here, however, that (as one would expect) death not only marks the departure of a kinsman, but is also the circumstance through which, when that kinsman was married and had children, the surviving spouse becomes widowed, and heirs become executors. Sons may become breadwinners for their mothers, and brothers for their younger brothers and sisters. Although one still has "parents" in the kindred, the death of parents confers a new social personality on the children, as does marriage, because one does to an extent inherit the social personality of the deceased parent. This is why in the allocation of housing land, a section should go to the unmarried members of a sibling set which has been orphaned.

If a married person dies, both his and his spouse's kin attend the funeral. This raises the general question of attendance, which will be considered now.

ATTENDANCE AND GIFT GIVING

Some relatives, especially those considered "close," are informed beforehand of the utu gathering. Especially for marriage and death, however, those close relatives constitute a small proportion of the people who come. These are not the by-invitation-only affairs with which we are familar in our own culture. People come after they hear, a practice which underscores both the lack of boundaries of the kindred, and the fact that the onus of maintaining the relationship is not primarily upon the person supervising the occasion but upon his kinsmen. Or rather, the matter is phrased in terms of reciprocity: So-and-so came to my wedding, I will go to his funeral. In one family that I knew rather well, the greatest anger I witnessed between the mother and her married eldest son was when the latter heard that a close relative was to have a first menstruation celebration but forgot to tell his mother. She said to her son, among other things, "Are you *kamoamoa?*" Kamoamoa means "overbearing, pushy, pretentious, trying to put oneself above others," and is a hard insult. The family of the girl who had menstruated and that of the mother and her son were quite close and frequently visited one another and attended one another's gatherings. Lack of concern for the gathering can be a sign that one does not consider one's kinsmen as worthy.

"The utu," a young man said somewhat hyperbolically, "is your foundation and your strength. If you did not have utu, you would sit lonely in your house. If you passed someone else's house, you would not be invited in. If you were in trouble you would have no one to go to." And it is at family gatherings that the relationships are displayed, that the kindred acts in part as a unit, that relationships which in fact may not have been much exercised are given tangible formulation.

On joyous occasions one does not ostensibly go only to join in the fun, but rather "to help the work." Part of the help consists in giving money to assist in the feeding of the gathering. Of course, the gathering is composed of the people who have also come "to help the work." One of my assistants commented that he attends many family gatherings because, "I am thinking of my children. If you have no children, you do not have to worry. The utu comes and helps you at your time" (that is, when you are supervising a gathering for your children). I objected that one might not arrange a gathering at all. "Maybe that is all right," he replied, "but if no one comes, it would be as if you were an outsider, and not a person of the land." Not only "people of the land" come; some are Gilbertese relatives of Gilbertese. And people without children do, in fact, attend these gatherings. The point is that if no one comes, it would be as if one had no utu, and if one had no utu, one's social personality would be critically incomplete.

If one attends a gathering and does not present a gift (usually of money), then it would be as if one were coming to eat, and nothing more. This is stated in an informative way through the traditional definition of the gifts of children who have been "adopted away."

As has already been noted, a child adopted away without having been given a piece of land (known as *te iria*, the accompaniment, or *te kan-oki*, the wanting to return) by his real parents is not supposed to behave in kinship roles with his "real" family, except insofar as his adopted parent (or parents) is also related to that family (which is generally the case). It is recognized, however, that blood is thicker than adoption and can triumph in the end, and that the adopted child may want to attend the marriage of his blood relatives. The problem is resolved by stating his gift of money, not as a "contribution" in the same manner as the utu, but as "the wanting to eat" (*te bia-amarake*). Here he is contrasted with those who contribute to "help the work" and contribute because they have a *right* to contribute and indeed to have their contributions accepted.[1] These gatherings are at least as much for those who give as for those who receive, although the people do not explicitly look upon it that way.

With the gift type "the wanting to eat," it is as if the returning adoptee were exchanging money for food *directly* which is in contrast to the delayed reciprocity of the kinship relationship. In explaining this, people point out that the returning adoptee is not actually coming because he wants to eat. "It doesn't *really* mean that." The statement of the gift is a kind of legal fiction at a time which calls for the demonstration of solidary ties, allowing for the expression of a tie which is on the one hand broken, but on the other hand unbreakable.

Utu gifts (*te birin utu*) are made by a person individually, or in combination generally with a sibling or siblings or first cousins. As one would by now

1. It is interesting to note here that when we collected descent-unit genealogies (see chapter 14), adopted children were sometimes included in their natal utu and were sometimes not. When they were included, it was often noted that they were "adopted away." Remembering the genealogical information in this case may keep the option of a relationship open but may also operate in the other direction, by providing an account of why a person does not and should not own land through a particular line. This point emerged in a conversation with Mervyn Meggitt.

expect, there is no formal stipulation of a boundary. Utu is as utu does. A sibling set may contribute in the name of their deceased parent through whom the connection is traced, the name of that parent being written down in the book or on the pieces of paper which record the gifts. Siblings need not contribute as a unit, and when they are married may give individually since they are productive responsible entities. I know of one time when an unmarried young man contributed separately from his mother, and the contribution was not marking a connection through his father. Mother and son were reported to be angry with each other, and not even living in the same house. Thus the nature of the solidarity of the givers among themselves can be stated as well as their solidarity with the recipients.

Especially at marriage, which is a much larger celebration than the others, the recording of the gift may indicate the path (*kawai*) of the connection. When giving a gift, I may say that it is from me on my father's side to you on your mother's side. You may make the surmise yourself and write it down that way. Or the gifts can be listed on separate pages, or under separate columns, not necessarily with the same degree of further specification on the different sides, with a tendency for greater specificity in the Banaban than the Gilbertese lines. As an example, at one large marriage, on the bride's side, the gifts were categorized by whether they were "to" her father (deceased, Gilbertese), her mother's father (deceased, Gilbertese), her mother's mother's mother (alive, Banaban), and her mother's mother's father (deceased, Banaban). For the contributions to the marriage of Karawa, a young man whose Banaban father and Gilbertese mother were alive at the time, the listings were made by his mother's utu (some of these relatives were designated as being on his mother's "male side" or "female side"), his father's utu, his father's mother's father's utu, and his father's mother's mother's utu. The amounts of money were summarized as from his father's utu on the "female side," his father's utu on the "male side," his mother's utu on "the male side and the female side," and "from the house."

"The male side" is *te itera-ni-mane* (*itera*, side, half; *ni*, of; *mane*, male, man) and "the female side" is *te iteran-aine* (*aine*, female, woman). One can divide one's kindred in this way, as "my male side" and "my female side," in describing a connection using those terms. For example: "He is 'my father' on my female side." The terms are also used, as we shall see, to describe the bride's utu (the female side) and the groom's utu (the male side) at marriage. ("Side" is also used in a more general sense. For example, if I suggest that you are related to X through Y, and Y is the wrong connection, you may say, "No, it's another side." Or if you have both Banaban and, say, Tarawan ancestors, you may refer to "my Tarawa side.")

In the delineation of the gifts to the marriage under discussion, there was also a category of gifts "from the house." The people in this category were the groom's siblings and his father's mother's sister's daughter, who had been living with them. The delineations illustrate the generally inner-utu character of the three-generational line; the isolation of parents as those through whom relationships are traced; and the coresidence relationship aspect of kinship, through the inclusion of the one collateral in the last category. At times there is a competitive element: whether the father's side or the mother's side will yield the greatest total.

The coresidence factor may be illustrated by another example. It was noted in the last chapter that when the Buakonikai Rorobuaka Society decided on a communal copra cutting, it was agreed that people who would soon be involved in the heavy expenses of family gatherings should be exempted. The general boundary adopted for exemption purposes included people with a grandparent who was a sibling of a grandparent of the celebrant. These people are expected to contribute more. A case that drew comment involved a man living in the same house as his deceased brother's daughter and her husband, and the latter's sister's daughter. The man is considered the elder of the house, and the girl, who was about to be married, lived there all the time. Someone mentioned his name as one of those whose Buakonikai land would be excluded from the communal copra cutting. He replied, however, that he should not be excused. A consanguine of the girl later commented that this was a shameful thing for him to do. It was shameful because it was as if he were saying: "The girl is living in my house, we are in an utu relationship, she is under my care, but she *really* is not my kinsman." This derives from the principles outlined in the last chapter.

If two people are related in more than one way, a person may present more than one gift, either by giving, for example, ten shillings and indicating that five is through one connection and five through another, or by giving five shillings each to two different people. At the death of Karawa's youngest child, his sister received the money for the connections to him; his wife's father, B, for those to B; and his wife's mother's father, C, for connections to C *and* C's wife (the child's mother's mother's mother).

One of the things that this division allows for is the tangible formulation of solidarity on one side and nonsolidarity on another. This same man, Karawa (whose family I lived with for some weeks in Uma village), for example, is engaged in a descent unit dispute with another utu on the question of traditional precedence in Uma village. Another Uma man, D, is related to Karawa's mother through D's father, and to Karawa's father through D's mother. The latter connection is the one involved in the dispute. When D gave a contribution to Karawa at a gathering, I asked Karawa to explicate it. He said that it was the relationship through D's father; he would not give on the other side because of the dispute.

Marriage is the only situation where the descent group collective gifts are presented, as well as the private gifts. Even here, however, I may make a gift as part of a descent group and also make a private gift. This is not necessarily because I am connected to the person through two different lines. The *same* line may be implicated in both gifts. One gift represents myself as, for example, part of the senior line of a descent group contributing to a junior line of the descent group. The other represents myself as a kinsman (although perhaps specified as belonging to the male or the female side) of the person in question. Although the genealogical relationship is the same, this illustrates how the descent group and the kindred are not the same thing.

The private gifts themselves illustrate how no special problems need be created by the "overlapping" of kindred. I can conceive of gifts from my mother's utu, and my father's utu, or even divide those into one or more levels, although they involve some of the same people. One may choose to emphasize one relationship, but one need not. Within the house of gathering, if there are people collecting the money for different utu of the celebrant, I can walk from one collector to another.

Not presenting a gift at all may be a statement of nonsolidarity, but unless there is a known breach, the situation may call for comment but still be uncertain. Yet even if there is a great deal of comment, the nongiver may appear at the next gathering of the family to reaffirm the relationship.

In marriage, the situation with regard to multiple relationships is somewhat different. The bride's side generally assembles in one house and the groom's side in another. There may be some movement between them, but especially as the time of marriage approaches, not much. Although one's physical body can be "in the groom's side" rather than the bride's side, this does not mean that one's social body (and the Banabans use the image of "body") is committed to one side rather than the other.

Murdock writes of the lack of "discreteness" and "separability" of the kindred at the time of a marriage.

> The Tenino of Oregon illustrate how conflicts in ceremonial obligations can arise in a sibless society. In this tribe weddings are solemnized by an elaborate series of property exchanges between the kindreds of the bride and groom. The relatives of the bride, of both sexes, bring clothing, baskets, bags, vegetal foods, and other articles produced in the feminine sphere of economic activity. Those of the groom bring horses, skins, meat, and other masculine products. Each participant then exchanges his gifts with a particular member of the other kindred. It nearly always happens, of course, that a number of people are related to both the bride and the groom, and are forced to decide on which side they shall participate: they cannot play two contra-

dictory roles at once. Moreover, the numbers in each party must be the same. These problems are settled only after protracted discussions among the parties concerned and persons in authority, and they not infrequently generate jealousy, friction, and injured feelings.

Under unilinear descent such conflicts could never arise. [Murdock 1949, pp. 61–62.]

Banabans do not have this elaborated series of exchanges between kindred of bride and groom at the same moment, although as we shall see there are some comparable institutions. Some people do "stay" at the house of one side rather than another although they are related to both, and in the church sit on one side of the church rather than the other. But a sibling may be on the other side, and the sibling unit is thus represented on both sides. (One may not attend at all and still be represented in this way: When I asked someone why he was not going to the family gathering of one of his utu, he replied that he did not have to go because another man, his mother's mother's sister's daughter's son, was attending. "My body is going." One of the links between the two men was, incidentally, adoptive.)

I do not know the Tenino ethnography, but it is interesting that there the numbers of people in the exchanging groups must be equal, and presumably the kindreds of bride and groom are never in fact all equal in number. One is led to ask the question of why "representation" is not used there, if indeed it is not. The jealousy, friction, and injured feelings are not *entailed* by the absence of unilineal descent but may be related to a formulation of sibling unity different from that among the Banabans. It is upon this formulation that bilateral descent symbolically rests. It should be noted that the unity of siblings does not necessitate that a sibling group choose up sides, or spatially separate themselves from other sibling groups. The presence of one implies the social presence of another. Although I may be at the bride's side and my sister at the groom's side, "our body" is on both sides. The maximal extension of relationships which this system allows is not compromised by the separation of units, because they are units of relationships rather than persons.

The exchange of multiple gifts between kinsmen connected in different ways; the presentation of gifts by one individual in two roles, as a kinsman and as a member of the same descent unit; the simultaneous articulation of solidarity and nonsolidarity; participation by proxy—these practices indicate again how options can be maximized. The double relationship between people, as consanguines and as affines, and the multiple memberships of the descent system, are part of the same complex. The "Cast your net wide" specification of the general value is built into the system.

Marriage creates affinal ties. At first birthdays, first menstruations, and some of the occasional gatherings, and in the activities within the kindred of bride and groom at marriage, affinal ties are displayed in the context of their consequence: the children who are equally kinsmen to both. Marriage, in the system of expectations, brings together the greatest number of people and those related most distantly. Death brings together fewer people, they may not be as distantly related, but the "range" of affinal ties assembled in one place may be the greatest in the series. For example, suppose my daughter has married a man and there is a death in his utu, of his brother's child. At the first birthday, first menstruation, or marriage of that child I have no role. He is "another utu." My daughter will probably be there because her husband will probably be there. If that child dies, however, there is a general expectation that some people from my utu will go to "support our child." At the occasion of death, perhaps those relationships contributing to life are invoked.

A number of the principles involved in who goes to these gatherings may be illustrated by a rather unusual but for that reason informative situation. Nei S is a middle-aged, widowed, adopted Banaban. She is a Gilbertese by birth. She was adopted as a child by a Banaban woman who was Nei S's mother's brother's wife.

Nei S's real father's brother, a very old man, was living on Rambi with her and her son. The old man died. There was not a massive attendance at the funeral, but the people who came were (*a*) from Nei S's adoptive utu, (*b*) from her Gilbertese utu, and (*c*) from her husband's utu.

Here, the old man was in a special position because he was essentially under the care of Nei S and her son. This is described as being "in her arms," or "in his arms." The people from her husband's utu were coming in recognition of their tie with her, manifest through her son, who is their kinsman. One man who presented a gift was a collateral "brother" to her son, through her husband. The man said that the gift was "to" the son, because the old man was in his mother's "arms." They were supporting and helping the mother. One gift giver was in the relationship of "the meeting" with Nei S.

Nei S's husband's family, who came to the old man's funeral, would not ordinarily go, for example, to a first birthday or marriage in *her* family, to an occasion involving people in the son's family not also related to them. But death can bring them together. The son's father's family was standing with him.

At the death of another man, a young man who was engaged to a member of the deceased's utu brought a gift. This was considered a proper thing to do. A relationship of affinity, creating new ties and perhaps leading to the creation of life, was brought to bear on the occasion.

At the death of Karawa's child, the people who presented gifts were kin either to Karawa or Karawa's wife, Nei Ngariki. One young man who pre-sented a gift, however, was in a special position. He is a Gilbertese and a relative (through a close Gilbertese connection) of B and C (see figure 5). His gift was "to" B.

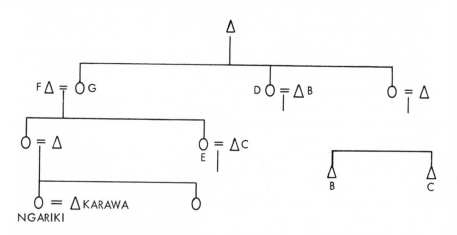

FIG. 5. LINKS IN A GIFT AT DEATH

Nei Ngariki's mother died when Nei Ngariki was young, and the latter was brought up by her mother's family, especially by Nei E and C, and Nei G and F. C and Nei Ngariki are in a father-daughter role relationship, and Nei E and Nei Ngariki are in a mother-daughter role relationship. The house-hold of C and Nei E is a coordinating household for this group. F and Nei G, B and Nei D, Karawa and Nei Ngariki, stay there at times. The inter-relating core is a tight unit of women, with the unusual feature that two brothers (B and C) married a woman and her niece (Nei D and Nei E). They all behave as utu to one another.

The Gilbertese lad sees B and C as his closest Rambi relatives, and he had resided with them. He and B are connected by blood and relationship (code); B and the ascendants of the child are connected by relationship only. In presenting the gift to B, the elder of the two brothers, the Gilbertese fellow was articulating the relationship, recognizing the death as a death in the family of a kinsman.

The giver was almost in a position of being "in the arms of" his relative. The "in the arms of" phenomenon, which we observed in the death de-scribed earlier, is the nurturance-coresidence aspect of relationship or code. There can be some ambiguities in it, as one would expect since the substantial link is missing. One ambiguity was observed when the Buakonikai man deferred from including himself among those to be exempt from the communal copra cutting. Another case will demonstrate the kinds of ambiguities which can exist.

A young Gilbertese man, G, was about to be married to a Banaban girl. There was a huge turnout on the girl's side for the marriage. On the boy's side, there was a problem. Some people thought that he had been adopted as grandchild by a Banaban woman but were not sure. He is a relative of her deceased husband, who was a Gilbertese, but also an adoptive brother of a prominent Banaban woman, Nei H. Nei H's husband was the brother of the woman who may or may not have adopted the boy.

Some considered the adoption to have been completed, and thus the proper person to give gifts to was the adoptive grandmother. But the boy had been "in the arms of" Nei H. It so happened that the marriage was to take place in Nei H's village, and her house was the house of gathering for the groom's side. The people who came were generally considered to be "coming" to Nei H, although there was still some confusion. The day before the church marriage, I related to some friends that Nei H's son had told me that the adoption had in fact occurred. An old man present said ruefully that he had given some money to Nei H, who is a kinsman of his through adoption. But someone else said that there was no error in the gift. The boy had been in Nei H's arms. It was proper, as is said, to "make worth of her" or "emphasize her" (*kabonganaa,* also "make use of") because of that.

Having considered the problem of what going to the gatherings means in general, and how transactions are conducted, we will now turn to the ritual statements of kinship and marriage encoded in the wedding sequence.

THE WEDDING SEQUENCE

In marriage ritual there are alternative kinds of performance. I will begin to discuss now the mode (which has alternatives within it) that is regarded as most customary. It is one among alternatives, but its status is such that it is the gauge against which others are measured.

The first menstruation rite may be regarded as anterior to this sequence. The girl's availability has been announced. And the full sequence, including the gifts from a wide-ranging group, is not properly operable if bride and groom have already been living together, or rather if the girl is known definitively to have already had sexual intercourse.

In the engagement, the first move is made by the groom's side, in sending a letter to the bride's side probably after some of the groom's close utu have met and discussed the proposed marriage. The bride's side, after meeting and discussing, indicate acceptance or rejection in a letter to the groom's side. Particularly appropriate letter carriers are people related to both sides. They can be counted upon to faithfully execute their responsibilities, and their arrival at the house of the prospective bride or groom creates no special difficulties there.

If the proposal is accepted, both utu become kautabo of one another. The relation of kautabo, as we have noted, is opposite to that of utu: kautabo proverbially visit only on special occasions (at least for some time after the marriage), show great reserve, and are loath to make requests of one another. Terms appropriate to in-laws are used after the engagement.

The next step is that a party from the groom's side goes to the bride's side to discuss such details as the date of marriage, whether the two next steps of the full sequence ("the buying" and "the summons") will be activated, and other arrangements for the wedding. The male journeys to the female, because that is what males do: "The man journeys, the woman sits." The male side is expected to arrive with some decisions already made, but the place of marriage (significant if bride and groom are of different sects) is by the same principle up to the girl, according to the most "proper" practice. In the sending and returning of the letter, it was the male who took the initiative but the female who had the veto; in the present step, "the man decides," but there is something reserved for the woman.

One of the things that may be decided is whether from then until the wedding, the girl or boy will attend such public occasions as national holiday celebrations with some of the other side's utu (but not with each other). This interim is a particularly difficult period, and the utu can both watch over and demonstrate the new relationship with the prospective spouse at these occasions. Now some engaged young men visit the houses of their prospective brides, but this is not Banaban custom. One of the explicit reasons for the separation is the fear that they will run away ("They can't wait"), thus taking the matter entirely out of the hands of their utu. A bad report about the behavior of either boy or girl after engagement, or an argument between kautabo, can threaten the marriage.

At this journey of the male side to the female side, the groom and his parents in the model generally do not go themselves, nor in some views ought their parents' siblings and the latters' children to go. It is the utu more "from outside, the people who lift you up." It is more proper for the boy and his parents to go if something is wrong, if there is a threat of the engagement's being broken.

The standardized form of "the buying" is that a few members of both utu meet in the store to buy food and other things for the wedding. The groom's kinsmen may protest that the buying is their job, the "work of the man." Before the wedding also, if this has been agreed upon, each side will buy some of the wedding dress for the in-marrying spouse, which is given during "the summons." At the time the clothing is purchased the utu has not yet presented its gifts, and it is the responsibility of the parents and perhaps their siblings to buy it.

In "the summons," a delegation from the groom's side calls for the bride the day before marriage, and vice versa. Each utu has by now been feasting and preparing for several days, and the gifts have been presented. The bride spends the night at the groom's place, and the groom at the bride's. In the buying and the summons, the emphasis is on exchange; in the preceding steps, on the initiative of the male. The sequence is male to female (the proposal), female to male (the acceptance), male to female (the arrangements), and then a combination. At the wedding itself in church and especially the feasting in church afterwards, each side sits on a different side of the building. There are "conductors" or "conversationalists" (similar to bridesmaids and groomsmen) between whom the bride and groom sit: the bride between those from the groom's side (representing both father's and mother's utu), and vice versa. The food from both sides is combined.

Feasting and dancing may go on there for a while. People from one side call those of opposite sex from the other side to dance with them. Old people do this especially, and with humor. This is a departure from the reserve of kautabo, and here, as well as in some of the later steps when members of both utu meet (as in conducting the couple from one side to another), there are sexual overtones to the encounters between sides. As the relationship between descent units is modeled on and a consequence of the relationship between siblings, the relation between kindreds in this context is modeled on and is a consequence of the relationship between spouses. At the wedding feast, one practice may be invoked which is considered customary. Food is thrown about and liquid items are poured over other people. Although the wedding feast is a time of combination, the possibility of this practice perhaps marks it as a "liminal period" in Turner's sense (see Turner 1969). The usual care and attentiveness to food is abandoned, as is the usual form of respect behavior. People behave in a manner which is in a sense "anti-structural"; they are behaving as *people* at a time when a marriage has been legitimized (by a cultural act) but not yet consummated (by a natural act).

After the church activities are concluded, the couple go to the bride's side, where feasting is still going on. The order is reestablished, male to female. Perhaps around midnight, the couple go to the groom's side, also still feasting, and stay for two or three days. Part of the point of this is to see whether the bride is a virgin. If she is, the groom's side may parade themselves the next day anointed with coconut oil. When the bride's side sees this or hears about it from a "spy" (who can be someone belonging to both sides, or the spouse of a person from the bride's side who belongs to the groom's side), they too rejoice. They have given what was promised; the groom's side has received it. It indicates also that the bride's mother has been a good teacher of her daughter, has carried out her responsibilities: Good girls do not have sexual relations before marriage. They do not "go around," which is what the male does, but "stay in the house," which is what the female does.

The couple stays at the groom's side until the girl is "strong" again. The presumption is that first intercourse is strenuous for her. The next step is "the return" to the bride's side, with the couple perhaps carrying a small present from the other side. A few members of the sending side may accompany the couple to the receiving side on these moves between houses. If these people are unrelated to the receiving side, and to a lesser degree have no spouse staying there, they are "held" for a while by that side, treated as kautabo, but perhaps in the allusive sense.

By this time some of the utu have left. The parallel to the prewedding transaction has now been completed: male to female, female to male, male to female. But the emphasis in the prewedding set is on the initiative of the male; in the postwedding set, more on the higher position of the female.

This is also indicated in a procedure not considered a necessary part of the sequence, but a possible one. While the couple is at the groom's side, the bride's side may send a few representatives to summon the groom "to spend time with them" before the utu disperses. At the one occasion when I observed this, there was first a refusal by the groom's side to send him, and some of the bride's side were angrily talking about breaking up the marriage. It was as if they had not found her a virgin. (An excuse offered for the groom's parents was that they were Gilbertese and "didn't know the custom.") The bride's side gave him new clothing and took him to a film showing that day, which was also attended by the bride surrounded by the groom's side (a parallel to "the summons"). This was considered rather ludicrous to many people. "They are already married and they can't even talk to each other!" But the people commenting ironically were the same people who had directed the proceedings. The groom's answering the summons, or rather the agreement of the groom's side to it, was clearly an obligation. After the film, the couple returned to the groom's side.

It is here that the norm of uxorilocal residence, as phrased, is relevant. The proverbial phrase denoting the principle is "the burae [strands, body hair] of the skirt." This recalls the traditional costume at first menstruation. The man may be described as having been "caught by the strands of the skirt." This is first a continuation of the last step in the sequence considered thus far, the series of relations of alternating direction beginning with the marriage letter. After the period at the groom's side, the couple goes to the bride's side. The man goes to the woman's side and "stays" there; it is his "proper place."

Second, since his sexual rights over his wife are continuing, since the relationship is continuing, so are his obligations to his wife's utu, which granted those rights. He "works for" his wife's family, particularly his wife's father. After I described to a friend the American custom as one in which the couple ideally live on their own and the man is under no such economically phrased obligation to his wife's family, my friend remarked humorously: "In that way the man cheats. He sleeps with the girl, and eats, too." That is, he just concerns himself with his own and his wife's food and not with that of his wife's utu.

In "working for" his wife's parents, the man "repays her debt to them" for bringing her up. He has already to some extent repaid his own debt to his parents because he could perform a wide range of arduous tasks when young. The girl could not; her husband does it for her. There is even an alternate norm that the husband should give his wife the money he makes, and it is hers to dispose of, to her own parents if she is so inclined. In this situation a man is "lucky" if his wife favors his parents also.

The working agreement is glossed in such comments as: "It is good to have many daughters because then you will have many sons," that is, sons-in-law, or, "You are unlucky if you have only sons; they will all go away."

The man "going" and the woman "staying" is in general a feature of the principle that the man is the "journeyer" and the woman the "sitter." "The man goes about, the woman stays in the house." This does not mean that they cannot or even should not live alone or with the man's family. It is a proverbial way of stating the kinds of obligations entailed by marriage, which can be met by the man residing with his wife's kin, giving them money, or giving them other gifts. It is the encoding and application of the concepts of maleness, femaleness, and exchange in the marriage context.

The discussion of the "responsible entity" suggests an expectation that a couple will live with their children in their own place. It is understood as European custom, although the Maudes refer to a married man building his own house. In any case it should be noted that people move back and forth among households at various times, and there is not the same rigid normative stipulation about residence which occurs in some other cultures. Typically the Rambi household at any one time is composed of a couple and their children, often with an assortment of kin related to either husband or wife or both. People may feel taken advantage of by long-staying kin, but as long as the members of a household are connected in some not too

distant way by consanguinity or affinity, it is a matter calling for little comment. Prolonged coresidence, enactment of the code, is often sufficient for
others to regard the members of a household as "an utu."

The claims of both utu are expressed in what follows marriage in this customary model and is consistent with the principle that any two succeeding
steps in the whole sequence will articulate the interests of both utu. The idea
is that the first child should be named by the groom's side and while young
perhaps even spend more time with the paternal grandparents. The second
child is similarly involved with the female side, and so on.

The marriage sequence is the paradigmatic Banaban "cultural performance" in part because it articulates, physically and dramatically, the nature
of consanguinity and affinity. At the wedding, the kindreds of bride and
groom act as units, overcoming in certain contexts their own relations of
affinity as they gather about the product of those relations, the bride or
groom. And the kindred of one spouse acts—dances—in a relationship of
affinity with the kindred of the other spouse. The affines let their hair down,
as it were, and enact the sexuality which is the origin of the relationship between them. In this sense, with the dancing and the joking and suggestive
"holding" of a person from the other side seen passing by, the kindred acts
as a spouse.

The relationship is there for all to see and know about. These activities
are the activities through which tangible expression is given to consanguinity
and affinity. They are socializing devices. I suggest that lingering behind
them, however, is a problematic element.

THE RELATIONSHIP OF BONDS

The rituals associated with marriage constitute a denial of the independent nature of the conjugal bond, and most obviously a statement of particular and general consanguineal solidarities. In the feasting before marriage,
the parents of bride and groom take a backseat position, as may their grandparents. They serve those who come to honor their obligations. The affairs
are managed by elder kinsmen. The sequence of events from engagement to
marriage, and some events afterward, directs attention to two related points:
first, that in marrying, a person is not detached from his kindred but continues as a person with consanguineal rights and obligations. Second, that in
marrying, a person contracts a set of obligations toward, and may receive
rewards from, a new body of people.

The suspicion that makes the dramatization of these points necessary is
twofold, or rather there are two aspects to it: that the conjugal bond might
take primacy over the consanguineal bond, and that the person may be led
away from his own kindred to that of his spouse. The problem is that the

relationship of consanguines, and the relationship of spouses, is phrased in part in the same terms: diffuse solidarity. One solidarity potentially qualifies that of the other, and we are dealing with a situation in many ways similar to that outlined by Radcliffe-Brown (1952) in his discussion of joking relationships and expanded upon by Aberle (1961) in his analysis of the Navaho, but here in a purely bilateral system.

One further aspect of the marriage ritual deserves comment in this context. We have already observed how a person may represent his sibling or other kinsman. This representation applies to descent unit and kindred activities, among others. In kindred activities, however, a person's spouse can be designated to represent him or can be considered to represent him. A person may go to the first birthday of the child of a member of his deceased spouse's utu if he has, through his children, maintained his relationship with that utu. At a first birthday, a person might come for a spouse unable to come. But more salient to the present discussion is that at "the summons," for example, spouses of members of the utu can be sent as a part of the delegation. This is particularly appropriate if the sender is also related to the other side, which may be the case. One is sending out spouses of the utu, representing the utu, to summon a new spouse of the utu. One relationship of affinity is being invoked in the creation of another. The utu is perhaps trying to show that consanguinity and affinity can be harmonious. This kind of representation, by spouses, is impossible in the descent group context: there the line is drawn, or rather that draws the line.

We also discussed earlier the ideas concerning "equivalence," from the level of the utu as a whole to that of siblings. Siblings of the same sex are most "just the same." But at the same time they are not really so. There are differences not only in age and sex, but also in alternative commitments arising from marriage. Looking outward from the marriage bond, it is a question of alternative commitments arising from consanguinity.

Marriage does introduce a potentially qualifying solidarity, but it was also observed earlier that siblings are expected to fight although they will make up in the end. For, as is well known in anthropological studies, the people whose solidarity is supposed to be the greatest are often also those between whom the greatest competition occurs, or the greatest opportunities for differences of interest occur. There are two issues, for example, which are known to divide brothers: land and women. The people despair of their inclination to envy (*te bakantang*), with the result that the progress of the community is impeded because when someone sees another person "up" (for example, because that person is educated) he might see himself "down." They also despair of their inclination to sexual jealousy (*te koko*). On the latter one man remarked, "It is a bad sickness. With it, it is as if you had no family, no siblings."

The fundamental insight was articulated by Shakespeare: "The nearer blood, the nearer bloody." Kinsmen are, alas, also persons, and as persons they can be expected to behave in ways which are inappropriate to kinship. The individual must therefore hedge his bets: not only by casting his consanguineal net wide (while protecting the inner circle), but also by securing his affinal net. Your spouse's parents, for example, are not only in a position of authority and in the position of creditors, but are also in a position to give your spouse or even your own children greater or lesser amounts of land.

As we noted in the last chapter, the relationship between the equivalence of siblings and the nature of marriage is articulated in the eiriki ("sibling-in-law of opposite sex") relationship.

The conventionalized pattern of joking between eiriki consists in allusions to the sexual desirability of the other party, or more directly to the possibility of sexual relations. The allusions have varying degrees of subtlety, depending in part on the comic ability of the jokester. This is qualified within the sibling group by the factor of age, which connotes authority. There is a certain inappropriateness in joking to (or in having sexual relations with) an elder sibling's spouse. The elder sibling and his spouse may be thought of somewhat as playing paternal and maternal roles.

We can identify a group of jokes as eiriki jokes, and these need not be between the eiriki themselves. Although I cannot document this, I suspect that the jokes are rarer among full siblings of a sexually active age. There the jokes may hit too close to home. A few examples will indicate the nature of the humor.

(1) A party of people were traveling on the island Land Rover, which serves as intervillage bus. As a young man was getting off at his stop, a middle-aged woman called out to him, "Wouldn't you like to come with me to my village? Why are you getting off here?" He was a "brother" of her husband. (2) A man was about to leave for the house of his brother, and commented to his group of male friends, giggling, that he was "going to see the child, Nei Z." Nei Z is his brother's wife. "The child" can be used in jest to allude to a woman sexually, and is also a euphemism for virgin. Others joined him in his laughter. (3) In a house-building gang, one man often informed a coworker when the latter's brother's wife was passing by on the road, to the general amusement. (4) A man was about to leave his house to play cards, when a "brother" asked him, "Aren't you afraid to leave your wife alone?" They both laughed. (5) A man was jokingly complaining to his wife about her inability to cook and suggested that she send for her sisters to perform the tasks of which she was incapable. His wife assumed an attitude of mock stern disapproval. (6) At another time, the woman just

referred to commented that it did not really matter if her husband died while fishing, because he had an elder brother who would take care of her. This was so funny that she could hardly contain herself while saying it.

In the first case, a woman addressed the joke to her eiriki, and he was the butt of it. In the second, a man addressed the joke to a group of male cronies, about his eiriki. In the third, a man addressed it to another, about the latter's eiriki. In the fourth, a man addressed it to his "brother," about the latter's wife. In the fifth, a man addressed the joke to his wife, about her sisters; in the sixth, a woman addressed it to her husband, about his brother. Rather than as a joking relationship, eiriki is better conceptualized as a joked-about relationship or a humor generating relationship, and some of the people who joke about it are the eiriki themselves. When a joke is made, the eiriki is the person-not-to-be-embarrassed; the person-not-to-take-offense is the relevant "sibling" or spouse.

When a person cracks an eiriki joke to his "sibling" or his "sibling's" spouse, it articulates the fact that the "sibling" has not left the fold, that his spouse is not exclusively his own concern but is also involved with the family and that this must be acknowledged. When the spouse makes the joke, he articulates his recognition of the situation, and because of it he can look to that family. A woman who runs away from her husband after an argument might go to her family or to his. This aspect of the eiriki relationship is a statement of obligations and possibilities, a dramatization of the fact that neither spouse nor sibling can have his cake and eat it too, alone.

The structural aspects of this part of the eiriki message are, again, that marriage does not remove a person from his kindred, which has claims over him and his spouse, and that the in-marrying spouse recognizes this and can look upon his affines as an alternative line of support.

It is not generally expected that actual sexual relations will take place between eiriki, who in the humorous context can be referred to as "spouses." This does not mean, however, that a woman, for example, might not *suppose* that her husband desires sexual relations with her sisters and, if given the chance, would deviate from a normal course of faithfulness. In the extreme case, she might suppose that he would like such relations with any attractive woman. It is the factor of structural equivalence which directs special attention to her sisters. And if a person learns that his spouse has had sexual relations especially with an elder sibling, as a good sibling he might take it philosophically. Not everyone, however, can be expected to be a paragon in this way, and if the cuckold is angry, there are other people who will find the occurrence hysterical. The whole situation is seen as an irony—siblings are "just the same," although on the other hand of course they are not—but there is irony at a second level.

The two explicit sources of morality recognized are custom and (Christian) religion. According to Banaban folk history, the present joking aspect of the eiriki relationship is only a shadow of what it once was, which was the availability of one's unmarried eiriki for sexual relations. This, however, has been specifically prohibited by religion. Tradition defines a practice which religion condemns; each system defines a different way of behaving. The situation thus presents two interrelated contradictions: between the personally desirable and the socially desirable on the one hand, and between custom and religion on the other. They are related because that which people at least believe to be considered personally desirable by *other* people, is also permitted in custom. It is natural to want to take advantage of opportunities for sexual adventures. Other conflicts between religion and custom are also seen with wry amusement: as unfortunate, perhaps, but thoroughly understandable. In summary: (1) Since structural equivalence obtains, there is potentially a sexual aspect to the relationship between eiriki; (2) actual sexual relations are permitted in custom but prohibited by religion; and furthermore (3) custom is more in key with human nature, and the lack of fit between what is "good" and what is "desired" is comical.

I noted that a third party might crack an eiriki joke, or an interested party where other interested parties are not in the audience. It is in these contexts most obvious that the message dramatized in the eiriki relationship is being laughed *at*. In addition to the sexual aspect, or as another aspect of the same thing, it is that the definitions of kinship situations do not provide a neat ranking of solidarities between the utu and the married couple. The eiriki pattern is a comically ironic commentary on this.

People can joke about affinal relationships other than eiriki. For example, someone said something uncomplimentary about a man's wife's brother, and the man interjected, in jest, "If you are going to talk about my brother-in-law that way, I can kill you." Social structural incongruities are one of the sources of humor, and this applies beyond the relationships discussed here. Incongruities are perceived as ironic, and as comic when they are regarded as being inherent in the situation or as inevitable. Joking about affinity is a special case of this.

There are several things, then, that are being laughed at: the social structure, the conflict between what is good and what is desired, and the related conflict between Christianity and custom. Considering the jokes *ensemble*, there is a consistent reaction to the incongruities in the relationship between consanguinity and affinity in the kinship domain; between two differentially conceived moral systems; and finally, between morality and human nature. These are all inherent, expectable incongruities, and such things in general are seen ironically and confronted comically.

It was observed in chapter 12 that the term *tinaba* was reported for earlier

Banaban culture as a counterpart in proximate generations of eiriki and nga-ni-bu in the same generation. The term is known on Rambi and is occasionally used in jest. The role meaning of tinaba is sexual relations with spouse's "parents" of the same sex as spouse, especially collateral ones. There is an observation in the Maude-Grimble papers that tinaba was not a Banaban custom, although apparently the term was used.

I have heard that both wife's "sisters" and "mothers," and husband's "brothers" and "fathers" are people with whom sexual relations do not bring the same opprobrium as they do with spouse's junior kinsmen. (In fact, the term sometimes used jokingly to allude to a tinaba type of relationship, or another illicit one, is *natina* [to treat as child]. The aptness of this may come from two directions: first, as a transformation of tinaba; second, "the child" [*te tei*] can be used allusively and is a euphemism for virgin.)

With spouse's sibling of the same sex it is a feature of their identity with spouse. With spouse's elder consanguines, it may be a feature of their generation as that which is implicated in the disposal of sexual rights, and as the authority figures, of emphasizing the claims of the utu as a whole on the in-marrying spouse. When you marry you are to a limited extent, as someone put it, "the utu's."

The most proverbial tinaba relationship is between a man and his nephew's wife. The analytically difficult element here is that tinaba, as far as I could tell, is ideally proscribed and actually little practiced among Banabans. It is generally regarded as a Gilbertese rather than a Banaban phenomenon, and one is under the impression that the meanings of male and female roles are different in the Gilberts. Both Banabans and Gilbertese on Rambi state that the woman is more highly valued by the Banabans, and in residence "the woman follows the man" in the Gilberts, whereas the reverse is true among the Banabans. The form of tinaba is, however, consistent with Banaban utu norms in the sense that the envisioning of its possibility is an articulation to the young man by his utu that the position of the wife is not only that of a person drawing him into her utu as its worker, but that she is also the utu's. It is an articulation to the young woman that her husband, even sexually, is not exclusively her own.

There are some tinaba jokes which are similar to the much more highly developed complex of eiriki jokes. As an institution known about, there is another and perhaps even more fundamental message of tinaba. Perhaps it is a kind of diacritical on different-generation affinal relationships. By stating that the relationship between generations is somewhat similar to that within generations, by stipulating sexuality, it keeps the lines of consanguinity and affinity drawn in a situation where a person might be "absorbed" into another utu.

The position of the interrelationship of consanguinity and affinity emerges

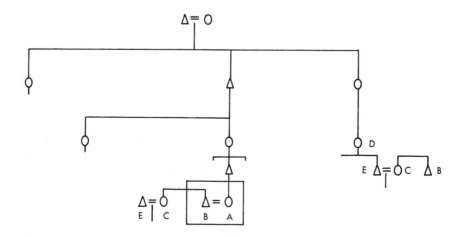

FIG. 6. A CONTROVERSIAL MARRIAGE

when one considers unusual marriages. One kind of unusual marriage is where the spouses of "siblings" are closely related to each other, but not as "siblings." In one case the second marriage almost did not occur, and I would like to describe it briefly. The circumstances were reported to me by a friend, S, involved in the proceedings by being related (see figure 6) to the father of Nei A through Nei A's father, and to the father of B and Nei C.

The marriage in question was that between B and Nei A. E and Nei C were already married. The proposed marriage of Nei A and B was objected to by Nei D, who, as an elder of Nei A's utu, was part of the group considering whether to accept B's proposal of marriage to her. Nei D objected to the marriage because her son, E, is married to B's elder sister. "She refuses to have Nei A treat E's children as her children." The relationship of Nei A to the children of E and Nei C through E, her "father," is that of sibling. The relationship of Nei A to the children of E and Nei C through her husband, B, would be that of "mother" to "child." The analytic point is first that the marriage of E and C has implications for the relationships between other members of their utu. If there are further marriages, that particular one could be cited as having to be taken into account. If Nei A were a "sibling" of E, rather than E's "child," however, there would be no problem.

While at home, S told his own mother that Nei D's objection was meaningless. His mother asked, "If E's child defecates, would Nei A clean it up?" Nei A is presented as being in something of a dilemma of choice. Is she the children's mother or sibling? "That doesn't make any difference," S replied to his mother. He said that his own elder daughter cleans up after her own siblings, and there was nothing wrong with that. The roles of mother and sibling are not so structured that they are mutually exclusive on this point.

In Nei D's objection, the assumption was that Nei A's affinal relationship to the children of E and Nei C could take precedence over her consanguineal relationship to them. If the relationships were of the same kind, there would be no cause for complaint. Since they are of different kinds, there is. The best solution is to prevent the situation from arising at all. The relationship between the kindred and spouse relationships is such that one can never be quite sure which will take priority. Since the definitions are diffuse, when there is a concrete situation calling for a statement one way or the other, the results cannot be predicted. The situation, however, does not in fact call for a statement one way or the other. Nei D's objection, first accepted, was later ignored.

S's own feeling about the true reason for Nei D's objection was phrased in terms of the kind of situation that might arise if these people resided together. Nei C is B's elder, but B is "the man," and his father favors him. B is the last-born, but the last-born is often the proverbial favored child, as a complement to the general seniority of the first-born. B may get more of his (and Nei C's) father's property than Nei C will. B will act in a sense as successor to his father. This, S suggested, would decrease E's authority. Nei D was really thinking of her son and her son's authority position over his wife. That position might be compromised by the entry of her brother, the favored child and the male, into the situation.

Let us return now to a further consideration of the eiriki relationship. There are aspects to it more pedestrian than the three levels of irony analyzed. The jokes allude to the eiriki as potential "replacements."

As we have said, if a person dies and especially if he has had children, it is ideal for his or her sibling to marry the surviving spouse "to care for the children." And from the point of view of the deceased spouse's utu, by "giving," for example, the surviving husband one of his wife's sisters, it is also insured that his land will "stay with the utu," that is, not be reduced through inheritance by children with a woman of another utu. This is the phrasing, rather than a desire for general purposes to continue a relationship with another utu.

Since a person's sibling's children are also "his children," he can also be expected to care for and love them as a "stranger" would not. But even here the problem can arise of a person giving more attention to his own children. The bad step-parent is a well-known figure. A person ought to treat his spouse's children by a previous marriage, or his deceased sibling's children, as his own. If he does not, it is reprehensible but understandable. After the death of a woman with many children, an old woman referred to the general plight of children when their parent remarries, and said that one man who is "always praised in conversation" is a resident of Tabiang who, after divorce, did not remarry, because he was thinking of his child, who stayed with him.

This is of course the point on the position as responsible entity of the child when his parent remarries, although it still may be said that the parent is really the responsible entity. The child should get a housing section of his own, with his siblings, since there might be trouble with the step-parent. A similar case is a person's separation from his siblings as responsible entity when he marries. A new factor has been added to the situation, a new solidarity which might threaten that of the utu: that of spouses, and their children if any.

Spouse solidarity is similar to utu solidarity in its diffuseness, and as the brother is proverbially "toddy-cutter and fisherman" for his sister, and the sister "coconut-oil maker" for her brother, so too between husband and wife. The marriage situation is different, however, in the potential impermanence which goes along with sexual relations. Common substance is lacking. This is not ideal impermanence, but one cannot act on ideals. Thus the plausibility of the notion of two housing sections for spouses: to insure not only against eviction by the spouse's utu at his death, but also against the possibility of divorce or separation. In death or divorce, the relationship with spouse's utu may end but need not if the surviving spouse keeps up the relationship. A prerequisite for keeping up the relationship generally is not remarrying, except of course to a "sibling" of spouse. If the relationship is terminated with the death or divorce of spouse, one can find sanctuary with one's own utu. But this is not the ideal procedure either. And it still makes sense to use such an eventuality to back up a claim for another quarter-acre. This reflects both the status of landholder in the community concepts, and the fact that marriage confers a distinct social personality upon the individual.

The fact that matters generally associated with consanguinity can creep through the marriage bond is illustrated by two rare (as far as I know) kinds of occurrence: a variant of child adoption, and lands trusteeship.

The spouse of one's deceased child might be adopted as child. This is regarded as new on Rambi. In one of two such cases, the adopted daughter of a childless couple told them before her death not to grieve because there was someone who would replace her: her (Gilbertese) husband. Some of the mother's kinsmen are not very happy about this adoption.

In the other case, a deceased Banaban woman's non-Banaban husband was adopted after his wife died, "to look after the children." He "replaced her." The man later remarried, to a Gilbertese, and he is reported to be giving Ocean Island land to the children of his second marriage. Some of his first wife's relatives observed that this was improper. The purpose of the adoption according to them was to insure his position as guardian of the children, and he was made custodian of their lands for this reason. The adoption, in this view, was not an unequivocal one, and he was transgressing its terms. Court action may occur in a case such as this.

There are three cases known to me where a person was made "trustee" for some or all of his spouse's Ocean Island land. In one case, the eldest son of the family related it as follows: When his father died, he and his siblings met to discuss the division of their father's lands. They decided to place a few lands under their mother's name. This was to help her maintain her livelihood and would perhaps reduce the children's amount of trouble in supporting her. The speaker thinks that he was the first to do this on Rambi. It is not Banaban custom, and the people at the Lands Court said so when he went to register the lands. In the second case, some land was given to a Gilbertese mother as trustee for similar reasons.

The third case stipulated a woman as trustee for her deceased husband's land. Her father explained the situation as follows: the land could then not go to her husband's *utu*. The children were "in their mother's arms," and the *utu* agreed that she should be trustee. Her husband had not made a will, and she was "like one who closed her husband's estate," her husband's *mwi* (inheritance, remains, trace). If he had made a will there would have been no problem. Without a will, the position of the children vis-à-vis their own father's kin is secured.

It may indeed be the case that the solidarity of the spouse bond vis-à-vis that of the consanguineal bond has been increasing among the Banabans. But there is evidence that the trustee phenomenon was not completely unknown on Ocean Island. From Maude's records for the 1931–32 Lands Commission, a case is listed where a woman on her deathbed declared that her second husband "was to be caretaker" for her son's lands because her brother "had not been kind to her."[2]

Thus it is possible, if unusual, for a person to represent his spouse with regard to Ocean Island land. This seems to run contrary to the blood and mud hypothesis. Or does it? We note that spouse adoptions are in fact adoptions. And the trusteeships are in fact trusteeships.

It is indeed possible, as I have noted, that the solidarity of spouses has increased in strength. If so, there is no better way than through land to ar-

---

2. There is another case where a man had some lands which were his wife's and were to be partitioned among the children. But here, the initial listing could have been an error or deception.

ticulate solidarity, identity, and unity. On the other hand, such developments may not be as surprising as they seem, even to the Banabans. Recall that

$$\text{Blood : Land :: Identity : Code}$$

and

$$\text{[Blood + Land] : [Nurturance + Residence] :: Identity : Code}$$

If one should take a generalized notion of identity to include spouses, or even only a generalized notion of kinship, it becomes possible to put together elements that would otherwise be separate.

I have already indicated that the marriage sequence exactly as described need not be enacted. It is supposed to apply in any case only for a virgin girl. The furthest variant in one direction is for the marriage really to have been arranged beforehand between elder kinsmen of the bride and groom. It is now generally supposed that the prospective couple first decide to marry, and then the boy at least tells his parents, and thus the letter is sent. In any case, the girl will be consulted when the letter is received.

The furthest variant in the other direction is elopement: *te birinako*, literally "the running-away," and couples do from time to time actually run away. Either they were caught up in the passion of the moment, or the families of one or both of them were against the marriage, or they did not want to be bothered with the whole complex of custom which I have described. It is too annoying and too expensive. Some people have ostensibly tried to spread the word that fewer people should come to family gatherings than in the past, but to little avail. The reciprocity accounts are hard to cut into.

With an elopement, the utu has in effect been ignored if not actually opposed. The groom's family might take a certain satisfaction, in that they are getting something at a reduced price. With the rumor of an approaching elopement, the bride's parents and brothers may try to use force to keep the lovers apart, or to return their kinswoman, if she has already departed.

If an elopement occurs, even if anger flares, the matter is generally expected to settle down after a while, especially after the birth of the first child. After all, they are your utu.

The middle-range variants center more on what happens before and after the ceremony rather than during it. By "during the ceremony" I am not referring here to the church practices (which are different for different churches) but to the bringing of food and money by relatives and the "confrontation" of kautabo. These are the essential elements, and these seem to be relatively stable. (It is more complex when people get married outside the island, but I will not go into that here.)

I will look at the marriage of a young Methodist pastor as an example of a variant. Because he was a pastor and a confessed "progressive" it may seem an inappropriate example, but it is in fact the most appropriate example. He got away with doing what he wanted to do.

He went himself to talk to the girl's "grandfather," her closest relative on Rambi. His fiancée was in another room in the house and was serving food. He brought the ring and some money with him. They talked, ate, and the old man agreed. Then the pastor put the money on the table in gratitude. They made the arrangement for the time of marriage, which was about a month later: sooner than in many other cases. His adoptive father was angry because he did not follow the custom; his father is conservative on matters like this.

The two customs of "the buying" and "the summons" were ignored, but he did buy her veil and she bought his jacket. The gift giving and church ceremony were as usual except for a greater involvement of church people; we will turn to this kind of thing soon. After the ceremony they went to his house. A "sister" of his real father stayed in the house the first night.

The custom model is not mandatory, although while not enacting it, people probably are aware that they are not enacting it (and others comment upon it). The ritual especially on either side of the actual wedding ceremony can expand and contract, as kinship terms and terms for kinsmen can expand and contract in usage, as the circle of recognized kin can expand and contract through time and context. That the range of elements clustered around the basic symbols can expand and contract in action is a fundamental characteristic of the total kinship system, and this characteristic is itself part of the option-maximizing complex.

Not enough is known of actual marriages on Ocean Island to discern directions of change, on this short-term basis. If as some Banabans assert, however, the younger people are taking things more into their own hands (and especially if the lack of prewedding communication, except in highly stylized contexts, between the affianced couple is becoming mollified), then something at a more than surface level is changing. Given these trends, what is changing is the age-sex-authority system so that it more approximates the modern Western system. That is how the people themselves see it. That would go some way to explaining why the greatest variation would be in the events on the two sides of the wedding ceremony, because they are largely about the age-sex-authority complex as manifested in the sphere of kinship.

These changes and variations are not, however, in kinship qua kinship. And they also reflect the increasing importance of the person as a social unit.

One must, however, treat the people's statements on changes with extreme care. Like many others, they tend to see the past as uniform and the present as diverse if not falling apart. There might always have been a wide range of ways of getting married which were tolerated at the very least. As long as the basic point is made—the transformation of relationship into substance, of differentiation into equivalence, of exchange into sharing; the nature and contrast of utu and kautabo, the relationship between the consanguineal and the marriage ties—there is no reason why an enlivening range of variation in ceremonial practice cannot exist. There is more than one way to slice a wedding cake. Or, however you slice a wedding cake, you still end up with the same thing, slices of wedding cake.

And perhaps one need not be overconcerned with detailing a particular, rigid system because of the redundancy built into the system which exists. A couple who elope might still crack eiriki jokes and hear them. They might have first birthdays, and other celebrations, for their children, and for that matter attend the most proper weddings or funerals of relatives. If "the system" does not get you in one place, it will get you in another. And if the system does not get you through one channel, or one sense, it will get you through another. At large marriages, for example, participants see, speak, sing, hear, smell, taste, dance, and touch important elements in the ritual structure. One might hazard the speculation that the mobilization of all the senses is part of the ritual design, and that this functions (as Vern Carroll has pointed out) in general to make the communication redundantly efficient, and in particular to hammer the messages home to individuals whose susceptibility to communication through one channel is greater than communication through another channel. The "cultural performances" are dramatic in part because they are multi-media events, drawing together the items of custom (for example, eiriki jokes) which are less general in their sensory orientation.

This McLuhanesque point may illuminate the discussion in chapter 2 of ritual aspects of the descent system. The complexity of the goods and services flowing along the ritual circuits might be related to the fact that the system considered in toto functions as a cultural multi-medium. And the point may also deepen our understanding of such well-known phenomena as commensality, which use particular senses to get the message through. Perhaps in the future we will have studies of ritual which carefully decipher the orchestration of the senses. We cannot account for the fact that certain ritual structures are dramatically multi-media events by some general principle at this time, because some peoples seem more austere than others in their approaches to the senses. Comparative research should tell us what it is all about.

THE INTEGRATION OF TIES AND DOMAINS

Family gatherings do not only implicate kinsmen and the spouses and perhaps coresidents who trail along after them. Friends can come and give money. It is said that particularly in the earlier days on Rambi, Gilbertese from the same island might go to some of the core gatherings. Thus a man would go to the wedding of another because they were both from Tarawa, for example, and they were people not recognizing a genealogical link.

I am concerned here, however, with the relationship between the utu and the church in the gatherings. Before we consider that, the general set of relations which informs it must be outlined.

We have already discussed the relationship between utu and church at the level of symbolism: God and the Creator Father, and the family of Christians. And now, the most proper context in which to form an utu of men (marriage) is in the utu of Christians. And indeed, the central sacrament, Holy Communion, is an internalization of substance.

We have raised the issue of the "Keep your options open" value as structuring some aspects of kinship (as well as political and economic) behavior. Are there analogues in religion? People cannot "belong" to different sects as they can to different utu, although they can be implicated in some activities of one sect while being members of another. An important thing culturally, however, is that faithful church membership maximizes one's options in the Other World, and to some extent in This World. And the lingering credibility of some traditional religious beliefs might be interpreted as an attempt to keep one's cognitive and affective options open, as the lingering viability of the descent system keeps one's social options open.

At the level of religious organization, there are parallels between family and church in the way sex and age roles are played out. But we are concerned here with more direct points of contact. The first is affiliation. People are considered to belong to a sect if they regularly attend its services, have been baptized into it, converted into it, or it is the sect of both their parents.[3] When parents belong to different sects, the affiliation of their children is something to be worked out between the parents. The general assumption is that one starts out in the religion of the parents. If young children are baptized, it is generally that sect into which they are baptized.[4]

3. The dogma of the Pentecostal church, according to its local teacher, stresses baptism when the child "is old enough to know what religion means." But even there young children may be considered as affiliated when their parents are.

4. Perhaps both this fact and the more general role meanings of kinship terms were implicated in a notice from the Methodist Sunday School group asking support for their fund-raising bazaar. The notice included the words, "We want to be helped, ourselves, your children and grandchildren, in this work of ours."

Fund-raising is an instance of economic circulation. If I were more sensitive to the economy I would have investigated it more closely in the field, because it is relevant to the matters under discussion. For example, I was told at one large marriage that a man was fined (perhaps in kava) for some reason, and I was fined myself for appearing late at the festivities. The legal system features fines, and some churches may make use of this device. I can say little more than that.

It is always recognized, however, that a person can change his religious affiliation. This may be ascribed to personal conviction or a baser, political motivation. It may also be ascribed to the fact that a child goes to live with a relative who belongs to another sect or marries someone in another sect. Indeed, as we observed earlier, the "man follows the woman" principle can be invoked to state a norm that when the affianced coupled are of different sects, the marriage should take place in that of the woman.

In religious organization, the household and the responsible entity can be units contributing to collective sect activities (and also village activities).

In religious action, some families say graces before their meals and hold evening prayers that include hymn singing in their homes. And in some sermons and other religious rhetoric (including at marriage), the values of correct kinship behavior are stressed. (One local agnostic proclaimed that those who invented religion were very smart. It makes people behave in the right way. Without it, they would not.)

Marriage and death call for standardized activities by religious functionaries "from the book," but there is more to them than that. Religious functionaries attend many family gatherings. They may come of their own accord to wakes to sing hymns and comfort the aggrieved. To other gatherings they are invited. The two explicit bases of morality, God and Banaban custom, are thus joined, as are the specific kinship and religious ties of individuals. A person is also "honoring" the pastor and deacons of his church, and the latter share in the joy or sadness of the occasion. In strong church families other coreligionists may come to some occasions and present gifts.

The marriage of a church official calls for special efforts on the part of the members. When the Buakonikai pastor was married, village congregations presented collective gifts, and the Tabwewa church youth group went to sing. We have already noted the fact that when the son of the Gilbertese Catholic teacher (who was acting for his father, who was away in a hospital) was married, Catholic adults were called upon to present gifts of money. Another wedding illustrates the relationship of sectarianship and kinship in this context.

At the postmarriage celebration, the Catholic choir performed at the head of the church meetinghouse. Facing them, the groom's kinsmen were sitting on the left, and the bride's on the right. Many choir members were themselves kinsmen of the young couple. But they were performing as members of the choir, representing the church. Just as concrete spatial separation need cause no special problems with overlapping membership or multiple affiliation for ties of the same kind (kinship), it need cause no special problem for ties of different kinds (kinship and religious).

During the wedding of the teacher's son, a group of Pentecostals sang their own songs at the feast at the bride's house. Neither the bride nor her parents were Pentecostals. But some very close relatives of the bride were, including an elder with a role in directing the entire proceeding. At the death of the bride's sister's child, the year before, her Pentecostal relatives sang Pentecostal hymns, and her Methodist relatives sang Methodist hymns. These events occurred in contexts (marriage, death) of both the religious and the kinship domains. The activities emphasized both religious difference and kinship solidarity at the same time.

But beyond this apparent harmony lies the possibility for serious trouble. Religion is universalizing, custom particularizing. Religious solidarity is ideally the solidarity of those who acknowledge a common, general truth, a common identity, derived from the author of Creation, and a common code for conduct. In this, combined with its nature as a personal and free commitment, lies its strength and the possibilities for the expression of both interchurch hostility and unity. And religious groups are the most clear-cut exclusive membership groups.

At family gatherings specific religious and kinship ties may be assembled in one place and the mutual relevance of the kinship and religious domains articulated. But there can be conflict because of membership in different sects. While the partisans are heartily involved in the conflict, it may dramatize to others how the two domains should not be allowed to interfere with one another. At one first birthday, for example, there was a great deal of difficulty because the child's father's mother was a Methodist and the child's mother's parents were Pentecostals. The parent themselves were Pentecostals, but this was an affair involving not only themselves but also their utu. It was a question of the role of different church functionaries and where the feast would be held.

People clearly recognize and bemoan the possibility of religion dividing kinship solidarity. As Rev. Tebuke Rotan put it, "In the time of a 'family gathering,' the utu comes. But if they argue on religion, that can break it up: father and children, brother and sister." Religious differences interfere with the performance of proper kinship behavior of other kinds as well. The point is not only that kinsmen may be divided by nonkinship principles, but also that such division is considered rather surprising. Kinship is so fundamental, so a priori, that interference from another solidarity calls for comment. The breakup of religious groups because of kinship-related conflict is not so surprising. (Many people account for the origin of the Seventh Day Adventist and Pentecostal churches in terms of descent unit arguments with people who were also leaders of the Methodist church. In this line a Methodist remarked, "When people have a bad feeling, they form up a religion.")

Religious and kinship solidarities, the dividers of each other and of everything else, are dividers in different ways, since as we have frequently observed, religion embodies a universalistic scheme of values, and kinship a particularistic one. Even when religious membership or difference originates as a cloak for something else, other people are brought in on other grounds and a religious momentum builds up. It is precisely when coreligionists act divisively in consonance with their more diffuse solidarity (for example, in mutual support on political issues) that other people get the sense that religion is overstepping its boundaries. Nondivisive relationships among coreligionists (such as fishing together) do not form instances of overstepping. The problem is partially one of incomplete differentiation and may be a permanent one.

This raises the question of historical development again.

THE PROBLEM OF HISTORY

Information on kinship ritual and relations other than descent, beyond what is reported in chapter 1, is quite fragmentary. Grimble's paper, "From Birth to Death in the Gilbert Islands" (1921a) gives a general picture for the Gilbert group and makes some specific references to Ocean Island. Even by that time, however, Grimble was "piecing together the fragmentary acounts [the Gilbertese] gave of things as they used to be" (1921a, p. 25).

In order to grapple with the problem of ritual change, I would have to introduce a great deal of material on traditional Banaban mythology. I have decided to leave the discussion of mythology for another time and so will make only a few observations. I will also draw from items other than Grimble's paper.

The rule that "the fourth generation goes free" with regard to incest has had a great deal of stability. Acceptable polygamy and the male initiation which Grimble described have disappeared. Important utu ritual which apparently surrounded birth may have been partially shifted to first birthday. First menstruation has been transformed (1921a, pp. 41–44), as has death (1921a, pp. 44–53).[5] Let us look a little more closely at marriage and begin with Grimble's discussion of the Gilberts in general.

> Children might be betrothed at a very early age, sometimes before birth. Two friends not yet married would sometimes make a compact that if they should ever beget children of opposite sex, they should marry one another.

5. Since Webster's book is much less available than Grimble's article, I quote what Webster had to say about death on Ocean Island: "On the decease of a native, his friends meet together; his body is ornamented with feathers and carefully oiled, after which a great feast takes place, and on these occasions liberty is given for everyone to speak their mind freely, which gives rise to no small amount of scandal and depreciation of each other's character, especially amongst the weaker sex" (Webster n.d., p. 48). If this single report is faithful, it would delineate a somewhat "anti-structural" (in Victor Turner's [1969] sense) character for death ritual.

When the girl child whose fate had thus been arranged was born, she was taken by the parents of the prospective husband and brought up by them.

But most often marriages were arranged by the negotiation called *te mata-mata, the envisagement*. When a father saw that his son was likely to become a strong and healthy man (*maiu*, meaning *full of life*, is the Gilbertese term), he would send his own or his wife's brother to the father of the girl desired in betrothal. This envoy would broach the subject and sometimes, but not always, leave a small present of food behind; on his departure the girl's parents would take a few days to decide upon the proposal. If they decided against it, a message to that effect would be dispatched and no offense taken on its receipt.

But if they regarded the match with favour, they would send one of their brothers to invite the boy's parents to visit them. As soon as possible after receipt of this invitation the couple would pay their call, and on arrival would be taken by their hosts to the land that was intended as the bride's marriage portion. On their return home it was their turn to consider. If the marriage portion did not satisfy them they would acquaint the girl's parents with their opinion, and this might lead to a perfectly peaceful breaking off of negotiations.

If however, all seemed satisfactory, the boy's parents would send their brother to bring the girl to their house, where she would remain sometimes for a number of years until she was ripe for her marriage. The act of transferring her from household to household was called, somewhat ungallantly, *te iaaki*, which means *the gathering-up-of-rubbish*.

The envisagement stage was now complete and the definite link of *kainro*, or *betrothal*, established between the boy and girl. This could only be dissolved by common consent of the contracting parties; if one desired to do so without consulting the other, it must be prepared to pay for the privilege by the forfeit of a large piece of land, though in some cases the fine might be reduced to a seagoing canoe with sail, bailer and steering-oar complete. [1921*a*, p. 29.]

If this was indeed the general practice in the Gilberts, three things suggest themselves. First, the going back and forth between the sides is probably a pattern of antiquity in the area (although not, of course, limited to it). Second, the "marriage portion" in land is unreported for the Banabans: land seems to maintain itself as more of an intra-utu concern. Third, and most interestingly, the Banaban pattern may have differed from the Gilbertese most significantly in the position of women. I know nought of "the gathering up of rubbish," and, according to the Maudes, land was passed only when the boy broke up the engagement.[6]

The possibility of before-birth betrothal which Grimble mentions, and the

---

6. Lest the Gilbertese appear patriarchal by the contrast, I should quote Grimble: "Divorce, unlike marriage, was effected without formalities. It might lead to the surrender of land forfeits on one side or the other, but there was no fixed custom by which bonds were dissolved or penalties assessed. For a man to put away his wife he had simply to eject her from his house; equally well a woman might dissolve the partnership by returning to her parents, who, if there seemed good cause, would har-

betrothal soon after birth which the Maudes mention for Ocean Island in particular, are suggestive of marriage as, if not alliance, at least allying. In his book *We Chose the Islands,* Grimble (1952, pp. 17, 39) refers to an "arranged marriage" that took place in premission times, and one that almost took place in the early twenties. (At the same time there was, incidentally, a name-changing ceremony in which Grimble was involved, during which the mother's side and father's side of the central figure sat in different places.) Perhaps the situation has always been as it is now: particular families can purposely set out to build connections for poltical reasons, or to marry a child to another who is land-rich or prestigious for other reasons, including having precedence in the descent system. The genealogies show a number of "ancient" marriages which make it appear as if people with high descent unit status positions had arranged marriages to one another. This is a possibility which the system allows but does not entail. And now, some people are looking to education and the holding of good jobs, as well as to land, precedence, and general good behavior, as positive attributes for a good match for their children.

In a discussion of marriage in the Gilberts, Grimble describes at length the "generally known" practice.

> A house for the reception of the bridal pair was first built on the land of the bridegroom's father, by the boy's kinsmen. From the outside this house looked like a large thatch, of which the eaves rested on the ground and the ridge was some 14 feet high. From the inside, which was accessible through doors in the gables, the thatch was seen to be supported by corner studs of coral rock about 2 feet in height. The floor space was about 18 by 18 feet; it was shingled with small white stones and covered with mats. Overhead, there was a loft or attic, of which the floor was so low that a man could not stand upright in the lower room; this was accessible through a small square trap in the middle.
>
> In the lower room on a given day the families of the bridal pair came together, as soon as the sun had passed his zenith. When all were present and silent, the bride was brought into the house by her mother, mother's sister, mother's mother, or adoptive mother. The girl and the old woman immediately mounted into the loft, and there the younger was stripped of all her clothing and laid upon a new sleeping mat especially woven for the occasion. Thus she was left, awaiting the arrival of her groom.
>
> As soon as the bride was known to be ready, the boy was brought by his mother or father's sister into the lower room. Aided by pushes and encourage-

---

bour her and take her part in any unpleasantness that might ensue. The right to decide in such a matter was thus accorded as freely to the wife as to the husband, and this is a fair indication of a woman's general status in the Group, where mother right and father right seem to have impinged upon one another and eventually come to a compromise" (Grimble 1921a, p. 33).

ment from all his nearest female relations he climbed into the loft; there he stripped off his waist mat and threw it down among the waiting people. As soon as it was seen to fall the whole audience broke out into clamorous exhortation to both the young people, beseeching them to cast off coyness and quickly to consummate the union. Nevertheless, the bride's kinsfolk would have been much disappointed and ashamed had she surrendered herself without demur to the embraces of the bridegroom, for that would have denoted a lack of modesty unseemly in a well-born maiden. Without moving her mat, it was therefore customary for her to resist the advances of her mate, and to intimate to those below that she was doing so by struggling of which the reverberation could not fail to reach them.

At the moment when her virginity left her she emitted a single piercing scream. Soon after, the bridegroom would call from above, and at that signal his mother would mount into the loft. There she would at once search for traces of blood on the girl's sleeping mat and having found them, would cry in a loud voice, *'Te tei!' 'Te tei!' (A virgin! A virgin!)* She then descended alone to exhibit the mat to all eyes, whereupon, taking up the cry of the old woman, the father and uncles of the bridegroom rubbed each a little of the virgin's blood upon his cheeks, where it would remain for the rest of the day. The mat was afterwards carefully burned in order that no enemy of the family might obtain it and, by using evil magic upon the blood, curse the bride with barrenness.

Throughout the ceremony, an old man on behalf of the bridegroom and an old woman on behalf of the bride sat under the eastern rafters of the house mumbling auspicious or protective charms; and always before proceedings began, the girl and the boy were given philtres to drink, which were made of cocoanut milk mixed with infusions from the bark of the *ango* tree (*Prenna taitensis*), and the orange-coloured petals of the *kaura* flower (*Wedelia strigulosa*). Of these ingredients, the last banished fear, the second promoted true love, and the cocoanut milk was a protection against foreign magic.

While the united families were rejoicing below, the girl and the boy dressed themselves in *riri* (kilts of cocoanut leaf) made by the bridegroom's mother's and father's sisters, anointed their bodies with oil from the same source, and girt themselves with dancing mats provided by the mother's and father's sisters of the bride. Then they descended from the loft. On their appearance a feast began which lasted for three days, and a great dance was given in which the young couple formed the *kabi* (keel), or leading pair.

On Banaba (Ocean Island) matters were rather differently arranged. A girl was married to her betrothed a few months after she reached the age of puberty, if the boy's initiation into manhood was by then complete. The test of virginity was the same as that described above, but the couple was housed in a hut while the families were assembled outside. They lay on a bed made of a single cocoanut leaf screen built up of two parts. The half on which the boy lay was made by his relatives, that on which the girl reclined was made by hers. The two halves were joined together by roughly knotting the edges. When the ceremony of marriage was over, the two were obliged to live in the house until the girl was pregnant, or until it was evident that she was barren; during this time of waiting they went entirely naked nor were they allowed to set foot outside. No sleeping mats were given them other than the wretched things of cocoanut leaf above mentioned; these were renewed every day, and the old ones hung up under the eaves of the house to form a screen against sun and wind. The object of this Spartan treatment was to encourage the couple to beget a child quickly and so earn their freedom. When at last the girl became pregnant they were allowed to don clothes and to live in the communal dwelling of the husband's family [*sic*].

If, on any island of the Gilbert Group, a girl was discovered at the marriage ceremony to have failed in the test of virginity, the bridegroom's mother, on establishing the fact, would cry aloud, *'Te kara! Te kara!' (An old woman! An old woman!)* and proceed to drag the poor naked creature from the loft. Below, the incensed families (her own in particular) would fall upon her and mercilessly beat her into the open air. On Banaba, exceptionally, she might be saved by her husband's love if she consented to disclose the name of her former lover, in which case the seducer would be made to forfeit land in expiation of his offense. But as a rule the unhappy girl was disowned from the moment of detection; she was branded with the name of *nikira-n-roro* (lit., the *remnant of her generation*) and earned her living by the favour of promiscuous suitors. [Grimble 1921*a*, pp. 31–33.]

Grimble's language is slightly ambiguous, in that one does not know exactly how much of the description before the paragraph explicitly about Ocean Island applies to Ocean Island. The coming together of the two families, the role of female kin before and after consummation of the marriage, and the stress on virginity all bear observation.[7]

In the description of the Banaban ceremony, the "Spartan treatment" is of course dramatic. It recalls Turner's remarks about ordeal behavior during many *rites de passage:* "The implication is that for an individual to go higher on the status ladder, he must go lower than the status ladder" (Turner 1969, p. 170). And to go higher on the status ladder, the couple must perform their duty for both their utu: assure continuity. It is also interesting to note the joining together of the rough coconut mats, as the two people are joined and their utu join in a common interest. But the "half on which the boy lay was made by his relations, that on which the girl reclined being made by hers." There was not a "crossing over." The possibility of love triumphing over the lack of virginity is suggestive of a recognition of the integrity of the married couple which may have transcended that in the Gilberts.

---

7. Webster, however, reported information differing in some respects: "No man in Panapa has more than one wife. When a young man is paying his address to a girl, he affixes a band of leaves round his ankle. The children are frequently betrothed as husband and wife when very young. On arriving at a certain age, they are united by a formal marriage ceremony. The age at which these nuptials take place is generally that of fourteen. The young couple sleep together several nights before marriage. The nuptials are consummated by extensive feasting, and a meeting of friends and relatives, as well as certain other ceremonies at which the old women officiate" (Webster n.d., pp. 47–48).

For the Gilberts in general, Grimble notes a category of concubitants which reminds us of the eiriki pattern (Grimble 1921*a*, p. 28). On the general problem of same-generation affines there are statements in the Grimble and Maude papers, probably taken from an old Banaban, which I will now present, slightly modified.

The nga-ni-bu, it will be recalled, were the spouses of siblings of same sex, or the siblings of opposite sex of spouse. The bun-uma alluded to literally means "spouse of the house," and is a form occasionally heard now to describe the married state; in the description here it is a woman.

(1) The nga-ni-bu (male): His role: He could have sexual relations with his brother's wife. She will be content whether she wants them or not, but if her husband hears about it, he might become angry (or "fight"), or he might not because the man is a member of the utu. But if he is not a member of the utu, the husband and his utu will really become angry, and land could go from the man who meddled with the woman.

(2) The nga-ni-bu (female): Her role: She will sit quietly in her house and not meddle with another man. And if it is seen that she is involved with another man who is not a member of the utu, the members of that utu can rise up and seize land of the meddler. And one other way: that woman is sent out of that utu, and her child is held from her. And if there are two children, she takes one with her and one stays. And she is finished with that utu and cannot return to it.

(3) The role of the kainuma (husband's sister) was to "be jealous for her brother." She watched over the conduct of her brother's wife and was considered to have specially the duty of preventing sexual relations between her kainuma and her unmarried brothers.

(4) The bun-uma: Her role: She will sit quietly and perform the role that she should before her husband, or her husband's utu. She will not joke toward young men or any man. But if she has a way which is seen to do something which is bad before the utu, she can be beaten and called upon not to do that thing again. And if she does it again, she can be sent away from that utu not to return.

The reader will be immediately struck by what may be an assumption of residence with the man's family. I suspect that the source of this information was one of the prime sources which lead the Maudes to the assertion of "patri-local residence," by which they imply residence in the man's hamlet. This troublesome matter was considered in chapter 2.

The ambiguity about anger in the case of eiriki relations, the right of the male to have them but the duty of his sister to prevent them, seem to add up to a picture of, in sociological terms, a "stand-off" between the unity and solidarity of the utu on the one hand, and the unity and solidarity of the couple on the other. As was noted earlier, the strength of the latter in the ladder of solidarities may be increasing. But the difference, based on the limited information we have, would be a difference of degree rather than kind.

The change in kind has probably not been in the definitional nature of utu itself, but rather in the fact that other institutions have developed which not only have taken over some functions previously performed in the kinship context but also have created new functions. The "environment" of the utu is totally different from what it was a hundred years ago. How the utu relates to other things (church, politics)—some of which are things which differentiated out of utu—is locally problematic and perplexing. At the same time, the people feel that there is something about utu which is unchanging, and they are probably right. The very flexibility built into the surface manifestations of kinship behavior, the range of variation which is possible without compromising the essential definitions of kinship, may have allowed the Banabans to have one conceptual anchor through an otherwise tumultuous history.

14

Kinship and Ritual II:
The Descent System

Descent, Kindred, and Affinity

Let us assume that the principles now governing the organization of the kindred and kindred ritual are the same principles as those obtaining in the traditional culture. We can then compare the kindred model and the descent unit model.

The loss of status as a kinsman in the code sense through failure to behave as a kinsman, is paralleled by the loss of rights in the descent unit through failure to exercise them.

Both kindreds and descent units can be treated as units conceptually, irrespective of overlapping membership. Where a particular context calls for physical separation of the units in descent unit activities, the unity and equivalence of siblings, which is a feature of the general kinship system, permits "participation by proxy" in more than one. For kindred activities, to representation by siblings or other kin is added representation by spouses. (Such representation now also applies in the domains of political and religious organization.) Descent unit organization manifests the unity of siblings; kindred organization, of siblings and of spouses.

Distinctions within both the descent unit and the kindred illustrate the operation of the same kinds of kinship and nonkinship symbols which connote division of responsibility, or responsibility differentially scaled. Lineality and collaterality is paralleled in the custodianship of rights of precedence through primogeniture, all relating to the conception of the sibling unit. Closeness and distance to the person in general is paralleled in the implications of closeness and distance to the ancestor.

The criterion of generation, applicable in both, is not so easily seen as an "importation" in the same way as, for example, sex, although it is conceptually related to age. Equivalence and identity are internal to the general kinship system; they are the "irreducibles," and the symbols of them, common blood and land, are the symbols of kinship in general.

The distinction of the "male side" and the "female side" in the kindred, reckoning up, is paralleled in the distinction between "descendants of the male" and "descendants of the female," reckoning down. The descent unit conception of the male as having the speaking rights and initiative is paralleled by that of the male side as having the initiative in marriage transactions. The conception of the rights to water-caves as lodging in the female is paralleled by the conception that "the woman sits." "The word" is spoken of as "moving"; the water-caves are unmoving.

Sex and age are conditioning roles in the sociological sense. They appear in most contexts, and this relates to their complementary nature. To take the example of sex: The diffuse obligations of utu membership are essentially toward other members of the utu, rather than toward unrelated utu. The relations of men and of women are not phrased in this way. Their obligations are toward society as a whole, and toward members of the *other* sex (see Lévi-Strauss 1960). The role of each is phrased in terms of the other.

The same idea is expressed in adoption: adopting a boy if one has only a girl; adopting a girl if one has only a boy. The idea is also reflected in two views of the practice of infanticide in pre-Christian days. These are that either only two children were allowed to survive, a male and a female, or that the desired number was three. In the latter case, if the first three children were of the same sex, the third and his successors would be killed until one of the opposite sex was born, thus completing the sibling set. Three as a number connoting completeness is manifest in ritual contexts also.

Those who say that the old custom involved infanticide do not feel constrained to comment when sibling sets of six or seven people appear in genealogies. The essential message is that life on Ocean Island was so precarious that people even had to dispose of their children, and in disposing of their children of course had to keep a male and a female.

Are there just parallels between the descent unit and the kindred, or is there something more? Do we only find the manifestation of the same principles in two planes of the kinship domain? I think not. The argument was presented in chapter 2 that the descent system operated fundamentally as a ritual system. It transmitted basic and important messages about the nature of the society and the nature of the world. The formal orientation of the relations it created was functionally specific rather than diffuse. Recall the case of the Uma water hole cited in chapter 2. Banabans today like to speak of "the anger of Banaba," meaning in general that an argument may have erupted traditionally but was settled by a boxing match, or in the descent context that an argument over rights need not affect (ideally) other relations between the people involved. One is impressed with the *contextualiza-tion* of descent relationships, which is another side to functional specificity.

Given the argument about ritual function, specificity, and contextualization, it is reasonable to hypothesize that one of the major functions of the system was to teach about kinship behavior and how other things related to kinship behavior. The descent units are ideally perpetual; this feeds into the nature of kinship as an enduring solidarity. Not all kinsmen, however, enact kinship behavior; the system records this fact and its consequences. Consider also the kinds of relationships enshrined: parent-child, sibling-sibling, brother-sister. The system spelled out the nature of those relationships. It spelled out how persons created roles, which were then complicated and interfered with by persons again. Generation, birth order and age, maleness and femaleness, closeness and distance, identity and relationship, appeared on a more cosmic stage. The system thus did not rationalize kindred relations and dyadic relations; it provided a larger and historic framework which informed those relations.

The descent system accomplished even more than that. Although a comparison between descent unit and kindred conceptions is valid, the functional contrast in ritual terms is with affinity.

In chapter 2, the Durkheimian idea was mooted that the existence of interrelated units in the model gave the authority of society as a whole to the messages being encoded in the system. A lower-level raison d'être relates to the nature of kinship itself. The descent units which were constituted were not only interrelated units; they were also *exchanging* units. Down to the lowest level within the units, exchange operated.

Descent ritual statements and affinity ritual statements thus take elements out of the complex of elements which is utu and show their interrelationship with one another in two ways: by a set of transformations, the one the reverse of the other, and by a set of alignments. The system operates as diagramed in figure 7.

The utu complex includes identity and relationship, equivalence and differentiation, sharing and exchange. The descent model takes identity of kin (through blood and land) and shows how it is transformed into relationships. It takes the equivalence of kin, particularly siblings, and shows how that equivalence becomes differentiated. It takes the sharing of kin and shows how sharing is transformed into exchange, to the point of exchanging sibling descent units.

The affinity model takes off from married couples in particular and affines in general and leads to the production of children. In this sense relationship

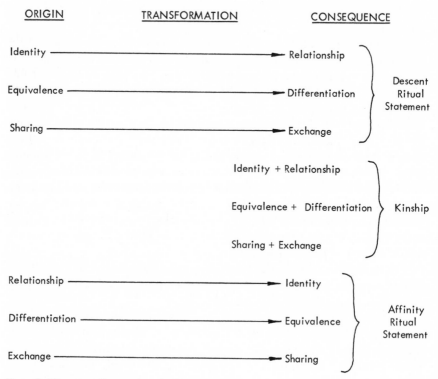

FIG. 7. KINSHIP, DESCENT, AND AFFINITY

is transformed into identity, differentiation into equivalence, exchange into sharing.

But all those elements are present in utu. Here they are interordered.

THE CURRENT DESCENT SYSTEM

I now want to discuss the current models of the descent system and their relationship to action. The models which people now have of the system as it used to be are probably more highly systematized. Some entirely new things may have been added; other things have probably been dropped. This is a problem because one of the sources for reconstruction has been current notions and practices. But on the basis of internal and comparative evidence, I have concluded that the fundamental "grammar," of patterned relationships between kinship, descent, locality, ritual circulation, precedence-complementarity, and person systems, is the same.

In chapter 2, certain definitional matters were raised which relate to the analysis of descent systems. It will be recalled that in the relationship between catagories, units, and groups, a special problem is created when the personnel in one does not equal the personnel in the other. This is the condition represented by the unequal sign. It was observed that following through the relationships precisely brings up a tangle of problems. In the two-island case (Ocean Island and Rambi), the tangle is worse.

One of the key problems is what place locality has in the unequal sign. We are still concerned with Ocean Island locality, the old hamlets and districts. But at this point we will deal with the current Rambi conceptions of Ocean Island locality in relation to descent and ritual, conceptions which embrace both the Ocean Island past and the Rambi present. On Rambi the hamlets do not exist as concrete localities. Those localities exist through memory, and through the people who belong to the categories, units, and groups associated with them. The old village districts as localities have some existence in their conceptual association with the four Rambi villages. (I should note here that current genealogies generally show between five and nine generations from living adults back to the hamlet founder, with between one and seven generations from the hamlet founder to the district founder.)

Let us look at what might appear to be a borderline case. It will be recalled that the situation often arises where people belong to more than one hamlet, either in the same district or in different districts. In some cases there is simply no more to be said about it. In others, there is a differentiation of participation. Figure 8 illustrates this.

In figure 8, Nei Tabotu's descendants, *according to one source,* represent the family in the affairs of Buakonikai, and Nei Tearia's descendants in those of Tabiang. As a senior descendant of Nei Tabotu explained, Nei Tabotu went to Buakonikai, and Nei Tearia stayed at Tabiang, as was decided by the family. If there is an affair at the Tabiang meetinghouse, the Tabotu line plays no role in the making of decisions. This does not mean, however, that they have no land in Tabiang, or that they are in any sense not kinsmen of the others, but only that with regard to the ceremonial activities of the unit, although still members of it, their rights are exercised by "their sister."

Another kind of situation arises within Tabiang district, where the two senior hamlets, descended from the first sibling set from the district founder, Nei Anginimaeao (and this is the first level of ramification within Tabiang district) are Tabiang hamlet whose ancestor is Nan Tetae, and Te Abauareke hamlet, whose ancestor is Nan Tetae's next sibling, Na Borirai. Tabiang has the right of "the word," and Te Abauareke is Tabiang's "worker" and "messenger." (The division of labor can be further elaborated by giving Te Abauareke the work associated with the sea, such as

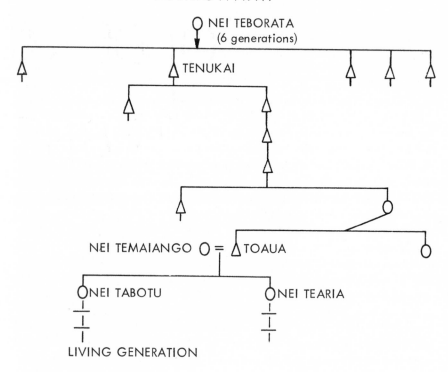

BUAKONIKAI

NEI TEBORATA
(6 generations)

TENUKAI

NEI TEMAIANGO ⚪ = △ TOAUA

⚪ NEI TABOTU   ⚪ NEI TEARIA

LIVING GENERATION

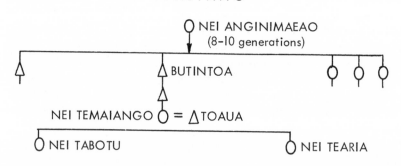

TABIANG

NEI ANGINIMAEAO
(8-10 generations)

BUTINTOA

NEI TEMAIANGO ⚪ = △ TOAUA

⚪ NEI TABOTU   ⚪ NEI TEARIA

FIG. 8. UTU REPRESENTATION

fishing for a meeting, and Etanibanaba, the hamlet of the third sibling, the work of the land, such as collecting drinking coconuts for such a meeting.) The senior descendant of Nan Tetae, a woman, married the second or third (this is disputed) child of Na Borirai. This family, of six generations' depth, belongs equally to Tabiang and Te Abauareke, but as descendant of the first-born in Tabiang, its position is more senior there than in Te Abauareke.

While I was on Rambi, there were several meetings to resolve the dispute within Te Abauareke about who was the second-born and who was the third-born, and members of that family attended and spoke. I was later questioning one of its elder members about the Te Abauareke situation, and he said that he really did not know very much about it, because his family did not have much to do with Te Abauareke. If there was a meeting, they stayed on the higher, Tabiang side. I asked him whether it would not be possible for him to send a brother to the Te Abauareke side. Yes, he replied, some people do this and it is possible, but "it would look as if we were trying to hold everything for ourselves."

The point we are dealing with here is that of overlapping membership, and the fact that it does not necessarily present a special problem calling for a special solution. But it *can* be a matter explicitly recognized that permits a range of variation in solutions. One of these is through representation, grounded in the equivalence of siblings, which is one of the bases of the whole system.

It may be tempting to look at the first case as a case of localized lines, and this is how the lines are thought of. But all of the people in those lines did not, and do not, live in those localities. Are they nonlocalized localized lines? One line has no role in the decision-making activities of the line in the other district, but they are being represented. They are committed by the decisions made by their kin, just as I am committed by decisions made by the United States Congress, although I am not a member of it.

There are, however, a number of cases that not even I can argue away. In the genealogy from a district founder one has the familiar pattern of a couple of generations where only the descendants of the eldest of a sibling set are given. What happened to the others? "Who knows," some people say. Others—or sometimes the same people—privately approach and tell one that *they* are the descendants, they really are members, but have been "wiped off" by vicious kin, hungry to maintain ritual rights for themselves. (Scheffler's term "co-optation" is particularly useful here; see Scheffler 1965.)

More disturbing are cases where, when the genealogy is being recited, someone is left without listed descendants and, on inquiry, one is told that that person "married to Uma," for example, or "married to" a particular hamlet. The implication is that the person did not concern himself with the affairs of the genealogy-giving unit and is out of it as a group. In such cases they are out of it as a *concrete group,* but there is some ambiguity about whether or not they are out of it as a *conceptual group.* The identity is there, but the code is questionable. In the "married to" instance also, the people may turn up at the ethnographer's doorstep and protest. They do not think they should be out of it as a group. We thus have descent groups as dissent groups, and this begins to specify the function of the whole thing on Rambi. To this we shall return shortly.

On the analogy with "kindred-based action groups" (Freeman 1961), these dissenting groups may be termed "descent-based action groups." And this structural feature may not be entirely unlike that which obtained in the traditional system, as was suggested in chapter 2. Even traditionally it may have been the case that as one moved away from the senior lines the groups became units and perhaps categories. Some, however, may have had the status of groups. The group aspect is not, and perhaps was not, directly predictable from genealogy. Now other ties—such as church, factional, kindred—combine with descent ties to ground the activity of groups.

The identity of individuals as members of descent units is not only relevant to situations where the unit acts as a group. There are certain things one might not say before a person because he is a member of a certain unit, even if the unit never does anything at all as a group, and there are certain behavioral characteristics of a person that one may explain by the fact that members of a unit to which he belongs are disposed to behave in that manner.

Other than argument, what are descent group activities on Rambi? It will be recalled that there were activities between hamlets, and activities within hamlets. One current set of activities which is an internal function is the presentation of gifts at marriage, *te biribai* (*biri,* contribute, run; *bai,* thing, property, right). One kind of biribai was described in the last chapter: gifts to kinsmen as kinsmen. In the other kind of biribai, the gifts are presented as those of one constituent hamlet descent group line to another. We will now take up this part of the biribai process and will use the example of the hamlet of Te Abauareke in Tabiang as a model for the system, and some of the matters of controversy that can arise within it. One of these is illustrated in the genealogy itself: the birth order of ancestors (see figure 9).

If someone in, for example, line four is to be married, and there is a whole figure of ten pounds for the group gift, then the elder of the first line, as senior of the whole group, informs each of the other lines (except four) that it is responsible for raising two pounds as "his gift to his siblings." The people of line four do not contribute in this way; they are the recipients.

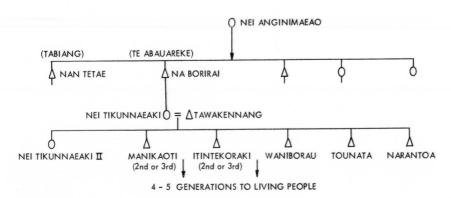

FIG. 9. UNITS IN MARRIAGE GIFTS

Within each of the other lines, the contribution is ideally subdivided *per stripes,* with some allowance often being made for nonproductive people to opt out. The receiving line, however, need not know who in the contributing lines paid and who did not. It is a collective gift, and they are confronted as a whole. The point that it is a collective gift of units of relationship is also manifested in the fact that since there are marriages within Te Abauareke, one person may make more than one contribution, as a member of different lines. Such a person may feel himself victimized, and sympathy for him may be expressed by· others, but there is no honorable way to escape.[1]

Another kind of person who may be faced with a large contribution is one who is in a line with few members. People in such a position are often expected to have more land than others. Thus the biribai system may not only in general spread the resources about, but also redistribute the moveable resources of those with larger landholdings and thus have somewhat of an equalizing effect.[2]

The gift is not presented by the entire group. The proverbial pattern is that a few days before the actual marriage, by which time many of the relatives of the bride have already arrived at her house, and similarly for the

1. During my stay, this group was considering a suggestion by one of its members, the Banaban Trust Fund Board treasurer, that the payments be adjusted so that an individual with multiple ties would not be victimized so much. The suggestion was received sympathetically, and if it is accepted, will represent a moving up in priority of economic values.

2. It was observed in chapter 2 that some sub-units have more than one ancestor. Unfortunately I do not know how the biribai would be affected in such cases.

groom (the two groups are not "combined" until the actual marriage ceremony), Te Abauareke "journeys" to greet its kinsman. This means that a group consisting of one or more representatives of each line but the one in which the marriage occurs, arrives at the house of meeting, finely dressed and wreathed. In addition to the money, which they have not yet showed, they may also bring cigarettes and matches to be given to the gathering and receive cigarettes and matches themselves. Some of these items have presumably been substituted for things from the land.

This, "the arrival," is one of the most stylized of procedures. When the group arrives their feet are washed, they are anointed with coconut oil and given new wreathes to wear, as they sit along a wall of the house. The house itself becomes quiet, and small children who may be scurrying about the middle of the room are whisked away. After a period of strained silence, an old man in the house addresses the group by asking, "If you please, where do you journey from? The road from where?" Someone from the visiting group replies, "The road from Te Abauareke." This subtype of biribai is known as "the road"; the image is apt in a genealogical sense and it underscores the solidarity of the group irrespective of where its members happen to reside.

The old man may but need not then ask them to recite the genealogy linking their lines with the line of the person being married. If he does, and if this is done to his satisfaction, he affirms them as coming on a proper road. He "recognizes them." The gift is then presented to that old man, or perhaps to the parent or other relative of the person to be married. If the genealogy has not been recited, then acceptance of the gift itself constitutes recognition of the relationship. Polite conversation and a meal follow, and the group leaves. They depart not necessarily from the area but from their roles as members of "the journey." The journey here is spoken of as being similar to the visit of affines (kautabo), where the household also must present the best mats and food for them, and behave with great respect. The analogy has meaning in another way since those arriving are coming as members of the group, but the relationship has not yet been recognized. The initial exchange of cigarettes and matches is also similar to the behavior of affines before marriage. This may be a feature of the meta-ritual component discussed in the last chapter. Indeed, everything enacted in the descent system has a heavy meta-ritual component today.

Overlapping membership need present no special problem here either. The lines act in presenting their gifts through representatives. It is even feasible for the same person to be part of more than one journey, since the journeys are independent of one another. I observed one instance where a girl was part of the journey of two different descent units involved in the same marriage. When I called this fact to the attention of a man nearby he indicated that this was not really correct practice, although no one spontaneously manifested surprise. I did not, alas, follow up the matter.

There are also no transactions between the descent units of the bride and those of the groom, as descent units. This is a matter entirely *within* the group, and it defines its limits.

There is some opinion that "in the old days" there was biribai between hamlets, which suggests a fission process. But the general conception of this is as an affair among the people of one hamlet, one place. The way these gifts are presented is indicative of the state of solidarity within the unit at the time. One of the reasons given for why many units do not engage in collective presentations is their size: practically the whole island would be involved. Another reason is intra-unit quarrels: "If they are angry, how can they journey?"

At one marriage that I attended in the line of Nei Tikunnaeaki II, there were two journeys from Te Abauareke: one from the descendants of Na Itintekoraki (see figure 9), and one from Na Manikaoti and the other siblings. When a marriage is not in the most senior line, it is the most senior line which should organize the collection of money. When a marriage is in the senior line, it is the next most senior line which should do it: a junior substitutes for an elder sibling. At this marriage there was the problem of who was the second: the Itintekoraki group claims that he is, and the Manikaoti group, supported by the other sibling lines, claims that it is Manikaoti. The Itintekoraki people would not recognize those of Manikaoti as the proper ones to collect the wedding money, and so they journeyed on their own.

This may be a moment in a process of fission, although if they were to opt out, the Itintekoraki people would then have to biribai among themselves if they were to have any real collective existence in the system at all. Recall from chapter 2 the point that validation of the position of the unit is required from the outside, from groups with which it is linked. It is instructive to note here, however, that Itintekoraki married the senior woman of Tabiang hamlet (see figure 10), and speaking on that side, some members of the group claim that only they, to the exclusion of the siblings of their ancestor, have important rights of ritual precedence in Tabiang, which suggests a related fission process there. What makes the data difficult to interpret sociologically is that one does not know whether in fact they are trying to exclude the others, or whether it is the others who are trying to secure a position for themselves which they did not have before.

The nature of the descent system will be clearer if we examine the kinds of evidence used to support the claims in the Itintekoraki-Manikaoti dispute.

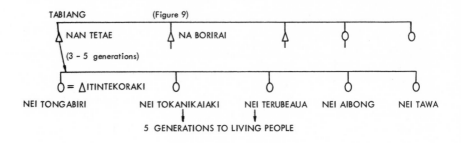

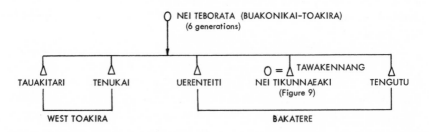

FIG. 10. A DESCENT UNIT DISPUTE

Since I am illustrating rather than taking sides, I will present the arguments on the Manikaoti side only. (Another motive for presenting this is to convince, perhaps, those who are skeptical of the possibility of existence of a system such as this, that people can in fact take it seriously.)

The argument as summarized by J, an elder of the Manikaoti line, first involved statements made by Tekoruru, an elder descendant of Nei Tikunnaeaki II, which is the senior or first line of Te Abauareke (see figure 9).

Tekoruru said that he was with his grandfather at the time of a large meetinghouse assembly on Ocean Island. He saw Tamuera, a descendant of Manikaoti, dividing the food. If Tamuera was not the proper person to do it, why did the elders descended from Itintekoraki not object at the time?

Tekoruru also referred to a time when a certain visitor was an "official guest" at Tabiang, and he (Tekoruru) got together the gift of Te Abauareke for the occasion and gave it to Tawita, Tamuera's son, to take to the elder descendant of Nan Tetae, of the senior hamlet of Tabiang. (Tamuera's line, incidentally, is a component of both Tabiang and Te Abauareke, but this makes no difference.) Again, why did the Itintekoraki people not object?

He also said that his grandfather had told him that Nei Tikunnaeaki II stayed in one house, and her brothers in another, and that if she had a message to send to them, she would call Manikaoti first, who would then tell Itintekoraki.

As seen from figures 9 and 10, the only daughter of the ancestor of Te Abauareke married a man from Bakatere in Buakonikai. A woman descended from this man's brother, also part of Bakatere, was asked to whom in Te Abauareke she would send "the word" if there were a message on family affairs. She replied that she was told by her elder to send the word to Tekoruru (of the first line), but if Tekoruru was not there, to Nan Tawita (of the Manikaoti line).

J indicated how these points prove the case for Manikaoti as second-born: the first-born stays at the hamlet, and has the right of "the word," or precedence and initiative. The second-born has the right of doing "the work," such as carrying messages and dividing the food in meetings, for the first-born. He cited the cases of the word staying with Nan Tetae (the first-born) at the hamlet of Tabiang, and Na Borirai (the second-born) having the right of the work. Within the hamlet of Tabiang, he cited Nei Tongabiri (the first-born) as having the right of the word, and Nei Tokanikaiaki (the second-born) as having the right of the work.

The argument is then clear. Since the descendants of Manikaoti are known to have done the work, and since no objection was raised to their doing it, they did it by right. Who has the right to do the work? The descendants of the second-born. Therefore it follows that Manikaoti, and not Itintekoraki, is the second-born.

There are well-known cases where the first-born does not in fact have the right to the word, and the second-born to the work. These are situations calling for special explanation by a special series of events which occurred in their time. Without such special historical facts to command, one can reason in terms of the norm, since it always was.

Another aspect of the idea of descent and the activities of descent units is revealed in a comment J made when an old member of the Itintekoraki group, who had appeared at a previous meeting, did not appear at the next one. He was afraid to be found out in his lies, J remarked, because he was afraid of what might happen to him. J went no further than that. In a similar vein, on my return to Rambi after my first visit, someone whispered that two people whom he said had lied at the time of genealogy-collecting had died in the interim. Part of this is the special traditional status of the meetinghouse and activities associated with it. Since such activities involve descent units, which are in turn associated with the hamlets of the district, it is understandable in straight Durkheimian terms.

But there is another and more elusive aspect to it. It recalls a time when a

Gilbertese man was telling an old story at a wake in the Pentecostal church meetinghouse. He was interrupted by a question from his listeners and refused to continue. The comment was made that this was the "true way" of the meetinghouse and old stories. Once there is an interruption, once the continuity is broken, it is impossible to go on. There might be dire consequences. More directly relevant to the descent question, people repeatedly say that if the occasions arose where descent unit rights were in fact exercised, especially if there were a true meetinghouse, there would be no argument. The proper person would do the proper thing, and all would see it. This is a manifestation of what I will call the "integrity of pattern" and is familiar to students of ritual.

The genealogy is a whole, beginning at the beginning and temporarily stopping at the present, and the property of the unit whose genealogy it is. The differentiated rights vested in a unit are a pattern, a self-realizing one, which, once the button is pushed, must proceed to its foreordained conclusion. The telling of an old tale can be the same. Once the pattern is interfered with, the whole point has been lost.

A common remark on the biribai process is that it cannot stop, even when the people of one unit intermarry. Banabans regard this situation with humor: We marry one another, they say, but the biribai goes on and on anyway. The basis of the joke is, I think, that the parents and grandparents of bride and groom do not utuna one another in the diffuse sense after the marriage of their children or grandchildren, but kautabona one another. A marriage between two relatives is referred to by two expressions. The first is "It returns"; as one Banaban said, "The utu returns to the utu." The image may perhaps be understandable in terms of both genealogical lines and land. The second expression is "it is broken." What may be broken is the expectation of the diffuse solidarity of the kinship relationship. There is some feeling that in the old days marriages within the descent unit did not occur, although they are visible in the genealogies. There are also a few local reports that in the old days people tried to marry close relatives for reasons of land. Notions of both exogamous and endogamous marriage are consistent with notions of maintaining the solidarity of the unit. It may indeed be the case that the units when they were more important were also smaller, both in number of members and in generational depth. If they were smaller in generational depth, then the operation of the three-generation rule against marrying one's kin would have the practical effect of making intra-unit marriages less likely. In the contemporary system, at any rate, even with intra-unit marriage the descent aspect of the relationship is uncompromised: *"It goes on and on."*

Dorothy Lee (1959) refers to something like this integrity of pattern in her discussion of the Trobriands, as a contrast to lineality. Among the Banabans the pattern is lineal itself, but similarly, there is value in the pattern through its eternity. Interfering with it creates disorder (by definition), and a mysterious punishment may be meted out to the offender.

One cannot, however, count on mysterious punishment. Complementary to the idea of pattern integrity is the notion that when there is a question of one's rights, one must make sure that they are recognized, and this is accomplished by exercising them. In a meeting on that Te Abauareke dispute, a man on the Manikaoti side said that if the other side indeed had the rights they should have raised them before. Addressing the meeting at large, he proclaimed, as I indicated in chapter 2, "Banaban custom tells that if there is something that is yours, you touch it, or somebody else will." If you do not exercise your prerogative, the pattern as a whole will not collapse. There is someone else to move in, perhaps someone waiting for the chance. A person or unit not originally the right one can play a part if the right one has withdrawn, and in that case, the filler of the gap may become the right one himself.

Marriage contributions and ritual rights are aspects of the system calling for a definite drawing of boundaries. Although there may be arguments about the genealogy, there is ideally a generation in which the descent unit begins and membership ends. The hamlet is a "place" (on Ocean Island), and a place means the lands of that place. This is land in the symbolic sense discussed earlier. Not everyone of the hamlet owns land there. Although two hamlets may be in the same named district descended from one ancestor, the people of them are not in this sense people of the same place. Tabiang is one place, Te Abauareke another. The common land of the common place symbolizes the solidarity, the closer relationship, between them as opposed to those of other places, and it is within this group that the marriage contributions occur.

The remarkableness of continuing marriage contributions when marriages do occur within the unit is a feature not of the organization of descent units, but of kindreds, for the hamlet boundary also defines, very roughly, the unit within which diffuse genealogy-related kinship relationships are expected to take place. This only applies, of course, where there are hamlets. As mentioned earlier, people who are kinsmen do not necessarily have a hamlet relationship in common.

Those hamlets engaging in the collective biribai tend to have linking genealogies. Even with a linking genealogy, anger or size may constrain the biribai process (see above). There are other complicating factors. A genealogy may feature one or two members of a larger ancient sibling set who are identified by hamlet, but whose descendants are obscure. Individuals may recognize a particular original ancestor, but not as one of the five early figures. Or a hamlet ancestor may be said to be a child of one of those figures, but people make the assertion rather tenuously. Individuals known as people of a hamlet may not recognize an actual relationship with one another. Or they may recognize a connection as being from a hamlet ("He is my 'father' from the hamlet of Nakieba"), but little more. Marriage gifts here are made on an individual or small-group basis. Some of these "hamlets," and lines with genealogies deemed very incomplete, are not generally thought of as part of the intra- and inter-district system and are not profitably considered descent units at all.

The relationship between descent and the two localities of Ocean Island and Rambi is a complex and ramifying one. I do not know about the conduct of the biribai process on Ocean Island. It is considered custom. On Rambi, as I have indicated, "the journey" is to the site of marriage, and the site of marriage may not be in the Rambi village associated with the Ocean Island village district of which the hamlet was part. Besides, hamlets from more than one district may be journeying to the same marriage.

When I held genealogy meetings, the proper site for them was generally the meetinghouse in each Rambi counterpart of the relevant Ocean Island village district, or the house of one of the elders of the district. But of the ongoing meetings that were theoretically trying to straighten out the Tabiang dispute discussed, the first were in Tabiang, but the last I attended was in the house of a Tabiang elder living in Tabwewa.

The meetinghouses of the villages, or the church meetinghouses which function as village meetinghouses also, have not entirely escaped the aura of the descent system. The idea of the meetinghouse and its formality is a transformation of that system. It is the place where visitors are officially welcomed into the village. As the theoretical collective center of the village, it is where they are greeted and given feasts, and where arrangements are made for their sleeping. But the association of the buildings with the churches complicates matters for non-Methodists.

In certain intervillage affairs a traditional order of districts is recognized, but erratically, and this is probably on the wane.

Rambi rumor has it that even when the Uma church meetinghouse was constructed, the right people (by descent) did the right thing. While the new Tabwewa church meetinghouse was under construction, one man told me that if I was still on Rambi for the opening, I would see the "true custom." When I asked others if custom would be practiced, they said maybe yes, maybe no.

The situation that reigns is in part illustrated by an incident reported to me. Once in 1965, a man whom I will call Luke sought and was given permission to speak before the council. He said he was communicating the dissatisfaction of the people of Uma over the rumor that Karawa I. Eri, one of the two Uma councillors, was being considered to go to England as part of a delegation to protest British handling of the phosphate issue. Luke, a resident at that time of Tabiang, and Karawa are well known as senior members of two related Uma-based descent units, each claiming that it is the most senior Uma unit. Karawa was one of the few people openly supporting the Banaban Adviser in the controversy discussed earlier and was marked to be purged by the Rorobuaka Society, of which Luke was a member. His declaration that the villagers were restless was interpreted as involving both things.

At the council meeting, Paul, the other Uma councillor, is reported to have said that the council "does not know Luke," that is, does not recognize his right to speak on behalf of the village. That was a councillor's right. Luke, in anger, replied by asking if they did not know Nan Tenikoria, the Uma ancestor among whose descendants Luke counts himself as senior. He said furthermore that he did not hear Paul's name in the Uma genealogies; he was really a Tabwewan.

The councillors, many of whom were Karawa's political opponents, did not act positively on the complaint. But Paul did go from house to house in Uma asking people to sign a paper indicating whether or not they were in favor of Karawa's going to England. He may have anticipated the results because in general he stands with Karawa and was in fact nominated by him. Of the few who opposed Karawa, Luke's close relatives were prominent, and the matter died there, at least for the moment.

The point is that this was a "village matter," which is why if what Paul did was a calculated risk, it was a risk that, as Uma councillor, he could take. Councillors are village representatives, and other grounds for representation ought not to interfere. The issue may be stated symbolically as that of whether the Rambi village is a continuation of and stands for the Ocean Island village, or it does not. The "solution" is that at least in those village functions connected with the council domain, the two entities should be distinct.

Intrahamlet activities are the most easily transportable. Some attempts have been made, however, to revive other aspects of the system. Certain individuals have, from the beginning, apparently tried to convert the functionally specific kind of authority of the traditional system into a more diffuse kind of authority on the new island. This has been moderately successful in the case of individuals who could combine other qualities with their descent prestige. The more influential figures gather up as many strands of relationship and solidarity as they can: descent, kindred, religious, village, economic.

In 1948, however, there was more of a collective operation. The Adviser reported that on the Governor's first visit to Rambi, the "right of dealing with visiting vessels" was invoked. The Governor's boat was met by certain canoes, and the people brought him ashore.[3] Some traditional games were also played in the old manner. By 1960, the year before my first visit, the Adviser said that the Maudes' 1932 article itself has been used in a Tabwewa dispute over precedence. We will shortly examine the question of why people bother with the system at all, but its revival at the time of the Ocean Island Lands Commission and the 1927–31 phosphate dispute, and the 1948 period when independence was being sought, suggest that some version of the traditional system reappears to give tangible support to the definition of the community's boundaries. Even when traditionalists give anti-modern arguments, the attention of the community is more intensely focused on matters of land, feeding into the direction of more political action.

I will not detail here the various disputes which occur, from time to time, over the traditional system. The traditional system is a vehicle for conflicts of other kinds (for example, political), and old feuds from it feed into conflicts of other kinds (for example, religious). I must here record my own participation and effect in the situation, which developed to a point where further inquiry on descent matters became almost impossible, and thus a number of clearly visible loose ends were left.

Soon after arriving on Rambi, I met a man who told me of a meeting which was to take place in Tabwewa village, where I was to work first. Members of two groups were to discuss a dispute between them.

This Tabwewa dispute over traditional matters is of such complexity that I will make a few points but will not go into its details (and will merely assert that it spilled over into church and political organizations).

The reader is referred back to pp. 94–96. One of the groups participating in the dispute was constituted of descendants of the woman referred to in the document as the "hereditary high chiefess" of Tabwewa. A photograph of her is the frontispiece of Ellis's (1935) *Ocean Island and Nauru,* which denotes her as the old "queen." People know about this.

Her great-grandson was listed in a genealogy in an appendix to the Maudes' 1932 article as "chief." His granddaughter and other relatives were participants in this dispute, during which a copy of the Maudes' article was used, as it had been before. (Information from the article was used in another dispute by a contending party whose case it supported. The article, and to a lesser degree written genealogies, have helped to make the structure more explicit. However, people can always impugn the writer's sources of information.)

---

3. Holland to Chief Secretary, WPHC, 11 September 1948, Holland Papers.

My knowledge of the Gilbertese language was minimal at the time of the Tabwewa dispute under discussion, but it seemed that the explicit points at issue were whether the line referred to was really in the position of genealogical seniority set out in the article, and whether it was in the position of ritual precedence. Its members were not publicly proclaiming themselves to be chiefs, as far as I could tell, but the question of kingship and chiefship was on people's minds. People took many occasions to tell me that on Ocean Island there had been neither kings, queens, nor chiefs.

In general, the Banabans resent the fact that Europeans decided there was a chiefly system on Ocean Island. They understand that by the word *chief* the European means a person with an almost unlimited authority over his subjects, where nothing could be further from the truth on Ocean Island (and the Maudes had in fact *not* made this error). Some people, the Banabans believe, are trying to perpetuate the old system in order to pervert it: they want to be chiefs. This is at times ascribed not only to the general perverseness of human nature, buttressed by European misunderstanding, but also to contact with Fijians.

There are many personal friendships between the Rambi people and Fijians, and prominent Fijian leaders are widely admired. The Banabans often characterize the Fijian chiefly system in such a manner that its hierarchical nature contrasts radically with their own more egalitarian way of life. This is not to suggest that the Banabans want to change the Fijian system. Both the Fijians and the Banabans are entitled to their own custom, in the local view, and in fact the Banabans sympathize with the perceived continuity of Fijian tradition.

On Rambi, when people are taking down the alleged seekers after diffuse status who ground at least part of their claim in the descent system, the accusation is sometimes made that the status-seekers want to be like Fijian chiefs, and the Fijian word *ratu* is used. The *ratu* is often posited as one before whom dependents must behave with obeisance, as one who can order people around, and one to whom tribute is paid. This reference to the Fijian chiefly system may operate as a negative sanction. That system represents what Banaban society is not like, what it should not be like, but what some status-hungry people want it to be like. The Fijian chiefly system is fine for the Fijians, but not for the Banabans. The formulation of images of Fijian society (and similarly notions about islands in the Gilberts) is a means through which the Banabans clarify their self-conceptions, and both those conceptions are probably transformed in the process.

To return to my work in Tabwewa: Upon inquiry the disputing groups appeared to be bilateral descent groups, and in order to understand them, I thought the collection of genealogies would be useful. Besides, everyone knows that anthropologists collect genealogies. My interests included the functioning of the Rambi Island Council, and exploring the kin relations among the councillors and other leaders seemed a relevant part of the study. I might add that at this point I had had very little formal training in kinship or in field methods.

In discussing research plans with my Banaban assistant, I mentioned genealogies and started explaining what they were by drawing part of my own. I later learned that there was a Gilbertese word for genealogy, *te kateiriki*. My assistant was quite impressed with the idea.

I was then living with a family in Tabwewa, and my assistant's house was the first to the south, over a small tidal stream. Next day he came and reverently produced a piece of paper with part of his own genealogy on it. He said that he had worked on it for a long time, and it was a truly amazing and wonderful thing, showing his descent all the way back to the ancestral spirits of Ocean Island.

He indeed started with the spirits, and in drawing the genealogy did not indicate *all* of the descent lines he knew, but only those stemming from the ancestor of one Tabwewa hamlet. He knew his relationship to other units, and these appeared on other genealogies, but he drew this one in his own house in his own time, and as I learned later, although he recognized his belonging to other groups, this was the one which he chose to emphasize.

Old men and old women were in most cases considered to be the authorities on matters genealogical. We were directed to some of them to see how much they knew and were willing to tell. For the old people, some said, were not talking. They were guarding their knowledge.

It was thought proper that as I was in Tabwewa, I should start with the descent units traditionally associated with Tabwewa. We did get information from the old people. But then some people came to me and said, in effect: Taking genealogies is a very good idea, but not in the way you are doing it. A person may "make a mistake" or lie outright in his own house, giving information which would raise his own position and lower that of others, or exclude them altogether. The only thing to do, they said, was to hold meetings of the groups, some of which had been meeting and airing points of argument just before I came. The theory was that in public the truth would out. And if the truth did not emerge of its own accord, I, the anthropologist, would arbitrate. It was a good thing that someone was coming who could straighten out what was bothering the people so much. I declined this responsibility.

Nevertheless there emerged a series of meetings in the villages, led by their island councillors, after consultation with elders. I sat at the side taking notes and asked some questions. Many Banabans were taking notes too. The councillors advertised the sessions in advance, and some put up notices in the stores to give members living in other villages a chance to come. It was not long before it seemed to me that the amount of time being spent on these genealogies, and the recitation of traditional rights which sometimes occurred, was a bit excessive. But once started the process could not be stopped. I had pushed the button.

People from individual lines often tried to work out their own differences first. The information was going to be written down, so they were concerned to get it right. There were fifty to seventy people present in the largest meetings of whole districts, which were held in the meetinghouses.

The form of the meetings was generally as follows: The councillor called it to order and said a few words on its purpose and worthiness. It was good to broadcast the information among the people. In the case of the descendants of Na Kouteba, a Buakonikai district founder, for example, he first asked, "Did Na Kouteba have issue?" An elder answered, "He had issue." The councillor next asked, "Who were the children of Na Kouteba?" They were named by an elder, and then the descendants, line by line. Many disputes occurred.

When one argument arose about which of two groups possessed a set of ritual rights, the people, as usual, called for remembered cases of their exercise on Ocean Island. One man said that Eri (who had died on Ocean Island) had exercised them, and called, "Where is Eri?" He was looking to Eri's grandson to speak. On other occasions, when we came to a particular near ancestor whose descendants were not yet included in the genealogy, the leader of the meeting did not always call out, "Where are the descendants of X?" but at times, expecting the elder of the line to speak up, "Where is X?" The ancestor is alive through his descendants. One way of asking who the descendants are, or referring to the descendants, is by using the term *kanoa* (contents). The contents of X are his descendants.

An incident of interest occurred in one village. When it came time for the recitation of a particular line, Taekana (I am using some fictitious names), a man of about forty, started giving it. Rewi, a leading leader, interrupted him loudly, saying, "What right do you have to speak on that line?" The meetinghouse became quiet. Taekana replied, "I am speaking for Nei Nikawai." Rewi then shouted angrily across to him: "You have nothing to do with the matter; leave the meetinghouse!" and Taekana was silenced.

The issue was this: Taekana is a Gilbertese married to Nei Nati. Taekana is extremely interested in genealogies and custom, and his wife is spokeswoman for a group in which she is a member of the most senior branch.

Her mother, through whom she attained this position, is deceased. The oldest living member of the group is Nei Nikawai, who is Nei Nati's mother's father's father's brother's daughter: her "grandmother." Nei Nikawai would have been an appropriate person to speak. But she is very old, gets about and speaks very little, and Nei Nati is the usual spokeswoman.

Taekana was not allowed to assert himself in this context. A person can represent his spouse in some kindred and other matters, but not in a context such as this. That explains one of the reasons for having such contents.

At another meeting, when the day's recording was concluded, an old woman sitting on the edge of the meetinghouse broke out in tears. Another sitting next to her addressed the group, saying that the old woman was very distressed, and sought the help of those present. Rewi told her to speak her piece, and the people of the meeting would try to help her. Her complaint was this: She knew she belonged to that unit but her name did not appear on the genealogy. She knew because of her ownership of a piece of land in the appropriate district on Ocean Island. But she did not know the genealogy. Thus she suffered shame.

Rewi asked her how she acquired the land, and she recited the line up to her great-grandmother, but could go no further. There were two known women with the same name as her great-grandmother, which added to the confusion.

Rewi asked the others present for enlightenment, and got none. He then asked the old woman, "With whom do you biribai?" She uttered a name and motioned toward a highly respected old woman on the western side of the meetinghouse, to whom Rewi turned and asked, "Do you biribai with her?" The woman replied that she thought she did. The old woman had thus gone a halting step toward establishing part of her case but still had to find the proper connection with the other old woman, since they might be related through an entirely different descent unit. At this point the meeting broke up, and Rewi said he would look into his own book of genealogies for further illumination.

Three factors in claiming connection appeared: (1) being an acknowledged part of the genealogy; (2) owning a piece of land in an area associated with the unit, and (3) participating in biribai on known occasions in traceable ways.

The case of the old woman also indicates the disadvantage a person is in who does not know his genealogy. If a land dispute arises between two people and one knows the genealogy and the other does not, the former has a better case. The same applies to any other kind of dispute involving descent. Participating in the biribai is, among other things, a way of accumulating a treasure house of evidence for future reference. Some claim that on Ocean

Island genealogies were in fact not recited during the biribai; they did not have to be because everyone knew his place. Concern with the biribai now is at times explained by concern for the genealogy, which is in turn explained by concern for accurate knowledge bearing upon one's land rights.

When nothing is written or printed, this knowledge comes from sources one considers reliable, or possibly reliable. If a person claims to belong to a certain descent unit, or to be in a certain line, and others rebuff the claim, their denial by implication impugns the claimant's source of information. Almost inevitably the claimant says, "My 'old men' and my 'old women' told me so." Politely the person may be told that his honored elders made a mistake. When he is not around it may be remarked more strongly that the old man was a liar. One's kinship identity is tied up with the integrity of one's forebears; casting doubt upon the one is casting doubt upon the other.

The meetings we held resurrected lost kin, and a marriage held after their conclusion had a massive biribai participation. One descent group appeared which others said had never done anything before, and which did not descend from its claimed ancestor. Attempts were made again to resurrect the games system, but with results which satisfied hardly anyone (although they may have provided momentary catharses). This is a predictable feature of such resurrection. The system had been reality-tested erratically. It was being resurrected to serve some purposes different from those which it had served before, but also some of the same purposes, if with a different content. After a session ostensibly called to settle a dispute between two groups, I asked a friend privately if he thought such meetings would really end in agreement. The problem was not only in the meetings, he said. Irrespective of what was stated there, one did not know what a disputant might tell his child secretly in his own house. The father, for example, might claim that a unit to which he belonged had the right of dividing food in the meetinghouse, and he, as elder, was the proper executor of the right. (And perhaps the potential distribution of rights affects parent-child relations.)

Listening to people talk of enacting the old culture, one is reminded of the music of the late 1920s. The experience that many have of it is only through records and films; they equate the sound as it came to them through recording devices with the sound as it was originally played. And, indeed, it may be the case that the memories of many who actually lived through that period, who danced to the music and sang with the songs, have been altered to conform with the transformed rendition. If so, any attempt on their part to perform the melodies again would be colored by this transformation, by the deliberate, flattened, and faintly echoing quality of a sound at one remove.

The information which came to light during my activities may be a significant input to the kinship scene for a while. It was serving a demand for clarification, which in specific cases may have meant the hope by an individual that *his* version would be accepted and validated. He was testing it out. Yet it seemed that, as the situation developed, the meetings had dramatized the impossibility of achieving consensus. I noted above that the council had earlier sought to put a moratorium on the exercise of such rights because they led to so much dissension. The meetings we held further articulated the fact that the traditional system had completely fallen apart as a social system, whatever hopes individuals might nourish. It was being tested out and was being found wanting. If on Ocean Island there had been a model of social structure which was enacted as a drama, on Rambi there are individualized models (but with similar if not identical grammars) of both that model and its enactments. One finds a set of changing myths, parts of which are individually and collectively, at no fixed intervals, converted into dramas. Absence makes the mind grow.

In terms of concrete, acting social groups, the descent groups are noisesome phantoms of the social order rather than indispensable parts of it. Although the descent system is a *system of social classification* not everyone knows which descent units he belongs to. But people do know that the units are, that the system of classification exists. Few groups actually biribai in the "old style." A musical analogy again sounds to mind in contemplating ritual rights. If a person owns a violin he is not ipso facto a musician. We can regard people as violinists, timpanists, and flautists without their making up an orchestra. An orchestra will, however, be composed of violinists (first, second. . .), timpanists and flautists, among others. We can think of the argumentative descent groups as being composed of the owners of the instruments, or at least those who claim to be owners of the instruments, some of whom meet from time to time to discuss which among them are the musicians, and what the scoring is of the composition which they might sometime play. They very rarely even get to the stage of full rehearsal. At a performance, likely as not, cacophony reigns, or there might only be mother in the front row to applaud. The cumulative effect is that people think that maybe they should take up another line of work.

The tone I have adopted is not specific to myself. Banabans joke about the system—although those who joke may be angry disputants in another context. Much ado about nothing; a great deal of fuss and trouble with little to show for it. Why, then, bother with the thing at all? I refer the reader back to the discussion in chapter 2 and the opening of this chapter. The models of the model still give some information of the same kind, and I will not repeat much of what is there. Understanding the relation between people and places, space and time, on traditional Ocean Island is understanding the descent system. It is an obvious identity symbol, the repository of Banaban custom. Enactment is an enactment of Banaban-ness, which must be seen in the context of the phosphate issue and political ambitions, the presence of Gilbertese in the community and the location of the community in Fiji. But the symbol is best kept at one remove lest it divide more than unite. The biribai system, the most currently operative part, what there is of it, is a rite to articulate solidarity and breach; to give form to the distinction between kinship and descent and between consanguineal and affinal kin; to spell out the nature of reciprocity and siblingship; to assert precedence and have precedence affirmed but in the context of mutual obligation and the possibility of having precedence in one place but the lack of it in another; to acknowledge or deny claims and have claims acknowledged or denied; to give, receive or withhold information; to redistribute resources. The biribai system, like the whole thing, is tied up with the genealogies, which are tied up with kinship and the distribution of land. Or, blood and mud.

The system as a whole serves some as a vehicle for the fantasy of having status, where the means toward status advancement are uncertain or blocked —especially, perhaps, for women. Simple pride plays a large role. Some have a hope for genuine status advancement through the system and may try to arrange marriages with the right people. Others see the possibility of status advancement for some undefined time in the future and think they should keep their options open. Others see the possibility of *others* making claims, and feel they must be prepared to fight those claims if they are unjust and maybe even present their own. The system schools in the maximizing of options, and its very lingering on is a manifestation of the "Keep your options open principle." The system is a vehicle for taking people down, or raising people up. It is a vehicle through which objects of solidarity can be added to strengthen the bonds between some kin. It is a vehicle through which hostility can be expressed in a defined context. It is a vehicle for rhetoric. It even has a utility as something to deny, giving a self-assurance of social and religious progress.

The descent complex provides a set of *theories* of tremendous power— even if their applicability is now on the wane—about the ways in which the social world was (and may still be) put together, and the ways in which individuals are put together. Whatever role the concrete aspects of the system (such as the ritual details) may have in motivating people to concrete action, the theories can be brought into play post hoc by people in order to explain action.

The system helps you know and may even help you prove you are a

Banaban, with Banaban blood and Banaban land, or only Banaban land, and all that Banaban blood and land imply. Even if it fails as a social system, the penumbra with which it surrounds kinship, villages, religion, and politics is a visible sign to all that Banaba is alive, if not well, and living on Rambi Island.

Conclusion: The Quest
for a Civil Religion

The Banabans have been a people in search of a paradigm—a paradigm to meaningfully comprehend and direct both the organization and behavior of people on Rambi *and* their relationship to the external agencies which in large measure superintend their fate. The traditional culture, or rather their newly articulated model of it, has failed culturally to provide a design of sufficient scope and has failed socially to ground a system of sufficient solidarity. Christianity has had the advantage of scope, but in that respect it may go too far, and there has been more Christian division than Christian unity. Neither paradigm produces rules specifiable in concrete situations which can cover the terrain over which urgent passage must be made.

In this situation individuals and social groups have turned to their cultural equipment and have derived from it pieces to creatively test out against themselves and the real world. Some of these pieces are the redefined traditional model, Banaban solidarity, individual or cooperative economic action, the church, the village, the family, the general notion of a differentiated system. The models which are being tested out have grown to include external models, conceptions of the ways in which other people behave, which make behavior more directable and understandable. At the same time, pieces begin to include other pieces, and the process which results is neither orderly in the social sense nor entirely satisfying in the personal sense. Testing out is a creative response, but in its duration produces an environment with the very characteristic of instability which the process is intended to reduce.

As models and concepts are tested out through their embedding in social processes, those models and concepts change. They may or may not change in a direction which allows of a generalized (but not too generalized) solution. Why they do or do not is a great unanswered question.

Although it may be a response to my demand for order, I do sense an emerging pattern which may not and perhaps even cannot work but which at least would have better pretentions to success. This is one pattern among many, and there is no a priori reason to expect its sovereignty.

Robert Bellah has recently discussed the notion of "civil religion" as it applies to the United States: "a collection of beliefs, symbols, and rituals with respect to sacred things and institutionalized in a collectivity" (Bellah 1964, p. 8). He is referring to the "public religious dimension" in political life in particular, and in general to "an understanding of the American experience in the light of ultimate and universal reality" (p. 18).

Bellah is analyzing a society with a differentiated polity. The concept of civil religion, as distinct from highest level values or just religion itself is perhaps only rightfully applied where the polity is as differentiated as it is in our own system. But since I am trying to cover my tracks by calling this an emergent pattern (a loose term)—it is simply too early to tell—I can justify extending the concept through the assertion that the polity has been becoming more highly differentiated.

If this pattern were to be encapsulated in a single credal statement (as opposed to the numerous concrete statements), it might look something like this:

"We hold these truths to be self-evident, that all Banabans are created equal, that they are endowed by their Creator and Banaban custom with certain inalienable rights, that among these are life, liberty, the pursuit of happiness, and the just recognition of their rights, as individuals and as a people, to Ocean Island land, within the British sphere if possible."

The document upon the form of which this hypothetical statement is based is not invoked facetiously; the people have been profoundly affected by its consequences.

The rituals through which this emergent civil religion are stated are many: colony holidays, Arrival Day, council meetings, greetings to visitors, church services, political meetings and letters, kinship assemblies, and stylized discourse. The symbols include God in general, Christ in particular and the Cross, the British Government as embodied in the Queen (pictures of members of the royal family adorn many houses), Ocean Island itself with its blood and lands, and the acts and objects which are tangible formulations of Banaban custom. The foundation for this civil religion was formed on Ocean Island (the inclusion of many minute details in part 2 is directed to informing this point), and it is in the process of articulation on Rambi. The high position of Ocean Island land and the phosphate which derives from it underscores the outlook toward more than casual visitors to Rambi Island: they must state where they stand.

The details also furnish the basis for the dramatic historical constructs which spell out this civil religion through time: A small island community living with its own custom, suffering from periodic drought. The transformation of darkness into light through the acceptance of Christianity (and, in the conception of some, the triumph through faith of the Christian God over local spirits). The discovery of phosphate and the coming of the government, changing material and political life as Christianity had changed spiritual life. The community now in the charge of a powerful and fundamentally good master, whose agents deceived and began to betray the Covenant with their charges, finally taking away their charges' patrimony; an act immoral on grounds both of custom and of Christianity, and thus creating an issue of immense power. Negotiations and more negotiations—they occupy somewhat the same position to the Banabans as our wars do to ourselves, except that we won and they lost. The beginning of concerted opposition, later courageously led by one man, Rotan, in the face of some others still blinded by the ignorance of their forefathers. The thought of an almost promised land for justice and rebirth. Abandonment, dispersion, and cruelty in the war, but almost miraculous survival. Arrival in the new country, but to find tents instead of houses, dissension instead of unity, poverty instead of riches, repression and ambiguity instead of freedom and certainty. Being left to one's own resources. Rotan asserting his leadership to keep the community together and to realize its ambitions—hero to some, and to others far from it. Attempts to make a go of it with unfamiliar things and methods. Making a lands settlement and deciding to stay; the boundary making and returning. Becoming copra cutters and gardeners, with even women working strenuously. Moving into new homes. Seeing the fruits of new construction and new religions. Seeing the first blessedly numerous Rambi generation growing up but becoming Europeanized. Subdividing lands. Always seeking, hopefully with the help of government officials but denied it, the righting of past wrongs; the amelioration of present injustices; the securing of a peaceful, comfortable, and distinctly Banaban future.

These are the symbols, the rituals, the sacred history. What are the problems?

A Catholic leader could say in public assembly with others applauding, "There is one God, one Christ, one thought," but there is always the danger of the Christ of the creed suffering at the hands of religious intolerance. Banaban custom, which is so closely tied to Banaban identity, blood, and land, may not yet be generalized enough. Liberty is an option-maximizing idea without established boundaries, making strong collective structure and concerted long-term collective action difficult. Banabans are equal, but they own different amounts of capital—literally—in the Banaban estate.

Christianity and Banaban custom do have the appearance of becoming more generalized. A Rambi identity seems to be emerging. A measured acceptance of a need for centralized planning might be emerging. If the Banabans are to remain a significantly bounded and distinct community, the one great difficulty with this complex as a civil religion is Ocean Island land itself. It can unite people in their sense of grievance. It has the promise of maximizing all options and all values simultaneously, since success in the phosphate dispute would in the local perspective give people the money with which to do whatever they want (and would give tangible form to their identity). This very belief complicates the development of institutional means for coping with other problems that exist. And uncertainty about many aspects of the phosphate situation complicates the orderly specification of the value on phosphate itself.

The phosphate cannot be as easily generalized as custom, or Christianity, or freedom. It is, among other things, a resource which is mined and produces money and will some day no longer be mined and produce money. The more generalized orientations have the possibility of being specified and institutionalized in social structures that people could live with. Ocean Island land, through phosphate, is relatively instrumental in its nature but at a high level of generality in the system. Unless the Banabans change their position, or win their case, while the phosphate lasts (and perhaps even after its exhaustion) it stands able to be more than a medium of symbolic exchange between Ocean Island and Rambi; between the Banabans and the world; between the individual and the community; between past, present, and future; between kinship, nationality, village, and church. It stands capable of collapsing the rest of the structure into itself.

Epilogue

Toward the end of my stay on Rambi, and since then, Banaban delegations have attended various conferences in connection with the phosphate issue. The royalty has risen and the offer of a grant from the British Government made. In 1968, Rotan Tito, as Chairman of the Rambi Island Council; his son, Rev. Tebuke Rotan, as Manager of the Rambi Island Council; and their new lawyer, A. D. Patel (also Leader of the Opposition in the Fiji Legislative Council), went to New York and petitioned the United Nations Committee on Colonialism for the independence of Ocean Island (but not Rambi). The attempt failed.

APPENDIX 1

Map of Ocean Island (Banaba)

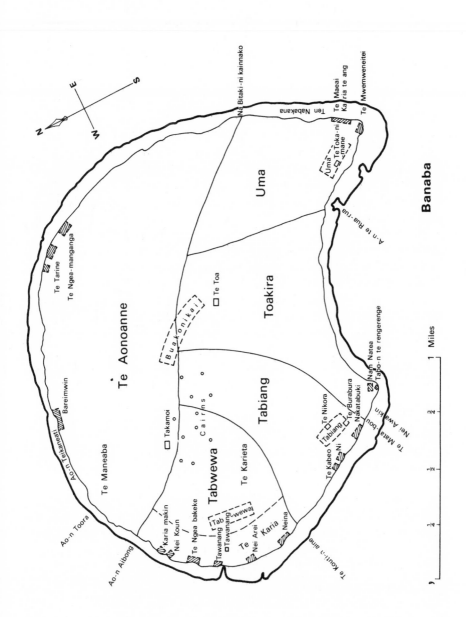

APPENDIX 2

This was the manner of the land in former days: it was not divided up among the people. It only began to be divided up when the canoes came from Beru, bearing Nei Angi-ni-maeao and her brother Na Kouteba, with Nei Te-Borata and Na Mani-ni-mate.

Nei Angi-ni-maeao and Na Kouteba were the dividers of the land. They stood on the foreshore; they separated; Na Kouteba paced the shoal water eastward, to fetch a circle round the land; and Nei Angi-ni-maeao paced the shoals westward.

So Nei Angi-ni-maeao measured the foreshore to westward, from the place called Na bitaki ni kainnano to the place called Te Rua-rua. This was the first portion, and she gave it to Na Mani-ni-mate. She said to him,

"Tiku	*i ao-n*	*te ora aei*	*n amarake*	*i maai-u."*
Remain	on	this foreshore	to feed	before me.

(i.e., Continue to use all edible things cast up on this foreshore until I claim them back from you.)

Again, Nei Angi-ni-maeao measured the foreshore from the place called Te Rua-rua to the place called Te Mata bou. That portion she gave to Nei Te-Borata saying, "Take this foreshore and use the food of it until I claim it back from you."

And for herself Nei Angi-ni-maeao measured off the foreshore from Te Mata bou to the place called Ao-n te maiango: that was her own portion. And behold, she returned to her houseplace at Tabiang, and remained there. She had two children, Na Borau and Nei Angi-ni-maeao the younger.

Nei Angi-ni-maeao the younger had a child, Na Kataburi.

This account of the partition of Banaba was obtained by Mr. Grimble from Nei Beteua, a direct descendant of Nei Angi-ni-maeao.

Na Kataburi had a child, Na Borau the younger.

Na Borau the younger had a child, Nei Angi-ni-maeao, and she had five brothers.

Na Borau the younger arose to pace out his foreshore. He came to the northern boundary, at a place called Ao-n te maiango. Thence he went forward until he met a man, who invited him to go home with him; but he refused and went forward again along the shore, until he came to a place called Ai-bong. There he met another man, whose name was Nan Teraro. This man invited him to go and live awhile in his house.

So Na Borau the younger followed Nan Teraro home, to live with him. But when they came to Nan Teraro's house, it was not ready to be lived in, for it was being floored; so Nan Teraro took the remnants of the material of the house of his brother, Na Ning, and began to finish his floor with that. But while he was at work, his brother Na Ning called to him, saying "Sir, send thy guest to me, for my house is ready for him to live in." So Na Borau the younger left Nan Teraro, and went to live with his brother Na Ning. There he remained, until the advent of his daughter Nei Angi-ni-maeao, who had come out in search of him.

When Nei Angi-ni-maeao found her father Na Borau with the man Na Ning, she approached him, and asked him to return home again. But he said to her,

"Tai	*kuri*	*moa*	*ni*	*kair-ai*	*ba*	*N*	*na*
Do not	be in haste	first	to	lead me away	for	I	shall

iangoa	*aro-u*	*nkai*	*I*	*mena*	*i rou-n*	*teuaei."*
consider	my attitude	now that	I	am domiciled	with	this man.

(i.e., Do not hastily call me away before I have repaid the courtesy of this man in entertaining me thus.)

And his daughter said to him, "I know nothing about it; the matter is in thy hand."

And Na Borau considered, and after a while he said to his daughter, "Woman, these things shalt thou give this man:

Wa-m n tieke,   *ao kana-m te amarake,*
Thy prior right to board strange vessels or canoes, and thy right to take the

            ao kabira-m te ba,   *ao mwe-m te kaue,*
peace offering of food, and thy right of anointing with oil, and thy right of

ao kana-m te ika te on ke te kua,
garlanding the stranger who arrives, and thy right to take the turtle or the

ke kana-m te ika te urna,   Ba
porpoise stranded on the foreshore, or thy right to the stranded urua fish. For

arom ni bane aikai   a bon tiku i rou-n teuaei,   ba e uot-ia
all these thy customary rights indeed remain with this man, for he assumes

ba te mane.   Ao ruoia-m,   ao taeka-n ao-n te
them, being a male. And thy right to ordain the ruoia, and governance of the

aba, ao katika-ni   kora-n ao-n te aba,   ao boni buki-ia arei i rou-m."
land, and drawing the measuring cord across the land, indeed such matters
are in thy hands.

And as Na Borau told her, so did Nei Angi-ni-maeao, for these things,
which Na Borau gave away to Na Ning, were not given away in very truth.
For when Na Borau spoke to Na Ning and apportioned him his foreshore,
he said to him,

"Tiku,   amarake   i ao-n   te ora anne i maai-u."
Remain,   feed   upon   this foreshore before me.

(i.e., Remain with thy foreshore rights until I claim them back from thee.)
Therefore the foreshore rights were not given away in very truth.

So Nei Angi-ni-maeao returned to Tabiang, and she appointed to each
of her five brothers a portion of the foreshore of the island.

Then the brothers of Nei Angi-ni-maeao arose in battle against the people
of Tabwewa, for they disputed the kingship of the people of Tabwewa. And
behold, they won the kingship; and the decision was that the brothers of Nei
Angi-ni-maeao should rule over the land. This they did, and they upheld all
the judgments of their father Na Borau concerning the foreshore rights.

Nei Angi-ni-maeao had a child, Nang Konim;

Nang Konim had a child, Nan Tetae; and Nan Tetae's brothers were
Borirai and Boi-n te Iti.

And these were the deeds of Nan Tetae. The man Kamtea came to him
one day, and told him that the people of Tairua had taken his land. The people of Tairua lived on the north side of Banaba, and they were eaters of
men. So Nan Tetae told Kamtea that he must not give way before them.
Kamtea went back to his land, and he saw that his boundaries had been

pushed back to the place called Te I-Namoriki. So he told his people to move them again to their former place. They did so, but afterwards the people of Tairua came and seized the land again.

So this was the judgment of Nan Tetae: he said to Kamtea, "Prepare thy torches of dried leaf, for we will fight with them from the sea." And he also told the people of Uma and Buakonikai that there would be a fight at sea.

And when night came, they fought with the people of Tairua from the sea. But there was no decision in that battle.

And so the judgment went out again that there should be a battle on the summit of Banaba. First came Nan Tetae with his brothers; then came three or four of the people of Uma; then came the people of Buakonikai and also the people of Tabwewa, to fight the people of Tairua.

Na Karobeing was the leader of the people of Tairua, and it was said of him that he was skilled in the *wawi* (death magic).

The fight was fought. Nan Tetae and his people were victorious, and only two of their side were killed.

This then was the word of the people of Tairua to Nan Tetae about the land of Kamtea: "We have no share in it, for it is in thy hands." So Nan Tetae took the land, together with the water-cave called Te Ba.

Then Nan Tetae returned to Tabiang. There he had a child, whose name was Nam Baia.

(Then follows the genealogy of the Chiefs of Tabiang.)

APPENDIX 3

The Hamlets of Banaba

Tabwewa District
Te Karia
  Taekarau
  Kabi-ni marata
  Tabongea
  Namanai
  Tekerau
  Aobike
  Te Maiu
  Ao-n te marae

Te Karieta
  Mangati
  Uma na kainnako
  Karongoa
  Te Kainga
  Ao-n te bonobono
  Tabo-n te marae
  Karibariki

Mixed Karia and Karieta
  Aurakeia
  Marakei
  Te I-Namoriki

Tabiang District

Nokuao	Tarakabu	Tabiang
Te Aba uareke	Tabo-n te marae	Nei Rao
Te aba ni mate	Tabo-ni buota	Buariki
Oraka	Tabo Matang	Taiki
Eta-ni Banaba	Buki	Tangi-n te ba
Bare bongawa	Bare buairake	Te Aba-n aine
Ata-ni Banaba	Neingkambo	Te Kammamma
Nakieba	Nanimanomano	

Te Aonoanne District

Te Mara-ni kaomoti	Te Ababa	Norauea
Te Katuru	Toka mauea	Te Aka
Te Maeka-n anti	Bakatere	Taborake

340

Ao-n natiabouri   Ao-n te katoutou   Te Angaba
Terike

Toakira District
Toakira maeao   Te Bubunnai   Nakieba
Toakira mainiku   Te Kamaruarua   Tangi-n te ba
Niniki   Nei Tang   Te Uma reburebu
Te Roko-ni borau

Uma District
Nang Kouea   Te Maneaba   Naria kaina
Rariki-n te kawai   Te Mangaua   Bwibwi-n toora
Naruku   Te Tarine   Ata-n te Maneaba
Te Reineaba   Tonga i-eta   Tabo-n te ba
Te Toka   Te Wae   Te Uma-ni mane
Te Rawa i-eta   Bare tarawa   Te Rawa i-nano
Nuka   Aoniman   Ao-n te marae
Te Banga-ni U   Taboiaki

APPENDIX 4

Tabwewa District
  Karia Makin (used by Te Karia)
  Nei Koun (used by Te Karia)
  Te Ngea bakeke (used by Te Karia)
  Tawanang (used by Te Karia and Te Karieta)
  Nei Arei (used by Te Karieta)
  Neina (used by Te Karieta)
Tabiang District
  Te Kabeo
  Ni
  Nakatabuki
  Tabo-n te rengerenge (situated on Toakira land but used by Tabiang)
  Nam Natea (situated on Toakira land but used by Tabiang)
Te Aonoanne District
  Bareimwin
  Te Tarine
Toakira District
  Te Ngea manganga (situated on Te Aonoanne land but used by Toakira)
Uma District
  Te Maeai
  Karia te ang
  Te Mwemweneitei

In conversation, the word *ao-n,* meaning "on" or "situated upon," is used before the names of terraces. Thus one speaks of Ao-n tabo-n te rengerenge and Ao-n Arei.

APPENDIX 5

I. Three funds
  A. The Banaban Royalties Trust Fund (or Banaban Fund)
  B. The Banaban Provident Fund
  C. The Banaban Landowners (or Landholders) Fund
II. History of phosphate licenses
  A. Shortly before annexation in 1900, the Pacific Islands Company applied for a guano license for Ocean Island. It was suggested that the company should make own arrangements with natives concerning their guano deposit rights (if any).
  B. By an agreement dated 3 May 1900 with "the King and people of Ocean Island," the company obtained sole right to work phosphate deposits for 999 years, for £50 per annum.
  C. By Crown license dated 2 October 1900, Pacific Islands Company granted official sanction for Ocean Island activities for 21 years from 1 January 1901, for annual rent of £50 to the government.
  D. By a license dated 13 August 1901 superseding (C), the period was extended to 99 years and a royalty of 6d. per ton made payable to revenue from 1 January 1906, in place of the annual rental.
  E. In 1902 the Pacific Phosphate Co., Ltd., was formed as a subsidiary of the Pacific Islands Company, and a further license (otherwise identical) transferred Ocean Island working rights to this company.
  F. In 1920, the interests of the Pacific Phosphate Co. were acquired by the British Phosphate Commissioners (partner governments: Australia, New Zealand, United Kingdom).
III. History of land agreements
  A. 1900–13. Mining land was acquired by direct negotiation and agreement with individual owners for a fixed sum, apparently

This outline is slightly modified from notes by official sources.

343

averaging about £20 per acre which, with £50 per acre under
(B) above, was the natives' sole consideration.

B.   In 1913, negotiation between government, company, and landowners resulted in a further 145 acres being acquired by agreement
at £40–£60 per acre (according to position and quality), which
went direct to the landowners, as compensation for food-produc-
ing trees destroyed, plus 6d. per ton royalty on all phosphate
shipped from 17 December, which became the old Banaban Fund.

C.   In 1931, a further 150 acres was resumed under Mining Ordinance
no. 4 of 1928, with the following terms of settlement:

1.   Rental of 2s. 6d. per acre, paid to colony revenue;

2.   Payment for landowners' surface rights of £150 per acre
(Banaban Landowners Fund), with interest paid annually
to landowners or descendants;

3.   2d. per ton royalty to Banaban Provident Fund until it reaches
£175,000;

4.   8½d. per ton royalty to be held in trust for Banaban community (new Banaban Royalty Trust Fund);

5.   £20,000 transferred from old Banaban Fund to Banaban
Provident Fund;

6.   Annual lease payments to owners (up to £3 per acre) and
compensation for coconut trees cut down (up to £2 for fully
grown tree) in an additional 27¾-acre area of nonmining
land.

IV.   Banaban annuities

A.   These were first suggested by Grimble in 1931.

B.   After long discussions and negotiations with parties involved,
agreed to in final form by 1937. The agreement provides for payment from Royalties Trust Fund of:

1.   Annuities to all Banabans of £8 for adults and £4 for children, and

2.   Additional annuities to landowners of lands in 1913 or 1931
areas of £2 for less than one acre, £4 for 1–2 acres, £6 for
2–5 acres, £8 for 5–10 acres, £10 for 10 acres and over.

V.   The Banaban funds

A.   The old Banaban Royalties Trust Fund

1.   This fund was built up between 1913 and 1931 by 6d. royalty
at (III. B.). The terms of agreement provided for royalty being devoted to "the general benefit of the natives." After 1941
only interest on capital sum was to be paid to landowners.

      2.   In actual practice money has been deducted from this fund for annually recurrent Banaban services.

      3.   Interest was payable yearly to landowners under 1913 agreement (up to time of payment of 1937 annuities).

      4.   £20,000 was taken in 1931 to form nucleus of Banaban Provident Fund.

B.   The new Banaban Royalties Trust Fund

      1.   This fund was built up by money from 8½d. royalties at (III. C.4.) from 1931.

      2.   Since payment of annuities in 1937 the above funds have been amalgamated under the name of the Banaban Royalties Trust Fund (or Banaban or Common Fund).

C.   The Banaban Provident Fund

      1.   This fund was created in 1931 by a transfer of £20,000 from the old Banaban Royalties Trust Fund—see (V. A.4.)—and was

      2.   Built up by 2d. royalty at (III. C.3.).

D.   The Banaban Landowners Fund

      1.   This fund was built up in 1931 as at (III. C.2.).

      2.   It consists of £22,500, i.e., £150 x 150.

      3.   Capital remains invested while interest is paid annually to landowners concerned.

VI. Financial considerations

A.   British Phosphate Commissioners pay 1s. 4½d. per ton of phosphate exported. It is distributed in the following manner:

General Revenue	6d.
Banaban Provident Fund	2d.
Banaban Royalties Trust Fund	8½d.
Total	1s. 4½d.

B.   During 1937–38 payments from Banaban Royalties Trust Fund were:

Annuities to Banabans	£4,340
Annuities to Landowners	902
Banaban Services	3,557
Total	£8,799

REFERENCES

Aberle, David
1961   Navaho. In David M. Schneider and Kathleen Gough, eds., *Matrilineal kinship*. Berkeley: University of California Press.

Bellah, Robert
1964   Religious evolution. *American Sociological Review* 29:358–74.
1965   Epilogue. In Robert Bellah, ed., *Religion and progress in modern Asia*. New York: Free Press.
1966   Civil religion in America. *Daedalus* (Winter 1967):1–21.

Campbell, J. K.
1966   Honour and the devil. In J. G. Peristiany, ed., *Honour and shame*. Chicago: University of Chicago Press.

Carroll, Vern
1966   Nukuoro kinship. Ph.D. dissertation, University of Chicago, 1966.
1970   Adoption on Nukuoro. In V. Carroll, ed., *Adoption in Eastern Oceania*. Honolulu: University of Hawaii Press.

Cheyne, Andrew
1852   *A description of islands in the western Pacific Ocean*. London: J. D. Potter.

Christian, F. W.
1899   *The Caroline Islands*. London: Methuen.

Colson, Elizabeth
1953   *The Makah Indians*. Minneapolis: University of Minnesota Press.

Dumont, Louis
1961   Caste, racism, and "stratification": reflections of a social anthropologist. *Contributions to Indian Sociology* 5:20–43.
1964a   Nationalism and communalism. *Contributions to Indian Sociology* 7:30–70.
1964b   A note on locality in relation to descent. *Contributions to Indian Sociology* 7:71–76.
1969   Provisional statement for Wenner-Gren Symposium no. 46, Kinship and locality, at Burg Wartenstein, Austria, 23 August–1 September 1969.

Eggan, Fred
1960   The Sagada Igorots of Northern Luzon. In G. P. Murdock, ed., *Social*

structure in Southeast Asia. Viking Fund Publications in Anthropology 29:24–50. Chicago: Quadrangle Books.

Eisenstadt, S. N.
1964   Social change, differentiation and evolution. *American Sociological Review* 29:375–86.

Eliot, E. C.
1938   *Broken atoms.* London: Geoffrey Bles.

Ellis, Sir Albert
1935   *Ocean Island and Nauru.* Sydney: Angus & Robertson.

Fanon, Frantz
1967   *Black skin, white masks.* New York: Grove Press.

Frankenberg, Ronald
1957   *Village on the border.* London: Cohen & West.

Freeman, J. D.
1961   On the concept of the kindred. *Journal of the Royal Anthropological Institute* 91:192–220.

Geertz, Clifford
1957   Ritual and social change: a Javanese example. *American Anthropologist* 59:32–54.
1959   Form and variation in Balinese village structure. *American Anthropologist* 61:991–1012.
1964   Ideology as a cultural system. In David Apter, ed., *Ideology and discontent.* New York: Free Press of Glencoe.
1965   *The social history of an Indonesian town.* Cambridge, Mass.: M.I.T. Press.
1966   Religion as a cultural system. In A.S.A. Monographs 3, M. Banton, ed., *Anthropological approaches to the study of religion.* London: Tavistock Publications.

Gluckman, Max
1962   Les rites de passage. In M. Gluckman, ed., *Essays on the rituals of social relations.* Manchester: Manchester University Press.

Goodall, Norman
1954   *A history of the London Missionary Society, 1895–1945.* London: Oxford University Press.

Goodenough, Ward
1964   Componential analysis of Könkämä Lapp kinship terminology. In W. Goodenough, ed., *Explorations in cultural anthropology.* New York: McGraw-Hill.

Goodsell, Fred F.
1959   *You shall be my witnesses.* Boston: American Board of Commissioners for Foreign Missions.

Greenberg, Joseph
1966   *Language universals.* The Hague: Mouton.

Grimble, Sir Arthur
1921a   From birth to death in the Gilbert Islands. *Journal of the Royal Anthropological Institute* 51:25–54.
1921b   Canoe crests of the Gilbert Islanders. *Man* 21:81–85.
1923   Myths from the Gilbert Islands, II. *Folk-Lore* 34:370–74.
1931   Gilbertese astronomy and astronomical observations. *Journal of the Polynesian Society* 40:197–224.
1933   The migrations of a pandanus people. Polynesian Society Memoir 12.
1952   *We chose the islands.* New York: William Morrow; London: John Murray.
1957   *Return to the islands.* New York: William Morrow; London: John Murray.

Halligon, Contre-Amiral J.
1888   *Six mois à travers l'Oceanie.* Brest: Soc. An. d'Imprimerie "L'Océan."

Handy, E. S. Craighill
1927   *Polynesian religion.* Bishop Museum Bulletin 34. Honolulu.

Hanson, F. Allan
1970   *Rapan lifeways.* Boston: Little, Brown.

Horton, Robin
1967a   African traditional thought and Western science, I. *Africa* 37:50–71.
1967b   African traditional thought and Western science, II. *Africa* 37:155–87.

Inder, Stuart
1965–66   The Ocean Islanders; 2. Resentment on Rabi. *New Guinea and Australia, the Pacific and South-East Asia* 1(4):53–56.

Kennedy, D. G.
1931   Field notes on the culture of Vaitupu, Ellice Islands. *Journal of the Polynesian Society* 40:285–319.

Kirsch, A. Thomas
1970   The Thai Buddhist quest for merit. In John McAlister, Jr., ed., *Southeast Asia: the politics of national integration.* New York: Knopf (in press).

Kroeber, A. L.
1917   Zuni kin and clan. Anthropological Papers of the American Museum of Natural History, vol. 18, pt. 2. New York.

Kroeber, A. L., and Kluckhohn, Clyde
1963   *Culture: a critical review of concepts and definitions.* New York: Vintage Books.

Kroeber, A. L., and Parsons, T.
1959   The concepts of culture and social system. *American Sociological Review* 24:246–50.

Lambert, Bernd
1963   Rank and ramage in the Northern Gilbert Islands. Ph.D. dissertation, University of California (Berkeley), 1963.

Langdon, Robert
1965–66 The Ocean Islanders; 1. A quite scandalous document. *New Guinea and Australia, the Pacific and South-East Asia* 1(4):42–52.

Lee, Dorothy
1959 Codifications of reality: lineal and non-lineal. In *Freedom and culture*. Englewood Cliffs, N.J.: Prentice-Hall, Spectrum Books.

Lerner, Daniel
1958 *The passing of traditional society*. New York: Free Press.

Lévi-Strauss, Claude
1960 The family. In Harry L. Shapiro, ed., *Man, culture, and society*. New York: Oxford University Press, Galaxy Books.
1963 Social structure. In *Structural anthropology*. New York: Basic Books.

Levy, Marion J., Jr.
1962 Some aspects of "individualism" and the problem of modernization in China and Japan. *Economic Development and Cultural Change* 10:225–40.
1965 Aspects of the analysis of family structure. In Ansley J. Coale et al., *Aspects of the analysis of family structure*. Princeton: Princeton University Press.
1966 *Modernization and the structure of societies*. 2 vols. Princeton: Princeton University Press.

Levy, Robert I.
1970 Tahitian adoption as a psychological message. In V. Carroll, ed., *Adoption in Eastern Oceania*. Honolulu: University of Hawaii Press.

Lundsgaarde, Henry P.
1966 Cultural adaptation in the Southern Gilbert Islands. Ph.D. dissertation, University of Wisconsin, 1966.
1968 Some transformations in Gilbertese law: 1892–1966. *Journal of Pacific History* 3:117–30.

Mahaffy, A.
1910 Ocean Island. *Blackwood's Magazine* 188:569–85.

Mannoni, [Dominique] O.
1964 *Prospero and Caliban: the psychology of colonization*. New York: Praeger.

Maude, H. C., and Maude, H. E.
1931 Adoption in the Gilbert Islands. *Journal of the Polynesian Society* 40:225–35.
1932 The social organization of Banaba or Ocean Island, Central Pacific. *Journal of the Polynesian Society* 41:262–301.

Maude, H. E.
1946 Memorandum on the future of the Banaban population of Ocean Island, with special reference to their lands and funds. Suva, Fiji: Western Pacific High Commission.
1953 The cooperative movement in the Gilbert and Ellice Islands. *Proceedings,*

Seventh Pacific Science Congress (Auckland and Christchurch, 1949), 7:63–76. Christchurch: Pegasus Press.
1963   The evolution of the Gilbertese *boti*. Polynesian Society Memoir 35.
1968   *Of islands and men.* Melbourne: Oxford University Press.

Memmi, Albert
1967   *The colonizer and the colonized.* Boston: Beacon Press.

Morison, Samuel Eliot
1944   Historical notes on the Gilbert and Marshall Islands. *American Neptune* 4:87–118.

Moss, Frederic J.
1889   *Through atolls and islands in the Great South Sea.* London: Sampson Low.

Murdock, George P.
1949   *Social structure.* New York: Macmillan.

Northcott, Cecil
1945   *Glorious company.* London: The Livingstone Press (LMS).

Oliver, Douglas L.
1958   An ethnographer's method for formulating descriptions of "social structure." *American Anthropologist* 60:801–26.

Parsons, Talcott
1964   Evolutionary universals in society. *American Sociological Review* 29:339–57.
1965   General Introduction II, An outline of the social system; Introduction to part 2; Introduction to part 4. In Talcott Parsons, et al., eds., *Theories of society* (one volume edition). New York: Free Press.
1966   *Societies.* Englewood Cliffs, N.J.: Prentice-Hall.

Radcliffe-Brown, A. R.
1952   *Structure and function in primitive society.* Glencoe, Ill.: Free Press.

Read, K. E.
1955   Morality and the concept of the person among the Gahuku-Gama. *Oceania* 25:233–81.

Reay, Marie
1959   *The Kuma.* Carlton: Melbourne University Press for Autralian National University.

Sabatier, Révérend Père Ernest
1939   *Sous l'équateur du pacifique.* Paris: Editions Dillen.
1954   *Dictionnaire Gilbertin-Français.* Tabuiroa, Gilbert Islands: Sacred Heart Mission.

Sahlins, Marshall D.
1962   *Moala.* Ann Arbor: University of Michigan Press.

Scarr, Deryck
1967   *Fragments of empire.* Canberra: Australian National University Press.

Scheffler, Harold
1965   *Choiseul Island social structure.* Berkeley and Los Angeles: University of California Press.
1966   Ancestor worship in anthropology: or, observations on descent and descent groups. *Current Anthropology* 7:541–51.

Schneider, David M.
1961   The distinctive features of matrilineal descent groups. Introduction to David M. Schneider and Kathleen Gough, eds. *Matrilineal kinship.* Berkeley: University of California Press.
1965   Some muddles in the models: or, how the system really works. In A.S.A. Monographs 1, *The relevance of models for social anthropology.* London: Tavistock Publications.
1968   *American kinship.* Englewood Cliffs, N.J.: Prentice-Hall.
1969a   Kinship, nationality and religion in American culture: toward a definition of kinship. In Robert F. Spencer, ed., *Forms of symbolic action,* pp. 116–25. Proceedings of the 1969 Annual Spring Meeting, American Ethnological Society. Seattle: University of Washington Press.
1969b   Componential analysis: a state-of-the-art review. Wenner-Gren Symposium, Cognitive studies and artificial intelligence research, at University of Chicago Center for Continuing Education, 2–8 March 1969.
1969c   A reanalysis of the kinship system of Yap in the light of Dumont's statement. Wenner-Gren Symposium no. 46, Kinship and locality, at Burg Wartenstein, Austria, 23 August–1 September 1969.
1970   What should be included in a vocabulary of kinship terms? *Proceedings, Eighth International Congress of Anthropological and Ethnological Sciences* (Tokyo and Kyoto, 1968) 2:88–90.

Schneider, David M., and Roberts, John M.
1956   *Zuni kin terms.* Laboratory of Anthropology, Notebook no. 3, Monograph 1. Lincoln: University of Nebraska.

Silverman, Martin G.
1966   Symbols and solidarities on Rambi Island, Fiji. Ph.D. dissertation, University of Chicago, 1966.
1967a   The historiographic implications of social and cultural change: some Banaban examples. *Journal of Pacific History* 2:137–47.
1967b   Participation by proxy. *Journal of the Polynesian Society* 76:215–17.
1969a   Maximize your options: a study in symbols, values, and social structure. In Robert F. Spencer, ed., *Forms of symbolic action,* pp. 97–115. *Proceedings of the 1969 Annual Spring Meeting, American Ethnological Society.* Seattle: University of Washington Press.
1969b   Land as a medium of symbolic exchange: the Banaban case. Wenner-Gren Symposium no. 46, Kinship and locality, at Burg Wartenstein, Austria, 23 August–1 September 1969.
1970   Banaban adoption. In V. Carroll, ed., *Adoption in Eastern Oceania.* Honolulu: University of Hawaii Press.

Singer, Milton
1959   The great tradition in a metropolitan center: Madras. In Milton Singer, ed., *Traditional India.* Philadelphia: American Folklore Society.

Turner, Victor
1967   Symbols in Ndembu ritual: *and* Ritual symbolism, morality, and social structure among the Ndembu. In *The forest of symbols*. Ithaca: Cornell University Press.
1969   *The ritual process*. Chicago: Aldine.

Wagner, Roy
1967   *The curse of Souw*. Chicago: University of Chicago Press.

Webster, John
n.d. (1866)   *The last cruise of the Wanderer*. Sydney: F. Cunninghame.

Wood, C. F.
1875   *A yachting cruise in the South Seas*. London: King.

Woodford, C. M.
1895   The Gilbert Islands. *Geographical Journal* 6:325–50.

INDEX

Aberle, David, 281
Adoption: and kinship, 233–36, 245, 247, 257–58, 262–63, 268, 272–73, 275, 288–89, 304; on Ocean Island, 27, 33, 44, 53–54, 57, 61, 71–72, 74, 76, 130–31, 140, 142–43, 152; on Rambi, 180, 200
Affinity, 19, 179, 224, 233, 247–328 passim; and affinal terms, 245, 247–56 passim, 259–61. See also *Butika; Eiriki; Kainuma; Kanoanikainga; Kautabo; Nga-ni-bu; Tinaba*
Age, 70, 72, 94, 159, 201, 203, 206, 242, 245, 261, 281–82, 291, 303–4
Alliance, 57, 61, 67, 298
American Board of Commissioners for Foreign Missions, 88, 91, 93, 114–18
Ancestor, 24, 28, 30–31, 34, 40, 52–57, 59, 61, 87, 88, 94, 95, 104, 152, 171, 211, 221–22, 225, 237, 238, 303, 307, 310, 313, 317, 318, 322, 323, 325
Annuity, 139, 140, 141, 145, 149, 152, 165, 168, 192, 193, 194, 196, 199, 221, 226, 344–45
Arundel, John T., 99, 100
Auriaria, 24, 30, 57, 87
Authority, 11–12, 17–18, 52–59, 63, 67, 77–78, 94–95, 97, 134, 166, 198, 201, 203–5, 305, 319, 321; governmental, 103, 144; of males and elders, 62, 77–78, 102n., 198, 241–45, 251–53, 282, 285, 287, 291
Autonomy, 18, 93, 105–6, 122, 136, 147, 150, 161, 177, 179, 190–91, 195, 200, 207, 219

Banaban Adviser, 162–63, 165, 166, 169, 176, 182, 184, 185, 187, 191–94, 196, 199, 200, 219, 222, 319, 320

Banaban funds, 107, 110, 124–25, 145, 149–50, 168, 177, 192, 219, 223, 311, 343–45
Bellah, Robert, 20, 330
Beru, 25–27, 30, 40, 57, 69, 94, 95, 116, 118, 121, 134, 136, 336
Biribai, 310–13, 316–18, 324–27. See also Gift-giving
Blood (consanguinity), 5, 16, 17, 19, 53–81 passim, 106, 139, 144, 148, 155, 159, 207, 220, 222, 224, 231–328 passim. See also Substance
"Blood and mud" (blood and land), 72–79, 152, 155, 159, 207, 237, 240, 289, 303, 327
Boti, 35–37, 41, 47, 49, 52, 81
Boundaries, land, 26, 30, 44, 97, 127, 128, 130, 131, 144, 171, 172, 193, 200, 211, 226, 331, 337–38
Bralsford, H. P., 188, 119, 121
Britain, British, 6, 16, 108, 116, 122, 126, 133, 153, 166, 183, 185, 186, 188, 319. See also Government, British (colonial)
British Phosphate Commissioners (BPC, "the company"), 47, 113, 119, 123, 125, 126, 127, 128, 131–34, 145, 146, 147, 149, 150, 165, 167, 170, 174, 175, 178, 186, 188, 192, 193, 194, 195, 206, 223, 343–45
Buakonikai: on Ocean Island, 26, 31, 34, 37, 46, 49, 50, 56, 65, 95, 96, 124, 171, 339; on Rambi, 180, 210–25 passim, 235, 270, 275, 294, 307, 315, 323
Butika, 247, 251–54, 260. See also *Kautabo*

Campbell, J. K., 205
Carroll, Vern, 292

355

Cartwright, C. G. F., 146
Categories, units, and groups, 54–55, 58, 307
Catholic, 93, 103, 114, 115, 118, 137, 178, 182, 211, 213–15, 232, 244, 246, 331
Ceteris paribus model, 55–56, 61, 62, 74
Channon, Rev. Irving M., 102, 114–17, 121
"Chiefship," 31–33, 41–43, 46, 52–53, 64–66, 88–89, 94–99, 112, 147, 321, 339; in allegory, 182–86
"Child": as euphemism for virgin, 282, 285; position of in social structure, 265–68, 273, 286–88; terms, 27, 142, 239, 245, 250
Christianity, 10, 17–18, 23, 58, 60, 85–105 passim, 116, 119–20, 122–23, 138, 148–49, 151, 154–55, 182, 190, 202–3, 206, 216–17, 256, 284, 293, 329, 331–32
Church: and civil religion, 329–32; council, 120, 121; and kinship, 232–33, 235, 237, 265–66, 293, 295, 302, 310, 320; meetinghouses, 316–18; on Rambi, 173, 177–78, 194–218 passim; and weddings, 272, 275, 277, 290–91
Clan, 30–31, 36, 40, 42
Code for conduct, 17, 19, 72–76, 79, 122, 130, 131, 139, 144, 150, 154, 155, 181, 187, 207, 218, 221, 224, 226, 227, 231–36, 238, 245, 246, 251, 261, 274, 279, 280, 290, 295, 305, 311
Colonies: colonial administration (bureaucracy, control), 10, 85, 112, 129, 140, 149, 151, 153, 206–8; colonial legitimization, 137, 330; colonial societies, 12–14, 16, 19, 81, 133, 227
Community, 18, 19; on Ocean Island, 32, 103–5, 108–10, 115, 125–26, 137, 140, 144, 148, 150, 153; on Rambi, 161–68, 173–75, 178, 180–224 passim, 246, 270, 275, 288, 320–21, 331–32
Community store. *See* Cooperative society
Competition, competitive, 137, 212, 214
"Conceptual circulation effect," 18
Consanguinity. *See* Blood
Cooperation, 41, 72, 145, 151, 204, 212, 214, 247, 264, 329
Cooperative society (community store, cooperative stores), 18–19, 139, 144, 150, 164–65, 173–77, 206, 210–13
Copra, 159, 164–65, 173–79, 196, 199, 202, 211, 217, 219, 235, 270, 275, 331
Cosmology, 70, 76, 78, 79

"Couple" (*tanga*), 248, 249, 255–56, 300, 302
Court, 129, 132–33, 165
Crabb, David W., 19
Credit, 176, 177, 179, 213
Custom, 5, 23, 106, 134, 146, 152–53, 181–82, 196–97, 204–8, 312, 318, 321, 323, 330, 331, 332; and Christianity, 17–18, 103, 137, 190, 197, 295; and "gatherings," 262, 266, 290; and land rights, 41, 94, 124, 126, 129–32, 144, 163, 168, 219–20, 222, 226, 289, 327; and morality, 284, 294; and villages, 212, 218

Dances, 33, 43, 49, 50, 60, 92, 118, 136, 137, 144, 181, 188, 212, 214, 218, 261, 271, 280, 292, 299
Death, 29, 44–45, 171, 255, 262, 266, 267, 270, 273–74, 288, 294, 295, 296
Debating society, 115, 116
Decisions, decision-making, 15, 19, 32, 161, 207, 276, 307, 309
Descent, 9, 15–17, 19, 40, 48–105 passim, 113, 123–24, 143, 147, 149, 152, 159, 175, 180, 185, 201, 210–12, 214, 218, 231–328 passim
Dialectic, double, 6, 7, 10, 16, 85, 86, 98, 106, 160, 226
Differentiation, 11–18, 55, 58, 63, 69, 81, 88, 92, 105, 123, 132, 144, 149, 150–53, 159–60, 164–65, 173, 177, 178, 184, 197, 206, 208, 209, 214–15, 224, 243, 265, 292, 305, 306, 329, 330
Division of labor, 48, 51, 61, 71, 264, 307
Drought, 23, 46, 64, 66, 68, 85, 87, 98, 107, 123, 149, 331
Dumont, Louis, 153
Durkheim, Emile, 71, 305, 315

Eastman, Rev. George, 117, 134, 136, 138, 147
Economics, 5, 15, 18, 41, 66, 68, 69, 77, 93, 106, 108, 115, 131, 136, 139, 145, 149, 151, 153, 163, 164–65, 169, 174, 176–79, 184, 194, 205, 213, 218–19, 279, 293, 311, 319, 329
Education, 115, 117, 120, 138, 149, 204, 212, 221, 298
Egalitarianism, 203–4, 207
Eggan, Fred, 240
Eiriki, 251–53, 260, 282–85, 287, 292, 301

Elders, 64, 96, 164, 201, 215, 217, 218, 220, 244, 262, 270, 280, 290, 295, 310, 318, 322, 323, 325

Eliot, E. C., 97, 109, 110, 111, 112, 113, 118, 126, 133, 145

Ellis, Sir Albert, 92–94, 96–99, 101, 102, 103, 108, 189, 320

Engagement (betrothal), 45, 78, 273, 275, 276, 296, 297

Equivalence, 63, 73, 240, 243, 247, 265, 281, 282, 283, 284, 292, 303, 305, 306, 309

Etiquette, 80, 81, 111, 112, 132

Europeans, 23, 26, 65, 85, 86, 87, 88, 97, 101, 107, 110, 112, 114, 118, 120–22, 128, 133, 134, 135, 137, 145, 150, 151, 152, 162, 166, 171, 187, 193, 203, 279, 321, 331

Exchange, 17, 49, 72, 76, 81, 126, 153, 225, 265, 266, 271, 272, 277, 279, 292, 305, 332

Exogamy, 28, 30, 316

Expansion-contraction model, 19

Family gatherings. *See* Death; Engagement; First birthday; First menstruation; Marriage; Ritual, meta-ritual; Weddings

Famine, 23, 44, 46

"Father," terms, 239, 240–41, 245–47, 253, 259

Fiji: relationship with Banabans, 168–69, 173, 177, 179, '181, 185–86, 190, 192, 195, 199, 205, 211, 212, 217, 221, 321, 327

Fiji Government. *See* Government, British (colonial)

First birthday, 262, 266, 272, 273, 281, 292, 295, 296

First menstruation, 262, 264–67, 272–73, 275, 278, 296. *See also* Menstruating women

Fish, 34, 40, 41, 49, 56, 60, 63, 87, 98, 99, 101, 115, 134, 146, 147, 202, 296, 309

Fisherman, 44, 76, 77

Food, 29, 37, 41–44, 46, 52, 56, 60, 62, 72, 95, 99, 147, 148, 152, 176, 210, 264, 266, 277, 279, 290, 291, 297, 315, 325, 336

Freedom, 202–7, 332

Freeman, J. D., 55, 300

Friendship, 45, 130, 134, 179, 187, 233, 235, 257, 292

Frigate-birds, 38–39, 45, 77

Games, 33, 39, 42–43, 47, 50, 56, 60, 61, 71, 95, 127, 132, 212, 320, 325

Geertz, Clifford, 6, 7, 9, 10, 14, 180, 216

Genealogies, 26, 32, 33, 52–57, 62, 67, 70, 113, 130, 131, 143, 147, 234, 238, 245, 252, 253, 255, 257–60, 271, 293, 298, 304, 307, 309, 310, 312, 315, 317–25, 327, 339

Generalization, 12, 209, 266, 329, 331, 332

Generations, generational, 63, 70, 123, 198, 199, 236, 238–42, 253, 260, 270, 285, 296, 301, 303, 305, 309, 316, 317

Gift-giving, 41–43, 64, 95, 232, 259, 262, 265, 267–75, 277, 278, 279, 291, 294, 297, 310, 311, 318. See also *Biribai*

Gilbert and Ellice Islands, 3, 18, 23–27, 30, 38, 85, 88–89, 94, 97–98, 100–101, 103, 116–18, 121, 123, 129, 134, 136, 145, 147–48, 150, 160, 166, 185, 187, 189–92, 196, 199, 232, 254, 262, 296–97, 300–301, 321

Gilbertese, 86–87, 93, 147, 183, 247, 268, 285, 293, 316, 323; in Banaban social structure, 75, 121, 140, 143, 162–63, 171, 175, 178, 196, 200, 220–21, 223–24, 257, 269, 273–75, 278, 288, 327; laborers, 93, 97, 99, 113–14, 118, 133–34, 143, 163; language, 16, 23–24, 133, 141, 146, 167, 182, 204, 231, 234, 248, 254, 260, 297, 321–22; myth, 77–78, 113; social structure, 30, 31, 33, 35–36, 40, 42–43, 53, 66, 68

Gluckman, Max, 265

Goodenough, Ward, 238

God, 106, 126, 148, 189–90, 207, 246, 247, 293, 294, 330–31

Gossip, 208

Government, 8–9; British (colonial), 4, 18, 46, 81, 93–94, 100–101, 103, 111, 118, 119, 122–23, 126, 131–34, 139–40, 146, 149, 152, 164, 168–70, 173–74, 176–79, 181–82, 184–93, 195–97, 199, 205–6, 212, 218–19, 330, 333; native, 46, 66, 92, 101, 103, 120, 134, 149, 164, 166 (*see also* Rambi Island Council)

Goward, Rev. W. E., 116, 117

"Grandchild," terms, 239, 240–42

"Grandparent," terms, 239, 240–42, 250–51, 259

Greenberg, Joseph, 233

Greeting (welcoming), 66, 95, 214, 262, 330. *See also* Visiting ships; Visitors

Grenfell, Richard, 109, 115, 116, 117

358 INDEX

Grimble, Sir Arthur, 16, 24, 26, 53, 60, 67, 77, 79, 80, 87–89, 94–95, 110–13, 119, 120, 123–25, 128, 134, 187, 253, 259, 285, 296–98, 300, 301

Half-Banaban, 140, 141, 143, 144, 193
Hamlet, 27–31, 34, 53, 56–63, 71, 81, 104, 152, 210–11, 219, 237, 307, 309, 310, 313, 317, 318, 319, 340–41
Hannah, Rev. Percy, 134, 135, 137
Hanson, F. Allan, 79
Heirship, 57
High Commissioner for the Western Pacific, 124–25, 127, 145–46, 167. *See also* Western Pacific High Commission
History, 5–7, 9–11, 14–16, 24–26, 48, 51, 71, 85, 92, 105, 106, 160, 161, 164, 165, 180, 181, 203, 209, 210, 212, 259, 284, 296, 331, 343
Horton, Robin, 13
Household, 27–28, 58, 236, 238, 279, 280, 294
Housing, 211, 219, 221, 223–27 passim, 288
Humor, kinship, 246. *See also* Joking relationships

Identity: Banaban, 19, 106, 139, 144, 150, 152, 207, 226, 327, 331–32; in social structure, 17, 72–75, 130, 155, 160, 203, 218, 221, 224, 227, 231, 233–38, 243, 246, 255, 261, 265, 290, 295, 303, 305–6, 310, 325
Incest, 233, 296
Independence, 4, 190–91, 320, 333
Individual, 13, 15, 17, 53, 58, 105, 140, 150, 152, 153, 168, 184, 189, 191–93, 196, 202, 204–8, 215, 219, 222, 223, 232, 238, 256, 310, 326, 327, 329, 332. *See also* Person
Infanticide, 304
Inheritance, 43–46, 53, 63, 74, 76, 95, 129, 130, 150, 167, 183, 185, 221, 229, 287, 289
Initiation, 28, 296, 299
Institutionalization, 11–15, 17, 61, 153, 180, 205, 207, 208
Integral model, 160, 163, 164, 178–80, 216
Integration, 11, 13, 15, 17, 18, 20, 93, 159, 160, 201, 207, 208, 264

Japan(ese), 147, 166, 174

Joking relationships, 18, 250, 251, 252, 257, 280, 281, 282, 283, 284, 287, 292, 316, 326

Kainuma, 251–53, 260, 300
Kanoanikainga, 249
Kautabo, 247, 251–55, 260, 263, 276–78, 290, 292, 312, 316. See also *Butika*
Kindred, 28, 46, 72, 131, 200, 237, 238, 249, 253, 266, 267, 269, 271–73, 277, 280, 281, 283, 287, 303–6, 316–17, 319, 324. See also *Utu; Koraki*
"Kingship," 89, 94–99, 103, 321, 338
Kinship. *See* Affinity; Blood; Code for conduct; Descent; Kindred
Kirsch, A. Thomas, 59, 208, 217
Kluckhohn, Clyde, 9
Koraki, 235, 245
Kouti magic, 28, 31, 38–39, 47, 78, 80
Kroeber, A. L., 9
Kuria, 127
Kusaie, 147

Labor, 4, 100, 103, 117, 119, 122, 135, 147, 217; Chinese, 113, 114; Fijian, 162–63; Gilbertese (*see* Gilbertese); labor relations, 100, 114; Solomon Islands laborers, 162
Lambert, Bernd, 261
Land, 4, 5, 16–19, 159, 208, 240, 255, 268; and kinship, 281–345 passim (*see also* "Blood and mud"); on Ocean Island, 21–155 passim, 161–62, 167–68, 170–72, 180–81, 184–88, 193, 195, 209; on Rambi, 163, 167, 169, 195, 200, 210–27 passim, 267. *See also* Locality; Phosphate
Langdon, Robert, 96, 100, 107
Law, 99, 101, 103, 120, 133, 144, 153, 165, 166, 169, 184, 186, 197
Lawyer, 182, 185, 195, 200, 246, 333
Lee, Dorothy, 316
Lerner, Daniel, 136
Lévi-Strauss, Claude, 78, 304
Levy, Marion J., Jr., 202
Literacy, 90, 91
Locality, 14, 17, 48, 53–59, 64, 66, 70, 72, 76, 79, 81, 104, 105, 139, 141, 144, 149, 150, 152, 160, 165, 210, 306–9, 318. *See also* Place; Space
London Missionary Society (LMS), 18–19, 93, 118–21, 134–36, 147, 162, 175, 178, 214

Lundsgaarde, Henry P., 99, 101, 260, 261

Mahaffy, Arthur W., 66, 107
Marked and unmarked categories, 233–34, 236
Marriage, 28–29, 45, 54, 57, 59, 67–68, 95, 114–15, 143, 165, 183, 201, 223–25, 229–328 passim
Maude, H. C. and H. E., 16–17, 23–48, 51, 52, 58, 62–64, 67, 69, 71, 75, 77, 80, 85, 99–101, 103, 104, 121, 123–25, 128–33, 138, 145, 164, 165, 174, 184, 259, 260, 279, 285, 289, 297, 298, 301, 320, 321
Meeting (*te bo*), 61, 235–36, 238, 273
Meetinghouse (*maneaba*), 29–34, 36, 41, 43, 47, 49, 54, 60, 62–63, 80–81, 105, 111, 132, 139, 201, 212–13, 215, 217–18, 307, 314, 316, 318, 323–25; church, 92, 212–13, 316
Menstruating women, 28, 77, 78, 80. *See also* First menstruation
Methodist, 93, 181–82, 189, 194, 198–200, 203, 213–14, 215, 217, 232, 246, 247, 290, 293, 295, 318
Mission, missionaries, 66, 85, 88, 90, 92, 98, 101–4, 109, 114–23, 134, 137, 150, 152, 207, 212, 266. *See also* American Board of Commissioners for Foreign Missions; Catholic; London Missionary Society
Models, 6, 16, 18–19, 135, 151, 153, 161, 180, 191, 207, 227, 326, 329
Money: for copra, 211; for the council, 199; for gifts, 232, 264, 266–68, 270, 279, 290–91, 293–94, 312–13; for land and phosphate, 94, 98, 103–5, 123, 125, 132, 140, 144, 149, 168, 184–85, 332; and rights, 128, 189–91, 194–96; for work, 217
Morality, 90, 91, 94, 190, 203, 206, 284, 294
Moss, Frederic J., 86
"Mother," terms, 231, 240–42, 246, 253, 258, 259
Murdock, George P., 271, 272
Myth, 6, 24–25, 77, 78, 113, 116, 253, 296, 326

Names, 28, 52, 80, 211, 298
Nationality, 153–55, 163, 178, 223–24, 332
Nauru, 6, 16, 77, 86, 101, 120, 121, 134, 135, 145, 147, 151, 153, 160, 191
Naylor, A., 96–97
Nei Anginimaeao, 26, 30–31, 36, 40, 68, 70, 307, 336, 338
Nei Tituabine, 30, 34, 40, 59, 87, 171
New Zealand, 113, 122
Nga-ni-bu, 260, 301
Nuka, 172, 175, 179, 210–13, 215, 261
Nurturance, 74, 75, 76, 81, 155, 274, 290

Ocean Island Lands Commission, 31, 106, 129–32, 134, 136, 139, 144, 147, 150, 221, 289, 320
Old man (*unimane*), 29, 52, 64, 116, 132, 187, 198, 214, 245, 312, 322, 325. *See also* Elders
Oliver, Douglas L., 9
Opposition, 18, 106–38 passim, 178, 331
Options, maximizing, 15–17, 19, 70–71, 89, 104, 164, 179–80, 206–8, 209, 213, 224, 256, 272, 291, 293, 327, 331, 332
Outsiders (strangers), 5, 29–30, 40–41, 49, 52, 95, 247, 258, 263, 268
"Overlordship" of Tabwewa, 27, 40, 95. *See also* "Chiefship"; "Kingship"

Pacific Phosphate Company, 37, 95–114, 121, 122, 343
"Parents": in allegory, 183, 186; terms, 241
Parsons, Talcott, 11–12
Patrilineal, 28, 42, 52, 77
Patrilocal, 28, 52, 301
Pentecostal, 214–15, 246, 265, 293–95, 316
Person, 7, 17, 58, 70, 81, 202, 204, 206–8, 226, 237, 256, 306
Phosphate, 4–7, 10, 18–19, 23, 47, 81, 85, 92–111, 113, 121–22, 125, 131–32, 134, 138, 149–209 passim, 219, 220, 319–20, 327, 330–33, 343–45
Place, 7, 80, 81, 210, 238, 317, 327. *See also* Locality; Space
Pluralization, 256
Politics, 4, 5, 12, 15, 17–19; on Ocean Island, traditional, 57–58, 63–69, 77; on Ocean Island, colonial, 81, 93, 96, 105–37 passim, 139–40, 145, 150–51, 153; on Rambi, 160, 163, 165, 173–205 passim, 214–20, 293–94, 296, 298, 302–3, 320, 327–28, 330–31
Population, 23–24, 26, 65, 67, 87, 91, 102, 107, 162, 259

Power, 48, 58, 63, 64, 66–68, 77, 89, 95, 112, 196, 206, 331
Precedence, 17, 51, 52, 66, 67, 71, 204, 215, 270, 298, 303, 313, 315, 321, 327
Precedence-complementarity system, 17, 48, 61–63, 90, 242, 306
Prestige, 49, 66, 132, 204, 205, 319

Quayle-Dickson, Capt. J., 107, 108, 110, 112, 133

Radcliffe-Brown, A. R., 71, 252, 281
Rambi Island Council, 18, 164, 170, 174–79, 183–84, 190, 193–94, 197–201, 208, 210–12, 222, 330, 333; councillors, 170, 183, 197–98, 319, 322–23
Read, K. E., 203
Reay, Marie, 205
Reciprocity, 267, 327
Religion: civil, 329–30; and change, 89, 106, 117, 119, 122, 135, 139, 145, 150–51, 153; and division, 211, 214, 320; and kinship, 260, 265–66, 303; and morality, 260, 284; and opposition, 177; in social structure, 12, 15, 17–20, 69, 91–92, 102–3, 136–37, 149, 154–55, 161, 165, 181, 199–201, 206, 212, 294, 327–28; and solidarity, 216–18, 295–96, 319; and style, 126, 182, 187, 246; traditional, 59, 66, 69; and values, 207, 293–94
Resettlement, 14–16, 18–19, 108, 110, 147, 148, 153
Residence, 28–29, 48, 52–53, 58–59; and adoption, 75, 154; and kinship, 274, 279–80, 290, 301; and land, 72, 76, 141, 144, 155, 163, 167, 193, 221–22; and marriage, 236–38, 253, 270; on Rambi, 211, 220, 226; and separatism, 121, 149; uxorilocal, 279
Resident Commissioner, 87, 97, 99, 100, 106–11, 118–20, 123–24, 128, 133, 137, 141–42, 144, 167, 187, 222
Responsible entity, 224, 269, 279, 288, 294
Rights: and adoption, 75; of councillor, 319; fishing, 128; of hamlet, 29, 52, 62, 71; of "king," 97; of kinship unit, 54, 57, 60–61, 68, 70, 74, 113, 251, 303, 307, 309, 315–17, 323; over land, 4, 72, 98, 111, 125, 128, 138, 140, 142–43, 150, 167, 170, 181, 185, 187–89, 325; of men and women, 62–63, 304; to phosphate, 94, 200; of precedence,

67; sexual, 279, 255; of Tabwewa, 40–41, 43, 66, 95; over visiting ships, 320
Ritual (ceremonies): and adoption, 304; amusements, 50–51, 212 (see also Games); ritual circulation, 17, 48, 50, 55, 56, 58, 59, 64, 68, 69, 92, 152, 306; and civil religion, 137; distribution, 49; functions, 69, 305; and kinship, 19, 61, 70, 231, 261, 264–66, 275, 296, 309; and locality, 307; and magic, 38, 78; meta-ritual, 265–66, 312; rights, 57, 313, 317, 321, 323, 326; unit, 53. See also Boti; Family gatherings; Hamlet; Kouti magic; Meetinghouse; Spirit house; Terraces
Roads, 194–95, 206
Roberts, John M., 201, 246, 255
Rorobuaka, 28, 39, 198, 199
Rorobuaka Society, 198, 205, 216–17, 235, 270, 319
Rotan Tito, 109–13, 123–26, 135, 139, 140, 145, 147, 164–65, 175, 176, 188, 189, 194, 197–98, 215, 218, 331, 333
Royalties, 121, 125, 127, 139, 168–70, 185, 186, 191–92, 194, 195, 333, 344–45

Sabatier, Révérend Père Ernest, 244, 254, 260
Samoa, 25–26, 63, 68, 117, 216
Sanctions (punishment, penalty), 44–46, 65, 124, 130, 131, 144, 191, 317, 321
Saunders, M. J. C., 182, 183, 186, 200
Scarr, Deryck, 96, 100, 107, 110
Scheffler, Harold W., 309
Schneider, David M., 7–9, 17, 55, 71–73, 153–55, 159, 201, 246, 247, 255
School, 91, 102, 103, 113, 115–18, 134, 165, 200, 211
Sea, 4, 62, 70, 76–79, 309
Second World War, 18, 139, 149, 166
Segregation, 121, 151
Seniority, 52, 61, 62, 63, 239, 287, 313, 321
Separatism, 121, 149
Seventh Day Adventist, 200, 214–15, 295
Sex: differentiation by, 32, 43, 70, 76–78, 94, 198, 203, 223, 239, 242–43, 247, 264, 281, 304; role of women, 39, 61–64, 80, 92, 102n., 264–65, 276, 278, 285, 300–301, 304, 327; sexuality and sexual intercourse, 39, 45, 78, 237, 260, 275, 277–78, 280, 282–85, 288, 301

Shakespeare, W., 136, 326.
"Siblings": behavior of, 63, 242, 257, 263, 281, 286–87; position of in social structure, 242, 253, 262–63, 269, 272, 281–82, 303, 309, 327; terms, 242–47
Silverman, Martin G., 15, 57, 93, 143
Singer, Milton, 262
Social structure, 12, 13, 16, 17, 30, 48, 67, 87, 105, 153, 202, 206, 214, 226, 227, 277, 284, 321, 326, 332
Solidarity: Banaban, 135, 150, 164, 177, 181, 190, 199, 329; and gift-giving, 268–72, 312–13, 317; of groups on Rambi, 201–5, 207, 213–16, 295–96, 319; of kinship, 54, 58, 67, 72, 90, 159, 224, 233, 242, 246–47, 281, 288, 295, 301, 305, 316–17, 327; national, 154, 159; of spouses, 281, 288–90, 302
Song, 171, 182, 188, 204, 295
Space, 17, 70, 72, 79, 80, 81, 105, 214, 234, 294, 327. *See also* Locality; Place
Spirit house (*uman anti*), 29, 30, 31, 34–37, 41, 42, 47, 49, 59, 63, 81, 211
Spirits, 27, 49, 57, 59, 322, 331
"Spouses": position of in social structure, 223–24, 255, 281–83, 287, 288, 289, 303; terms, 248–54, 260
Statement of Government Intentions Regarding the Banabans on Rambi ("Covenant"), 126, 167, 185, 189, 190, 331
Status, 80, 105, 152, 154, 160, 163, 224, 226, 261, 275, 298, 300, 303, 321, 327
Store, company-owned, 98, 110, 119, 151, 152, 179; private, 179, 213. *See also* Cooperative society
Substance, 17, 72–75, 154, 155, 224, 233, 274, 275. *See also* Blood
Succession, 32–33, 52, 62
Surface and undersurface, 125, 140, 150, 185
Suva, 160, 179, 181, 182, 190, 200, 235
Symbol, 7–8, 49–51, 106, 126, 133, 153, 207–8, 216, 266, 293, 319, 327, 330
Symbolic systems, 7–9, 18–19, 90, 93, 105

Tabiang: on Ocean Island, 26, 31, 34–36, 40–41, 46, 49–50, 57, 65, 88, 95–97, 104, 111–12, 119, 129, 139, 338–39; on Rambi, 210–12, 215, 222–23, 288, 307, 310, 313–14, 317–19
Tabwewa: on Ocean Island, 25–26, 27, 30–31, 33–34, 37–38, 40–43, 46–47, 49–51, 53, 57, 62, 64–66, 68, 94–98,

102, 338–39; on Rambi, 178–79, 210, 212–13, 215, 218, 221, 223, 225, 294, 318–22
Tairua, 25, 70, 338–39
Tarawa, 30, 99, 147, 148, 160, 259, 293
Teacher, 88, 89, 92, 98, 118–22, 135, 136, 144
Te Aonoanne, 26, 31, 34, 35, 41, 340, 342
Tebuke Rotan, Rev., 188–90, 197, 216, 295, 333
Te Karia and Te Karieta, 25, 31, 34, 41–44, 49, 50, 51, 56–57, 68, 340, 342
Telfer-Campbell, W., 99, 100
Terraces, 28, 31, 33, 37–38, 59, 80, 342
Testing-out process, 14–15, 18, 160, 164, 179, 202, 206, 218, 326, 329
Tinaba, 260, 284
Toakira, 26, 31, 34–35, 41, 341, 342
Trees, 34, 77, 94, 99, 100, 104, 107, 108, 115, 126, 127, 128, 344
Turner, Victor, 71, 277, 300

Uma: on Ocean Island, 26, 31, 33–35, 37, 41–42, 46, 49, 50, 56–57, 60, 65, 88, 95–96, 109, 119, 171, 339; on Rambi, 178–79, 182, 194, 210, 212–15, 218, 222–23, 225, 247, 270, 304, 309, 318–19,
United Nations, 4, 189, 191, 198, 333
Universalism, 151, 174
Universalizing, 94, 150, 206, 295, 296
Utu, 28, 46, 52, 60, 231–316 passim

Values, 11, 12, 14–15, 17, 19, 49, 68, 72, 81, 100, 109, 125, 128, 151, 161, 170, 189, 192, 195, 201, 204–8, 209, 216, 293, 330, 332
Villages: on Ocean Island, 24–27, 31, 40–41, 56, 59, 63, 64, 68, 90, 92, 96, 99, 104–5, 115, 121, 128–29, 132, 135–37, 147, 149, 318–19; on Rambi, 159, 175, 177, 197, 200–204, 206, 210–27 passim, 237, 246, 294, 318–19, 323, 328–29, 332. *See also* Buakonikai; Nuka; Tabiang; Tabwewa; Uma
Violence, 196, 201
Virginity, 272, 278, 282, 285, 290, 299, 300
Visiting ships, 23, 40, 41, 56, 64–66, 85, 86, 95, 96, 320, 337
Visitors, 49, 61, 85, 86, 92, 201, 212, 276, 312, 314, 318. *See also* Greeting

Wagner, Roy, 265
Wakaya, 145, 146, 147
Walkup, Capt. Alfred C., 66, 88, 89, 91, 92, 98, 99, 101, 102, 117
Water-caves (*bangabanga*), 31, 46, 59, 60, 61, 63, 64, 66, 68, 77, 92, 109, 125, 304, 339

Webster, John, 64, 296, 300
Weddings, 257, 275, 276, 277, 280, 290, 292–93, 294, 299, 313
Welch, Rev. Clifford, 135, 136
Western Pacific High Commission, 185, 190, 197. *See also* High Commissioner for the Western Pacific